ROYAL NAVY
HANDBOOK
1939–1945

ROYAL NAVY HANDBOOK

1939–1945

DAVID WRAGG

SUTTON PUBLISHING

First published in the United Kingdom in 2005 by
Sutton Publishing Limited · Phoenix Mill
Thrupp · Stroud · Gloucestershire · GL5 2BU

British Library Cataloguing in Publication Data
A catalogue record for this book is available from the British Library.

ISBN 0-7509-3937-0

Typeset in 10/13pt New Baskerville.
Typesetting and origination by
Sutton Publishing Limited.
Printed and bound in England by
J.H. Haynes & Co. Ltd, Sparkford.

CONTENTS

INTRODUCTION

'Command of the sea is the indispensable basis of security, but whether the instrument that commands swims, floats, or flies is a mere matter of detail.'
Adm Sir Herbert Richmond, Statesmen and Sea Power, OUP, 1946.

Despite years of economic depression, in June 1939 the Royal Navy and Royal Marines totalled 129,000 men, which could be expanded by a further 73,000 men from the Royal Naval Reserve and the Royal Naval Volunteer Reserve. Today, in a period of economic prosperity and many uncertain dangers, the Royal Navy and Royal Marines numbers just about a third of its 1939 strength. Admittedly, we have lost the burden of empire, but all too often the responsibilities of the past come back to haunt us, whether it be in providing humanitarian aid – as most recently following the tsunami that caused devastation across the Indian Ocean, or simply during the hurricane season in the Caribbean – or maintaining an armed intervention as in Sierra Leone. It is clear that today we would be hard put to repeat the Falklands campaign of 1982, and even that was a close-run thing, with ships lost because of the lack of airborne-early-warning aircraft. In 1939 the United Kingdom had the world's largest Merchant Navy, and we still had the remnants of it in 1982, but today a British-registered deep-sea vessel is a rarity, so there is no longer the trained back-up of seafarers to allow the rapid expansion of a fleet, and no longer the same opportunity to 'take ships up from trade' when a crisis occurs.

Of course, technological change has also helped reduce the number of ships and manpower needed. Modern warships do not need to spend years in refit simply to have their engines changed, or months to have boilers cleaned. The presence of helicopters aboard frigates and destroyers also helps. Yet from 2006 until 2012 the fleet will be without fighter air cover, and in recent years this has comprised just two squadrons, each of only eight aircraft, with only two of the three aircraft carriers active at any one time. The dependence on costly nuclear-powered submarines is also a weakness, as smaller, conventional submarines are not only cheaper and better for training, they are also much better for many tasks, including the insertion of special forces and operations in shallow waters. In one sense, it might not matter that for the first time in more than 200 years, the Royal Navy is smaller than the French navy, but in others it does. France does not claim to be a maritime power, yet most of our trade is by sea. We also have extensive offshore waters to protect, both for fisheries purposes and because of the importance of North Sea oil.

Recent events such as the Anglo-American intervention in Iraq also show that France does not view the world in the same way. Yet politicians constantly demand more from the armed forces while providing less, and in the case of the Royal Navy, the construction of new ships is not an operational question, but a political matter, so that the present government can safeguard its majority.

If one is to draw a parallel between the 1930s and the situation today, one shines through clearly. Between the two world wars, the 'ten-year rule' applied, meaning that there would be ten years in which to prepare for a major war. Today, much the same attitude is taken. But modern equipment takes much longer to bring to service. In fact, by the time the Eurofighter Typhoon 2000 reaches operational service in the Royal Air Force, more than twenty years will have passed since the first flight of its antecedent, the British Aerospace Future Combat Aircraft. In the meantime, the role for which the aircraft was designed has gone, and much time and taxpayers' money has been spent re-inventing the wheel, simply so that work and technology can be transferred to European partners who have a different requirement. An earlier in-service date and new aircraft carriers cap-able of handling conventional take-off and landing aircraft might have meant that this fighter could have been a formidable addition to the Fleet Air Arm's capabilities.

Today we are also looking at ten years plus for new ships, against three in the 1930s. Yet modern technology should mean that ships are easier to design and construct, with modular installation of equipment. All too often we are told that ships are simply 'platforms' for weapons and aircraft.

Looking at the world today, we see a heavily armed China emerging not only as an industrial power, but – while that country lacks democracy and maintains territorial ambitions – a regional, if not global, threat. The increasing centralisation of power in Russia also threatens a return to the dark days of the Soviet Union, which many Russians mourn as they face the uncertainties of life in post-Communist Russia. A modern ten-year rule is even more danger-ous than it was during the 1930s, when just six years passed between Adolf Hitler's assumption of absolute power and war breaking out. We no longer have the cer-tainties of a known danger, as during the Cold War. After all, no one waking up on the morning of 11 September 2001 realised what that day would bring, and its implications.

ACKNOWLEDGEMENTS

In researching and compiling any book such as this, an author is heavily dependent on the help and assistance of many others. In particular, I am indebted for the provision of photographs and other material to Lord Kilbracken, who, as John Godley, flew as an RNVR pilot; to 'Bill' Drake for photographs of his service; to my cousin David Wragg (yes, there is *another* David Wragg) for photographs of his late father's submarine service during the Second World War; to Mrs Marjorie Schupke, for photographs of her brother, Sub Lt (A) Gordon Maynard, RNVR, who lost his life in action while flying with no. 1836 Squadron off HMS *Victorious*; to my late father, Lt S.H. 'Harry' Wragg, RN, for his collection of wartime photographs and other material.

Inevitably, official and semi-official sources have also been invaluable. Like many other researchers, I am grateful to Debbie Corner, Keeper of Photographs at the Royal Navy Submarine Museum at Gosport; Jerry Shore, Assistant Curator and Archivist of the Fleet Air Arm Museum, and his enthusiastic team; and to the Photographic Archive team at the Imperial war Museum.

No work on something as vast as our wartime Royal Navy can cover every inch of ground, and for those whose appetite is whetted by this book, I would draw their attention to the bibliography at the back. There are accounts of the war at sea from every perspective, including the all-important personal accounts, as well as volumes of sheer factual matter, essential for the serious student and the modeller alike.

David Wragg
Edinburgh
Summer 2005

CHAPTER ONE

THE ROYAL NAVY IN 1939

The Royal Navy of England hath ever been its greatest defence and ornament;
it is its ancient and natural strength; the floating bulwark of the island.
Sir William Blackstone (1723–80)

'Finally, let it be remembered that when the present naval re-armament is completed in about 1940 our figures will still be 21 capital ships as against 68 in 1914, 69 cruisers as against 103 and 190 torpedo craft as against 319.

'With the exception of Germany, every other leading navy will be substantially stronger than before the last war.'

So wrote Lt Cdr E.C. Talbot-Booth, editor of the magazine *Merchant Ships*, on the eve of war in 1939. The period between the two world wars had not been good for any of Britain's armed services, and it certainly had not been good for the Royal Navy. The First World War had marked a turning point. The nation that had prided itself on maintaining a fleet that was the equivalent of any other two foreign navies, the so-called 'Two Power Standard', had nearly been brought to its knees by a combination of the German U-boat menace and the reluctance of the Admiralty to institute a convoy system. The search for a decisive sea battle had led to the Battle of Jutland in 1916, but this proved to be anything but decisive. On paper, the Royal Navy had lost, suffering heavier casualties in men and ships than the German navy, although a strategic victory could be claimed, since the German High Seas Fleet put back into port and never

ventured out again. The introduction of convoys and a sea blockade of Germany eventually meant that it was the Germans who were brought to the point of starvation.

STRUGGLING BETWEEN THE WARS

After the war, the Washington Naval Treaty of 1922 meant that the best the Royal Navy could aspire to was the 'One Power Standard'; in other words it would be limited to the size of the navy of one other nation. In fact, the Treaty was very specific, for its provisions allocating maximum tonnages to each navy of the signatories meant that the other navy was to be that of the United States. In addition to the Treaty's stipulating a maximum tonnage of ships for the main navies, it also imposed restrictions on the total tonnage for each type of warship, and maximum tonnages for individual vessels as well, with cruisers limited to 10,000 tons, for example; capital ships were limited to 35,000 tons and aircraft carriers to 27,000 tons, although both the British and Americans were allowed two carriers of up to 33,000 tons each. Both the Royal Navy and the United States Navy were limited to a total warship tonnage of 525,000 tons, while Japan, a First World War ally, was limited to

The importance of the battleship to the Royal Navy in 1939 was borne out by the construction of a new class of ships, one of which was HMS *Anson*, seen here in June 1942. *(IWM A10134)*

315,000 tons, and France and Italy to 175,000 tons each. These limitations had some unexpected results, with all three of the largest 'treaty navies' having battle-cruisers in excess of their permitted tonnage, and all three took the option of converting two of these ships to aircraft carriers, although the Japanese lost one of their battlecruisers while it was under conversion, as a result of an earthquake, and converted a battleship instead.

The statistics tell one story, but there were practical differences that meant that the state of the Royal Navy was worse than it might have been. The first of these was the determination of successive British inter-war governments to tighten the Washington restrictions and drive down the tonnage of ship-types to much less than that allowed under the treaty, aiming at a figure of around 8,500 tons for a heavy cruiser and 23,000 tons for an aircraft carrier. Not surprisingly, the future Axis powers took an opposing view, and consistently understated their tonnages. At the London Naval Conference of 1930, the Japanese attempted to obtain parity with both the UK and the USA. Four years later, Japan formally notified the other Washington Naval Treaty signatories that she no longer considered herself bound by its restrictions. German desire for rearmament became increasingly clear after Hitler came to power in 1933, although the Paris Air Agreement of 1926 had already removed the restrictions on German commercial aviation and aircraft manufacture. The London Naval Treaty of 1936 paved the way for the reconstruction of the German navy, restricted by the Washington Naval Treaty to a coastal defence force, granting Germany a total tonnage equivalent to 35 per cent of that of the Royal Navy, although within this figure, what can only be regarded as an oversight or collective memory loss allowed Germany parity with the Royal Navy in terms of submarines! The Germans even managed to build extra ships once new tonnage was permitted, ordering the battlecruiser *Gneisenau* secretly.

The second problem was that the Royal Navy had lost its aviation element, the Royal Naval Air Service, with the creation of the Royal Air Force on 1 April 1918. So it happened that between the wars, the navy that had invented the aircraft carrier and had come to know more about the operation of aircraft from ships than any other navy, found itself providing aircraft carriers for an air force to use. Many have drawn attention to the poor state of British naval aircraft at the outbreak of war, and some have blamed this on the Air Ministry, even though it too suffered from severe financial constraints until the late 1930s. The real problem, however, was the loss of experienced naval aviation personnel to the RAF in 1918. While the Fleet Air Arm of the Royal Air Force had included a number of naval airmen, especially for the catapult lights aboard battleships and cruisers, most naval officers knew little about aviation and cared even less. It was the Admiralty who believed that high-performance aircraft could not be operated off aircraft carriers. By contrast, in the United States Navy, with control of its own air power, even including the shore-based, long-range maritime-reconnaissance aircraft, there were senior officers such as Read and Towers with a real understanding of naval aviation.

In fact, this leads us to another weakness of the Royal Navy between the two world wars. It had quickly forgotten the teaching of Lord Fisher that the future of naval warfare would be in the air and under the sea. It still clung to the belief that future war at sea would see major fleet actions dominated by the battleship, and officers continued to be taught the 'lessons' of Jutland.

So, here we have it. A navy that had played fair and abided by its treaty limitations, hampered by tightly drawn public purse-strings and by a zealous and unwarranted desire to reduce ship-sizes on the part of the body politic, facing opponents who had consistently ignored their treaty obligations and whose expansion plans had never been limited by money, but by shipbuilding capacity and the availability of raw materials.

The impact of all this on the individual serviceman should not be underestimated. Across-the-board pay cuts during the financial crisis of 1931 resulted in mutiny among ratings aboard the ships of the Atlantic Fleet at Invergordon on the east coast of Scotland. Officers without a ship or a posting ashore awaiting them all too frequently saw their careers interrupted by a spell on half-pay, and this was a danger of service life for officers as senior as rear admiral! Half-pay was not abolished until 1938 and in that same year, faced with the need to increase recruitment and improve retention rates, officers over the age of 30 years received a marriage allowance for the first time. The Women's Royal Naval Service, the 'Wrens', was also reintroduced.

The outbreak of war did not come as a surprise to the Royal Navy, which had expected war from October 1935 onwards, after Italy had invaded Abyssinia (present-day Ethiopia), and indeed many in the Mediterranean Fleet at the time were surprised and disappointed that the League of Nations did not sanction war with Italy. The successive crises over Czechoslovakia and Italy's seizure of Albania had also increased tensions.

Around the odd corners of naval bases and even merchant ports, former warships could be found 'hulked' as accommodation and training vessels for the Royal Navy, and sometimes as home to divisions of the reserves. This is HMS *Eaglet. (IWM A29000)*

A BLUE-WATER NAVY

The world's navies are generally divided into those that are 'blue water', or ocean-going, or 'brown water', which means that they are limited to coastal duties or perhaps a largely land-bound sea, such as the Baltic or the Black Sea. The Royal Navy has always been the consummate blue-water navy, with a worldwide reach, while also retaining the tasks that fall upon a brown-water navy, such as fisheries protection and, in times of war,

keeping ports open through minesweeping. By contrast, the United States Navy was largely able to overlook many of these tasks, except minesweeping, because of the existence of the United States Coast Guard, in many ways a brown-water navy, which belonged to the US Department of Transportation during peacetime, but came under naval control in wartime.

By 1939, the Royal Navy had been through a number of reorganisations. The Grand Fleet of the First World War had become first the Atlantic Fleet and, later, the Home Fleet. The Inskip Award of 1937 had seen naval aviation handed back to the Admiralty, which formally took control of the Fleet Air Arm in May 1939.

In 1939, the distribution of the Royal Navy was:

The Home Fleet, which was the largest single administrative formation.
The Mediterranean Fleet, with its bases at Malta, Gibraltar and Alexandria.
The China station, essentially meaning Hong Kong.
The East Indies station, mainly centred on Singapore.
The American station, meaning Bermuda.
The African station, based on Simonstown, near Cape Town in South Africa.
The West Indies station.

On the outbreak of war in 1939, the Home Fleet was the strongest element within the Royal Navy. The commander-in-chief was Adm Sir Charles Forbes, who had 5 battleships, 2 battlecruisers, 2 aircraft carriers, 3 squadrons with a total of 15 cruisers, 2 flotillas each with 8 or 9 destroyers, and some 20 or so submarines. The main forward base for the Home Fleet was Scapa Flow in Orkney. Scapa had been neglected since the previous conflict, and it was only as late as April 1938 that the Admiralty had decided that Rosyth would not be adequate for the coming conflict. All too soon, Scapa itself was to prove insecure, but in any case this was more of an anchorage than a base, lacking the heavy repair facilities available at Rosyth. On the other hand, Rosyth, on the north or Fife banks of the Firth of Forth, was too far south, about twelve hours' steaming from Scapa.

Also in home waters and in addition to the Home Fleet, another two battleships and two aircraft carriers were based in the English Channel, with three cruisers and a destroyer flotilla, while another two cruisers and a further destroyer flotilla were based on the Humber. Further escort vessels were based on Plymouth and Portsmouth.

Under wartime pressures, new North Atlantic and South Atlantic commands were created. There were also six home commands: Orkney and Shetland, Rosyth, Nore, Dover (created in October 1939), Portsmouth and Western Approaches. The last-named was initially at Plymouth, but soon moved to Liverpool. The China station became the British Eastern Fleet on 2 December 1941, with its own commander-in-chief, and was augmented by ships that had previously been allocated to Force Z. After the fall of Singapore and the Japanese attacks on Ceylon (now Sri Lanka), the British Eastern Fleet moved its headquarters to Kilindini, or Mombasa, in British East Africa (now Kenya). Operations in the Indian Ocean were helped by a secret refuelling base at Addu Atoll (now known as Gan).

Despite this network of fleets, commands and stations, it was to be the British Pacific Fleet that eventually became the most powerful when it was formed late in the war and, despite the title, it operated as part of the US operation against Japan as Task Force 57, part of the US Fifth Fleet. The two best-known 'forces' operating independently of the fleets were Force H, based on Gibraltar, convenient both for operations in the Atlantic and the Mediterranean, and the small Force K, based on Malta.

In addition, the Royal Navy had far closer links with the navies of the British Empire than would be the case today, when these relationships have largely been overtaken by those with Britain's allies within the North Atlantic Treaty Organisation, NATO. There were differences, however, and the Canadians, for example, took a far more independent view than say the Australians or New Zealanders. Nevertheless, the four main Commonwealth navies were the Royal Australian Navy, the Royal Canadian Navy and the Royal Indian Navy (which had been known as the Royal Indian Marine as late as 1935), as well as the New Zealand Division, which later under wartime pressures became the Royal New Zealand Navy. None of the other colonies maintained a naval force, although locally recruited personnel were present in many cases. While officially Egypt was an independent kingdom, it was still at this time run virtually as a colony by the United Kingdom, and the Royal Egyptian Navy was commanded by a British admiral.

In 1939, no other navy had such a spread of responsibilities as the Royal Navy. The French came closest, with the need to maintain ships in the Mediterranean and the Atlantic, as well as a small naval presence in their colonies, but as a far weaker force. Much can be noted from the fact that instead of 'fleets', the Marine Nationale was divided into Atlantic and Mediterranean Squadrons, as well as a Far Eastern station (in French Indo-China).

The Royal Navy and Royal Marines in June 1939 totalled 129,000 men, of whom just under 10,000 were officers. To bring it up to maximum strength in wartime, it could depend on recalling recently retired officers and ratings, as well as two categories of reserves, the Royal Naval Reserve (RNR) and the Royal Naval Volunteer Reserve (RNVR), which between them provided another 73,000 officers and men in 1939. The Royal Naval Reserve consisted mainly of people drawn from the merchant navy, often bringing with them outstanding navigation and ship-handling capabilities, although, of course, there were other branches, notably marine engineering. The Royal Naval Volunteer Reserve consisted of

people from all walks of life, and was to undergo massive wartime expansion, since most wartime recruits went into this servce. The old saying was that Royal Navy officers were 'gentlemen trying to become sailors, RNR officers were sailors trying to become gentlemen, and the RNVR were neither trying to become both'! Doubtless, RNR officers from the smarter shipping lines, such as P&O, would probably have refuted any suggestion that they were not gentlemen.

Included in the 1939 total were 12,400 officers and men in the Royal Marines. The Royal Marines had a number of roles aboard ship, including security and the RM Band Service, but on cruisers and battleships they also manned X turret, one of the after gun-mountings. The Fleet Air Arm included a significant number of RM pilots and some observers. As early as 1923, the Admiralty had received the recommendations of the Madden Committee, one of which was that the Royal Marines should have a more ambitious role, raising a striking force based on amphibious warfare and also a mobile force for defending overseas naval bases. These far-sighted recommendations were ignored, probably as a result of financial constraints, until war broke out, after which they were to form the foundation of the Royal Marines Commandos.

The demands of war saw the RNVR grow to 48,000 officers and 5,000 ratings. Many RNVR personnel rose to command corvettes, minesweepers and destroyers; others took command of Fleet Air Arm squadrons as that element of the RN expanded rapidly. By mid-1944, the RN had reached its peak strength of 863,500 personnel, including 73,500 of the Women's Royal Naval Service. Many of the lower-deck personnel in wartime were conscripts called up under the National Service Acts for 'hostilities only'. In many cases, when merchant shipping was

The pressures of war meant that anything and everything that could be used was pressed into service, including this unlikely looking vessel, the *Duenna*, a motor patrol yacht seen here off Plymouth. *(IWM A19336)*

taken up from trade, the ships' companies were signed up under special articles so that they became part of the Royal Navy and subject to naval discipline, with temporary naval ranks, although they retained certain Merchant Navy terms of service, such as danger money for working in a war zone.

The Royal Navy's wartime casualties amounted to 50,758 killed, with another 820 missing, presumed dead, and 14,663 wounded. The WRNS lost 102 killed and 22 wounded, mainly in air raids. By contrast, the Merchant Navy lost 30,248 men through enemy action. One crucial difference between the two navies was that while ratings in the Royal Navy were paid less than their Merchant Navy counterparts, their pay continued if their ship was lost, while their better-paid Merchant Navy opposite numbers had their pay stopped immediately

their ship was lost and not reinstated until they signed on to a new ship. This could be a serious loss of money for men who might have spent considerable time in an open boat, and then much longer after being rescued being taken to a port, where there might or might not be a ship looking for their services.

While many bases, including Singapore, had been neglected during the years of peace and recession, so too had many of the roles that the Royal Navy was to be called upon to perform, including combined operations. Deficiencies included the lack of suitable craft to place troops and their equipment ashore, and this shortcoming was only just beginning to be corrected as war broke out. It was not until Churchill came to power that the importance of combined operations was stressed, and in

July 1940 he set up a special directorate to develop this form of warfare and to ensure that men were trained and equipment developed. Fortunately, Admiralty control of the Royal Marines made the task easier. Had this been done earlier, it is tempting to think that the outcome of the Norwegian campaign would have been different. Some historians blame the proponents of air power for the lack of attention paid before the war to 'combined ops', with the air-minded claiming that seaborne landings were hazardous and at risk from air attack, but the culprit was really the extreme cheese-paring inflicted by successive governments, aided and abetted by the 'peace in our time' lobby.

Before the war, Area Combined Head-quarters, or ACHQs, were established close to Plymouth, Chatham and Rosyth, with all three services represented, but in reality these were mainly aimed at improving RN–RAF Coastal Command cooperation. As the war progressed, this system was extended to foreign stations. The Western Approaches ACHQ was moved in 1941 from Plymouth to Liverpool.

The fleet that went to war in September 1939 consisted of twelve battleships and battlecruisers, including HMS *Hood* ('The Mighty Hood', which despite its battle-cruiser designation had been the world's largest warship for many years), 7 aircraft carriers, of which 4 were either in reserve or earmarked for early retirement, 2 seaplane carriers of little use in the carrier age, 58 cruisers, 100 destroyers, 101 other escort vessels, 38 submarines and 232 aircraft. This compared badly with the 61 battleships, 2 aircraft carriers, 120 cruisers and 443 destroyers, plus many sloops for convoy protection with which the Royal Navy had struggled to maintain control of the seas in the previous global conflict. Yet by 1945, this fleet was to grow to 61 battleships and cruisers; 59 aircraft carriers; 846 destroyers, frigates and corvettes; 729 minesweepers; 131 submarines; 1,000 minor vessels and landing craft and 3,700 aircraft.

Much has been made of the contribution to Britain's armed forces of the dominions and colonies but, in terms of equipment, this was insignificant in 1939. None of the dominions could offer battleships or aircraft carriers, and in fact had relied heavily on the imperial power for defence. In the event of a threat from Japan, Australia and New Zealand had been promised the support of the Royal Navy. No one seems to have considered the possibility of fighting three nations, a war on three fronts, while there was still time to do something about it.

By contrast, the German navy, or Kriegs-marine, in 1939 had 2 old battleships, really the old coastal defence ships permitted under the Treaty of Versailles, 2 battle-cruisers, 3 armoured cruisers, 3 heavy cruisers, 6 light cruisers, 22 destroyers, 20 torpedo boats and small destroyers, and 59 submarines. The three armoured cruisers, or in German terms *panzerschiffs* (armoured ships), were known to the British as 'pocket battleships', in reality a description invented by the British media and a term not used by the Germans. Still under construction at the outbreak of war were the two battleships *Bismarck* and *Tirpitz*. In reality, the German navy was unprepared for the outbreak of war in 1939, having been assured by Hitler himself that war with the British Empire would not start until 1944 or 1945, with a major fleet battle probably not due until 1948. The Germans' long-term planning for the war at sea centred on what was known as Plan Z, which had replaced the earlier plans X and Y. This called for a significantly stronger fleet with 6 battleships, 8 heavy cruisers, 4 aircraft carriers, 17 light cruisers and 223 U-boats. The U-boat figure was actually increased further under pressure from Dönitz, head of the submarine force. To put Plan Z into perspective, by the time of its completion, the Royal Navy would also have been much stronger, with at least six more aircraft carriers and several new battleships and cruisers. Another factor was that both the Germans and the Italians had internal problems to overcome before they could press ahead with completion of the aircraft carriers, as in both countries the air forces insisted that all air power should be under their control.

The Italian navy was stronger still, and as Italy did not enter the war until June 1940, that has to be the relevant date for comparison. The Italians had 6 battleships and 7 heavy cruisers, 14 light cruisers and a coast defence ship, no less than 122 destroyers and torpedo boats and 119 submarines.

On this basis, the Royal Navy was outnumbered and outgunned by the opposition, even without the need to dilute its strength through maintaining a worldwide presence. The Imperial Japanese Navy was not to be an opponent until December 1941, by which time the United States was also in the war, but by that date, the Japanese could boast 10 battleships, with 2 still building, 8 aircraft carriers and 18 heavy cruisers, 20 light cruisers and 108 destroyers, as well as 65 submarines. The Japanese navy was the only Axis navy to have aircraft carriers; both the Germans and Italians had such ships planned, but although construction had started and was well advanced, it was never completed. An unusual feature in the Japanese navy was the inclusion of aircraft-carrying submarines, something long abandoned by the Royal Navy after the loss of the experimental *M2*, and even more unusual was the fact that some of the Japanese submarines could carry two aircraft.

Looking at navies in terms of the numbers of ships and manpower is not enough. In 1939, the Royal Navy had radar, the Italians did not. The Royal Navy also had ASDIC, or sonar as it would now be called, which was far superior to the hydrophones used during the First World War. In fact, the Italian navy did not expect to fight at night! In addition, the Royal Navy had the advantage of belonging to a maritime power that had a substantial merchant fleet and a large fishing fleet, an obvious source of experienced manpower and, in an emergency, ships as well. Many passenger liners became armed merchant cruisers, and while this concept proved to be a failure with heavy losses whenever these ships were confronted by the real thing, the trawlers lifted from the fishing fleets did sterling service on convoy escort duties and minesweeping, while the smaller fishing vessels helped to carry out the many small but important tasks around harbours and anchorages. Ferries were also called up, with those for the Isle of Wight handling minesweeping, while the continental and Channel Islands ferries often found themselves working either as troopships or as hospital ships. The Merchant Navy also provided the ocean rescue tugs that did so much to help warships and merchantmen in distress, being positioned at strategic locations around the British Isles and sometimes abroad as well, and these were also responsible for moving the sections of the Mulberry harbours required for the support of forces put ashore in the Normandy landings.

ADMIRALTY

The big difference between the Royal Navy and the British Army and the Royal Air Force was that the Admiralty was not simply the power that directed the Royal Navy: unlike the War Office and the Air Ministry, it was also an operational headquarters

Getting to hospital or a hospital ship was far from being a comfortable experience. This is a naval ambulance launch, fitted to carry six patients, but they were exposed to the elements. *(IWM A19140)*

every hour of the day and every day of the year. While the Royal Navy did have local commanders with substantial delegated authority, usually designated as the flag officer (flag rank being the Royal Navy's equivalent to a general officer in the British Army, or air rank in the RAF), there would often be a commander-in-chief over and above any flag officers. The term 'flag officer' meant those holding the rank of rear admiral and above. As an example, the Mediterranean Fleet had a commander-in-chief, with subordinate flag officers for cruisers, destroyers and aircraft carriers; on the other hand, Force H, based on Gibraltar, had a flag officer and enjoyed considerable autonomy, moving between the Atlantic and the western Mediterranean as the strategic position required. As the war

developed, not only was there a commander-in-chief for the Home Fleet, but also one for the Western Approaches as well.

As an operational as well as an administrative HQ, the Admiralty could, and did, send orders to individual COs aboard their ships over the heads of their local c-in-c, justified by the developments in naval intelligence. Indeed, the withholding of information by the Admiralty had contributed to the unhappy outcome of the Battle of Jutland in 1916, and that lesson had been learned. The Admiralty included an Operational Intelligence Centre (OIC), and this was to prove especially successful in countering the U-boat threat.

A long-established institution, the Admiralty dated from the reign of Henry VIII, and long before the Second World War was controlled by the Board of Admiralty, which itself had replaced the earlier post of Lord High Admiral. First Lord of the Admiralty was a political post and its holder a member of the Cabinet; at the outbreak of war the post was held by Sir Winston Churchill. The naval officers on the board were led by the First Sea Lord, who was also the Chief of the Naval Staff. The other sea lords were the Second Sea Lord, responsible for personnel; the Third Sea Lord or Controller of the Navy, responsible for ship building and repair, including the naval dockyards; the Fourth Sea Lord, responsible for victualling and supplies and the naval hospitals; and the most recent addition to this select group, the Fifth Sea Lord, in charge of naval aviation. Appendix I shows the constitution of the Board of Admiralty at the beginning of the war.

The First Sea Lord was supported by the Vice-Chief of the Naval Staff, who had wide-ranging responsibilities including intelligence, planning, communications, hydrography and navigation, and by three Assistant Chiefs of the Naval Staff, otherwise known as ACNS, who had responsibility for home, foreign and trade matters. In addition to these individual roles, each ACNS would also look after local defence, operations, training, gunnery and minesweeping.

The way in which this structure worked can be best shown by the example of the Western Approaches Command. This had responsibility for the Battle of the Atlantic and for the convoys, putting it under the direct responsibility of the ACNS (Trade). The Admiralty Trade Division planned routes for the convoys, working with the Submarine Tracking Room at the Admiralty, itself part of the Naval Intelligence Division. The allocation of merchant ships to convoys was the responsibility of the Naval Control Service, which had a presence in each merchant port.

Escort vessels were organised into groups under the control of Western Approaches.

Within the fleets, major warships such as battleships, battlecruisers, cruisers and aircraft carriers, were organised into squadrons, each of which could have two or more ships. Smaller warships such as destroyers, minesweepers and submarines were organised into flotillas, again with varying numbers of ships, although destroyer flotillas often seemed to consist of five vessels. A destroyer flotilla would be subdivided into two divisions. Within 'forces', the squadron and flotilla distinction was usually dropped, so that Force K, for example, based on Malta at the height of the siege, consisted simply of two cruisers and two destroyers for part of its existence. A submarine flotilla often operated independently and could have any number of craft, while submarine commanders usually had considerable delegated authority; there was none of the centralised direction that characterised the German U-boat fleet and which soon became a liability, since once the German 'Enigma' codes were broken the constant stream of signals could be decoded and signals traced to reveal the location of submarine wolf-packs. Later, the Admiralty became heavily involved in combined operations, and when the time came Combined Operations took over landing ships and landing craft.

THE WHITE ENSIGN

The white ensign – the standard of St George with a Union flag in the upper left quarter – is today synonymous with the Royal Navy. This is because from very early times English ships wore the cross of St George, although at times this was combined with other devices, for example during the Tudor period, when the green and white stripes of the Tudors sometimes also appeared. After the start of the Stuart period and the union of the English and Scottish crowns, the Scottish saltire and the cross of St George were combined, and the resultant flag flown from the masthead, while English and Scottish ships continued to wear their own national colours as well. In 1634, the combined flag was reserved for the use of the sovereign's own ships, although this was in abeyance during the period of the Commonwealth when Cromwell had warships revert to the cross of St George. In 1801, following the union with Ireland, the cross of St Patrick was added to the flag to create the Union flag as we know it today. As time wore on, a smaller version of the Union flag was carried on the bowsprit – smaller so as not to interfere with the rigging – and this became known as the jackstaff.

Meanwhile, the King's fleet was divided into three squadrons, with the senior or centre division wearing the red ensign and the second-most-senior, or van, division wearing the blue ensign, leaving the junior or rear division as the white division, with a white ensign. At that time, the white ensign was simply a white flag with the Union flag in the corner. Unfortunately, the French naval ensign was also white, so to prevent confusion with what was, after all, Great Britain's most usual opponent, the red cross was added. The system of having three different ensigns for the Royal Navy was itself troublesome, and quite irrelevant when ships were deployed singly or in small numbers. At Trafalgar, the entire fleet fought under the white ensign for the first time as Nelson was the vice-admiral of the white squadron. Ensigns were always worn at the stern.

After Trafalgar, the red ensign became the flag worn at the stern on ships not owned by the Crown, while the blue ensign became the flag for the Royal Naval Reserve and, later, the Royal Fleet Auxiliary, as well as one or two other select users. Masters of merchant vessels who were members of the Royal Naval Reserve were allowed to fly a blue ensign on their ships, but this right was normally only exercised on a Sunday. The new Union flag, strictly only ever a 'Union Jack' when flown on a warship, once again became the preserve of vessels owned by the Crown, with ships in private ownership supposed to fly a white jack, that is a Union flag with a white border. The white jack has become something of a rarity, largely because the practice grew of merchant vessels flying their house pennant on the jackstaff.

The practice grew of the white ensign and Union Jack being flown only on ships in port or at anchor, with the white ensign flown from the masthead when at sea. Certainly, this became more practical with aircraft carriers and other ships operating aircraft over the stern. As with all other British national and service flags, these have been flown only in daylight when they can be seen – hence the practice of hauling down flags at dusk and raising them again at dawn – contrary to the practice in most countries.

When two or more members of the Board of Admiralty are aboard a ship, the Admiralty flag could also be worn from the peak, this was based on the old flag for the Lord High Admiral, a gold foul anchor on a red background.

An admiral would fly a simple St George's cross when aboard a ship, his flagship of course, while a vice-admiral would fly a flag with a red ball in the top quarter closest to the mast, and a rear admiral would have a flag with a red ball in each of the two quarters closest to the mast. Commodores would fly a simple pennant with the cross of St George.

When on convoy duties, the convoy commodore, who could be a Merchant Navy master or a naval officer not necessarily of commodore rank, flew a pennant with a blue cross.

CHAPTER TWO

NO PHONEY WAR AT SEA

In the wreck of the continent, and the disappointment of our hopes there,
what has been the security of this country but its naval preponderance?
William Pitt, 2 February 1801

On looking back at the Second World War, one often hears mention of the 'phoney war', that period between the outbreak of war in September 1939 and the German invasion of Denmark and Norway the following April, when nothing seemed to happen. The Germans called this period the *Sitzkrieg*, the 'sitting war', which was far more accurate as the opposing armies sat on opposite sides of the French Maginot Line. For the mass of the population, but especially for the civilians, little seemed to happen after war was declared on 3 September 1939.

There was no such thing as a phoney war at sea. On 3 September 1939, the very day that war broke out, the liner *Athenia*, 13,500 tons, was torpedoed off the Hebrides, without the warning required by the Hague Convention. Out of the 128 who lost their lives, twenty-eight were Americans, giving Hitler the opportunity to argue that the ship had been the victim of a British attack intended to sour relations between Germany and the United States. Later, the U-boat commander was to claim that he had mistaken the ship for either a Q-ship or an armed merchant cruiser.

Whatever view one might take of these arguments, the Germans were determined to bring the war home to the Royal Navy at the outset. During the first months of the war, losses at sea became all too commonplace. Just two weeks after the start of the war, on 17 September 1939, after flying had ended for the day, the aircraft carrier *Courageous* was torpedoed by *U-29* and sunk while on an anti-submarine sweep. The carrier sank in just twenty minutes, taking 500 men with her, many of whom would have been trapped below decks in the dark. Submarine sweeps were wasteful and hazardous, akin to looking for a needle in a haystack, given the available intelligence at the time. Worse was to follow. It was to be small consolation that the first German aircraft to be shot down, on 26 September, was accounted for by fighters from *Ark Royal*, for on 14 October, *U-47* penetrated the sheltered anchorage at Scapa Flow in Orkney and torpedoed the battleship *Royal Oak*, which sank with the loss of 833 lives. The submarine had fired two salvoes, each of three torpedoes; two torpedoes of the first salvo missed, and the one that made contact failed to explode properly, but forty-five minutes later a second salvo exploded under the battleship, detonating her magazine.

November was no better, for on the 23rd of that month, while on convoy escort duty, the armed merchant cruiser *Rawalpindi*, a former P&O liner, was sunk by the German battlecruisers *Gneisenau* and *Scharnhorst* off Iceland. This was an unequal contest between the finest ships in the Kriegsmarine at the time and a ship that not only lacked the firepower, armour and speed of her adversaries, but was also unable to match their rate of fire and gunnery direction.

This succession of losses was reversed before the year ended with the first British victory of the war. The brighter news came from the South Atlantic when, on 13 December, the cruisers *Ajax*, *Achilles* and *Exeter* encountered the German pocket battleship, or *panzerschiff, Admiral Graf Spee*, which had been engaged in commerce raiding, near the mouth of the River Plate. Despite being outgunned, the three cruisers used superior tactics that caused the *Graf Spee* to divide her fire, and managed to damage her to the extent that she had to seek refuge in Montevideo, in neutral Uruguay. Here, she was allowed three days for temporary repairs, but instead put all but a skeleton crew ashore and sailed on 17 December, simply to be scuttled. Had she not taken that course, her opponents were ready to resume the Battle of the River Plate. Many theories have been advanced for this success, including the inability of the German ship to direct her fire in two directions simultaneously, or that she might have mistaken the two light cruisers, *Ajax* and *Achilles*, for destroyers.

Hunting for commerce raiders was slightly easier than chasing submarines, especially since a growing number of British ships had radar; moreover, battleships and cruisers at the time still carried seaplanes for aerial reconnaissance, although obviously the support of an aircraft carrier was far better. The danger was that the heavier armed units of the Kriegsmarine could usually outgun the cruisers sent to catch them: 11in guns were far superior in range and in the damage that they could inflict to the 8in guns of a heavy cruiser, let alone a light cruiser's 6in main armament. British cruisers on foreign stations were exercised in dealing with a German surface raider, and by a curious twist of fate, during one such exercise in 1938, the heavy cruiser *Exeter* had played the part of a German pocket battleship.

The Germans believed that their *panzerschiffs* could only be countered by a British capital ship, but this was far from true. Perhaps it showed some foresight that before the outbreak of war, one of the *Graf Spee*'s sisters, *Deutschland*, was renamed *Lützow* because someone thought of the impact on the nation's morale if *Deutschland* was sunk. In 1940, the *panzerschiffs* were redesignated as heavy cruisers.

As early as 16 October 1939, the Luftwaffe had mounted a raid on British warships moored in the Firth of Forth. On this occasion the need to avoid civilian casualties was very much in mind. The nine Junkers Ju88 bombers of *Kampfgeschwader* 30 had as their target the battlecruiser *Hood*, but finding her in Rosyth Dockyard, turned their attention instead to the two cruisers *Edinburgh* and *Southampton*, and both ships were bombed. Although the damage to *Edinburgh* was slight, *Southampton* received a direct hit from a 1,100lb armour-piercing bomb that went through the port side before travelling down through three decks and out through the starboard side, after which it exploded causing further damage to the ship. Had the bomb exploded before it emerged, the ship could have been lost.

The concern for civilian life was not to last long, and at the height of the 'Blitz', the

Royal Navy's three main home bases at Chatham, Portsmouth and Plymouth were to be heavily bombed.

A pleasing footnote to the end of the *Admiral Graf Spee* came in the New Year. On 14 February, the *Graf Spee*'s supply ship, the *Altmark*, carrying British prisoners, merchant seamen from ships sunk during the commerce raids, was boarded by men from the destroyer *Cossack* in Jøssingfjord and the 303 prisoners set free. *Altmark* had sought refuge in Norwegian territorial waters after being challenged by *Cossack* while at sea, and the British destroyer had earlier been barred from entering neutral Norwegian waters by that country's destroyers as neither ship should have been there. Captain (later Rear Adm) Philip Vian withdrew immediately after releasing the prisoners. The Norwegian government sent a strong protest to London against what it regarded as high-handedness on the part of the Royal Navy, but even so, allowed the *Altmark* to continue her passage to Germany. Many believe that the '*Altmark* incident' was a factor in encouraging Hitler to invade Norway, but far more important was the need to secure the Norwegian ports and coastline essential for convoys bringing iron ore from Sweden, especially in winter, when the Gulf of Bothnia froze. No doubt he also felt that seizing both Denmark and Norway would also weaken the British blockade.

While the Royal Navy had been quick to introduce a convoy escort system on the outbreak of hostilities, having learnt the harsh lessons of the First World War, German naval operations were seriously inhibited at first by both the blockade and the need for submarines and surface raiders to sail around the north of Scotland and through the Denmark Strait to reach their operational waters. The fall of France gave the Germans established naval ports with open access to the Bay of Biscay and

beyond. The more direct route from Germany down the North Sea and through the Straits of Dover was judged to be too risky – a factor that was to be made good use of later when planning the audacious 'Channel Dash'.

Meanwhile, the Royal Navy had also spent the first few months of the war engaged in other activities. The widespread belief in 1939 was that the fighting, once it started, would see a repeat of the trench warfare of the First World War, but in any case, the territorial integrity of France had to be defended from the almost inevitable German assault. Between September 1939 and June 1940, half a million men and 89,000 vehicles were moved to France across the English Channel, without loss. Despite fears that German U-boats would intervene, only one passed safely through the Straits of Dover. So successful were the defensive minefields laid by the Royal Navy that during October 1939, by which time the last of 3,600 mines had been laid to create a barrier, three U-boats were lost.

Nevertheless, the Second World War saw the Royal Navy at a disadvantage on the other side of the British Isles, where it felt the loss of its bases in the Irish Republic. Even though they were supposed to be available under treaty, the Navy was deprived of the use of Berehaven in the south and Lough Swilly in the north. The latter was relatively easy to replace, with nearby Londonderry, across the border in Northern Ireland, becoming a handy substitute, with the advantage that it also had airfield facilities to the east at Eglinton, now known as Derry City Airport. The Western Approaches would have benefited from the base at Berehaven, as would the Atlantic convoys, but Devonport, near Plymouth, remained operational despite heavy German aerial attack; moreover, new bases, more conveniently sited, grew at

Milford Haven near the western extremity of South Wales, as well as further north at Liverpool and on the Clyde in Scotland.

Other steps were also taken to improve the security of merchant vessels, so that by March 1941 the Admiralty Defensively Equipped Merchant Ship (DEMS) organisation had equipped 3,434 ships with anti-submarine guns and had also put one or more close-range anti-aircraft guns on 4,431 British and Allied ships. Initially, naval ratings and army gunners were seconded, but later merchant seamen were trained to take their place.

NORWAY

The Royal Navy found itself presented with a challenge by the German invasion of Denmark and Norway. Denmark was over-

Narvik, April 1940, showing the poor visibility and inclement weather that confronted those involved in this operation. In the middle ground is the destroyer HMS *Eskimo*, damaged in the second battle. *(IWM A25)*

The cruiser HMS *Cairo* at Narvik. She was one of several elderly cruisers converted to anti-aircraft duties. She was lost on the famous Malta convoy, Operation Pedestal, in August 1942. *(IWM N331)*

whelmed quickly as German forces swept over the border and an invasion fleet was sent directly into the harbour at Copenhagen. Intervention by Britain and France was simply not possible. Norway was a different case, where defence was aided by the terrain and by the loss of key German commanders in the invasion, which also gave the Norwegian government time to move out of Oslo and organise resistance by the country's small armed forces. Alerted to the impending invasion, the Royal Navy had already started to mine Norwegian waters on 8 April, the day before the invasion started. An Anglo-French expeditionary force with an initial 13,000 men was quickly assembled and by mid-April British and French troops landed in Norway, with the landings covered by the aircraft carrier *Furious*, which then moved to the role of aircraft transport while the newest carrier, *Ark Royal*, took over protection of the landing fleet and forces ashore. The Mediterranean Fleet aircraft carrier *Glorious* was immediately recalled to home waters, and the carrier *Eagle*, in the Indian Ocean, was ordered to the Mediterranean.

With few good airfields available ashore, the Norwegian campaign was ideally suited to carrier operations, had sufficient ships been available together with aircraft of adequate performance. As it was, the Luftwaffe gained the upper hand as early as 10 April, when it mounted an attack against ships of the Home Fleet south-west of Bergen, sinking a destroyer and causing minor damage to the battleship *Rodney* and three cruisers, *Devonshire*, *Glasgow* and *Southampton*, the last of these only recently repaired after her earlier encounter with the German airmen.

The battle was far from one-sided, however, and an even greater success was scored against the German fleet that same day. Blackburn Skuas of nos 800 and 803 Naval Air Squadrons flying from HMS *Sparrowhawk*, RNAS Hatston, on Orkney, attacked and sank the German light cruiser *Königsberg* at Bergen, the first major warship to be sunk by naval aircraft. The aircraft used bombs, just 500lb apiece; a light cruiser was probably the limit of their

The withdrawal from Norway was marred by the loss of the aircraft carrier *Glorious*. This photograph was taken the day before, with recently landed RAF Hurricanes still ranged aft on her flight deck.

capability as the bombs would have bounced off the armour of a battleship, or perhaps even have broken up. Still on 10 April the Royal Navy proved that it could give a good account of itself again, with the first destroyer action in Narvik Fjord: British destroyers sank two German destroyers and several merchantmen, but two of their own number were also sunk. Far more successful was the second destroyer action at Narvik, often referred to as the 'Second Battle of Narvik', with the battleship *Warspite* and nine destroyers sinking the remaining eight German destroyers on 13 April.

Nevertheless, a combination of factors, including some reluctance to press home attacks by forces ashore, meant that the Norwegian campaign was gradually being lost to advancing German forces, and the decision was taken to abandon Norway in order to reinforce British and French forces as the Battle of France developed. In fact, the withdrawal and disengagement from fighting was sufficiently difficult that few if any of the resources freed from the Norwegian campaign were able to be redeployed in France.

The evacuation was covered by aircraft from both *Ark Royal* and *Glorious*. The RAF squadrons ashore were ordered to destroy their aircraft, since these did not have sufficient range to fly home, and evacuate their personnel. Despite having no carrier deck-landing experience, the pilots of the Hurricanes decided to save their aircraft by flying them to the carriers. Despite her shorter deck, *Glorious* was chosen because her larger lifts meant that the aircraft could be struck down into her hangars without having to have their wings removed. As the Hurricanes lacked arrester-hooks sandbags were attached to weigh down the tailwheels and the aircraft were landed successfully aboard the ship.

Short of fuel, *Glorious* left Norway on 8 June and steamed westwards at a stately 17 knots, which her commanding officer considered fast enough to save the ship from submarine attack. Despite the absence of radar aboard, her captain did not order aerial reconnaissance to be flown, nor even order a lookout from her crow's nest. All of her aircraft were struck down, while bombs and torpedoes were removed and returned to the magazines. Her sole protection was an escort of two destroyers. On to this peaceful scene at 16.00 appeared the two battlecruisers, *Scharnhorst* and *Gneisenau*, among the few German ships to be fitted with radar. Both ships opened fire at 28,000 yards with their 11in guns, with *Glorious* having no chance of firing back. The carrier increased her speed and the order was given to launch her aircraft. As additional boilers were fired up, the five remaining Swordfish were brought up from the hangars and made ready to launch a torpedo attack. At 16.15, the Germans scored their first hit on the carrier, destroying the aircraft, which were still without their crews, and, the range having been found, further shells then penetrated the flight deck and exploded among the Hurricanes in the hangar below. Within minutes, the hangar deck was an inferno as fuel left in the Hurricanes ignited and their ammunition exploded. At 17.00 a salvo destroyed the bridge, but by this time the ship was a pillar of smoke, despite having increased her speed to 27 knots. The destroyer escorts, *Ardent* and *Acasta*, were both lost making a desperate torpedo attack on the *Scharnhorst*, which was damaged by one of *Acasta*'s torpedoes.

An hour later, *Glorious* slipped beneath the waves. It is believed that as many as 900 of her combined ship's company and embarked RAF aircrew of 1,500 may have survived the attack, but just thirty-nine men survived two days in cold water, without food or drink, before they were rescued.

In the first twelve months of war, the lack of sensible precautions had cost the Royal Navy two of its scarce carriers, by coincidence sister ships. The run of bad luck continued, for on 13 June, when fifteen Skuas of 800 and 803 squadrons embarked in *Ark Royal* were sent to attack the *Scharnhorst* and *Gneisenau* at Trondheim, they flew into heavy AA fire from the ships and also met a strong fighter defence; the Skua, 'more dive-bomber than fighter', stood little chance against such opposition, so that eight of the fifteen aircraft were shot down and their crews either killed or taken prisoner. Although one survivor likened the operation to the Charge of the Light Brigade, the operation was far less successful, since when the *Scharnhorst* was struck by a bomb, it failed to explode.

DUNKIRK

The Royal Navy organised the evacuation of the British Expeditionary Force in Operation Dynamo, coordinated by Admiral Sir Bertram Ramsay at Dover. The operation moved 338,226 British and French troops to the south of England. Inevitably, most of the ships used were civilian-owned and manned, including not just merchant vessels and fishing boats, but private craft as well, many of which did sterling work moving troops from the beaches and the shallows out to ships moored in deeper water, although two-thirds of those evacuated were taken off the harbour's east mole straight on to ships. Meanwhile, other warships were used to keep German naval units, and especially E-boats,

The Southern Railway Channel Islands ferry *Isle of Jersey*, taken up and used as a hospital ship during the Battle of France. Despite the clear markings, many of these were attacked by the Luftwaffe. *(IWM A111)*

from the evacuation fleet, and to provide anti-aircraft cover during the period of the evacuation. Nothing larger than a destroyer could get close enough to help, but the Fleet Air Arm also assisted by lending several of its Swordfish squadrons to RAF Coastal Command to provide short-range reconnaissance and anti-shipping measures.

Operation Dynamo officially started on 26 May, although by this time 28,000 rear-echelon personnel had already been evacuated. Part of the problem was that the safest route from Dover to Dunkirk to avoid the many shallows and sandbanks in the English Channel entailed ships crossing from Dover to Calais and then sailing northwards along the coast to Dunkirk, exposing the rescue fleet to artillery fire and aerial attack. Two more-northerly routes

were also used, but one of these had to be abandoned as it was dangerously exposed to attack by U-boats and E-boats. The evacuation was not announced to the public until 29 May. The worst day for aerial attack was 1 June, after which Admiral Ramsay banned daylight passages. The last sailings were on the night of 3/4 June, when most of the 53,000 French personnel were rescued.

The Dunkirk evacuation was costly, with nine British and French destroyers and eight troopships lost, and out of the officially recorded 848 civilian vessels and small naval craft, no less than 72 were lost to enemy action and another 163 lost in collisions, with 45 damaged. Yet, while Churchill rightly reminded the British people that 'wars are not won by evacuations', the loss of a third of a million British and French soldiers would have been a shock that could have completely undermined the ability to continue the war, and public morale might not have survived the trauma.

DEALING WITH THE FRENCH FLEET

The fall of France immediately meant that the British Empire was on its own in the war, and nowhere was this felt more strongly than in the Mediterranean and in North Africa. Worse still, in the closing stages of the Battle of France, Italy had entered the war, with the long 'leg' of Italy almost bisecting the Mediterranean and Italian forces within easy reach of the Mediterranean Fleet's main base of Malta. While the Germans had not conquered the whole of France, largely because of Italy's late entry

into the conflict, the creation of what was effectively a puppet state by the Vichy French meant that the allegiance of the surviving French navy units could not be taken for granted. It was bad enough to lose an ally with its ships and seamen; worse still would have been to have them transferred to German control. Those French ships that had escaped to Portsmouth were quickly seized on 3 July under cover of darkness, while measures were put in hand to neutralise the ships sharing Alexandria in Egypt with the Royal Navy, repatriating most of their crews and ensuring that the guns could not be used. The big problem was the fate of the substantial number of major fleet units at ports in France's African territories, divided between Oran, sometimes known as Mers El-Kebir, in Algeria and Dakar in West Africa.

The guns of the battleship HMS *Rodney* frame the battlecruiser HMS *Hood*, just returned from the Mediterranean in 1940. *(IWM A111)*

Tackling the French fleet was an unwelcome task for the Royal Navy, whose personnel were all too aware that until recently this had been an ally. Vice Adm Sir James Somerville, in command of Force H based on Gibraltar, was anxious to avoid a battle with the French. On 3 July, he presented his opposite number at Oran, Admiral Gensoul, with an ultimatum, demanding that the French warships be handed over or neutralised, by which he meant that they should be non-operational. Force H included the aircraft carrier *Ark Royal*, commanded by Capt Holland, who was sent to meet Gensoul, flying in a Fairey Swordfish seaplane from a battlecruiser. The British ultimatum was rejected, leaving Holland to fly back to his ship, on which the arrester wires were removed to allow the seaplane to land safely on her deck.

Somerville now had no option but to attack the French fleet and the shore installations. A single burst of gunfire from one of his battleships blew an army barracks off the crest of a hill. Supported by an attack by aircraft from *Ark Royal*, in just fifteen minutes Force H blew up the old French battleship *Bretagne*, crippled the battleship *Provence* and the battlecruiser *Dunkerque*, both of which had to be run aground to prevent them sinking; but the battlecruiser *Strasbourg* and six destroyers managed to escape to Toulon. Force H's ships were completely undamaged in this short action, although the thin flight deck of the British carrier would have been vulnerable to heavy shell fire.

On 8 July, the small aircraft carrier HMS *Hermes* and two heavy cruisers attacked the rest of the French fleet at Dakar, damaging the battleship *Richelieu*. On this occasion, the French did not attempt to escape, doubtless because this would have meant sailing past Gibraltar, a high-risk strategy, and the force at Dakar remained intact until a further attempt was made to destroy it by the Royal Navy in September, when the French fought back and heavy damage was suffered by both navies.

Truly, the Royal Navy was on its own.

CHAPTER THREE

BATTLE OF THE ATLANTIC

*The decisive point in warfare against England lies
in attacking her merchant shipping in the Atlantic.*
Dönitz to Raeder, September 1939

Traditionally, the protection of trade has always been one of the most important tasks of the Royal Navy, whether from piracy or enemy action. In wartime, effective trade protection normally entailed a convoy system. Convoys were not a twentieth-century invention. They were used to protect Roman shipping against Mediterranean pirates, by the Spaniards to protect shipping

to and from their American colonies, and by the British during the Napoleonic wars. The Royal Navy was severely criticised for its reluctance to instigate a convoy system during the First World War, but eventually was compelled to do so.

In addition to adopting the convoy system, the Royal Navy also went looking for the enemy. While anti-submarine sweeps

The destroyer HMS *Express*, damaged by a mine in 1940, with her bows and forecastle blown away, shortly before she was taken in tow by HMS *Kelvin*. *(IWM A534)*

Exercises involved firing blank ammunition, including torpedoes. This is a dummy torpedo after it has reached the end of its 'run', bobbing nose-up in the water. *(IWM A1398)*

were abandoned for some time after the loss of the aircraft carrier *Courageous*, until the number of escort carriers and escort vessels to accompany them, together with Ultra intelligence, made this safer and more effective, much attention was also given to commerce raiders. Ships were deployed to the South Atlantic and to the Indian Ocean in particular. Indeed, this was the role being undertaken by *Eagle* in the Indian Ocean when she was recalled to the Mediterranean to replace *Glorious* after the start of the Norwegian campaign. It was also the role of *Exeter*, *Ajax* and *Achilles* when they found and destroyed the German pocket battleship, *Admiral Graf Spee*, off the River Plate in December 1939.

For many senior naval officers, the Second World War meant once again looking for a major fleet engagement. This was unlikely from the outset. The German navy was not expecting war to come so soon, and neither of its large battleships was ready, while for the most part the *Kriegsmarine* harboured its surface fleet, both literally and figuratively, relying heavily on its submarines and E-boats. In the Far East, the Royal Navy was in no shape to tackle the Japanese head-on. It was outnumbered and lacked the balanced fleet that was essential for success. The small forces that did confront the Japanese in the beginning were wiped out. Only later in the war did the Royal Navy succeed in taking the offensive to the Japanese, by which time the enemy was in no state for a fleet action and the burden fell upon the Fleet Air Arm.

The statistics for Second World War convoys were impressive. During the war years there were 2,889 escorted trade convoys to and from the UK, with a total of 85,775 ships. There were in addition another 7,944 coastal convoys, comprising 175,608 ships. This latter figure has to be put into perspective, for after the fall of France, coastal convoys did not operate through the English Channel because of the danger of enemy attack, and instead their cargo became yet another burden for the railways. It should also be remembered that since the same ship would, while it survived, take part in many convoys, the chances of a ship surviving the war were much less than these figures might suggest.

Although it would be foolhardy to ignore the protection offered by a convoy and its escorts, the convoy system was not compulsory and not universally accepted. Fast troopships, such as the former liners *Queen Mary* and *Queen Elizabeth*, sailed alone, relying on speed to keep them safe. Many of the ships lost from convoys were stragglers, ships that for one reason or another could not keep up with the rest of the convoy and so became vulnerable to attack.

The convoy war was the reason for many innovations. Destroyers were seen at one and the same time as too important to risk on convoys, and their design, intended for high speed, made them uncomfortable at convoy speeds in the open ocean, so the small but cheap and cheerful corvettes of the Flower class soon appeared. The need for dedicated anti-submarine or anti-aircraft vessels also saw the reinvention of the frigate, a type of ship that had gradually disappeared in the late nineteenth century. Armed merchant cruisers were conversions of passenger liners, but soon proved vulner-

able to enemy cruisers and although they did sterling service, their role was sacrificial until later, when the surviving ships became auxiliary anti-aircraft cruisers. More useful were the catapult-armed merchant ships, the CAM-ships, with a solitary fighter to provide air cover, but since this couldn't return to the ship and either had to fly ashore or, more usually, ditch, this was very much a single-shot solution. Better still were the merchant aircraft carriers, MAC-ships, with converted tankers carrying three Fairey Swordfish and grain-ships carrying four, which were used in the anti-submarine and reconnaissance role. Most effective of all were the escort carriers, initially merchant ships converted to carry aircraft; later versions used merchant hull designs and were laid down to be escort carriers, but were capable of conversion for merchant duties at the end of hostilities. Escort carriers could carry a mix of aircraft, fighters as well as anti-submarine types.

Not all convoys were the same. The hazards and the measures needed to protect them depended on the route. On the North Atlantic, the main threat to the convoys occurred in what was variously known as the 'Atlantic Gap', or the 'Black Gap', that part of the North Atlantic in which convoys were outside the protection of shore-based maritime-reconnaissance aircraft. The gap reduced steadily as longer-range aircraft became available, but land-based aircraft always suffered from the disadvantage that for every aircraft flying over and around a convoy, another had to be on its way back to base and yet one more was on its way out. At the base for these aircraft, there would be several more aircraft undergoing maintenance, refuelling and rearming while their crews took a well-earned rest. The presence of the venerable Swordfish with a convoy forced many U-boat commanders to remain submerged, so that they could not catch up with a convoy, and while the Swordfish often did attack and destroy a U-boat, in many cases the best results came from Swordfish and escort vessels working together. It was the convoy war and the need to protect trade that saw the birth of Canadian and Dutch naval aviation, brought into being as part of the Fleet Air Arm and at first fully integrated with it.

The impact of the MAC-ships was considerable. From May 1943 until VE Day, MAC-ships made 323 crossings of the Atlantic and escorted 217 convoys, of which just one was successfully attacked. The Swordfish they carried flew 4,177 patrols and searches, an average of thirteen per crossing, or one per day at average convoy speed. The problem of convoy protection had been foreseen before the war, and the need for a MAC-ship or something similar had been proposed, so it seems incredible that it took so long for the MAC-ships to appear. As it was, they arrived at virtually the same time as the escort carriers and had they been available in 1941, the war could well have been much shorter, and certainly less costly.

The convoys through the Bay of Biscay suffered similar problems to those on the North Atlantic once France had fallen and both the Kriegsmarine and the Luftwaffe had access to French bases. These convoys often divided at Gibraltar, with part of the convoy proceeding to Malta and, in the early days, Alexandria, while the rest would steam to destinations in Africa and beyond. Once the Axis made the passage across the Mediterranean all but impossible, convoys for Egypt also sailed via the Cape and the Suez Canal. This was taking the long way round and the much-lengthened route made heavy demands on shipping, and on the supply of escorts.

A weakness of the German U-boat campaigns was that the submarine commanders made and received a significant volume of radio transmissions, sending reports back to HQ and being given instructions. The Germans believed these communications to be secure, using their Enigma codes. Nevertheless, these codes had been broken by the British after a German submarine, *U-570*, had been captured by a British escort vessel south of Iceland in August 1941. The capture of the submarine was kept secret, although she was commissioned into British service as HMS *Graph*. The possession of the codes and British Ultra intelligence was a crucial factor in winning the Battle of the Atlantic, but it also provided significant advance warning elsewhere as well.

THE ATLANTIC CONVOYS

During the final four months of 1939, British and French shipping losses totalled 509,320 tons, concentrated entirely in the Atlantic and North Sea, although the Battle of the Atlantic did not begin in earnest until after the fall of France, which gave the Germans naval and air stations on the Atlantic coast.

The Battle of the Atlantic can be divided into four distinct phases:

1. The period from July 1940, after the fall of France, until December 1941, when the United States entered the war after the Japanese attack on Pearl Harbor.
2. January 1942 to March 1943, when the German U-boats were dominant, as numbers increased more quickly than the Allied countermeasures could destroy them.
3. April and May 1943, when the arrival of escort carriers and MAC-ships combined to inflict heavy and unsustainable losses on the U-boats, which were temporarily withdrawn, many of them for re-equipping.

The vessels taken up from trade included the all-important rescue tugs, which were positioned at strategic points ready to go to the aid of crippled ships, a hazardous task since these were easy prey for enemy ships, submarines and aircraft. Later, many of these tugs towed the Mulberry Harbour sections across the Channel after D-Day. This is HM Rescue Tug *Advantage* at Greenock. *(IWM A25721)*

4. The period from June 1943 to May 1945, with the closure of the 'Atlantic Gap' by escort carriers and ever longer-range maritime-reconnaissance aircraft, with growing losses by the U-boats.

At the outset of war in Europe in September 1939, Germany had just fifty-nine submarines, but the war years saw a total of 785 U-boats sunk. The total merchant shipping losses for 1940 alone amounted to 2,451,663 tons in the Atlantic and North Sea. Most of the North Sea was to be closed to convoys as a result, with Germany holding the entire coastline of mainland Europe from the North Cape to the Bay of Biscay. The two worst months were June, with 356,937 tons lost in the Atlantic, and October, when 361,459 tons were lost. To put this into perspective, the loss for the year was almost a sixth of the available tonnage of UK merchant shipping, although this would have been boosted by new construction and by vessels that had fled from the German occupied territories (Norway and the Netherlands both had considerable tonnages of merchant shipping, much of which escaped to operate with the British).

In the second half of 1940, from the end of August to the end of September, U-boats sank twenty-two ships from four convoys, a loss of 113,000 tons of shipping. This included, between 29 August and 2 September,

A tanker refuels HMS *Colombo* off Greenock using the line-astern method, which was both slow and more likely to be affected by bad weather than the abeam method favoured by the United States Navy. *(IWM A16661)*

six U-boats sinking ten ships totalling 40,000 tons from three convoys, HX66, OA204 and OB205. Later in September, five U-boats sank twelve ships totalling 73,000 tons from convoy HX72, which had sailed from Halifax, Nova Scotia.

This dire situation became worse in October. In the North Channel during the four days from 17–20 October, nine U-boats found the convoys SC7 and HX79, with a total of seventy-nine ships. Between them, the U-boats sank no less than thirty-two of the ships with a total tonnage of 155,000 tons, stopping only when they had exhausted their torpedoes. Just a few days later, on 23 October, just two U-boats accounted for no less than twelve ships, a total of 48,000 tons, from convoys SC11 and OB244. A further nine ships, 53,000 tons, were sunk from convoy HX90 by U-boats in December. To put the losses into perspective, during 1940 the average number of U-boats at sea in the operational zones each day was around a dozen. The massive build-up to a hundred or so U-boats patrolling daily was some time away. One authority on the wartime German navy, Jak Mallman Showell, maintains that two-thirds of the U-boat fleet, some 800 craft, never got within reach of the enemy, and that half of those that did only attacked four or fewer Allied ships. Most of the Allied losses were down to just 131 U-boats.

The U-boats were not the only predators. Armed and camouflaged merchantmen were deployed as auxiliary cruisers as early as April 1940, with *Atlantis*, *Orion*, *Pinguin*, *Thor* and *Widder* operating against Britain's trade routes, while in August the *Komet* managed to reach the Pacific by sailing north of Siberia. The term 'auxiliary cruiser' was hardly appropriate, as these vessels were Q-ships, disguised as merchantmen, sometimes from neutral countries, and only displayed their true colours, and

intent, at the last minute, making their operations more akin to piracy. During that second winter of war, the battlecruisers *Gneisenau* and *Scharnhorst* and the heavy cruiser *Hipper* operated in the Atlantic and, with the heavy cruiser *Scheer* in the Atlantic and Indian oceans, managed to account for forty-nine ships, or 271,000 tons of shipping, between October and March.

SINK THE *BISMARCK*

Although the hunt for the German battleship *Bismarck* is usually separated out from the Battle of the Atlantic, the ship's intended role was as a commerce raider and so her story blends in with that of the convoys in the North Atlantic. It was to be a serious reverse for Germany.

The two most impressive German warships were the sisters *Bismarck* and *Tirpitz*. The battleship *Bismarck* had an official net displacement of 42,000 tons and a full load displacement of 47,000 tons, although a post-war USN assessment put the latter figure at closer to 49,000 tons. A broad beam ensured that she had the stability to act as an effective gun platform in the open seas, and three screws gave her a maximum speed of 30 knots. Heavily armoured, the ship had two twin 38cm (approximately 15in), turrets forward and another two aft. Her reconnaissance aircraft were four single-engined Arado Ar196 monoplane floatplanes, capable of flying at almost 200mph. *Bismarck* had a complement of 2,200 men, including the admiral's staff and war correspondents.

In company with the heavy cruiser *Prinz Eugen*, on 18 May 1941, *Bismarck* left the German port of Gotenhafen (now Gdynia) for a commerce-raiding operation under the command of Captain Lindemann with Admiral Günther Lütjens in overall charge. There seems to have been some urgency about commencing the operation, code-named Operation Rhine Exercise, as the ship's fuel tanks were not completely full, a hose having given way and interrupted fuelling. Inexplicably, even when the two ships called at Korsfjord in Norway, the opportunity to 'top-up' the fuel tanks was not taken, although a shortage of heavy fuel oil may have been the reason. Soon after leaving Norway, the German ships were detected by the Royal Navy and shadowed by two heavy cruisers, *Suffolk* and *Norfolk*,

which, despite heavy seas, managed to track the Germans by using their radar. Vice Adm Holland took the battlecruiser *Hood*, and the new battleship *Prince of Wales*, planning to bring the Germans to action. In the Denmark Strait on 24 May, the four ships met in what was to be a classic naval engagement. Only minutes into the battle, *Hood* blew up with the loss of 1,500 men, leaving just three survivors, the explosion generally believed to have been caused by a shell from *Prinz Eugen* penetrating one of her magazines. The *Prince of Wales*, still not fully worked up, was forced to retire after taking several hits from the German ships. The engagement was not completely one-sided as *Bismarck* was hit three times, breaking the connections from the forward fuel tanks. The earlier decision to go to sea without completely full fuel tanks now became critical. Lütjens was forced to break company with the *Prinz Eugen* and head for St Nazaire, with Brest as an alternative, in occupied France.

Throughout this drama, the cruisers *Norfolk* and *Suffolk* had continued to track *Bismarck*. At 21.30, nine Fairey Swordfish from HMS *Victorious* found the *Bismarck* and launched a torpedo attack. As the aircraft approached, *Bismarck* increased her speed to 27 knots and started to zigzag while the ship's anti-aircraft batteries fired into the water ahead of them, raising massive water spouts that could easily account for any aircraft flying into them. The Swordfish had planned their attack from different directions so that, for the *Bismarck*, avoiding one torpedo meant putting the ship in the way of another. One torpedo dropped at close range hit the armour belt at the waterline amidships, doing little damage but killing a warrant officer and injuring six engineers. The attack was followed by a

A convoy sets sail, with the soldiers in the foreground undertaking lifeboat drill while the pre-war destroyer *Fury* steams past. Note the lack of camouflage at this early stage, and the prominent pennant number. *(IWM N42)*

The prime minister, Winston Churchill, on the quarterdeck of the battleship HMS *Prince of Wales* at Scapa Flow in August 1941, after his return from a meeting with President Roosevelt. He is talking to Admirals Sir John Tovey and, far right, Dudley Pound. *(IWM 4995)*

brief gunnery exchange with the *Prince of Wales*, but this was broken off in the fading light.

The following day, 25 May, Force H left Gibraltar under the command of Vice Adm Sir James Somerville, who had the aircraft carrier *Ark Royal*, the battlecruiser *Renown* and two cruisers. Contact with the *Bismarck* was lost early on 26 May, until an RAF Consolidated Catalina flying-boat rediscovered the ship. Early in the afternoon, in rough weather, fifteen Swordfish took off from the *Ark Royal*, while the cruiser *Sheffield* was ordered to maintain contact with the German ship. Unaware of the *Sheffield*'s

presence, as the Swordfish dropped out of the clouds they attacked her by mistake and she was only saved by her high speed and prompt evasive action, as well as faults in the torpedoes' magnetic detonators. Closing in on the *Bismarck* was Admiral Tovey, commander-in-chief of the Royal Navy's Home Fleet, with the battleships *King George V* and *Rodney*, accompanied by a destroyer escort. Tovey signalled Somerville that unless *Bismarck*'s speed could be reduced, he would have to withdraw *King George V* to refuel and leave *Rodney* on her own.

At 19.15, again in low cloud and poor visibility, a further strike by fifteen Swordfish

The sloop HMS *Aberdeen* hit the news when her crew rescued a dog that had been aboard a merchantman that was torpedoed. They adopted him as the ship's mascot, something that would not be allowed today! *(IWM A21708)*

was launched from *Ark Royal*, and on this occasion the torpedoes were fitted with contact detonators, which required a direct hit. Once again they appeared over the *Sheffield*, but this time looking for directions, and returned once more thirty minutes later for fresh directions. After they had flown off for the second time, the sound of heavy AA fire told those aboard the cruiser that the Swordfish had found the *Bismarck*.

Now under intense pressure, *Bismarck*'s AA armament was joined by her main and secondary armaments, firing into the paths of the torpedoes. Flying low, the spray of the heaving seas masking their landing gear and the cloud making a synchronised attack

from all directions difficult, the Swordfish pressed home their attack. Once again, the battleship zigzagged frantically, while the engine room was told repeatedly to stop, or to increase speed, or even to go astern, all in an attempt to avoid the torpedoes. This was all in vain: two torpedoes struck the ship, one immediately after the other, jamming the rudder and sending the ship into a continuous turn. All fifteen aircraft returned safely to *Ark Royal*.

Aboard the *Bismarck*, the situation was grave. In rough seas, the rudder would have to be cut off or blown off to allow her to manoeuvre using her engines. Taking the aircraft hangar door as a makeshift rudder was considered, but the sea state meant that this was impracticable. The steering flats had in any case been flooded by the massive hole in the hull. There were other problems: the explosion had closed a safety valve, shutting down the starboard engines, although this was quickly repaired.

The way in which good fortune plays a part in war was being demonstrated at the same time: the two British battleships passed *U-556* just as she was returning from a mission, but the U-boat had used all of her torpedoes, preventing her from adding a battleship to her score.

A night torpedo attack on the *Bismarck* by destroyers caused little further damage. On the morning of 27 May, *King George V* and *Rodney* engaged the *Bismarck* in a final gunnery duel of such intensity that a further strike by Swordfish was put into the air, but had to turn back because of the heavy rate of fire. The two British ships hit the *Bismarck* several times and after ninety minutes she was burning fiercely. Two cruisers then torpedoed the stricken ship, after which Capt Lindemann gave the order to abandon her. The cruiser *Devonshire* started to rescue survivors before one of them told his rescuers that U-boats were coming, causing the cruiser to move away. Whether this was a ruse to avoid becoming a prisoner of war and in the hope of being rescued by a German ship, we will never know, but as a result just 115 men survived from *Bismarck*'s ship's company.

THE ESCORT CARRIER ARRIVES

In 1941 the total shipping losses for the year fell to 2,214,408 tons in the Atlantic. The year started with more than 117,000 tons of shipping lost in January, while the following month, major action was seen, with a convoy battle off Cape St Vincent, at the extreme south-west of Portugal, between 8 and 11

February. The term 'battle' was not too strong for this action, which involved U-boats and German air and surface units. Action started on 8 February when *U-37* spotted convoy HG53 and promptly sank two ships, before her reports prompted the Luftwaffe to send five long-range maritime-reconnaissance aircraft to attack the convoy, sinking another five ships. *U-37* then turned to a third ship and, having sunk her, called for the heavy cruiser *Hipper*, which picked off a number of stragglers. Now active in the area and with no comparable British warship to stop her, *Hipper* found convoy SLS64 and sank seven ships.

In April and May, two more convoys were savaged by the U-boats. Between 2 and 4 April, six U-boats sank nine ships in convoy SC26, while between 19 and 22 May, HX126 was attacked by nine U-boats which sank another nine ships, and not surprisingly a new monthly peak of 363,073 tons was reached. Nevertheless, even without escort carriers to defend the convoys, the U-boats did not always have everything their own way. When convoys HX133 and OB336 were attacked by no fewer than fifteen U-boats between 20 and 29 June, with the loss of nine ships, the escort vessels were able to account for two of the U-boats and eventually drive away the remainder. Again, between 9 and 19 September, when the large convoy SC42 with seventy ships was attacked by fifteen U-boats with the loss of eighteen ships, two U-boats were sunk by the convoy escort. Size of convoy was in itself some protection, attracting a heavier escort and also forcing the U-boats to divide their fire. Between 19 and 27 September, convoy HG73 lost ten out of its twenty-five ships off Cape St Vincent, and worse was to come between 21 and 24 September when just three U-boats accounted for seven out of the eleven ships in convoy SL87.

Successful though the Flower class corvettes were, something larger was needed, especially for the Arctic convoys. This was the Castle class corvette *Leeds Castle*. *(IWM A25732)*

The emergence of the Soviet Union as an ally was a mixed blessing: this was to be an ally that demanded massive aid at a time when the British armed forces themselves were suffering shortages of equipment, and especially modern equipment, while the country was effectively bankrupt. There was some relief for the hard-pressed Royal Navy when, in September, the United States Navy started to escort North Atlantic convoys as far as the mid-ocean meeting point, officially to protect neutral shipping. This was yet another step just short of outright participation in the war; it was to be another three months before the United

States became one of the belligerent powers.

The escort carrier first became involved in convoy protection with convoy HG76, which sailed from Gibraltar to Britain on 14 December 1941 with thirty-two ships, including the CAM-ship *Darwin*. The Royal Navy's first escort carrier, HMS *Audacity*, was accompanied by two destroyers, four sloops and nine corvettes, which together made up the 36th Escort Group. The 36th was commanded by the then Cdr F.J. 'Johnnie' Walker (later Capt Walker), the Royal Navy's leading anti-submarine commander, in the sloop *Stork*. Against this convoy were the

One of the interim measures designed to get fighter cover for the convoys was the catapult-armed merchant ship, or CAM-ship, especially useful on the Russian convoys. The ships remained part of the Merchant Navy, carrying cargo; the pilots were usually from the RAF, although there were a few from the Fleet Air Arm. This is the *Empire Tide* with a Hawker Hurricane on the catapult. *(IWM A10115)*

seven U-boats of the *Seerauder* Group, which were guided on to the convoy by the Focke-wulf Fw290 Condors of 1KG40, based on Bordeaux. At dusk on 15 December, the most southerly of the U-boats discovered the convoy and was soon joined by a second boat. On the morning of 16 December, *U-131* was attacked by Wildcats flying from *Audacity*, before being attacked and sunk by destroyers. On 17 December, the destroyer *Stanley* was torpedoed by *U-434* and blew up, and in the frantic counter-attack led by Walker, *U-434* was depth-charged and forced to the surface, and then rammed and attacked by further depth-charges. The convoy escorts had by this time also sunk *U-567*, commanded by Endrass, one of

Germany's most experienced U-boat commanders. Nevertheless, the escort themselves suffered a bitter blow on 20 December, when *Audacity* was torpedoed and sunk by *U-751*. Nevertheless, despite the loss of the carrier, a destroyer and one of the merchantmen, four out of the seven U-boats were sunk.

Notable convoy actions in the Atlantic in early 1942 included convoy ONS67, which lost eight merchantmen to six U-boats between 21 and 25 February, without any losses among the U-boats. Then, on 12 and 13 May, just two U-boats sank seven ships from convoy ONS92. One of the worst convoy losses of this desperate year was that of convoy SC94, whose thirty-six merchantmen were attacked by seventeen U-boats between 3 and 11 August, with eleven ships lost for just two U-boats. The following month, between 10 and 14 September, ON127, whose thirty-two merchantmen had just six escorts, was attacked by thirteen U-boats, who accounted for seven merchantmen and one of the escorts, a destroyer, without any loss to themselves. October was little better: SC104 lost eight ships between 12 and 14 October, with *U-221* accounting for five of the merchantmen, although on this occasion three U-boats were sunk. Later, on 27–29 October, HX212 lost six ships in attacks by four U-boats.

Convoy SL125 was another convoy that suffered a cruel fate when off Morocco during 27–31 October 1942 with just four escorts to look after thirty-seven merchantmen. Ten U-boats found the convoy and sank eleven merchant vessels. It is hard not to believe that this convoy was a 'tethered goat', there to attract the wolf-pack, since the rush of U-boats to the convoy enabled the troop transports for the Allied landings in North Africa to pass completely unscathed.

Between 1 and 6 November, convoy DC107 lost fifteen out of forty-two merchantmen to attacks by thirteen U-boats, although two of the attackers were sunk by the escorts. No less than twenty U-boats were sent against ONS154 between 24 and 31 December, with the loss of another fourteen ships, some 70,000 tons of shipping, out of a total of forty-five.

Worse was to come in the New Year. Between 8 and 11 January 1943, convoy TM1, the first tanker convoy from Trinidad to North Africa, lost no less than seven out of the nine tankers with their valuable fuel, necessary to push the Axis out of Africa. Once again twenty U-boats were deployed between 4 and 9 February to attack convoy SC118, sinking eleven ships totalling 60,000

tons, although three of the U-boats were sunk by the escorts. Later that same month, between 21 and 25 February, ON166 with forty-nine merchantmen was attacked by a large wolf-pack of U-boats, with ten boats getting within firing range to sink fourteen ships totalling 88,000 tons for the loss of one U-boat. One of the largest U-boat packs came between 6 and 11 March, when SC121 with fifty-nine ships was attacked by no less than twenty-seven submarines, losing twelve ships while the U-boats escaped unscathed.

This period saw the U-boats at their maximum strength in the North Atlantic: from September 1943 to March 1943, there were more than a hundred craft in the area at any one time.

In March 1943 two convoys sailed from New York. The first, SC122, departed on 5 March with fifty-four merchantmen, followed by the faster HX229 with forty ships on 8 March, which was scheduled to catch up with SC122 on the 20th. Speed was, of course, a relative term, since the large ocean liners could cross the Atlantic in five days! It also has to be recognised that defensive measures against the U-boats did not simply consist of surface escorts and aircraft, whether carrier-borne or shore-based. The British had broken the German Enigma codes and by this time it was easier to divert convoys away from the waiting patrol lines of U-boats.

The attacks started on 16 March, when up to forty U-boats found HX229, and over two days the convoy lost ten ships. On 17 March, U-boats started to attack SC122. Plans for the two convoys to pass close together were abandoned and they spread out. In the days up to 20 March, a total of twenty-one ships were lost to both convoys, a total of 141,000 tons, with just one U-boat sunk. The attacks stopped once the convoys were within range of shore-based maritime-reconnaissance aircraft from Northern Ireland.

On 23 March, just a few days after the heavy losses suffered by the convoys SC122 and HX229, another convoy left Canada for the UK, but despite repeated attacks by U-boats, crossed safely to arrive on 8 April without a single ship being lost.

The third phase of the Battle of the Atlantic started with two successes for the U-boats. Between 4 and 7 April 1943, fifteen U-boats sank six ships, 41,000 tons of shipping, from convoy HX231, although this cost two U-boats. Then on 30 April and 1 May, *U-515* found a convoy off Freetown in Sierra Leone, and sank seven ships totalling 43,000 tons with nine torpedoes.

The success of *U-515*, while outstanding, was by this time the exception. In 1940, each U-boat on patrol sank an average of six merchantmen per month, but by 1942–3, it took more than two U-boats to sink a single merchantman.

Nevertheless, April and May 1943 are regarded as being a turning point in the Battle of the Atlantic. From this time on, the U-boats would be on the defensive. The successes of March and April turned to disaster in May, when more than forty U-boats were lost, many of them to aerial attack, while other losses were the result of collaboration between aircraft and surface escorts. Technical innovation would not be enough to ensure the survival of the U-boats. Schnorkels were progressively introduced from this time onwards to enable U-boats to recharge their batteries without surfacing, and indeed to run on diesel power under water. Heavier anti-aircraft armaments were also progressively introduced, although often at the cost of further reducing speed while submerged. In fact, attacking a U-boat that elected to remain surfaced in an aircraft such as a Fairey Swordfish, the obsolescent biplane operated from MAC-ships and the anti-submarine aircraft of choice for the British

and Canadian escort carriers, took some nerve. On the other hand, a fast, well-armoured aircraft such as those operated by the Royal Air Force and United States Navy was a different matter altogether and for most U-boat commanders, the crucial factor was just how fast they could dive, known to them as the 'Battle of the Seconds'. Even so, there were a small number of instances of a U-boat inflicting fatal damage on a land-plane, but the odds were against it, as their armament was too light and the firing platform unstable in the heavy Atlantic swell.

Between them, the MAC-ships and the escort carriers closed the 'Atlantic Gap', the 500 miles or so of mid-ocean that lay beyond the range of shore-based aircraft, forcing the U-boats to abandon their pack tactics. The impact on merchant shipping losses was dramatic, falling from fifty ships in August 1942 to just sixteen between September 1943 and May 1944, and only another five between then and VE Day a year later.

Allied anti-submarine operations also underwent a radical change during the fourth phase. Convoys continued to be escorted and to enjoy the close protection of one or two escort carriers, but now anti-submarine sweeps by 'hunter-killer' forces of escorts with one or two escort carriers also reappeared following American success with these techniques in the mid- and South Atlantic. To say that anti-submarine sweeps 'reappeared' is simply to recognise that this was the technique that had fallen into disuse following the loss of the British fleet carrier *Courageous* in September 1939, but this time the techniques were different. *Courageous* had had just two escorts to protect her; now, between four and six per carrier was more usual. More important, *Courageous* had been merely hoping to find a submarine, but the late-war task groups knew where they would find U-boats refuelling and taking on supplies from the supply submarines, replacing hope with a high degree of certainty. Direction finding could detect the radio 'chatter' between U-boats, including their signals to base, while the breaking of the German Enigma codes also meant that the location of the ocean refuelling and resupply points became known. Refuelling a U-boat at sea was difficult enough, transferring stores and ammunition between two low-lying craft rolling and pitching in a heavy mid-ocean swell was much more so, and the problems were compounded by hatches that were too small for efficient stowage of supplies, but big enough for large waves to enter. The submarines were now the hunted.

CHAPTER FOUR

WAR IN THE MEDITERRANEAN

*It takes the Navy three years to build a ship. It would take three hundred
to rebuild a tradition.*
Adm Sir Andrew Cunningham, Alexandria, May 1941

The most dangerous convoys were those across the Mediterranean in the struggle to sustain the defence of Malta. This situation was so bad that fast minelayers and large minelaying submarines were pressed into service to keep the Maltese islands going in between convoys, which often failed to get through. The operations of the fast mine-layers were known as the 'club runs', while those of the submarines were known as the 'magic carpet'. Even escort carriers were of little use in the intense fighting that these convoys suffered, and so the large fleet carriers and battleships had to be pressed into service.

BRINGING THE ENEMY TO BATTLE

Only in the Mediterranean was a major sea battle possible, but after the Battle of Punta Stilo, or Calabria, the Italian navy, the Regia Marina, kept out of the way.

The battle of Punta Stilo came after the submarine *Phoenix* had alerted Adm Sir Andrew Cunningham, Commander-in-Chief of the Mediterranean Fleet that the Italians had two battleships at sea. On 8 July 1940 the two ships were 200 miles east of Malta and steaming on a southerly course. Aerial

reconnaissance later found that the battle-ships were supported by six cruisers and seven destroyers, escorting a large convoy. Cunningham planned to put his ships between the Italians and the major forward base at Taranto.

On 9 July a Malta-based flying-boat found the Italians 145 miles west of the Mediterranean Fleet at 07.30. Further confirmation came from aircraft flown off from *Eagle*. By noon, the distance had closed to 80 miles, and it was not until then that the Italian Adm Campioni, racing to get under the air cover of aircraft based in Sicily, was alerted to the proximity of the Mediterranean Fleet by a seaplane catapulted from his own ship, the *Giulio Cesare*.

Other than *Warspite*, most of the British ships were outgunned by the Italians. To slow the Italians down, two strikes of Swordfish armed with torpedoes were launched from *Eagle*, with the first before noon and a second at 16.00, but failed to score any hits, missing the opportunity to slow the larger ships, or even sink a cruiser. Just before 15.00, two British cruisers spotted four of the Italian cruisers, who responded with their 8in main armament, outranging their British counterparts

Operation Halberd, September 1941, and three cruisers escort a convoy to Malta. Closest to the camera is HMS *Edinburgh*, with HMS *Sheffield* centre and HMS *Kenya* in the distance. *(IWM A5645)*

which had only 6in guns. Cunningham, ahead of his other two battleships in *Warspite*, raced to the rescue and at just under 15 miles, opened fire, forcing the Italians back behind a smokescreen. While *Eagle* and the two older battleships attempted to catch up with *Warspite*, two Italian heavy cruisers tried to attack the carrier, drawing further fire from *Warspite*, and *Malaya* and *Royal Sovereign*, which by this time had rejoined Cunningham. At 16.00, the two fleets' battleships were within sight of one another, and *Warspite* opened fire again, at a range of nearly 15 miles, almost immediately after the second Swordfish strike. The Italians replied with ranging shots straddling the British ships, but a direct hit on the *Giulio Cesare* at the base of the funnels by a salvo of 15in shells persuaded the Italians to break off the engagement under cover of a heavy smokescreen. Cunningham also turned, aware that his ships would not be able to catch the Italian ships and that there was the risk of submarine attack. Italian bombers finally arriving to attack the Mediterranean Fleet bombed their own ships by mistake, to the delight of the crew of *Warspite*'s Swordfish floatplane, in the air since before the start of the action.

This was the only battle in the Second World War when two full battle fleets actually engaged. The United States Navy was later to come close to such an action during the final stages of the Battle for Guadalcanal, but one of the two US battleships suffered an electrical failure and could not fire her guns. The Imperial Japanese Navy attempted to force such an engagement at Leyte Gulf, but again failed as carrier-borne aircraft took over. All other engagements either involved a single capital ship on one side or the other, or were between carrier-borne aircraft while the opposing fleets were out of sight and beyond gun range.

Typical of the actions between the British and Italian navies in the Mediterranean was that off Cape Spada in Crete on 19 July 1940. The two Italian light cruisers *Bartolomeo Colleoni* and *Giovanni delle Bande Nere* engaged the Australian light cruiser HMAS *Sydney* accompanied by five destroyers. The Italians had the upper hand at the start of this engagement as their ships outgunned the destroyers and outnumbered the British cruiser. But a direct hit by *Sydney* put the *Colleoni*'s boilers out of action, and she lost way, before sinking. While *Bande Nere* managed to hit *Sydney*, the Australian cruiser struck back and damaged the remaining Italian ship, which then took refuge in Benghazi, Libya.

The following month, on 15 August, expecting the Italians to move eastward to threaten the Suez Canal, Cunningham took his battleships and the heavy cruiser *Kent*, newly arrived, to bombard coastal positions around Bardia and Fort Capuzzo, near Sollum (now Salûm). RAF fighter support was added to that of *Eagle*'s own fighters operating from a shore base. The fighters accounted for twelve of the Savoia-Marchetti SM79 heavy bombers sent to attack the British ships. Something more typical of the war in the Mediterranean came a week later, on the night of 22/23 August, when destroyers were sent in to bombard the seaplane base at Bomba, west of Tobruk, and three of *Eagle*'s Swordfish, operating from a forward shorebase, attacked enemy shipping. The flight of three aircraft was led by Capt Oliver 'Olly' Patch of the Royal Marines. On arrival at Bomba, they found a large Italian depot ship, with a destroyer and a submarine lying on either side, while a second, larger submarine lay astern. Patch torpedoed and sank the latter, while the other two Swordfish attacked the submarine and destroyer lying alongside the depot ship, which also sank. Cunningham noted with satisfaction that it was 'a most daring and gallant effort on the part of our young gentlemen from the *Eagle*'.

We will look later at the famous attack on the Italian fleet at Taranto in November 1940, but this came between many attacks by the Fleet Air Arm against Italian shipping and airfields, and many operations in support of the British Army.

The cruiser *Ajax* had a busy war, certainly during the early years, and during the night of 11–12 October, she met four Italian destroyers and three motor torpedo boats off the coast of Tunisia. In the action that followed, a destroyer and two MTBs were sunk. On 27 November, Force H, with the battleship *Ramillies* and battlecruiser *Renown*, as well as the aircraft carrier *Ark Royal*, was escorting three fast freighters from Gibraltar to Alexandria when Admiral Campioni was sent with the battleships *Vittorio Veneto* and *Giulio Cesare* to intercept them. The Italians were spotted by British reconnaissance aircraft off Cape Teulada in Sardinia and Somerville moved Force H towards them. Both sides were supported by cruisers, five British against six Italian, and these clashed first. The elderly *Ramillies* soon fell behind, but *Renown* followed

Malta proved to be a worthwhile base for submarines, fully vindicating the Admiralty's confidence that it could survive as a base for offensive operations. Here are some of the U class submarines, smaller boats that proved their worth in the Mediterranean. Inboard is HMS *Urge*, alongside the famous *Upholder*. Note the difference in the bow design, as later vessels of this class were modified to improve seakeeping. *(RN Submarine Museum, Neg. 5804)*

closely on the British cruisers, and once she opened fire, the Italian cruisers withdrew behind their battleships, which then joined the Battle of Cape Teulada. *Ark Royal* sent her Swordfish to attack the Italians, and although no torpedo strikes were made, this was enough to encourage Campioni to break off the battle, having no aircraft of his own. At the end of the action, one Italian destroyer was badly damaged, as was the British cruiser *Berwick*. Nevertheless, the priority for Somerville had been the protection of the convoy.

As the year ended, on 18 December, the Mediterranean Fleet was able to send two battleships, *Warspite* and *Valiant*, to bombard the port of Valona in Albania, which was being used by the Italians for their assault on Greece. Two days later, Cunningham in *Warspite* visited Malta, to a warm welcome. It was to be the last visit that either the ship or the admiral could make for some time: the turn of the year was to mark a dramatic change in British fortunes.

JUDGEMENT AND VENGEANCE

An attack on the Italian fleet in its forward base at Taranto had been planned some years before the Second World War broke out, at the height of the Abyssinian crisis in 1935. At that time, the Mediterranean Fleet

During the Second World War, Malta was no longer a posting to be sought after. This is the destroyer HMS *Lance*, after a heavy air raid on 7 April 1942. A large hole can be seen in her hull, just above the waterline. *(IWM A9635)*

aircraft carrier was HMS *Glorious*. In 1940, the plan was revived, and originally it was intended that two carriers, *Illustrious*, newly arrived in the Mediterranean, and *Eagle*, should be used, giving a total of thirty Fairey Swordfish biplanes for the operation, and that the date for the attack should be 21 October, the anniversary of Nelson's famous victory at Trafalgar. Fate intervened, however, with first a serious hangar fire aboard *Illustrious* delaying the operation, and then with *Eagle* suffering extensive damage to her aviation fuel system as a result of the mining effect of near-misses by heavy bombs. In the event, a number of aircraft were transferred from *Eagle*'s 813

and 824 squadrons to 815 and 819 aboard *Illustrious*, giving a total of twenty-four aircraft for the operation. However, on the day before the operation, one aircraft ditched in the sea because of fuel contamination, and the next day the same thing happened again. In the end, it was discovered that one of the carrier's aviation fuel tanks had been contaminated by sea water, and all of the aircraft had to have their fuel systems drained and refuelled. Just twenty-one aircraft were available for the attack.

The operation was rescheduled for the night of 11/12 November 1940. The Swordfish carried extra fuel tanks – in the observer's cockpit for the torpedo-carrying aircraft (displacing the observer into the rearmost cockpit, since TAGs were not carried on the operation) and under the fuselage for the bombers and flare-droppers. The attack took place in two waves, with twelve aircraft in the first wave and nine in the second. Attacking against a heavily defended target, the first wave concentrated on the ships and the second wave on the shore installation. When the raid ended, three of the Italian navy's six battleships were sitting on the bottom of the harbour, although two eventually returned to service, while other ships were damaged and fuel tanks ashore set on fire. Just two aircraft were shot down and the crew of one of these, the leaders of the first wave, Lt Cdr Kenneth Williamson and his observer Lt Norman 'Blood' Scarlett (later Scarlett-Streatfield), taken prisoner.

The Italians were forced to move their warships away from Taranto at first, although the nearest port, Naples, was soon within reach of Malta-based Wellington bombers. Nevertheless, it was not long before the Axis powers were to show that they were also capable of inflicting serious damage on the Royal Navy, and this came on 10 January 1941, when Malta's vulnerability was brought home with a vengeance. The convoy codenamed Operation Excess ran into trouble early on, having been delayed from December, because of the presence of the cruiser *Hipper* in the Atlantic. The convoy was escorted towards Malta by Adm Somerville's Force H, and consisted of just four large merchantmen, three for Piraeus and one, carrying 4,000 tons of ammunition and 3,000 tons of seed potatoes, for Malta. From Alexandria with the Mediterranean Fleet came two merchantmen, one with general supplies and another with fuel, for Malta. It was always important in convoy planning to 'return the empties', and part of the plan

was to escort merchantmen from Malta to safety in Alexandria. Wellington bombers from Malta had raided Naples on the night of 8/9 January, damaging the battleship *Giulio Cesare,* and forcing her and the *Vittorio Veneto* to withdraw north to Genoa.

On Malta convoys, escorting warships usually outnumbered the merchantmen. Force H included *Ark Royal*, the battleship *Malaya,* the cruisers *Southampton, Gloucester* and *Bonaventure*, and five destroyers. The Mediterranean Fleet included *Illustrious,* and the battleships *Warspite* and *Valiant.* After initial skirmishes on 9 January, when Force H was bombed but *Ark Royal*'s Fulmars accounted for two bombers, the real action came at the handover the following day. The Axis reconnaissance aircraft knew of the Mediterranean Fleet's presence in the area, but the bombers had failed to find them until 10 January. Both carriers kept their Fulmar fighters on constant CAP.

On 10 January the Luftwaffe and Regia Aeronautica attacked, with most of their bombs aimed at *Illustrious.* Luftwaffe Stukas quickly scored six direct hits and three near misses on *Illustrious*, whose deck was designed to take a direct hit of 500lb, but the hangar lifts were much weaker than this. The ship was forced to put into Malta for repairs, where she remained prey to the attentions of the Luftwaffe and Regia Aeronautica until she was able to sail to the United States for repairs. Those of her aircraft that were airborne at the time of the attack managed to reach Malta, where for a while the Fulmars augmented the RAF Hurricanes in defending the island. Five of the carrier's Swordfish also survived to be based on Malta.

On 11 January 1941, the day after the severe damage to *Illustrious* during Operation Excess, the Luftwaffe found the two British cruisers *Gloucester* and *Southampton* in the Mediterranean escorting four merchantmen towards Alexandria. In the subsequent attack, *Southampton* had to be abandoned, although the four cargo ships managed to reach their destination safely.

Force H continued to do its best to maintain the pressure on the Axis forces in the Mediterranean. On 9 February 1941 Vice Adm Somerville, its flag officer, took the battleship *Malaya*, the battlecruiser *Renown* and the aircraft carrier *Ark Royal*, with a cruiser and ten destroyers as escorts, into the Gulf of Genoa, steaming into a relatively confined area close to the enemy's mainland. *Malaya* and *Renown* bombarded Genoa itself, while the *Ark Royal*'s aircraft bombed the port of Leghorn and dropped mines off the naval base of La Spezia. The Italian battleships *Vittorio Veneto*, *Giulio Cesare* and *Andrea Doria*, with three cruisers and ten destroyers, were sent to intercept Force H, which they heavily outgunned and outnumbered. For a while, it looked as if Somerville was to have the decisive naval engagement for which Cunningham had longed, but the Italian ships failed to make contact.

On 25 March Italian torpedo boats sank a tanker in the important anchorage at Suda Bay, Crete, displaying a courage and flair that was largely confined to smaller operations rather than those of the fleet. The next day, the torpedo boats inflicted such heavy damage on the heavy cruiser *York* that her captain had to run her aground to avoid sinking, but as she lay stranded the bombers of the Luftwaffe destroyed her.

Battle of Cape Matapan

The Germans were by this stage preparing to attack Yugoslavia and Greece, and pressured their Italian allies to cut British seaborne communications between Alexandria and Athens. Italian ships were thus sent into the waters south of Greece to attack British convoys. British aerial reconnaissance soon spotted the Italian ships. Cunningham intended to retain the element of surprise, and considerable effort was put into making it seem that the Mediterranean Fleet was staying in port, in the conviction that Alexandria was awash with Axis spies. Then, under cover of darkness, the fleet slipped out to sea late on 27 March.

The opening of the Battle of Matapan took place the following morning when, at daybreak, *Formidable* flew off aircraft for reconnaissance, fighter combat air patrol and anti-submarine patrols. They soon received two reports of cruisers and destroyers: in fact, Italian heavy cruisers were pursuing the British light cruisers. In order to rescue the British ships from this predicament, *Formidable* flew off six Fairey Albacores escorted by Fairey Fulmar fighters to attack the Italian ships, which were being joined by the battleship *Vittorio Veneto*.

While the Fulmar fighters shot down one of two Junkers Ju88 fighter-bombers that attempted to attack the Albacores, and drove the other one off, the six Albacores dived down through heavy AA fire to torpedo the *Vittorio Veneto*. No strikes were made, but they did force the Italian battleship to break off the pursuit of the British cruisers.

A second strike of three Albacores and two Swordfish, again with Fulmar fighters, was sent off, while two Italian bombers attempted to attack *Formidable*. *Vittorio Veneto*'s AA defences were surprised by the Fulmars' machine-gunning their positions and the bridge as the Albacores pressed home their torpedo attack. As the AA fire started to hit it, the leading aircraft dropped its torpedo 1,000 yards ahead of the ship. The torpedo struck the ship almost immediately after the plane crashed. The

Cruisers *Euryalus* (leading) and *Galatea*, on patrol in the Mediterranean, December 1941. *(IWM A7593)*

battleship was hit 15ft below the waterline, allowing a massive flood of water to gush in just above the port outer screw, so that within minutes the engines had stopped. Hard work by damage control parties enabled the *Vittorio Veneto* to start again, using only her two starboard engines, but she could only manage 15 knots.

A third air strike was then mounted by *Formidable*. When this arrived over the ship at dusk, they attacked the Italians, diving down through a dense smokescreen and then being dazzled by searchlights and the usual colourful Italian tracer barrage in an unsuccessful attack. Then an aircraft flying from Maleme in Crete spotted a heavy cruiser, the *Pola*, successfully torpedoing it

and inflicting such severe damage that she lost speed and drifted out of position. Once the Italian admiral, Iachino, realised what had happened, he sent two other heavy cruisers, *Zara* and *Fiume*, with four destroyers to provide assistance.

While the Italians were not expecting a night action, Cunningham knew that they were weak in night gunnery and intended to take advantage of this. By this time the opposing fleets were off Cape Matapan, on modern atlases usually referred to as Cape Akra Tainaron, a promontory at the extreme southern end of the Peloponnese peninsula. At first, Cunningham thought that the *Pola* was *Vittorio Veneto*. As his ships prepared to open fire, the Italian rescue force of *Zara* and *Fiume* sped across Cunningham's path and were illuminated by a searchlight from a destroyer. In the battle that followed, both *Zara* and *Fiume* and two destroyers were sunk by the 15in guns of the three battleships, while *Pola* was sunk in a torpedo attack from two destroyers.

The next morning, Cunningham had his ships pick up 900 Italian survivors before the threat of air attack stopped the rescue. Nevertheless, before leaving he relayed the position of the remaining survivors to Rome, saving many more lives.

Despite this success, on 6 April the Germans started their attack on Yugoslavia and Greece, accompanied as always by heavy Luftwaffe attack. One raid blew up a British ammunition ship in Piraeus, which took ten other ships with her and caused so much damage that the port was put out of action, causing major difficulties for the British expeditionary force ashore. By 23 April the

Suda Bay in Crete was one of the finest anchorages in the Mediterranean, and this is the ill-fated battleship HMS *Barham* taking on supplies. *(IWM AX28A)*

Greek army had surrendered, and the Mediterranean Fleet found itself evacuating British forces to Crete. Had Crete been used simply as a staging post, all might have been well, but the mistake was made of attempting to defend the island, despite the shortage of aircraft and the fact that the British had left most of their heavy equipment and their communications behind in Greece.

The German airborne invasion of Crete followed on 20 May, finding most of the British and Greek forces defending the island on the coast, expecting a seaborne invasion. Göring had persuaded Hitler that the Luftwaffe's paratroops could mount the invasion; the German army and navy were left to support it. In the event, despite the British forces' lack of weaponry and equipment, the invasion proved so costly for Germany that for a time Hitler forbade any further airborne assaults. The loss of paratroops and glider-landed troops was bad enough, but the Royal Navy seriously disrupted the convoys bringing troops and heavy equipment by sea, wiping out one major convoy and sinking the heavily laden, unwieldy caiques.

On the night of 21/22 May, the cruisers *Ajax*, *Dido* and *Orion* with four destroyers completely destroyed one convoy carrying troops and munitions. The Luftwaffe responded on 22 May with another crippling attack on the Mediterranean Fleet, sinking the cruisers *Fiji* and *Gloucester* and a destroyer, and badly damaging *Warspite* and the cruisers *Carlisle* and *Naiad*. Cunningham sent the battleships *Queen Elizabeth* and *Barham* with nine destroyers to attack Axis airfields in the Dodecanese, with attacks by aircraft from *Formidable*, but by this time the carrier's air power was seriously limited because of a shortage of aircraft, and she could do little to defend herself when the Luftwaffe turned its attentions to her, causing serious damage. In the end, despite the best efforts of all concerned, it was time for yet another costly evacuation, with the Mediterranean Fleet continuing to evacuate the last of the 17,000 British, Commonwealth and Greek troops beyond the deadline set by the Admiralty.

For the second time during the war in the Mediterranean, an aircraft carrier was damaged beyond local repair and *Formidable* had to be sent away. This time, there was no replacement available.

MIXED FORTUNES IN THE MEDITERRANEAN

The loss of Crete and Axis domination of the battle in North Africa saw British power at its lowest ebb. Before the war, Britain's leaders had been unwise in making promises the country could not keep to its empire, and in giving commitments to allies who were more likely to be a burden than additional support in the war against Germany and Italy.

Nevertheless, there was much that could be done and the Royal Navy was determined to make the most of its main base in the Mediterranean, Malta. The Mediterranean Fleet may have been removed to Alexandria, but Malta remained an offensive base, not only for submarines, but for the Fleet Air Arm as well. The campaign against Axis shipping started slowly, with so many other demands on the Royal Navy. During the first six months after Italy entered the war, from June to November 1940, they lost just four ships carrying supplies to North Africa, with a total tonnage of 11,104 tons. The level of losses rose during the winter: from December 1940 to March 1941, Italy lost thirty ships with a total tonnage of 109,089 tons. But this was not enough to stop the two divisions of Rommel's *Afrika Korps* from reaching North Africa with few losses.

Initially, two destroyers, *Lance* and *Lively*, operated from Malta, attacking Axis shipping, and in October 1941 they were reinforced by two light cruisers, *Penelope* and *Aurora*, forming Force K under Capt W.G. Agnew. Malta was also sheltering the cruiser *Ajax*, which was out of action. This was a small force with which to face the might of the Regia Marina. Had the Italians sent their battleships and heavy cruisers to sea, not to mention their substantial fleet of submarines, which on Italy's entry into the war had far exceeded those of Germany the situation for Malta would have been hopeless. The Germans had expected the Italian fleet to bombard Malta almost as soon as Italy entered the war, and follow this up with an invasion, but the opportunity passed.

Force K soon proved its worth. Persuaded by the Luftwaffe that the two cruisers were so badly damaged as to be out of action, on 9 November the Italians sent a convoy of seven ships to North Africa, with an escort of two cruisers and ten destroyers. Far from being confined to port, Force K turned up, and in the engagement that followed, all seven merchant ships were sunk, as well as a destroyer, with another so badly damaged that she sank later. Eleven days later, on 20 November, another convoy was spotted, with four ships escorted by two cruisers and eight destroyers. The two cruisers were badly damaged by torpedoes and the entire convoy beat a hasty retreat into Taranto. Two other ships were spotted steaming from Piraeus to join the convoy, and these were promptly sunk by *Penelope* and *Lively*. All this contributed to the loss of 54,900 tons of Italian shipping in November.

Other forces operating from Malta at this time included the Swordfish of no. 830 Squadron, while the RAF bombed targets in Sicily and mainland Italy. The outlook for the Italians was increasingly bleak. At one stage the Italians gave up trying to get convoys through to Libya, and on other occasions used what they euphemistically described as 'white ships', meaning hospital ships that would not be attacked by the British, to smuggle supplies through. Despite the frequent air attacks on Malta, Italian intelligence seems to have been poor, since the two cruisers in Malta were classified as battleships; or just possibly the power of Force K was inflated to account for the fact that on occasion every ship in an Axis convoy was sunk.

Despite the mauling given to their fleet at Taranto, the Italians remained reluctant to risk a major fleet engagement. They had attempted to attack Force K in the Grand Harbour at Malta using fast small craft loaded with explosives, but now they turned their attention to the Mediterranean Fleet at Alexandria. For the most part damage on the Royal Navy was inflicted by the Germans, as when *U-331* torpedoed the battleship *Barham* off the coast of Libya; the ship rolled over and sank rapidly, blowing up with heavy loss of life as 862 officers and men died. Cunningham had earlier rejected an Admiralty order that *Barham*, which had not enjoyed the same degree of modernisation as *Warspite* and others of the *Queen Elizabeth* class, should be scuttled in Tobruk harbour to stem the Axis advance, preferring to see her continue in an active role with the fleet.

Despite such setbacks, the Mediterranean Fleet continued to have its victories, as on the night of 12/13 December, again off Cap Bon, when three British destroyers and a Dutch destroyer, using the dark coastline behind them to make identification difficult, torpedoed and sank the two Italian light cruisers *Alberico da Barbiano* and *Alberto di Giussano* in a brilliant action, since the enemy guns should have been able to keep the destroyers at bay.

The Axis were forced to take increasingly desperate measures with ever-stronger convoy escorts. On 17 December, four Italian battleships, *Littorio*, *Caio Duilio*, *Andrea Doria* and *Giulio Cesare*, escorted by five cruisers and twenty destroyers, escorting a convoy to Tripoli, met Rear Adm Philip Vian with five cruisers and twenty destroyers escorting a Malta-bound merchantman. There was a brief gunnery exchange, before the Italian admiral, Iachino again, broke off as darkness fell. As so often before, the balance of armament rested with the Italians, and again, they failed to make the most of it.

Nevertheless, in warfare, especially when heavily outnumbered, misfortune is never far away, as on 18 December 1941, when Force K, which had so easily destroyed an Italian convoy in November, found itself in trouble, running into an Italian minefield off Tripoli. The cruiser HMS *Neptune* and a destroyer were sunk, while two other cruisers, *Aurora* and *Penelope*, were badly damaged.

That same night an Italian submarine surfaced in the darkness just over a mile from the entrance to the harbour at Alexandria, and released three two-man human torpedoes into the water. Fortunately for the attackers, as they arrived, the harbour defences were open for Rear Adm Vian's destroyers. The human torpedoes were intended for the battleships. In the small hours of the following morning, with some difficulty, one of the Italians, Luigi de la Penne, fixed his warhead to the bottom of the battleship *Valiant*, but he and his companion lost their human torpedo in doing this and had to swim to a buoy, from which they were rescued and taken prisoner by the British. Another pair, including Martellotta, managed to blow the stern off the tanker *Sagona* and also damage the destroyer *Jervis* lying alongside. Unable to

escape through the closed dock entrance, they went ashore, but were soon spotted and arrested. The third duo, Marceglia and his companion, fixed their charge to the bottom of the elderly battleship HMS *Queen Elizabeth* and also attempted to escape, hoping to be picked up by the submarine. They too were spotted and arrested trying to spend English £5 notes, which were no longer legal tender in Egypt. Even though he was detained aboard the *Valiant*, de la Penne kept silence until the explosion ripped open her hull and she settled on the bottom. The *Queen Elizabeth* suffered a similar fate.

It was simply the good fortune of the Royal Navy that both ships were in shallow water, and aerial reconnaissance showed them as if they were still lying undamaged at Alexandria. The crews of the human torpedoes had failed to return, so there was little to show that they had been successful. The discovery of one of the torpedoes also caused the Royal Navy to embark on its own programme of human torpedo development, nicknamed 'chariots'. Nevertheless, as a result of the attack and the airsea battles off Crete, by this time Cunningham did not have a single battleship or, more important, an aircraft carrier.

This was not the only blow, for on 13 November, off Gibraltar, *U-81* had torpedoed the last of the pre-war aircraft carriers, *Ark Royal*, knocking out her engine rooms, and she sank the next day, leaving Force H without an aircraft carrier as a result. The irony was that most naval officers had expected the '*Ark*' to succumb to aerial attack, given the thin plating of her unarmoured flight deck.

As the year drew to an end with the Mediterranean Fleet having suffered heavy losses, despite its successes against the Italian Navy, a serious problem developed for Malta: as the German advance across the

The cruiser HMS *Cleopatra* leaving Alexandria for Malta in June 1942. *(IWM A10478)*

Soviet Union faltered and stopped under the crushing cold of the Russian winter, many of the Luftwaffe's aircraft were re-deployed westwards where they could still operate. As winter closed in, the German air force returned to Sicily. Malta could not be allowed to continue to strangle Rommel's campaign in North Africa.

THE MALTA CONVOYS

When Italy entered the Second World War on 10 June 1940, Malta was isolated. Even before the war, it was clear that Malta would be a target as the islands sat on the cross-roads of the Mediterranean, roughly halfway between Gibraltar and Alexandria, and between southern Italy and Italian forces in North Africa. Malta was a fortress of the past, not the present, as the extensive fortifications had been built with earlier conflicts and armaments in mind. Because of the high population density and the thin soil, the islanders could only grow sufficient food to meet a quarter of their needs, and had

no fuel sources at all. This all led both the British Army and the Royal Air Force to the conclusion that Malta could not be defended, but the Royal Navy saw the island as being of strategic importance, and as a base for light forces and submarines. The Royal Navy won the argument and the armed forces stayed, while most British civilians were evacuated well in advance of the Italian declaration of war.

Convoys to Malta were far smaller than on the Arctic routes, reflecting the small size of the islands and the population of around 280,000 in 1940. There were other problems too, since port facilities were extremely limited; in peacetime the island had received most of its supplies on small ships – a case of little and often. At the outset, Malta depended on Gloster Sea Gladiators left behind by the carrier *Eagle*, three of which were flown by RAF pilots and became famous as *Faith*, *Hope* and *Charity*. Someone at the Admiralty sent a signal demanding to know why Fleet Air Arm property had been handed over to the RAF!

A converted whaler, HMS *Calm*, returns to harbour after conducting minesweeping in the eastern Mediterranean. *(IWM A13615)*

Later, aircraft were flown from carriers, including the USS *Wasp*, to provide Malta with a fighter defence, but at first these fighters were often destroyed as they landed to refuel and re-arm in the middle of almost continuous Axis air attack.

The infamous convoy Operation Excess in January 1941, which saw the aircraft carrier *Illustrious* crippled by the Luftwaffe, nevertheless resulted in all of the merchantmen in the convoy reaching Malta safely. It was not always to be the case. It also became apparent that Malta lacked the port facilities to receive and discharge the cargoes of a number of ships at once. When four ships were sent to Malta in March 1942, one was sunk offshore, a tanker was so badly damaged that she had to be towed into Marsaxlokk and the two that managed to reach the famous Grand Harbour were sunk at their moorings with most of their cargo still unloaded. Such was the desperation that grain damaged by the sea water was salvaged and made into bread.

Most famous of the Malta convoys was that of 10–15 August 1942, known to the Allies as Operation Pedestal, but to the Maltese as the 'Santa Marija Convoy', arriving in Malta on 15 August, the feast day of the Assumption of the Virgin Mary.

This was the largest of the Malta convoys; with fourteen merchant vessels, reflecting both the desperate plight of those on Malta and the reality that not all of the ships could make it. Under the command of Vice Adm Syfret, the escorts included the battleships *Nelson* and *Rodney*, with their 16in guns in three triple turrets forward, the aircraft carriers *Eagle*, *Furious*, *Indomitable* and *Victorious*, seven cruisers and twenty-seven destroyers. *Furious* was carrying forty-two Supermarine Spitfire fighters to be flown off to augment Malta's defences.

The fleet itself was largely dependent on forty-three Sea Hurricanes for its air defence, although it also had a number of Fulmars and Grumman Martlets. After passing Gibraltar on the night of 10/11 August, *Eagle* was torpedoed at 13.15 on 11 August by *U-73*. All four torpedoes hit the carrier, sinking her quickly, and her four Sea Hurricanes flying CAP at the time had to land on the other carriers. The elderly carrier, regarded as too slow for frontline duty, was no stranger to the Malta run, and had previously flown 183 fighters safely to the island from her deck.

Later that day, the Luftwaffe started the series of heavy aerial attacks that the convoy was to suffer on its run across the Mediterranean. The escort vessels sank a U-boat at 16.00, before another combined strike of a hundred aircraft attacked at 19.00, sinking a merchantman and so seriously damaging *Indomitable* that she was put out of action, leaving her aircraft to be recovered by *Victorious*. Later, the Luftwaffe attacked, sinking the cruiser *Cairo* and two more merchant vessels, as well as damaging the cruiser *Nigeria* and three other ships, including the tanker *Ohio*.

Darkness brought an attack by E-boats that sank another five ships, and so badly damaged the cruiser *Manchester* that she had to be sunk later.

This day was typical, with another ship lost to air attack and further damage inflicted on the *Ohio*, whose master ordered her to be abandoned; but before they could be picked up, the crew reboarded the ship since she was still afloat. The leading ships reached Malta on 13 August, but *Ohio*, aided by an escorting destroyer, did not arrive until 15 August, one of just five out of the fourteen merchant vessels to survive the ordeal. Undoubtedly those aboard showed outstanding courage, but luck played a part as another straggler was promptly despatched by a U-boat, and the ships that reached Malta were not bombed as they unloaded. *Ohio*'s cargo of fuel was to prove invaluable in the defence of Malta. Pedestal cost one aircraft carrier, two cruisers and a destroyer, with serious damage to two carriers – *Indomitable* and *Victorious* – and a cruiser.

CHAPTER FIVE

FIGHTING THE WEATHER AND THE GERMANS

The officer who shall have command of a convoy entrusted to him is to consider the protecting of it as his most particular duty, in the execution of which he is to be very watchful to prevent it being surprised, and very alert in defending it if attacked.
Regulations and Instructions Relating to His Majesty's Service at Sea, 1806

The entry of the Soviet Union into the war was brought about by the German invasion, Operation Barbarossa. Prior to that, the Soviet Union, if not actually an ally of the Germans, was an opportunistic co-belligerent in that the German invasion of Poland was followed by Soviet occupation of that country's eastern territories. In a further attempt to return to the limits of the tsarist empire, the USSR then went to war with Finland.

That the USSR was a demanding and unreliable ally was not in doubt, at least as far as the British were concerned. The Soviet dictator, Stalin, had ignored warnings about German intentions, so that the country's armed forces were not deployed effectively to resist an invasion. The Soviet armed forces were in any case relatively ineffectual having had the bulk of their senior and more experienced officers purged by Stalin, while most of their equipment was inferior to that available to the other warring nations.

On the other hand, the invasion of the Soviet Union immediately eased the pressure on the British war effort. It brought a welcome, but from the German point of view premature, end to the blitz on British towns and cities. It also eased the pressure on the Maltese islands. The vast size of the USSR and its large population meant that it absorbed German ground and air forces like a sponge. The need for the Germans to intervene in the Balkans to relieve the embarrassment of their Italian allies meant that the invasion started late, too late to achieve its objectives before winter set in, although the operation was also hampered by Hitler's decision to divide his forces into three rather than two. Even so, as Napoleon had discovered almost 130 years earlier, 'General Winter' once again proved to be Russia's most successful commander!

Nevertheless, the British felt the need to encourage their new-found Russian allies and stiffen their resolve. Many believe that Stalin would have ceded territory in an

attempt to reach peace with Germany, and this was indeed considered, which would have released German forces once again to fight in western Europe. On the other hand, the question that can never be fully answered must be whether Stalin could have survived the ignominy of allowing the Germans to keep Soviet territory and the natural resources that the Germans so craved.

PETSAMO AND KIRKENES

German possession of the ports of Petsamo and Kirkenes, north of the Arctic Circle, made it more difficult for Russia's new allies to send supplies, since the direct route through the Baltic was completely out of the question. Kirkenes was in a key location at the northern tip of Norway; Petsamo (modern Pechenga, in Russia) was originally part of Russia before passing to Finland, but was ceded to Russia again as the price of peace in the Russo-Finnish War of 1940–41.

The only possible means of making an impact on the German forces attacking the Soviet Union lay with the Royal Navy, and especially with naval air power. The Commander-in-Chief, Home Fleet was urged by Britain's wartime leader, Winston Churchill, to carry out an attack that would be 'a gesture in support of our Russian allies to create a diversion on the enemy's northern flank'. An attack on the two ports seemed to be the only way forward in 1941. The Royal Navy deployed one of its newest aircraft carriers, *Victorious*, and its oldest, *Furious*. Aircraft for the attack were Fairey

Albacore torpedo-bombers, complemented by Fairey Swordfish, escorted by Fairey Fulmar fighters. *Victorious* sent twenty Albacores from 827 and 828 naval air squadrons, escorted by Fulmars from 809 squadron. *Furious* sent nine Swordfish of 812 squadron and nine Albacores of 817 squadron, escorted by the Fulmars of 800 squadron.

Unlike the raid on Taranto, the operation had to take place in daylight because of the almost 24-hour summer daylight of the far north. German aerial reconnaissance was far more methodical than that of the Italians, and the carriers and the nature of the operation soon became known. The final approaches to the targets were also far more difficult.

Aircraft were flown off late in the afternoons of 22 and 25 July 1941, with those from *Victorious* going to Kirkenes, while *Furious* sent her aircraft to Petsamo. The aircraft from *Victorious* had to fly over a German hospital ship on the way in to the target and were ordered not to attack it, although, of course, those aboard could warn the authorities ashore. When they reached Kirkenes, the aircraft had to fly over a mountain at the end of the fjord before diving into the bay, where they found just four ships. After enduring heavy anti-aircraft fire from positions on the cliffs, the attackers were themselves attacked by German fighters, and most of them had to jettison their torpedoes in a desperate bid to escape. They managed to sink just one cargo vessel of 2,000 tons and set another on fire. The slow and lumbering Fulmars did well to shoot down four Luftwaffe aircraft.

Petsamo was even worse, for the harbour was empty. Frustrated aircrew could do nothing more than aim their torpedoes at the wharves, hoping to do at least some damage.

Action stations aboard the battleship HMS *Anson*, with men running to their posts in anti-flash gear and steel helmets. In the background are the hangar and a Supermarine Walrus amphibian. *(IWM A16503)*

The Flower class corvettes shouldered much of the burden of convoy escort duty, and some idea of the conditions facing these plucky little ships can be gained in this shot of HMS *Honeysuckle* coming alongside the escort carrier HMS *Trumpeter* in the Kola Inlet in early 1945. *(IWM A28203)*

Having received such a hot welcome for so little of any value in the target area, the attackers attempted to make their escape. This was easier said than done, for the aircraft were easy prey for the German fighters. The normal defensive drill in such circumstances was for the Swordfish or Albacore pilots to go right down on the water and wait, with the TAGs watching for the cannon shells hitting the water, and at the last second calling out to the pilot, 'hard-a-starboard' or 'hard-a-port'. Flying just above the surface of the water also meant that the fighters had to pull out early or risk a high-speed dive into the sea.

Victorious lost thirteen of her aircraft, while *Furious* lost three. Altogether, forty-four aircrew were lost, seven of them killed, the remainder taken prisoner. Had the losses at Taranto been on a similar scale, seven aircraft would have been lost rather than just the two. 'The gallantry of the aircraft crews, who knew before leaving that their chance of surprise had gone, and that they were certain to face heavy odds, is beyond praise,' remarked Tovey. 'I trust that the encouragement to the morale of our allies was proportionately great.'

CONVOYS TO RUSSIA

Grimmest of the convoy routes were those to Russia, sailing past occupied Norway and north of the Arctic Circle, where the

Even in wartime, accidents happen. This is the battleship HMS *King George V* at Iceland, with a massive hole in her bows after a collision with the destroyer *Punjabi*, which was cut in two and sank. *(IWM A9943)*

weather was as much an enemy as the Kriegsmarine and the Luftwaffe. A total of 811 ships sailed in the Arctic convoys to Russia, of which 720 completed their voyages, another 33 turned back for one reason or another, and 58 were sunk, giving a loss rate of 7.2 per cent. Of the ships that reached Russia, 717 sailed back (some were being delivered to the Soviet Union), and of these, 29 were sunk, a loss rate of 4 per cent. This was the price of delivering to Russia some 4 million tons of war stores, including 5,000 tanks and more than 7,000 aircraft.

The problems of keeping the Soviet Union, industrially and technologically backward and ill-prepared for war, in the conflict were many. Both the United States

and the United Kingdom went to great lengths to keep the USSR supplied. Most of the aid went from the United States to the USSR via the Indian Ocean and Persian Gulf, then overland from an Iranian port. Very little took the short route from west-coast USA to Siberia, partly because the USSR did not come into the war against Japan until August 1945, and partly because of the limited capacity of the trans-Siberian railway to move materiel to the western USSR where it was needed. Most attention has centred on the Arctic convoys from Scotland and Iceland to Archangel and Murmansk.

The only route for the convoys was around the northern tip of occupied

The cruiser HMS *Belfast* stands out clearly against the snowy wastes of Iceland in February 1943. *(IWM A15530)*

Norway to Murmansk and Archangel. In summer, the almost constant daylight left the ships open to attack from the air, and from U-boats and surface raiders. In winter, in the almost constant darkness with just three hours of weak twilight in the middle of the day, the weather was another hazard. One officer having difficulty eating a meal as his cruiser rolled to angles of 30 degrees consoled himself with the thought that life must have been even more difficult in the destroyers and corvettes, which rolled as much as 50 degrees, and sometimes even more! For the airmen, life was hard. The cold meant that they tried to wear as much as possible, limited only by the need to get into and out of the cockpit. Metal became

so brittle that tail wheels could break off on landing. In his book, *Arctic Convoys*, Richard Woodman explains that 'the sinking of a 10,000 ton freighter was the equivalent, in terms of material destroyed, of a land battle'.

The first convoy to suffer heavy losses was PQ13, which sailed on 20 March 1942 and was attacked not just by U-boats and aircraft, but also by destroyers from Kirkenes. Despite Ultra intelligence warning of the impending attack, which led to one destroyer being sunk and two damaged by the cruiser HMS *Trinidad*, the convoy lost five ships. The scale of the Luftwaffe attacks was considerable, with convoy PQ16 being attacked by no fewer than 108 aircraft on

27 May 1942, and contributed to the convoy's overall loss of seven ships.

Best known of the Arctic convoys was the ill-fated PQ17, which had sailed from Hvalfiordur, in Iceland, on 27 June 1942, without a carrier among its escorts, which might have prevented the tragic events that occurred. The key to the disaster was that the German battleship *Tirpitz*, in the Altenfjord, was observed by the Norwegian resistance preparing to go to sea on 4 July. The Admiralty had been aware that an attack was likely and the convoy was given a heavier escort than usual, but with nothing heavier than the cruisers in the distant escort. Ultra intelligence had revealed that the cruisers *Admiral Scheer* and *Hipper*, and possibly the pocket battleship *Lützow*, were also in the Altenfjord. Faced with the strong possibility that this powerful force could overwhelm the convoy escorts, the First Sea Lord, Adm Sir Dudley Pound, ordered the convoy to scatter and the escorts to return. This left the thirty-seven ships at the mercy of U-boats and the Luftwaffe; just eleven ships out of the thirty-seven in the convoy reached their destination, with the loss of 153 lives, 2,500 aircraft, 430 tanks and almost 4,000 lorries and other vehicles. *Tirpitz* had meanwhile remained in harbour, believing that the distant escort had included a battleship. When this was corrected following aerial reconnaissance, she left port with the other ships during the afternoon of 5 July, but returned to her berth when it was clear that the convoy was being destroyed.

The order to scatter the convoy remains one of the most controversial of the war at

Another cruiser, HMS *Jamaica*, on Russian convoy duty in late 1943. *(IWM A20388)*

sea. With hindsight, the entire convoy should have been turned back and brought under the protection of the heavy units of the Home Fleet. Had it not scattered, there can be no doubt that the *Tirpitz* battlegroup would have destroyed the convoy and the escort.

Convoy PQ18, departing on 12 September 1942, was the first Arctic convoy to have an escort carrier, the US-built HMS *Avenger*. She carried three radar-equipped Swordfish from 825 Squadron for anti-submarine duties as well as six Sea Hurricanes, with another six dismantled and stowed beneath the hangar deck in a hold, for fighter defence. The fighter aircraft were drawn from 802 and 883 squadrons. A Hurricane was aboard the CAM-ship *Empire Morn*. The convoy escort included the cruiser *Scylla*, two destroyers, two anti-aircraft ships converted from merchant vessels, four corvettes, four anti-submarine trawlers, three minesweepers, two submarines and a rescue ship, so that the escorts would not be distracted from their work to rescue survivors, a matter of urgency in the cold seas. Three American minesweepers being delivered to the Soviet Union also acted as rescue ships. The convoy itself consisted of forty-one merchantmen.

Seas were so rough that a Sea Hurricane was swept off *Avenger*'s deck, and the steel cables securing the aircraft in the hangar failed to stop them breaking loose, crashing into one another and into the sides of the hangar. Fused 500lb bombs stored in the lift-well broke loose, and had to be captured by laying down duffel coats with rope ties, to be quickly tied up as soon as a bomb rolled on to the coats!

With the escort carrier, PQ18 fared far better than the earlier convoy, but even so, no fewer than thirteen merchantmen were sunk, including two ammunition ships. Three U-boats were sunk by the escorts and aircraft working together, while out of a total of forty enemy aircraft shot down, the Sea Hurricanes accounted for five and damaged seventeen others. As one of the early convoys to have escort carrier support, it enabled important lessons to be learnt, one of which was that keeping a single fighter in the air meant having the replacement aircraft flown off while the plane in the air still had sufficient fuel for combat. Another was that the Swordfish, while invaluable in the anti-submarine role, could be forced back from their patrols by German aircraft and were not enough on their own.

CHAPTER SIX

OVERWHELMED IN THE FAR EAST

All delays are dangerous in war.
John Dryden, 1631–1700

On 7 December 1941 the Imperial Japanese Navy attacked the United States Navy in its forward Pacific base at Pearl Harbor and brought the United States into the war. While it can be argued that it would then have been only a matter of time before the United States would have declared war on Germany and Italy, Hitler made sure that no time was lost, declaring war on the United States himself. Any temptation for the United States to concentrate solely on the war against Japan was avoided as a result, and after much debate US policy-makers saw that the defeat of Germany and Italy had to take precedence over the defeat of Japan. The reason for this was that it was easier to engage German and Italian forces and attack targets in those two countries, while Japan was still at some distance and at first could only be countered by naval forces.

Nevertheless, for the Royal Navy the new situation meant that it had to fight on yet another front and in two more oceans, the Indian and the Pacific. Before the war, the British government had always assured Australia and New Zealand that in the event of hostilities with Japan, it would send a fleet into the area, and a substantial dockyard had been created at Singapore. Yet, with Britain engaged in the struggle against Germany and Italy, there was no substantial fleet left to protect the furthest flung of the dominions, and Singapore was only the fortress that everyone liked to pretend it was if a substantial fleet was present. Losses were not long in coming.

On 10 December 1941 Japanese aircraft sank the new battleship, *Prince of Wales* and the elderly battlecruiser *Repulse*, giving Japan complete control of the seas. Had the British been operating these ships as a properly constructed task group with a couple of aircraft carriers, the outcome might have been different, especially if the carriers had had high-performance fighters embarked. As it was, they had been intended to operate with just one carrier, the new *Indomitable*, but she had run aground and was not available. The force commander, Adm Tom Phillips, planned to attack the Japanese invasion fleet, and discounted the threat of aerial attack. He maintained radio silence, making it difficult for the RAF to offer air cover; moreover the RAF was heavily outnumbered by around four to one by Japanese aircraft, and had no modern fighters.

The lack of air cover was to be a problem that plagued British efforts in the Far East into 1942. As the Japanese swept across the

HMS *Exeter*, one of the victors at the Battle of the River Plate, fires her anti-aircraft guns at Japanese aircraft while escorting the last troop convoy to reach Singapore before it fell to the Japanese. The troops in the convoy would all have become prisoners of war. *Exeter* was sunk the following month in the Battle of the Java Sea. *(IWM A9698)*

Pacific, the Philippines and the Indonesian and Malayan territories, Australian, British, Dutch and United States forces combined in a desperate bid to hold back the tide, creating a new command known as ABDA – American, British, Dutch and Australian. On 27 February the Dutch Rear Adm Karel Doorman with a force of two heavy and three light cruisers and nine destroyers, including HMS *Exeter* and HMAS *Perth*, confronted two Japanese heavy cruisers and two light cruisers, supported by fourteen destroyers and aircraft from the carrier *Ryujo*, in the Battle of the Java Sea. Communications between the allied ships were poor and Doorman had no experience of commanding a fleet action. Even if he had, the odds were stacked against his force: lacking crucial air cover, he had also made the mistake of leaving the ships' reconnaissance aircraft ashore, since he expected a night action. Instead, the battle started during the afternoon and continued into the night. During the action, Doorman was killed, two Dutch cruisers and three destroyers were sunk, and *Exeter* was badly damaged and had to withdraw to Surabaya. The Japanese admiral, Tagaki, was criticised by his superiors for excessive caution during the battle, but suffered only one destroyer damaged.

During the night of 28 February, the two remaining operational cruisers from the Battle of the Java Sea, HMAS *Perth* and USS *Houston*, were sunk as they attacked a Japanese invasion fleet, though they sank four enemy transports. On the morning of 1 March, *Exeter*, with two destroyers, was

The battlecruiser HMS *Repulse* leaves Singapore for the last time, before being sunk by the Japanese. *(IWM A29069)*

intercepted and sunk as they attempted to escape to Ceylon (now Sri Lanka). The only ships not to be sunk were four American destroyers that managed to slip through the Bali Strait to Australia.

The Japanese had their sights on India, planning to drive the British out, but at sea the effective limit of their operations was attacks on Ceylon in April. On 5 April carrier-borne aircraft bombed shipping in Colombo Harbour, while out at sea, the cruisers *Cornwall* and *Dorsetshire* were attacked by fifty aircraft and sunk within minutes. On 9 April the carrier *Hermes*, escorted by an Australian destroyer, HMAS *Vampire*, was caught by Japanese carrier-borne aircraft and both ships were sunk within sight of the Ceylonese coast. That same day, there were further air attacks on Trincomalee ('Trinco' to the Royal Navy), while Japanese cruisers attacked merchant shipping in the Bay of Bengal.

Nevertheless, the war against the Axis powers east of Suez was far from one-sided, even at this early stage in the war. On 5 May 1942, in Operation Ironclad, British forces invaded the large island of Madagascar off the coast of East Africa, which was of vital strategic importance. Governed by the Vichy French, it provided a base for Axis commerce raiders in the Indian Ocean, and with the Mediterranean by this time virtually impassable, the island was on the long convoy route around the Cape of Good Hope and through the Suez Canal to Egypt. Fortunately, the Axis powers had been unable to give Madagascar the strong defence that it needed, simply because the Suez Canal was closed to them, as were the Straits of Gibraltar to all but submarines. The long sea route from Europe was also vulnerable to attack by British ships and aircraft from Gibraltar, Britain's West African colonies and, of course, from South

The heavy cruiser HMS *Cornwall* sinking after facing heavy Japanese aerial attack. *(IWM HU1838)*

Africa. Had Japan been so minded, it is possible that she could have seized and held Madagascar, at least for a time, but cooperation between the European and Asian arms of the Axis was weak by Anglo-American standards, and before long the Japanese were to have difficulty maintaining seaborne communications even within their Asian empire.

British forces were landed at Diego Suarez, in the far north of the island. Aircraft from eight Fleet Air Arm squadrons provided air cover and ground attack, operating from the two carriers *Indomitable* and *Illustrious*, the latter now back from her extensive repairs in the United States following her sufferings around Malta in January of the previous year. The carriers were part of a balanced naval force that included the battleship *Ramillies*, as well as two cruisers and eleven destroyers. While the landings took until 8 May to become fully established, little local resistance was met.

The only counter-attack of any importance was that by Japanese midget submarines against *Ramillies* on 30 May, while she was still at Diego Suarez. The elderly battleship was put out of action for several months. The following day, a similar attack on shipping in Sydney Harbour was foiled.

CHAPTER SEVEN

BREACHING FORTRESS EUROPE

The fleet and army acting in concert seem to be the natural bulwark of these kingdoms.
Thomas Moore Molyneaux, 1759

While invasion of Madagascar had been a step in the right direction and provided additional security for the Cape route, mainly for ships heading north towards the Suez Canal, it was well away from the harsh realities of the war and the vital objective of securing Axis defeat. This had to come through North Africa and southern Europe before a head-on clash in northern Europe could be contemplated.

OPERATION TORCH – THE LANDINGS IN NORTH AFRICA

In North Africa, the British Eighth Army inflicted a major defeat on the German *Afrika Korps* at the Battle of El Alamein, which lasted from 23 October to 5 November 1942. This was to be the first major British victory on land, although the Japanese were to be held in Burma, but it was also the last in which Britain fought alone.

Even before El Alamein, the Allies had planned landings in North Africa, to squeeze the Germans between British and American forces. The North African landings were known as 'Operation Torch', and involved landing almost 100,000 men in Vichy French territory, on the Atlantic coast

of French Morocco and in Algeria. In between these two large areas lay neutral Spanish Morocco. Responsibility for the operation was divided between the British, with the Eastern Task Force, and Americans, with the Western Task Force. The Allies now had Gen Dwight Eisenhower as Supreme Commander while Adm Sir Andrew Cunningham was Allied Naval Commander. Force H under Vice Adm Syfret, with the aircraft carriers *Victorious* and *Formidable* and three battleships, including the new *Duke of York*, defended the eastern flanks of the invasion force from the Italian fleet and German U-boats. The Eastern Task Force under the command of Rear Adm Sir Harold Burrough, with three cruisers, sixteen destroyers, the elderly aircraft carriers *Argus* and *Furious* and two escort carriers to cover sixteen transports and seventeen landing craft, put Maj Gen Ryder's 33,000 British and American troops ashore near Algiers. The landings to the north and south of Casablanca in French Morocco were covered by a Western Task Force, TF34, from the United States which had twenty-three transports to land 34,000 troops commanded by Maj Gen Patton; the landing fleet was protected by three American battleships, seven cruisers and

The Blitz, and hit-and-run raids in the Channel by E-boats, meant that many convoys started and finished on the Clyde. This is a fire-fighting ship at Gourock in 1942. *(IWM A7248)*

thirty-eight destroyers, with air support provided by the USS *Ranger* and four American escort carriers.

In between these two major task forces was a Centre Task Force that had sailed from Britain under the command of Cdre Troubridge, with two escort carriers, three cruisers and thirteen destroyers escorting twenty-eight transports and nineteen landing craft to put 39,000 men ashore at Oran in Algeria under the command of Maj Gen Fredendall, US Army.

Landings started at around 01.00 on 8 November at Oran, and then a little later at Algiers, while those in Morocco started at 04.30, with further landings at Safi, almost 200 miles to the south of Casablanca. In the days that followed, there were additional landings further east in Algeria at Bougie on 10 November, and after troops fighting east from Algiers joined up, at Bone on 12 November. The Algerian coastline extended well over 500 miles; the landings in French Morocco were separated from those in Algeria by some 350 miles of Spanish Moroccan coastline.

Coordination was helped by Troubridge's maintaining a signals team of more than a hundred personnel using a dozen radio wavebands, located in a former armed merchant cruiser, *Large*. An idea of the tight timescale in which this, the first big Allied invasion, had been put together can be gathered from the fact that *Large*'s staff officers had to use umbrellas when sheltering in what was supposed to be their accommodation aft of the bridge!

Despite the size of the operation, almost complete surprise was gained. Nevertheless, the rapid expansion of both navies also meant that there were problems with inexperienced aircrew. Aboard the American escort carrier *Santee*, there were just five experienced pilots, and she was to lose twenty-one out of her thirty-one aircraft during Operation Torch, with just one of the losses possibly due to enemy action.

The uncertain position of the Vichy French forces was highlighted by the campaign, as the commander-in-chief of the Vichy navy, Adm Darlan, was present in Algeria at the time. Darlan agreed to surrender if Marshal Pétain, the Vichy French dictator, agreed, but Pétain was preoccupied with stopping German forces from occupying Vichy France. In the end, Darlan accepted surrender, but the lack of firm orders from Vichy meant that many of his subordinate commanders continued to fight, and gained time for German forces to enter neighbouring Tunisia.

While the battleships and cruisers attacked French ships and shore installations, the aircraft from the carriers were sent to attack airfields. Initially, the attackers thought that they had taken the French air force by surprise, catching many of their bombers on the ground before daybreak. Allied aircraft, including many from the Fleet Air Arm, strafed Vichy airfields, in some cases making several strafing runs, a tactic to be forbidden later because the danger rose so rapidly after the first run. Nevertheless, a number of French fighter pilots managed to get into the air and there was some aerial combat on the first day. The commanding officer of 807 squadron from HMS *Furious*, a Seafire unit, was shot down and briefly became a prisoner of the Vichy French. He sat in a French general's office while they decided what to do with him, and when the French forces eventually surrendered, he was returned, going aboard the carrier just two days after being shot down – one of the shortest spells as a prisoner of war on record. Meanwhile, at Casablanca, aircraft from the USS *Ranger* and gunfire from a US battleship caused severe damage to the French battleship *Jean Bart*.

Vichy resistance in North Africa ended on 9 November in Oran. The surrender persuaded the Germans that they should finally occupy Vichy France, which they did, reaching Toulon on 27 November. Italian forces took the opportunity to invade Corsica.

The landings in North Africa marked the end of German and Italian ambitions in that continent, turned the balance of power in the Mediterranean and considerably eased the plight of Malta. They laid the foundations for the next step in the war – taking ground forces into Axis territory for the first time. These plans were not without controversy – the American Adm Ernest King wanted specific tasks to be allocated to both the British and the Free French; moreover he felt that the British Eastern Fleet at the time was serving little useful purpose and could be used to sever Japanese shipping links with Rangoon. At the Casablanca Conference in January 1943, King explained that, according to his estimates, just 15 per cent of the total Allied effort was being devoted to the war against the Japanese in the Pacific, and that this would not be enough to stop them from consolidating their gains. His view was opposed by Gen Sir

The destroyer HMS *Campbell* at speed. *(IWM HU1464)*

Alan Brooke, Chief of the Imperial General Staff, who felt that the Japanese were by this time on the defensive in the Pacific. The First Sea Lord, Adm Sir Dudley Pound, believed that the British could not send naval units eastwards without strong carrier air support.

Given Churchill's reluctance to engage in either a major assault in Burma or a direct assault on Europe from the British Isles, and King's concern that the troops in North Africa should not be left idle, eventually it was decided to mount a campaign against either Sicily or Sardinia. King strongly favoured the former.

OPERATION HUSKY – THE LANDINGS IN SICILY

Some time elapsed between the landings in North Africa and the first invasion of Axis territory – Operation Husky, the Allied landings in Sicily. This was not simply because of the time needed to consolidate the Allied position in North Africa and finally defeat the Axis forces there, it was also because of the need to avoid the winter weather, which even in the Mediterranean can be unpredictable and stormy. The irony was that when the operation did take place, it was hindered by unseasonably bad weather.

There had also been some disagreement among the Allies over exactly what the next step should be. The Americans and Russians would have preferred an invasion of France in 1943, but the British argued successfully at the Casablanca Conference that the time was not right. The British saw an invasion of Sicily not simply as a stepping stone for the invasion of mainland Italy; it would also clear the shipping lanes through the Mediterranean, finally relieving the pressure on Malta. Furthermore, in allowing sea traffic to the Middle East and Australia to use the Suez Canal once more, it would at a stroke free a considerable volume of merchant shipping, on one estimate giving the Allies the equivalent of more than a million tons.

As a preparation for the operation, the small Italian islands of Pantelleria and Lampedusa, to the west of Malta, were taken on 11 and 12 June 1943. The garrisons had surrendered following a heavy naval bombardment accompanied by raids by Malta-based aircraft of the RAF and the Fleet Air Arm. The scene was set for Husky, scheduled for 10 July.

For Operation Husky, two aircraft carriers were assigned – *Indomitable* and *Formidable*, from Force H, now under the command of Vice Adm Willis. The carriers were able to give close air support, but most of the 3,700 aircraft available to the Allies were based ashore, Malta being less than twenty minutes flying time from Sicily. Allied aircraft heavily outnumbered those available to the Axis forces, which had just 1,400 machines. The Allies gathered together a force of almost 3,000 ships for

The M class destroyer HMS *Matchless* on plane-guard duty, escorting an aircraft carrier to rescue any airmen whose aircraft might have ditched during flying operations. *(IWM A8347)*

the invasion, including 2,000 landing craft which included for the first time the new LST (Landing Ship Tank). However, the balance of power lay heavily with the defenders in manpower, with 180,000 Allied troops facing 275,000 in General Guzzoni's Italian Sixth Army.

Once again the Allied forces were divided into a Western Naval Task Force – this time under Vice Adm Henry Kent Hewitt, USN, tasked to land Lt Gen Patton's US Seventh Army on the southern coast of Sicily – and an Eastern Naval Task Force – commanded by Adm Ramsay, RN, and charged with putting the British Eighth Army ashore under Lt Gen Montgomery on the south-east point of the island. The main bases for the attack had to be in North Africa – Malta was far too small to host an operation of this size, although the island's three airfields were very much in the fray.

The weather on 10 July was bad, with high winds and heavy seas, so that at one stage postponement was considered. While the adverse weather may have lulled the defenders into a false sense of security, it also resulted in heavy losses among the paratroops and glider-borne forces. As before, Force H provided fighter cover for the landings, but apart from a single Ju88, discovered by two Seafires, which shot down one of the fighters, many Allied pilots did not recall seeing an enemy aircraft for the first four days after the invasion. The reason for the sluggish response from the Axis forces was quite simple: they had believed that Sardinia would be the most likely location for an Allied landing, even though Sicily was the most obvious springboard for an invasion of Italy itself and much closer to the Allied bases in North Africa and Malta. The only advantage of Sardinia would have been that it would have offered bases from which bombers could have attacked Italy and the south of France more easily than

from Sicily, and perhaps also allowed the later invasion of the Italian mainland to take place further up the 'leg' of Italy; but again, this would have meant a bigger leap than necessary for the Allies.

Nevertheless, a counter-attack did come on 11 July, spearheaded by German panzer divisions, but this was successfully repelled by the invasion forces, with the support of air power and a heavy bombardment by the major fleet units in Force H.

Unfortunately, it seems that the Allies became too relaxed: an Italian aircraft successfully attacked and seriously damaged *Indomitable* with an air-launched torpedo after those aboard mistook the plane for a Swordfish. Some at least of those aboard the carrier put the Italian success down to care-lessness, since the carrier was supposed to have the protection of a battleship acting as radar guardship. A chief petty officer spotted the aircraft approaching in the moonlight and called up to the bridge, 'Enemy aircraft approaching', only to be told not to worry as it was a returning Swordfish. The torpedo was dropped close to the carrier and blew a 30-ft gash in her side, forcing her to divert to Malta for emergency repairs, where she found that the Axis air forces were still capable of mounting a heavy aerial attack. *Indomitable*'s squadrons were disembarked prior to her arrival in Grand Harbour, and spent an uncomfortable spell in poor tented accom-modation at the height of the Mediter-ranean summer, while the Axis mini-blitz extended to the airfields.

It took just over a month for the Allies to secure Sicily, and it would have been an encouraging start to the assault on the Axis strongholds in Europe had not most of the German and Italian forces on the island been able to slip away across the Straits of Messina over several nights, so that 100,000 troops remained free to fight another day.

The destroyer HMS *Broke*, which was used to breach the defences at Algiers, coming alongside the cruiser HMS *Sheffield* to embark US troops for the invasion of North Africa, Operation Torch. *(IWM A12879)*

ON TO THE MAINLAND – THE SALERNO LANDINGS

If carrier-borne aircraft had been useful, but not essential, for the invasion of Sicily, they were vital for the next stage, the invasion of mainland Italy with landings at Salerno. Although Salerno was within range of aircraft operating from airfields in Sicily, it was only just within range for fighter aircraft, leaving a Spitfire with just enough fuel for twenty minutes on patrol above the beachheads, and far less if engaging enemy aircraft. The obvious solution was to station aircraft carriers off the coast to provide fighter cover.

Salerno was an attempt to shorten the war in Italy, and in this, as we shall see, it was

As the war progressed, the means of landing invasion forces became more sophisticated. This is HMS *Eastway*, a landing ship dock with a floodable stern to enable the launch of landing craft. *(IWM A20411)*

unsuccessful for reasons that might not have been fully foreseen at the time. Montgomery's Eighth Army had already crossed the Straits of Messina into Calabria on 3 September 1943, a relatively easy operation but one that left them at the very tip of the 'toe' of Italy with some considerable distance to move through hilly terrain, fighting German and Italian rearguard actions. Salerno was some 200 miles further north. The prospects at first seemed extremely bright, for on the same day that Montgomery moved into Calabria, an armistice was signed in secret at Syracuse with Marshal Badoglio's new Italian government, formed after Mussolini had been deposed in July. Negotiations for the armistice had been prolonged as at first the

Allies were suspicious of Italian objectives, but this did at least give the Allies time to plan their assaults on Salerno and Taranto, fully recognising that the Germans were likely to continue to resist, whatever the Italians decided. This was another reason for choosing Salerno – the hope that a substantial number of German troops would be cut off and unable to withdraw. The armistice was announced on 8 September, on the eve of the Salerno landings, but it might have been as well to have postponed the announcement another twenty-four hours, since the Germans were able to move quickly to seize Italian airfields, although the Italians for their part were able to move most of their fleet to prevent it falling into German hands. Had the Germans not known about the armistice in advance, the landings at Salerno could have been easier.

The landings at Salerno, Operation Avalanche, on 9 September were coordinated with a British airborne landing at Taranto to seize the port and enable Italian shipping there to escape to Malta. Vice Adm Hewitt landed Lt Gen Mark Clark's US Fifth Army in a landing fleet covered by an Independence class light fleet carrier and four escort carriers, as well as eleven cruisers and forty-three destroyers. Force H, still under Vice Adm Willis, had the battleships *Nelson* and *Rodney* and the aircraft carriers *Illustrious* and *Formidable*. Force V consisted of the maintenance carrier *Unicorn* operating in the combat role, with another four escort carriers (known in the Royal Navy as auxiliary carriers), *Attacker*, *Battler*, *Hunter* and *Stalker*, and was under the command of Rear Adm Sir Philip Vian. Meanwhile, the Mediterranean Fleet had escorted Italian warships to Malta, before supporting the Taranto landings with heavy gunfire from the battleships *Warspite*, *Howe*, *Valiant* and *King George V*. *Warspite* and *Valiant* were then redeployed to provide heavy gunnery support for the Salerno bridgehead.

While the two large armoured carriers were intended to defend the fleet and look for enemy shipping, the carriers in Force V were solely concerned to provide fighter support, with each escort carrier carrying a single squadron of thirty Supermarine Seafires, with their engines tuned to provide maximum power at 5,000ft instead of the usual 15,000ft, making it a very different aircraft from those at the North African landings almost a year earlier. *Unicorn* carried two squadrons, with a total of sixty Seafires. As in the North African landings, the aircraft would be used to provide air cover and also to provide ground attack against German troops and airfields.

The Seafire was a big improvement in performance over anything that the Fleet Air Arm had operated before, being faster than the Sea Hurricane, although less manoeuvrable and more difficult to repair; and it had folding wings. The modifications necessary for carrier operation meant that it was slightly heavier than the Spitfire, from which it was derived, and so a little slower. Before the operation, senior Fleet Air Arm pilots visited the RAF to discover the latest in fighter tactics and up-to-date intelligence on German aircraft. The RAF personnel were helpful, but this couldn't disguise bad news. The latest versions of the Messerschmitt Bf109 and the new Focke-wulf Fw190 were indeed formidable opponents, the latter aircraft also having the manoeuvrability that the Bf109 lacked.

Anxious to squeeze the last ounce of performance out of the aircraft, the Fleet Air Arm put in hand a programme of 'local modifications'. The exhaust manifolds were removed and replaced with exhaust stubs to reduce drag and increase the thrust from the exhaust. The knobs for catapult operation from carriers were also removed, further reducing drag. Good-quality furniture polish was somehow obtained, despite wartime rationing and restrictions on production of quality materials, and everyone, pilots included, spent hours polishing the leading edges of the wings to make the aircraft more slippery. Introduced between May and June 1943, in time for the invasion of Sicily, these changes gave the aircraft another 15 knots' maximum speed. The Seafire rarely needed catapult assistance during take-off. The Seafire suffered from two shortcomings. The first was that, in common with many British fighters early in the war, it was short on range. The second was its tendency to pitch forward on landing, at best damaging the propeller, at worst damaging the aircraft beyond repair.

The British carriers made a feint towards Taranto after leaving Malta, although in reality the assault on Taranto was covered by six battleships from Force H and the Mediterranean Fleet, and by aircraft from Malta. The announcement of the armistice saw the Italian navy leave its ports of La Spezia, Genoa, Castellamare and Taranto and steam towards Malta, being escorted by four of the Royal Navy's Mediterranean battleships, leaving the other two to accompany *Illustrious* and *Formidable* to Salerno. Despite the escort, the Luftwaffe mounted a heavy aerial attack against the Italian ships, sinking the new battleship *Roma* and damaging the *Italia.*

The aircrew aboard the carriers of Force V were awakened at 04.30 on the morning of 9 September. Several of those present recalled not having had much sleep and few had any appetite for the breakfast of eggs and bacon put before them in the wardroom. Among the first into the air before dawn were eight Seafires drawn from *Unicorn*'s 809 and 887 Naval Air Squadrons, with four aircraft providing high cover and another four low cover, looking out for enemy dive-bombers and torpedo-bombers respectively. The practice was for aircraft to carry extra fuel in drop tanks, extending their patrol time, and to use this first as the tanks would have to be dropped to reduce drag before engaging in aerial combat. That first day, there was little sign of the Luftwaffe, but the troops landing encountered fierce resistance. In the days following the invasion, a strong counter-attack was mounted by mainly German forces accompanied by heavy aerial attack by the Luftwaffe, so that the entire operation soon appeared to be in difficulty.

Life was difficult aboard the carriers, with Force V given a 'box' offshore in which to operate, flying off and recovering their aircraft. In practice, this box was far too small for the ships, giving the carrier commanders great difficulties as they charged from one end to the other. The situation was even worse for those in the air: with large numbers of aircraft circling within a confined space, the danger of a mid-air collision was very real as they waited to land on ships that were steaming close to one another. At times a light haze added to the difficulties.

As luck would have it, the whole operation took place in conditions of complete calm, with little wind – never more than 3 knots. The Seafire needed 25 knots of wind over the deck for a safe take-off or landing, but the escort carriers could only manage 17 knots. Arrester wires had to be kept even tighter than usual, as did the crash barriers two-thirds of the way along the flight decks. The calm conditions meant that judgement of speed over the water and height above the surface, on the approach to landing on the carriers proved extremely difficult. Looking for a means of easing the problems, Capt Henry McWilliams, commanding officer of the escort carrier HMS *Hunter*, asked Rear Adm Vian for permission to saw nine inches off the wooden propeller blades of the Seafires. Vian wisely decided that the personnel aboard the carriers knew more about the problem than he did, and gave his permission. The modification was relatively easy for the ships' carpenters to do and had little effect on the performance of the aircraft, while propeller damage during landing was much reduced. After initial trials, the entire stock of replacement propellers aboard the carriers was also treated in the same way.

In other ways too, it often seemed to be a case of learning through trial and error. The casualty rate among the Seafire pilots seemed to be unduly high in the air, not just in landing, as many seemed to be unable to bale out quickly enough. Learning the hard way, it was soon discovered that the RAF-

Not all 'landing craft' were actually used for landings. Some were fitted out to fire rockets or, as in this case, provide artillery cover as a landing craft, gun – large – or LCG(L). *(IWM A23754)*

recommended method of escaping from a Spitfire, rolling the aircraft and opening the canopy before undoing their seat belts and 'ejecting' (in other words, falling out) from the aircraft, did not work. Possibly this was because of the higher weight of the Seafire. Eventually pilots were advised to jump over the side of the aircraft, and the survival rate among those shot down improved immediately.

Turning their attention to the carriers, the Luftwaffe mounted intensive attacks during 11 September, forcing the ships to operate at full speed even when not flying-off or landing aircraft, and fuel consumption increased considerably. For the first time, the Germans used glider-bombs, saving their

aircraft from the intense AA fire put up by the fleet offshore. That evening, Vian was forced to signal Vice Adm Hewitt in overall command of the operation, 'My bolt will be shot this evening, probably earlier.'

Hewitt had just been briefed by Lt Gen Mark Clark on the situation ashore, and guessed that more air attacks were imminent. He signalled back, 'Air conditions here critical. Can your carrier force remain on station to provide earlier morning coverage tomorrow?'

'Will stay here if we have to row back to Sicily,' Vian confirmed.

Hewitt's guess proved to be right. He wasn't surprised to learn that the carriers were low on fuel, but he didn't realise that

In addition to self-propelled landing craft, there were also towed barges, such as this landing barge, vehicle, seen here after completing its work. *(IWM A24661)*

they were already on their emergency supplies. The reason for the difficulty was not so much the German attacks forcing the carriers to operate at maximum speed throughout the day, but that the planners had assumed that the Fleet Air Arm would be needed for two days, or three days at worst if the invasion met stiff resistance. After that, it was expected that airfields ashore would have been taken and would be available. As so often happens in warfare, everything was not going to plan. The airfields that would allow the RAF and USAAF to bring aircraft forward from their bases in Sicily were not available.

In the end, the carriers remained on station until 14 September, by which time the 180 Seafires had been reduced to just thirty, more by accident than the efforts of the Luftwaffe. One consequence of this was that many senior officers blamed the Seafire for the losses, rather than a combination of factors that had to include the difficulty in operating high-performance aircraft off

escort carriers with their short decks, lack of accelerators and low speed, in light wind conditions. The aircraft had its weaknesses and, as one naval officer put it, 'was too genteel for the rough house of naval flying', but it had its strengths too, including protective armour behind the cockpit. It was also true that the naval air squadrons had carried out far more than the planned number of sorties, despite the high accident rate.

ATTEMPTING TO BYPASS RESISTANCE – ANZIO

Even with land-based aircraft to support the ground forces, German resistance proved strong and was augmented by a number of Italian units who had refused to surrender. During the winter, the British and American armies, supported by Polish units, were stuck on the Gustav Line, and especially at the key strongpoint of Monte Cassino. In a further attempt to bypass German resistance, more

At the other end of the scale was this landing craft, infantry – large – or LCI(L). *(IWM A24665)*

landings were made at Anzio, south of Rome, on 21 January 1944, as part of a two-pronged attack, the other point of which was to be a renewed assault on Monte Cassino.

A relatively small force was put ashore by 378 ships, with air cover by the USAAF's Mediterranean Allied Tactical Air Force, commanded by Maj Gen John Cannon. The landings were intended to cut the German supply lines, and lead to the liberation of Rome. The forces went ashore easily enough, but then found that the Germans were quickly able to organise strong resistance. The landings were without carrier air

support, which may have contributed to the difficulty the invasion forces had in breaking out of their new bridgehead on 30 January, although the time spent consolidating their position ashore, rather than pressing ahead before German resistance could be organised, doubtless also contributed to the problems. It took four months. There were problems enough with the commanders ashore, and especially the American Gen Lucas, who concentrated on securing the beachhead rather than thrusting towards Rome, which prompted Britain's prime minister Winston Churchill to say that,

'We thought that we had landed a wild cat, but instead we have stranded a vast whale with its tail flopping about in the water.'

At the Admiralty in London, Cunningham, the new First Sea Lord, maintained that Churchill could 'rest assured that no effort will be spared by the navies to provide the sinews of victory'. Yet the Germans were able to mount a highly mobile and flexible defence and counter-attack, and deploy their heaviest artillery, including railway-borne guns such as the famous 'Anzio Annie'. Cunningham in his memoirs remarked that the prolonged assault on Anzio and the delay in linking up with other forces caused a heavy demand on shipping to maintain what was effectively a shuttle service of supplies from Naples, and at a time when the Allies were attempting to concentrate shipping for the Normandy landings.

OPERATION OVERLORD – THE NORMANDY LANDINGS

The Allied invasion of France on 6 June 1944, more usually known as Operation Overlord or the Normandy landings, was the largest invasion in history. The complexity of the preparation, including the

Preparations for Operation Overlord, the Normandy landings, involved the assembly of large numbers of landing craft of many different types, as this view of the quayside at Southampton shows. *(IWM A23731)*

Specifically designed for shore bombardment were the monitors. This is HMS *Abercrombie* after the war had ended. *(IWM MH4039)*

The cruiser HMS *Ajax* bombarding the Normandy beaches. Her 6-in guns would have little impact on the enemy gun positions, but would have been devastating against vehicles. *(IWM A24661)*

A destroyer, believed to be HMS *Cottesmore*, off the Normandy beaches. *(IWM A23892)*

building of two giant artificial harbours, called 'Mulberries', transported across the English Channel in sections, and the laying of an oil pipeline known as 'Pluto', must place in doubt the ability of the Germans to have mounted an invasion of Great Britain in 1940, especially since they lacked landing ships and landing craft and would have been reliant upon barges.

For the Royal Navy, involvement came before the landings, with surveys of the Normandy invasion beaches, of necessity conducted in great secrecy using midget submarines or X-craft. Next, the Navy was concerned with the assault phase of the operation, known as 'Neptune', which not only included manning landing ships and landing craft, but mine clearance, protecting the assault fleet from German air and naval attack, and providing heavy gunnery support for the troops on the invasion beaches. Naval gunnery is not simply an option for armies while they gain a sufficiently deep beachhead to be able to install and use their own artillery; it has the value of providing heavier-calibre weapons than those generally available to armies and, moreover, the degree of mechanisation of shell-handling means that the rate of fire from a single barrel of a naval gun can be the equal of a complete artillery battery. The Neptune phase lasted from 6 to 30 June.

After being postponed for twenty-four hours because of bad weather, the landing began at 06.30 on 6 June with five assault fleets, each heading for its assigned beach. Gold (which had one of the artificial harbours, at Arromanches), Juno and Sword were the

British and Canadian beaches, while those of the United States were Utah and Omaha. Meanwhile 23,400 British and US paratroopers were dropped inland, followed by glider-borne air-landed troops and airportable weapons.

On D-Day itself, 75,215 British and Canadian troops were landed from the sea on a succession of convoys that had formed up south of the Isle of Wight; 57,500 US troops were put ashore. Altogether, there were nearly 7,000 ships and landing craft, carrying 195,701 seamen, many of them British and Allied merchant navy personnel. Many of the landing craft served specialist roles, including some fitted with rockets for bombardment, or anti-aircraft weapons to protect the troops from aerial attack while they were at their most vulnerable as they waded ashore. The Royal Navy and Royal Canadian Navy together provided 79 per cent of the 1,213 warships involved, compared with 16.5 per cent for the United States Navy and 4 per cent for the 'free' navies of the European occupied countries. Overall, by the end of June, 850,279 men, 148,803 vehicles and 570,505 tons of supplies had been put ashore. Fifty ships were sunk and a further 110 damaged, many by mines, though others were affected by the severe storm of 19 June, which also wrecked one of the artificial harbours.

Adm Sir Bertram Ramsay was in overall command of the invasion fleet, with Rear Adm Sir Philip Vian in command of the British landing fleet. Heavy fire was provided by many of the Royal Navy's battleships and cruisers; a bombardment group consisted of *Warspite* and *Ramillies*, as well as twelve cruisers and thirty-seven destroyers. In reserve were further powerful ships, notably the sisters *Rodney* and *Nelson* with their 16in guns, and three cruisers. While the Allies had overall air control with some 12,800 aircraft of all kinds, including

transports, against just 319 of the Luftwaffe (although this rose to 1,000 within a week of the landings), it was still necessary to protect the flanks from German naval attack, and shore-based squadrons of the Fleet Air Arm were placed under the control of RAF Coastal Command, as had happened earlier during the Dunkirk evacuation.

Despite the relative weakness of the German air and naval forces, on the first night of the invasion, E-boats and German destroyers attacked from both the east and the west and, in a night battle, two German destroyers and one British destroyer were lost. Nevertheless, U-boats were kept away from the landing fleet. Mines, coastal artillery and aerial attack accounted for another four destroyers and three cruisers damaged, while a further cruiser was put out of action.

FRIENDLY FIRE!

The relatively low naval casualties during the Normandy landings make a subsequent event a couple of months later all the more poignant. On 27 August two of the Royal Navy's minesweepers were sunk and a third had its stern torn off after an attack by Hawker Typhoon fighter-bombers from nos 263 and 266 squadrons, Royal Air Force.

The First Minesweeping Flotilla was operating off the French coast near Cape d'Antifer when it was decided to move it to a new area, and details of the change were sent by signal and circulated to all interested parties. Later that day, another naval officer came on duty and decided to send the flotilla back to its original area of operations, and again details were sent by signal, but because of an error these were not circulated to the area naval headquarters, so they in turn could not communicate the change to the Royal Air Force. So it happened that when Allied radar spotted five ships sweeping in line abreast at noon

HMS *Dinard*, a former Channel packet steamer taken up as a hospital ship, prepares to leave Greenock in 1943. *(IWM A15151)*

on 27 August, it was immediately assumed to be a German formation. Not having been told of the change, Flag Officer British Assault Area, FOBAA, on learning about the ships, agreed that they must be German. Two of the ships were quite substantial, *Hussar* and *Britomart* having served as sloops on convoy escort duties, and of sufficient size, given the difficulty in assessing them from the air, to appear to be small German destroyers. A Polish airman flew over the ships in his Spitfire and misreported their position, but also reported that they seemed to be Allied vessels. FOBAA then attempted to contact the officers controlling minesweeping, but telephone lines were down and so no confirmation could be made. Next, FOBAA called for an anti-shipping strike and sixteen Typhoons of the RAF's 263 and 266 squadrons were ordered

into the air. On approaching the flotilla, the strike leader was immediately suspicious and suspected that he could see Allied ships, so he radioed questioning his orders, only to be told to attack. He subsequently queried his orders twice.

The attack began at 13.30, with a classic swoop out of the sun towards the first ship, HMS *Britomart*, the Typhoons strafing and firing anti-tank rockets, deadly against the thin hulls of minor warships. Within two minutes, the ship had lost its bridge and was listing heavily, while another, *Hussar*, was on fire. The immediate reaction of those aboard the ships was to assume that the aircraft were from the Luftwaffe, *Jason* signalling that she was being attacked by enemy aircraft, but as the planes roared away, the distinctive D-Day 'invasion stripe' markings could be seen, and another ship,

Salamander, fired recognition flares, forcing the leader of the strike to query his orders for the fourth time. Once again, he was ordered back into the attack, and at 13.35 dived down towards the warships, hitting *Britomart* yet again and strafing *Jason* while rockets went into *Salamander* and *Colsay*. Despite a large white ensign and a Union flag being draped over the stern of *Jason* as she fired further recognition flares, a third attack followed at 13.40 hitting *Hussar*, which exploded, and *Salamander*, whose stern was blown off by rocket strikes. As the stricken *Salamander* drifted towards the coast, a German artillery battery with 9.2in coastal guns opened up, forcing *Jason* to launch her small boats to tow *Salamander* out of danger.

The end result of the worst 'friendly fire' incident faced by the Royal Navy during the Second World War was that 117 officers and ratings were killed and 153 wounded. The whole sorry incident was covered up and only came to light when the papers were released by the then Public Record Office (now the National Archives) in 1994. The survivors of the two ships sunk were separated and ordered never to discuss or disclose details of the incident. At a subsequent court martial of three officers who were responsible for supervising the minesweepers and who had ordered them into the area without checking that details were circulated properly, one was severely reprimanded and another two were acquitted.

LANDING IN THE SOUTH OF FRANCE

By August 1944 the entire strategic situation in Europe had been transformed. Not only had German resistance been broken and Rome liberated, but Allied forces had broken out from their Normandy beachheads. The Normandy landings had been one of the few amphibious operations of the war not to have carrier air cover, as the Normandy beachheads were within range of airfields in the south of England and the sheer size of the invasion force and the constant stream of vessels across the English Channel meant that there would have been no room for carriers to operate their aircraft. A number of Fleet Air Arm aircraft had flown from shore bases in the south of England in support of the landings and the bridgehead, while naval aircraft also flew reconnaissance sorties and operated in the spotter role for the heavy guns of the battleships and cruisers covering the landings. The Italian campaign was maintained throughout this period because it forced the Germans to divert ground and air forces from the Normandy theatre.

Landings in the south of France were an easier option than landing in Normandy, which was just as well since logistically it would have been impossible to allocate the same quantities of men and materiel to the operation as had been achieved in the Normandy landings, which had even required the construction of two ports to keep the invaders supplied. Serious consideration had been given to an invasion of the south of France as early as August 1943, but the British had objected, declaring that it would divert resources from the advance through Italy, which they believed would lead to an invasion of Germany through Austria – a highly optimistic assumption given the intervening terrain! The south of France had then slipped down the Allied order of priorities as attention focused on the invasion of Normandy, through which France and the Low Countries could be liberated. Meanwhile further landings in Italy at Anzio had proved necessary.

The original name for the invasion was 'Operation Anvil', but this was later changed to 'Dragoon'. The south of France operation was seen as being less formidable than that in the north, since the Germans had not taken Vichy territory until late 1942, and not only did they not have the time to build anything on the scale of the famous 'Atlantic Wall' fortifications along the English Channel coastline, but the resources were also becoming increasingly scarce. By this stage in the war as well, interference from enemy naval forces could also be discounted. As a consequence, the fast armoured carriers of the Royal Navy were sent to the Pacific to join the United States Navy in taking the war ever closer to Japan, and instead the entire air defence and ground attack needs of the landing force were entrusted to the two navies, using nine escort carriers. The five British ships carried Supermarine Seafires again; the four American vessels operated the new Grumman Hellcat, a true carrier fighter aircraft. Heavy fire support was provided by three US battleships plus one each from France and the UK, which had deployed the veteran *Ramillies*, while the US Navy also provided three heavy cruisers. In addition to the nine escort carriers, there were twenty-five cruisers and forty-five destroyers.

The overall invasion fleet was once more under the command of Vice Adm Henry Hewitt who was to land Lt Gen A. M. Patch's US Seventh Army and Gen de Lattre de Tassigny's Second Free French Corps along the French Riviera between Baie de Cavalaire and Calanque d'Anthéor. Rear Adm Tom Troubridge commanded the British carriers and Rear Adm Durgin the US ships.

Landing on 15 August, more than 56,000 troops came ashore on the first day, and by 28 August, the key naval base of Toulon had been surrendered as well as the major port of Marseilles. The most notable feature of these landings was the limited effort from the Luftwaffe, leaving the naval airmen to provide support for the ground forces. One

pilot recalled having a good relationship with the US Army commanders who made good use of naval aerial reconnaissance.

The lessons of the Salerno landings had been learnt, with more aircraft carriers and adequate room to manoeuvre, while the carriers were able to retire to Corsica for replenishment and new aircraft, so there were none of the fuel shortages that had so nearly placed the Salerno operation in jeopardy. It was also fortunate that the weather conditions were ideal for carrier operations, with a breeze and gentle swell offshore.

For many of the American carrier pilots, it was their first experience of operational flying, and much attention was paid to minimising their casualties during the vital first sorties. Advice was given by senior and experienced British naval pilots, who provided briefings on the Luftwaffe and also on the anti-aircraft fire that might be expected. The Americans were warned about the dangers of flying in a tight formation or in a straight line, and that German 88mm AA fire was especially accurate between 9,000 and 11,000 feet, so that flying at these altitudes should only occur when an aircraft was climbing or descending. Allowing space between aircraft to weave safely was also suggested as important. Not all of this well-intentioned and sound advice seemed to get through to the USN squadrons, or if it did it seemed to be ignored.

The landings in the south of France were successful, putting additional pressure on German forces and providing yet another front on which German troops had to fight. They were followed soon afterwards in September and October by British naval forces, using nothing heavier than cruisers and escort carriers, cutting the German evacuation routes across the Aegean from Greece and destroying the remaining German naval units in the Aegean.

CHAPTER EIGHT

RETURNING TO THE EAST

Not by rambling operations, or naval duels, are wars decided
but by force massed and handled in skilful combination.
A.T. Mahan, Sea Power in its Relation to the War of 1812

After the invasion of the south of France, the naval war in Europe began to run down. There was some mopping up of enemy forces in the Adriatic, especially to hinder the Germans' retreat, plus mine counter-measures around the newly available ports of the Low Countries as Allied forces pressed on towards Germany, and, of course, continued operations against German convoys off Norway. Nevertheless, the main body of the Royal Navy was now free for operations against Japan.

The return of the Royal Navy to eastern waters was met with considerable reservations by some senior officers in the United States Navy. Many of these saw the British role at best as being centred on the reconquest of Burma. There was a feeling among some senior officers that they could finish the job without any British help. On the other hand, the British had strong political reasons for wishing to play an active part. They did not want to be seen to be leaving an ally on its own, or abandoning Australia and New Zealand. They also needed to put pressure on the Japanese, so as to take the strain off British forces fighting to protect India from Japanese attack in Burma. Finally, much of the territory overrun by Japan was British,

including Hong Kong, Singapore and Malaya, as well as Burma.

There were practical difficulties to be resolved, such as coordination and liaison, and this could be difficult with any large force, even within a single navy: in the Battle of Leyte Gulf, for example, parts of the United States Navy had not been where they were expected to be. A condition laid down by the US Navy was that the Royal Navy could not expect any use of American facilities in the Pacific theatre. Two of the senior American commanders, Chester Nimitz and Ernest King, felt that the British lacked the experience of mounting mass air attacks from carriers and the means of supporting a fleet so far from its bases. The British had little experience of putting together a modern fleet that was both balanced and adequate in strength, which was why they lost so many important ships early in the war. British ships also tended to be short on range, and some eye-witnesses could attest to the Royal Navy's slow progress when refuelling at sea, compared to the Americans. The distances over which the war in the East was fought have to be taken into account: from Japan to Singapore was about the same distance as Southampton to New York.

The wardroom aboard the escort carrier *Atheling*. The presence of ladies suggests that the ship is in port. The young officer on the right without a curl on his ring appears to be a constructor sub-lieutenant, a member of the Royal Corps of Naval Constructors. *(via Mrs M.J. Schupke)*

The British started to resolve these problems. They were able to use Simonstown in South Africa as a base, with South African Air Force airfields available for carrier aircraft disembarking as the carriers went into port. Ceylon provided a forward base with many naval air stations ashore, and there were others in southern India. Australia became another especially important base for the British Pacific Fleet, which used Sydney and Brisbane, both with air stations ashore. Nevertheless, the prospect of having additional ships and aircraft appealed to many other senior American officers. The problems of cooperation were resolved, partly by ensuring that at first the British Eastern Fleet operated in one area, while the US Fifth Fleet operated elsewhere. This did not mean that there was no cooperation, and British, Australian and New Zealand ships did sometimes operate with the Americans and under their command. Liaison officers were exchanged.

Cooperation on a small scale was attempted at first, so that the two navies could get used to each other. During spring

1944, the USS *Saratoga* was attached to the British Eastern Fleet, joining *Illustrious* for the early raids on Sabang in Task Force 70. This was to prove to be the ideal target for the Fleet Air Arm to hone its techniques on massed aerial attack. It was well away from the Americans and posed no threat to them, but it was also a useful target, on a small island off the northern end of Sumatra, with a harbour and airfields vital to the Japanese war effort in Burma. This was also to prove to be the baptism of fire for a new high-performance fighter for the Fleet Air Arm, the American Vought Corsair, sometimes described as the best American fighter of the Second World War.

This was not the first example of RN/USN cooperation in the east. The shortage of flight decks felt by the three carrier-operating navies during the Second World War resulted in some unusual compromises. One of these was that the British fast armoured carrier, HMS *Victorious*, second ship of the successful Illustrious class, spent much of the winter of 1942–3 being refitted at the Norfolk Navy Yard before going 'on loan' to the United States Navy, being given the temporary name of USS *Robin*. Until later she was relieved by the American interpretation of the fast carrier, the USS *Essex*, leadship of the class of the same name consisting of no less than twenty-five large carriers in all. The *Robin*, alias *Victorious*, operated with the US Pacific Fleet, and no doubt helped to improve interoperability between the two navies.

The escort carrier HMS *Ameer*. *(Via C.S. 'Bill' Drake)*

Among the ships involved in the Royal Navy's return to the East was HMS *Empress*, engaged in operations off Burma. *(Via C.S. 'Bill' Drake)*

The first attack on Sabang was made on 19 April 1944, with Corsairs escorting Barracudas, an aircraft that had seen action in Europe, notably against the *Tirpitz*, but which was to prove ill-suited to tropical conditions. Operating under the command of Admiral Sir James Somerville, the British Eastern Fleet was to be a thorn in the Japanese flesh. The initial raid was unexpected by the Japanese, and devastating, despite the poor performance of the Barracuda. These aircraft were quickly exchanged for the more capable and reliable Grumman Avenger, and both ships were able to launch a second successful attack in May, against an oil refinery outside Surabaya on the island of Java, with the loss of just one aircraft.

Operating together quickly exposed weaknesses in British organisation. The British carrier air group was smaller than that of the Americans, but even more important, the Fleet Air Arm had to learn the importance of a fast turn-round of aircraft on the flight deck and in the hangar. Fortunately, these lessons were learnt very quickly.

Completely integrated carrier operations by the two navies took time, but coordination became increasingly important and, as the war progressed, was much in evidence. The Americans also came to appreciate the strength of the Illustrious class carriers, especially under kamikaze attacks. As one American officer aboard a British carrier put it succinctly, 'When a Kamikaze hits an

American carrier, it's six months repair at Pearl. In a Limey carrier, it's a case of "sweepers, man your brooms!"'

Several targets fell particularly to the Fleet Air Arm. One of these was Palembang, with oil refineries and port facilities on the island of Sumatra. The most important of these was on 24 January 1945, in Operation Meridian I, and involved aircraft from 820, 849, 854, 857, 887, 894, 1770, 1830, 1833, 1834, 1836, 1839 and 1844 squadrons, operating from *Illustrious*, *Indefatigable*, *Indomitable* and *Victorious*. The Japanese were subjected to heavy attacks throughout December 1944, and January 1945.

As the war moved eastwards and ever closer to Japan, a British Pacific Fleet was formed, commanded by Vice Adm Rawlings. The entire operation was under overall American direction, with the BPF becoming Task Force 57, part of the US Fifth Fleet. Rear Adm Sir Philip Vian commanded the British carriers, and once again, these were *Illustrious*, *Indefatigable*, *Indomitable* and *Victorious*, although *Illustrious* had to be replaced by *Formidable* after suffering heavy damage from aerial attack. The squadrons included those already mentioned, with the addition of aircraft from 848, 885, 1840, 1841, 1842 and 1845 squadrons. The British also had the battleships *King George V* and *Howe*, five cruisers and escorting destroyers.

Changes continued to take place so that organisationally the British could match the Americans. The concept of the naval air wing had evolved in 1943, but in 1945 the Royal Navy formed the squadrons that were embarked in both the fast fleet carriers and the new light fleet carriers into carrier air groups. On a more practical level, changes to make interoperability between the two navies easier included modifications to the batsman's signals so that the two navies were in accord. Before this, some directions had precisely the opposite meaning!

The BPF, or Task Force 57 when part of the integrated Allied force, operated against the Sakishima Gunto group of islands, through which the Japanese ferried aircraft to Okinawa, and did much to cut Japanese reinforcements. On and off, the carriers sent their aircraft to targets in the Sakishima Gunto from 26 March to 25 May 1945, as the BPF took part in Operation Iceberg, the attack on Okinawa.

Operations in the Pacific, as the Allies closed in on the Japanese, had more than the usual hazards for the naval aviator, or even those additional hazards of flying over inhospitable terrain. The Japanese never felt bound to observe the rules of the Geneva Convention, and the fate of pilots shot down could be grim. Many squadron commanders wore uniforms of a lower rank as some means of protection against interrogation and torture, and to avoid providing a propaganda coup for the Japanese.

The role of the aircraft carriers in the US Navy's Task Force TF58 was to provide air support for the assault on Okinawa. The Royal Navy's TF57 had the role of protecting the left flank of the US Fifth Fleet, especially TF51, the escort carriers providing close air support for ground forces. The initial landings on Okinawa were on Sunday 1 April 1945, when the US Tenth Army landed with four divisions on the west coast of the island. A breakdown in the Japanese chain of command proved helpful, with initial resistance being light, but on 6 April British and American forces started to suffer from the attentions of the Japanese kamikaze suicide aircraft. In all, between 6 April and 29 May, 1,465 aircraft from one of the Japanese home islands, Kyushu, were used in ten massed kamikaze attacks, with another 250 aircraft from Formosa. On top of this, there were almost 5,000 conventional sorties. The main targets for the Japanese aerial attacks were the

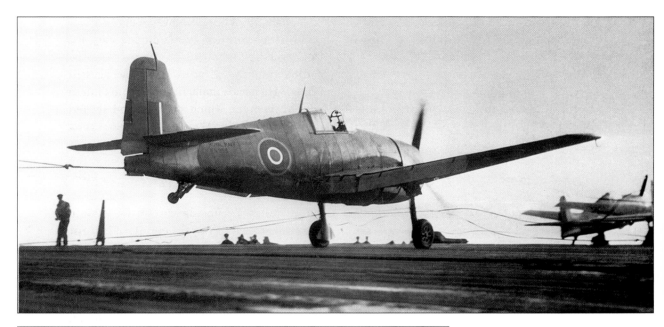

Above: Operations in the Pacific were helped by the involvement of high-performance aircraft intended for carrier operations, including the Grumman Hellcat. *(Northrop Grumman)*

Left: Another aircraft deployed mainly in the Far East was the Vought Corsair, sometimes described as the best fighter aircraft of the war, or as the 'bent wing bastard from Connecticut', as it could be demanding to land on a carrier flight deck. *(Vought Aircraft)*

ships of the combined British and American fleet, and in six weeks, twenty-six ships of destroyer size and below were sunk, and another 164 damaged, including *Illustrious*, *Formidable*, *Indefatigable* and *Victorious*.

Within days of the attacks starting, on 9 April, TF57 was ordered to attack airfields in northern Okinawa, while its role in attacking the airfields of the Sakishima Gunto was taken over by TF51. A pattern then developed, with the carriers striking hard at their targets, and then being rotated out of battle every few days to replenish their rapidly exhausted fuel and munitions. The demands on the ships of TF57 varied according to the overall strategic situation, so that by 4 May, TF57 found itself off Miyako in the Sakishima Gunto again. This was when *Formidable* was struck by her first kamikaze, which found the ship relatively lightly protected since the battleships, which could do so much to provide a dense curtain of AA fire around the fleet, were away shelling coastal targets. Unfortunately, the attack, at 11.31, came while the flight deck was crowded as aircraft were ranged for launching, and so while the ship merely suffered a two-foot dent in the flight deck near the base of the island, eight men were killed and forty-seven wounded. It might have been worse, the medical officer had moved the flight deck sick bay from the air intelligence office at the base of the island, and the AIO was the scene of many casualties.

Worse was to come. On 9 May *Formidable* was struck yet again. On this occasion, the kamikaze hit the after end of the flight deck and ploughed into aircraft ranged there. A rivet was blown out of the deck and burning petrol poured into the hangar, where the fire could only be extinguished by spraying, with adverse effects even on those aircraft not on fire. Seven aircraft were lost on deck, with another twelve in the hangar. The ship

refuelled and obtained replacement aircraft. Nine days later, on 18 May, an armourer working on a Corsair in the hangar failed to notice that the aircraft's guns were still armed. He accidentally fired the guns into a parked Avenger, which blew up and started another fierce fire. This time, thirty aircraft were destroyed. Even so, the ship was fully operational by the end of the day.

The BPF continued to operate alongside the US Fifth Fleet as the war was taken to the Japanese home islands. In the closing days of the war in the Pacific, the Fleet Air Arm was striking at targets in the Tokyo area, and it was then that it earned its second Victoria Cross of the war, again, like Esmonde's, posthumous. On 9 August Lt Robert Hampton Gray, RCNVR was leading a strike of Corsairs from *Formidable*'s 1841 and 1842 squadrons to attack a destroyer in the Onagawa Wan, when he came under heavy AA fire from five warships. He pressed ahead with his attack, even though his aircraft was damaged, and succeeded in sinking the destroyer before his aircraft crashed into the harbour.

Earlier, a small number of the Royal Navy's escort carriers had found their way to the Pacific, predominantly acting as aircraft transports and as maintenance and repair ships, but first, a number were also deployed to the Indian Ocean to provide trade protection. One of these was HMS *Ameer*, maintaining anti-submarine patrols in the Indian Ocean, through which convoys from the United States passed on their way to the Gulf, then usually known as the Persian Gulf, through which the bulk of supplies for the Soviet Union passed with transshipment to overland transport at an Iranian port.

Ameer was also present when Ramree Island, off the coast of Burma, was attacked by the Royal Navy and Royal Indian Navy in January 1945, a few months before combined amphibious and overland assaults saw the fall of Rangoon. The landing beaches were within the field of fire of Japanese artillery hidden in caves, but these were silenced by the guns of the battleship *Queen Elizabeth* and cruiser *Phoebe*, supported by *Ameer*'s twenty-four Grumman Hellcat fighters of no. 815 Squadron, allowing the island to be taken as a springboard for the capture of Rangoon in May.

Another operation was in the Netherlands East Indies in April 1945. Operation Sunfish on 11 April 1945, saw Force 63 attack Sabang and Oleheh, led by the battleships *Queen Elizabeth* and the French *Richelieu*, with the cruisers *London* and *Cumberland*, the latter leading the 26th Destroyer Flotilla, and including the escort carriers *Emperor* and *Khedive*. On 16 April the same force turned its attentions to Emmahaven and Padang. The two escort carriers shared no. 808 Squadron with its twenty-four Grumman Hellcats. The squadron was officially embarked in *Khedive*, but six of its aircraft were detached to *Empress* for some of the operations.

VE day in Europe, 8 May 1945, found HMS *Ameer* arrive at Colombo in Ceylon, with no. 896 Naval Air Squadron. There was little cause for celebration in the Far East, where American, Australian, British and New Zealand forces were gradually easing closer to Japan in the face of heavy resistance, and fiercer resistance still was expected if, as everyone believed likely at the time, the Japanese home islands would have to be invaded.

Neither the squadron nor the carrier was new to warfare. No. 896 had operated from *Victorious* and from the escort carrier *Pursuer* against the German battleship *Tirpitz*, which had spent almost its entire career tucked away safely in Norwegian fjords, menacing Allied convoys to the Soviet Union. *Ameer* had been engaged in trade protection duties in the Indian Ocean, having no. 845 Squadron embarked with its Grumman Wildcat fighters and Avenger bombers, before moving to a more combative role with no. 804 Squadron, whose Grumman Hellcats had covered landings on both Ramree Island, in Operation Matador, and Cheduba Island, Operation Sankey. Then 804's Hellcats had provided fighter cover for 888 Squadron on Operation Stacey as it conducted photographic reconnaissance over the Kra Isthmus, Penang and north Sumatra. At the time, this was seen as steady progress towards the eventual liberation of Singapore, with no one in South East Asia Command aware that Japanese surrender would first be forced by the use of nuclear weapons.

Later, 804 Squadron was to have its aircraft assigned to other escort carriers, including *Empress* and *Shah* for raids on the Andaman Islands and the coast of Burma, before returning to *Ameer* in June for attacks on Sumatra and Phuket in Thailand. No. 896, meanwhile, transferred to *Empress* to cover minesweeping off Phuket.

When Rangoon was eventually liberated in May, no. 807 Squadron, embarked in *Hunter*, provided fighter cover throughout much of April and May, and afterwards provided air cover for anti-shipping strikes. No. 809 Squadron aboard *Stalker* undertook similar duties.

SINK THE *HAGURO*

By spring 1945, the British were re-establishing themselves in Burma, and eventually, supported by the British Eastern Fleet, retook Rangoon from the Japanese, who were anxious to keep hold of the oilfields in Burma. The landings near Rangoon, Operation Dukedom, were covered by escort carriers including *Emperor*, although *Shah* would also have been involved had not a fault appeared with her catapult. The fleet was in Trincomalee on 9 May when Ultra intelligence discovered that a Japanese Nachi class cruiser was to leave Singapore the following day to evacuate the garrison in the Andaman Islands. Almost immediately, the fleet sailed, hoping to intercept the Japanese. Japanese reconnaissance, not always reliable, on this occasion did succeed in warning the cruiser *Haguro* and her destroyer escort, *Kamikaze*, that the Royal Navy was at sea, and the two ships returned to Singapore.

Ultra alerted the fleet that the two ships had sailed again on 14 May, and also confirmed that the Japanese supply vessel *Kurishoyo Maru*, escorted by a submarine-chaser, had successfully carried out an evacuation of the Nicobar Islands and was on her way to Singapore. The following day, the escort carrier HMS *Emperor* launched a strike of four Grumman Avengers from 851 Naval Air Squadron, commanded by Lt-Cdr (A) Michael Fuller, RNVR. The four aircraft were armed with bombs and attacked the two ships, but one aircraft was shot down by heavy AA fire, although its crew were able to take to their dinghy.

A second strike, again of four aircraft, was then launched from *Emperor*, led by Fuller, but one aircraft was forced to return with engine trouble. Two of the remaining aircraft then sighted five destroyers and spent thirty-five minutes trying to identify them, eventually deciding that they were friendly, which was fortunate since it was the 26th Destroyer Flotilla at sea in an attempt to intercept the *Haguro*. By this time, the two aircraft were short of fuel and had to return. This left Fuller on his own, with orders to search for the dinghy carrying the aircrew downed on the first strike. He jettisoned his bombs to increase range, but failed to find the dinghy as he had been given the wrong search coordinates; instead he found *Kurishoyo* and the submarine-chaser, and started to fly around them while fixing their position.

At this point, Fuller noticed two more ships some fifteen miles to the south of his position, heading north. Keeping out of AA range, he succeeded in identifying them as a Nachi class cruiser and a Minikaze class destroyer, before they changed course to the south-west having spotted his aircraft. 'She was very large and very black against a very dark monsoon cloud,' Fuller recalled later. 'An enormously impressive sight, just as a warship ought to look.' He was convinced that the Japanese were trying to remain unobtrusive, wanting to keep out of sight. Not being inclined to oblige them, he signalled the rest of the British fleet at 11.50: 'One cruiser, one destroyer sighted. Course 240. Speed 10 knots.' He maintained this flow of information for an hour before climbing directly over the *Haguro* at 12.50 to make a final signal, giving the direction finders with the fleet the chance of making an exact fix, before returning to the carrier to land with just ten minutes' worth of fuel left.

Haguro was still some considerable distance from the *Emperor*, but the carrier launched three more Avengers, which found the cruiser and dive-bombed her. They achieved one direct hit and another near miss. Their return flight of 530 miles was the longest attacking flight from any British carrier during the war, and the one and only occasion that a major enemy warship at sea was dive-bombed by British naval aircraft. The attack left *Haguro* only slightly damaged and heading for Singapore, but after dark she was finally cornered by the 26th Destroyer Flotilla and sunk by gunfire and torpedoes in the entrance to the Malacca Straits early on 16 May.

CHAPTER NINE

THE FLEET AIR ARM

They say in the Air Force the landing's OK,
If the pilot gets out and can still walk away,
But in the Fleet Air Arm the prospects are grim,
If the landing's piss poor and the pilot can't swim.
The Fleet Air Arm Songbook

The Royal Navy had taken an interest in the aeroplane as early as 1910, and despite the reservations of many senior officers, naval aviation played an important role during the First World War through the work of the Royal Naval Air Service. This was almost a 'service within a service' and at one time was given responsibility for the air defence of Great Britain, which may have been its undoing since overlap and duplication with the Royal Flying Corps, part of the British Army, led to the formation of an autonomous Royal Air Force on 1 April 1918. The new service inherited 2,500 aircraft and 55,000 officers and men from the Royal Navy, which contrasts with a total strength for the Royal Navy and Royal Marines of around 40,000 today.

The decision was one of those taken without any benefit of hindsight, and possibly also without a true understanding of the different requirements of naval and army aviation, or organic air power, and of strategic air power. There was an inability to consider the consequences, largely because so few understood the potential of air power. In the terms of creating a strong

strategic air service, the decision was right. In denuding the Royal Navy and the British Army of air power, organic air power, to fit their requirements, and in failing to force senior officers in both services to understand air power, the decision was wrong.

Aircrew and maintainers aboard the aircraft carriers and seaplane carriers or tenders all became members of the Royal Air Force, co-existing alongside the general service officers and ratings that formed the ships' companies of the carriers. The main exceptions to this arrangement were those concerned with the operation of seaplanes and flying boats operated from battleships and cruisers, who remained naval aviators, as did a small number sprinkled through the fighter and bomber squadrons. The aircraft embarked in battleships and cruisers provided the reconnaissance and spotter role for the guns of the fleet. Aboard the carriers, however, there was a demarcation line between the seafarers and the aviators. This was emphasised to a great extent by the system under which RAF stations in the Mediterranean and Far East included flights that could operate from aircraft carriers visiting those areas. In practical terms, units were under Admiralty control while afloat, and Air Ministry control while ashore.

Following the recommendations of the Balfour Committee of 1923, which examined Royal Navy and Royal Air Force cooperation, the Fleet Air Arm of the Royal Air Force was formed, with five squadrons belonging to what was then known as RAF Coastal Area, becoming Coastal Command in 1936. In 1937 it was proposed that the Fleet Air Arm be handed over to full Admiralty control. Nevertheless, the Admiralty did not formally take control until 24 May 1939. In between, in 1938, the Admiralty was authorised by Parliament to implement a 300 per cent increase in Fleet Air Arm personnel. While most of the RAF personnel serving with the Fleet Air Arm were to return to other postings within the service, around 1,500 transferred to the Royal Navy. One innovation introduced by the RAF that survived the handover was the squadron numbering system, which can be described briefly as being in the 7XX series for non-combatant and support squadrons, and the 8XX series for combat squadrons.

The authority for expansion may have seemed to indicate that the Royal Navy was finally equipping its Fleet Air Arm for war, but the reality was different. There were few naval aviators and maintenance personnel, hardly any naval air stations, and large numbers of these were to be built from scratch, with some, in unsuitable sites for the bombers and fighters of the RAF, transferred to naval control. There were no high-performance naval aircraft. For offensive purposes, the Fairey Swordfish biplane was to be the mainstay of the fleet, and for defensive purposes, there were two aircraft, the monoplane Blackburn Roc and the Gloster Sea Gladiator, another biplane! The RAF has been criticised for neglecting the

needs of naval aviation between the wars, but these were periods of acute financial stringency for all of the armed forces and as the Battle of France developed, the RAF lacked suitable aircraft itself to counter the rapid German advance. While attention normally centres on the obsolescence of so many of the Royal Navy's aircraft, the real problem was that an entire generation of senior officers with aviation experience had been lost with the transfer of many to the RAF, and so even among naval officers there was a widespread belief that high performance aircraft could not be operated from ships.

In home waters, the Fleet Air Arm's shore-based aircraft provided cover for convoys from the beginning of the war in Europe on 3 September 1939 until German surrender on 8 May 1945. At times Fleet Air Arm squadrons were placed under RAF Coastal Command control to ensure better integration. The FAA complemented the work of the RAF, with the latter using larger, twin-engined and, in due course, four-engined, long-range aircraft, while the FAA operated over shorter ranges, all that was necessary for the North Sea and English Channel.

The Fleet Air Arm started the Second World War with, according to the Imperial War Museum, 232 aircraft and 360 qualified pilots, with another 332 under training. The Royal Navy had seven aircraft carriers, of which four, HMS *Argus*, *Eagle*, *Furious* and *Hermes*, had officially been due to retire, but had been retained in service as the war clouds gathered over Europe. This meant that, while the first of the Illustrious class carriers was awaited, the best ships were the converted battlecruisers *Courageous* and *Glorious*, and the new *Ark Royal*. Not one of these three ships was to survive the first two years of war. There was also the seaplane carrier, *Albatross*, mainly used for training

The Grumman Avenger was a substantial and powerful carrier-borne bomber, and hence different from the biplanes with which the Fleet Air Arm had been equipped early in the war. *(Northrop Grumman)*

aircrew for the catapult flights aboard cruisers and battleships.

There were few Royal Naval air stations at the outset. HMS *Daedalus* at Lee-on-Solent, on the Hampshire coast opposite the Isle of Wight, was one of them. Not only was 'Lee' convenient for the ships of the fleet based at Portsmouth, it also had a slipway for seaplanes and amphibians. Yeovilton was under construction. The Fleet Air Arm also had lodging facilities at RAF bases.

Initially, the RN could not increase its pilot and observer strength without RAF cooperation, as basic and intermediate training was entirely in the hands of the RAF. Ground crew were also trained by the RAF. This created a bottleneck as the RAF struggled to meet its own needs, but fortunately it changed even before the United States entered the war with the introduction of the 'Towers Scheme', named after an American admiral, which enabled naval pilots and observers to be trained by the United States Navy at Pensacola in Florida. Observers were the Fleet Air Arm's navigators, so called because they had to do so much more than simply navigate, including observing the fall of shot in a traditional naval battle. Appropriately enough, they were known in naval slang as 'lookers'.

On many naval aircraft, there was a third member of the team, the telegraphist/air-gunner or TAG. These were always ratings, with the most senior on a squadron usually being a chief petty officer. Training for these was conducted in the UK and Canada.

After basic and intermediate training in the United States, the young pilots were given training in British practice, usually in Canada, where they could also receive their operational conversion training. Instilling the difference between British and American practice was important, with some deck-landing signals meaning the opposite! Finally, as the Royal Navy involved itself with the war against Japan, the American signals were adopted as standard.

The story of the Royal Navy's aviation during the Second World War is detailed in a companion volume, *The Fleet Air Arm Handbook 1939–1945*. Apart from the rating of the TAG, other differences between naval and RAF practice can be summarised briefly as:

- Pilots and observers were usually commissioned, although there were a few exceptions.
- It was rare for anyone commanding a squadron, no matter how many aircraft, to hold a rank higher than that of lieutenant-commander, the equivalent of a squadron leader in the RAF.
- Carrier air wings were also usually led by a lieutenant commander rather than a wing commander, or group captain as in the RAF.

- Training units were given squadron numbers, in contrast to RAF practice. These were always numbers in the 7XX series.
- There was no distinctive command structure for different types of squadrons on a par with RAF Bomber or Fighter Command, although groups of squadron numbers were allocated for different types of squadron.
- Command ultimately rested with the commanding officer of the ship or naval air station, as with the RAF, but above this, the next important person was the flag officer for a particular naval force or the commander-in-chief of a major fleet.

The rapid wartime expansion of the Fleet Air Arm, including the transfer of many RAF personnel, meant that training had to be abbreviated as far as possible, so that instead of becoming naval officers first and then aviators second, an air branch was formed with its members having a letter 'A' inside the curl on their uppermost ring of rank, whose members were effectively fliers who went to sea rather than sailors who could fly. The distinction meant that the members of the Air Branch did not have to be able to navigate a ship and stand watch, but it also meant that they were isolated outside the regular career structure, which was not a problem for the members of the Royal Naval Volunteer Reserve, but for the regulars meant that command of a ship and, for a few, the subsequent rise to flag rank, was denied.

Royal Naval Air Stations were all given ships' names as well as being known by their location, so RNAS Lee-on-Solent, for example, was also HMS *Daedalus*. Aboard carriers and at air stations, squadron commanders were under the ultimate control of the commander (flying), now known as commander (air), who would have a lieutenant-commander as his deputy. One innovation borrowed from the United States Navy around the time war broke out was the role of the carrier deck landing officer, or batsman, who would guide aircraft in to land on a deck that was often pitching and rolling. This was tiring and dangerous work requiring considerable concentration, but the batsmen, all former pilots, lost their flying pay on taking up their new role.

By the end of the war, the strength of the Fleet Air Arm had grown to 1,336 aircraft, with six large aircraft carriers (the elderly *Furious* was no longer operational), as well as the maintenance carrier *Unicorn*. The first five light fleet carriers were already in service, too late for combat but capable of overseeing the Japanese surrender of occupied territories and bringing home Allied prisoners of war. There were also forty escort carriers.

CHAPTER TEN

THE SUBMARINE SERVICE

For a city consists in its men, and not in its walls nor in its ships empty of men.
Nicias's speech to the Athenians at Syracuse

The Submarine Service had two things in common with the Fleet Air Arm. First, submariners and aircrew both received extra money, known as flying pay in the airmen's case, but more bluntly as danger money in the submariners'. Second, the two services had their origins at a time when neither was regarded as very respectable. Otherwise, airmen and submariners were a breed apart. Long before the war, the two had come together briefly with the ill-fated *M2*, Britain's only attempt at an aircraft-carrying submarine, whose aircrew, flying the diminutive Parnall Peto seaplane, were reputed to receive double danger money. The extra money was necessary to encourage sufficient men to volunteer for submarine service, which imposed extra dangers and many hardships.

Accommodation was even more cramped than on surface vessels, and the reason that so many British submariners opted for beards, known as a 'full set' in naval parlance, was the shortage of fresh water. A separate branch of the Royal Navy, the Submarine Service was organised into flotillas for control and administration, usually grouped around a base, such as the headquarters at HMS *Dolphin*, a 'stone frigate' at Haslar, or a submarine depot ship such as HMS *Forth*. There was never a set size for a flotilla.

Submarines were more than just another means of striking at enemy shipping. In contrast to the contemporary nuclear-powered submarine, which spends most of its operational life submerged, during the Second World War submarines spent as much time as possible on the surface, only diving when threatened or when needing to be concealed to make an attack, and even then many attacks were made on the surface if an unescorted merchant vessel appeared. The submarines of the period could cruise on the surface at a reasonable speed and their value lay in the fact that they had a far greater operational radius than a destroyer and made much more effective use of scarce manpower. In theory, they could get much closer to the enemy than a destroyer, without being detected.

MEDITERRANEAN 'MAGIC CARPET'

The popular view is that the submarine was at its most effective during the Second World War in the German U-boat campaign against Allied shipping. The U-boat campaign was undoubtedly effective, but the Allies also had their successes with the

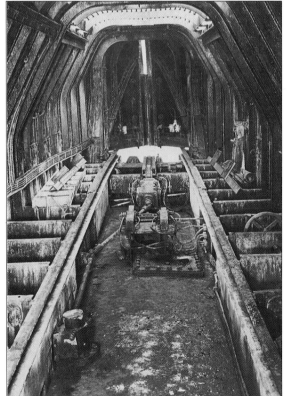

Above: Minelaying submarines posed some difficulties, including taking longer to submerge than ordinary submarines because of the additional buoyancy from the mines and the mine-tunnel. The photograph clearly shows the different profile of a minelayer. This is *Rorqual.* (*RN Submarine Museum, Neg. 8855*)

Left: An interior shot of the minelaying tunnel and rails, plus the release gear at the after end of the superstructure, again aboard *Rorqual.* Submarines such as this were invaluable cargo carriers at the height of the siege of Malta. (*RN Submarine Museum, Neg. 6978*)

submarine. The United States Navy virtually cut Japan off from its Asian empire and brought the country to the point of starvation, while the Royal Navy almost isolated Axis forces in North Africa from the supplies on which they depended, by a combination of submarines, surface vessels (especially those of Force K based on Malta) and air power, much of it naval. In the Mediterranean, submarines had other uses as well, helping to keep Malta in the war by bringing in supplies at a time when convoys could not get through. These were known as the 'Magic Carpet'.

This is not to suggest that the Mediterranean was a safe haven for the submarine, as its clear waters and relatively shallow depths meant that submarines could be easy prey. Within three days of Italy, entering the war, Italian warships sank three British submarines, *Grampus*, *Odin* and *Orpheus*. As the bombing of Malta intensified, submarines in port had to lie submerged in the harbour in the hope of being missed.

In 1941, Malta became a base for submarines. This was not without its difficulties, since most of the necessary supplies had been taken to Alexandria, but submarines operated from Gibraltar to Malta overloaded with torpedoes and other equipment until stocks were built up. The use of Malta as an offensive base was helped by the introduction of the new U class of submarines, smaller than most of the other classes, but ideal for the clear waters of the Mediterranean in which, all too often, sonar is not needed to spot a submerged submarine.

Among the more notable successes scored by British submarines were the torpedoing and sinking of the light cruiser *Karlsrühe* off Kristiansand during the Norwegian campaign, by *Truant* on 9 April 1940. Later, the pocket battleship *Lützow* was caught by *Spearfish*, commanded by Lt Cdr John Forbes, while she was on her way

from Norway to Germany for repairs to bomb damage. The submarine torpedoed *Lützow*, hitting her stern and putting her out of action, leaving her to be towed to Kiel by converted trawlers on 13 April 1941.

This was not the last success against a major German warship. The heavy cruiser *Prinz Eugen*, widely believed to have fired the shell that destroyed HMS *Hood*, and which had also participated in the celebrated Channel Dash in February 1942, was discovered in Norwegian waters by Lt Cdr George Gregory in *Trident* on 23 February 1942, and a well-placed torpedo blew off part of the ship's stern. A slow crawl with a temporary rudder to Trondheim for temporary repairs preceded a visit to Kiel for permanent repairs, putting the ship out of service for the rest of the year.

The clear waters of the Mediterranean had proved fatal for larger submarines, but the U class was better suited to the conditions (although the class had its origins in plans for a smaller training submarine), and of these, nine were deployed to Malta as the 10th Submarine Flotilla: *Undaunted*, *Union*, *Upholder*, *Upright*, *Utmost*, *Unique*, *Urge*, *Ursula* and *Usk*. *Usk* and *Undaunted*, nevertheless, did not survive long, but their place was soon taken by others of the same class. In addition to attacking Axis convoys and warships, these submarines were also ideal for landing raiding parties on the Italian coast, and on one occasion wrecked a railway line along which trains carrying munitions for the Luftwaffe bases in Sicily travelled.

The submarines were based at Manoel Island, which lay in the Marsamxett Harbour and was approached by a causeway just off the main road to Sliema, the island effectively dividing Sliema Creek from Lazzaretto Creek. Originally a fort designed to protect the outskirts of Valletta, which towered over the other side of the harbour, Manoel Island became a naval base, with

The Triumph, British submarine whose amazing exploit in crossing the North Sea with 18 feet from her bows by a German mine is told below. This picture was taken at her launching. The dotted line indicates the shape of her hull below water. Her smashed bow is shown by a wavy line.

Study this numbered key to the submarine Triumph as you read the story of her magnificent performance . 1. Bridge. 2. Mess deck. 3. Torpedo tubes. 4. Foremost bulkhead. 5. Where the bows were blown off. 6. Torpedoes. 7. The "small compartment." 8. Ballast tank. ("All the forward tanks were either open to the sea or missing altogether.")

► FROM PAGE ONE

TRIUMPH HOME WITHOUT HER BOWS

another the tube was crushed in pinning the war head.

Mercifully none of these 10 torpedoes went off.

Triumph thus found herself with no bows. She was in the Skagerrak, on the German side of the North Sea minefields, right inside enemy waters and 300 miles from home.

She could not dive, for all the forward buoyancy she should have required submerged had been destroyed. She was making water fast.

The pumps were kept running at their maximum capacity, and a rating was kept trying to plug the leaks with wooden plugs, felt, and anything else that was available, and the split foremost bulkhead was shored up.

In this condition Triumph started her long voyage home. She cleared the minefield and started off at about five or six knots. It seemed as if she was pushing half the North Sea along with that badly damaged bulkhead.

Later the weather got worse and she had to reduce to two-and-a-half knots for a whole day.

It was a desperately anxious day on the eastern side of the North Sea, unable to dive and expecting an air attack at any moment, for it was known that the damaged submarine had been sighted by a German reconnaissance aircraft.

Later the weather moderated and Triumph was able to work up to about 10 knots.

FIRST PATROL

On board the submarine was a young RNVR doctor who had gone out for his first patrol. It was almost miraculous that the mine had caused no casualties, but he made himself useful in coding and decoding signals.

Lieut.-Commander McCoy apologised for letting him in for such an unpleasant experience and remarked that it must be worse for him since he knew nothing of the capabilities of the submarine.

The young doctor replied: "All I know of submarines is what I've seen on the movies, where men are always struggling waist-deep in swirling water and the submarine always goes down—and, by God, they don't seem far wrong!"

From time to time during the long voyage home Triumph received encouraging signals from the Admiralty. "Aircraft escort is being sent." "Destroyers coming at full speed."

Just before our own aircraft arrived a Dornier sighted her and made as if to attack, but our planes got there in time to drive the Dornier away.

Two nights and one day after hitting the mine Triumph arrived at the Firth of Forth. When she docked it was discovered that the damage was much greater than anybody on board had thought.

Since her repairs she has been living up to her name and has

Submarine had its nose blown off
—18ft short—got home

WHEN the 1,090-ton British submarine Triumph struck a mine 18 feet of her bows were blown off, and there was a 12-foot split in her hull amidships. But she travelled safely home more than 300 miles across the North Sea— and has since torpedoed five enemy warships and five supply vessels.

The story of her escape from the mine was disclosed only last night by the Admiralty—nearly 21 months after it happened on Boxing Day, 1939.

It explains the announcement in April, 1940, that Lieut.-Commander John Wentworth McCoy, then her commander, had been awarded the DSC for "outstanding initiative, skill, and resource when a mine struck his ship."

Charging batteries

The crew were having lunch and Triumph was going slow ahead on the surface while charging her batteries. The first-lieutenant was on watch on the bridge.

It was a dark night with little moon but he sighted a very large floating mine just ahead. The helm was put hard over but before the submarine could alter course the bow lifting over a wave came down right on the mine.

There was a shattering explosion and a column of flame which temporarily blinded those on the bridge. The blast was severe but only one splinter hit the bridge and that did no damage.

She lurched and staggered

The submarine lurched and staggered and a pulse of pressure ran through the ship. The noise of the explosion was loud, but not shattering. Some of the soup was spilt.

The rear ends of the torpedo tubes had all been forced back about six inches, the foremost bulkhead was split right across and had been forced back with the tubes. There was a deep wrinkle right round the hull plating.

Several rivets were missing and a number of pipes as well as the torpedo tubes and the bulkhead were leaking.

Eighteen feet of the submarine was missing altogether.

In the torpedo tubes there were 10 torpedoes with war heads fitting and ready for firing. From one tube the whole torpedo was missing. In another all that remained was the after part of the torpedo. In

◄ BACK PAGE, COL. TWO

---

workshops and accommodation for resting submariners and for the artificers, the Royal Navy's skilled tradesmen. The submarines were moored alongside. Substantial AA defences were placed on Manoel Island, but being on the other side of Valletta from Grand Harbour did not spare the base from heavy aerial attack.

The campaign started in February 1941 with offensive patrols by *Unique*, *Upright* and *Utmost*. The first significant operation was in late February, when *Upright*, commanded by Lt E.D. Norman, sank the Italian cruiser *Armando Diaz*, one of two cruisers escorting a large German convoy. No doubt the Italians had committed two cruisers to this role to put on a show for their allies, but there were no major British warships in the area, and the cruiser, which posed no threat at all to a submarine, proved an ideal target.

Reconnaissance reports of large-scale shipping movements were received on 8 March, resulted in these three boats being sent to sea, even though *Utmost*, commanded by Lt Cdr C.D. Caylet, had only been in harbour for twenty-four hours. Despite this, the following day, *Utmost* found and sank the Italian merchantman *Capo Vita*. On 10 March, *Unique* sank another merchantman, the *Fenicia*. Later in the month, these submarines were at sea again, with *Utmost* finding a convoy of five ships on 28 March, and torpedoing and sinking the *Heraklia*, while the *Ruhr* had to be towed into port. The return voyage for the depleted convoy was no less eventful, when *Upright* torpedoed and severely damaged the *Galilea*, reported as being a straggler.

April saw *Upholder* join the flotilla, and for almost a year she and her commander, Lt Cdr Malcolm Wanklyn, played havoc with

Newspaper account of HMS *Triumph*'s encounter with a mine on Boxing Day, 1939. *(Collection of S.V. Wragg)*

The battered but triumphant
Triumph on her return to Rosyth.
(Collection of S.V. Wragg)

Mealtime aboard a submarine. 'Lunch' was at midnight, and known affectionately as 'big eats'. The nocturnal nature of much submarine work meant that, for the crews, day and night were reversed. (*RN Submarine Museum*)

the Axis convoys. From April 1941 to March 1942, this one submarine accounted for three large troop-carrying liners each of more than 18,000 tons, seven other merchant ships, a destroyer and two German U-boats, as well as damaging a further cruiser and three merchant ships. The first

two troop-carrying liners had been in a convoy of three approached by Wanklyn steering on the surface, who then skilfully fired a spread of four torpedoes at the ships. Two of the troopships managed to zigzag into the path of the torpedoes, with one sinking immediately, leaving the other to be finished off by Wanklyn when he returned the following morning. *Ursula* missed the third troopship, which managed to reach Tripoli safely. For his time in the Mediterranean, Wanklyn was awarded the Victoria Cross, the highest British service decoration, and the DSO. It was a sad day when *Upholder* was lost off Tripoli with all of her crew in April 1942.

For a period of about a year, the Malta-based submariners exacted a high price from the enemy, but opportunities could be missed. Probably more than any other type of warship, submarines need to practise 'deconfliction', largely because of the difficulty of recognising other submarines. 'Deconfliction' is the deliberate separation of friendly forces. In British submarine practice, this meant placing submarines to operate independently within designated patrol zones known as billets, and any other submarine found in that area was to be regarded as hostile. Yet off Malta there were often so many British submarines that it was necessary to impose an embargo on night attacks on other submarines, because of the difficulty in accurate recognition.

During the early hours of one morning in 1942, HMS *Upright* was on the surface when her lookouts spotted another larger submarine on a reciprocal course, and it was not until the two boats had passed that they realised that the other submarine was a large U-boat. A missed opportunity!

The Submarine Service tradition was to fly a 'Jolly Roger' on their return from an offensive patrol. This is that of HMS *Triumph*. Each bar denotes a ship sunk. *(RN Submarine Museum, Ref. 3079)*

Of course, there were many U-boats off Malta at the time, and no one will ever know if the Germans were working to the same rules, or whether their lookouts failed to spot the smaller British submarine. On another occasion, an Italian and a British submarine met each other at night on the surface, and after exchanging mutually unintelligible signals both dived,

Despite such missed opportunities, the submarines based on the other side of Valletta managed to account for 54,000 tons of Axis merchant ships between October 1941 and February 1942, as well as a destroyer and two submarines and two other ships near Taranto.

As already mentioned, the submarines were also used to carry supplies, a practice first attempted during the First World War by the Germans, who had established a company to operate merchant submarines to bring much-needed strategic materials from the United States and bypass the increasingly effective British blockade of German ports. The siege of Malta presented an opportunity for British submarines to show what they could do, carrying supplies on 'Magic Carpet' runs. At first the Axis grip on Malta was relatively light, and losses on the early convoys were few and far between, but by 1941 the situation was increasingly difficult and it became the practice for every submarine heading to Malta from both Gibraltar and Alexandria to attempt to carry at least some items of stores in addition to their usual torpedoes or mines. The 'Magic

Almost the entire crew of a U class submarine, in this case HMS *Uproar* in 1941. The lieutenant on the right of the photograph is a member of the Royal Naval Reserve. *(Collection of S.V. Wragg)*

HMS *Tantivy* proudly wears her 'Jolly Roger' as she returns to HMS *Dolphin*, the main base for submarines at Haslar, Gosport, after a successful tour of operations in the Far East in April 1945. *(IWM A28238)*

Carpet' submarines, however, were the larger submarines, and included the mine-laying submarines *Rorqual* and *Cachalot*, the fleet submarine *Clyde* and the larger boats of the O, P and R classes. The tragedy was that had not an unfortunate accident deprived the Royal Navy of its sole aircraft-carrying submarine, *M2*, some years before the war, that boat's hangar would have made an ideal cargo hold. In fact, the Royal Navy could have used the French submarine *Surcouf*, a large 2,800-ton boat also with a hangar, but never did so even though she was with the Free French rather than Vichy forces. Some have surmised that doubts over the reliability of her crew might have been behind this, but it is more likely to have been a failure of the imagination, since the crew could have been taken off and a British one installed – but in any event, *Surcouf* was eventually lost in the Caribbean.

The *Porpoise* class minelayers and *Clyde* were especially effective as supply ships, with plenty of room between their casing and the pressure hull for stores; sometimes one of the batteries would be removed to provide extra space, as happened on *Clyde* at least once, and the mine stowage tunnel was a good cargo space. *Rorqual* on one occasion carried 24 personnel, 147 bags of mail, 2 tons of medical stores, 62 tons of aviation spirit and 45 tons of kerosene. Inevitably, there was much unofficial cargo, a favourite being gin for the wardrooms and messes in Malta, and even Lord Gort, the island's austere governor, was not above having a small consignment of gramophone records brought out to him in this way. Cargo was sometimes carried externally in containers welded to the casing.

The operation was not without its problems, and the size of cargo that could be carried, while impressive in itself, could never compare with that of an average merchant ship, at this period around 7,500 tons compared with the 200 tons or so of a large submarine. This was a measure of the desperation of Malta's plight. For the submariners, there were problems with buoyancy. On one occasion *Cachalot* had so much sea water absorbed by wooden packing cases stowed in her casing that her first lieutenant (i.e. second in command) had to pump out 1,000 gallons of water from her internal tanks to compensate. Fuel was another hazard. In July 1941 *Talisman* carried 5,500 gallons in cans stowed beneath her casing; on other occasions fuel could be carried in external fuel tanks. When carrying petrol in cans, submarines were not allowed to dive below 65 feet, while aviation fuel in the external tanks meant that fumes venting in the usual way constituted a fire hazard, so smoking was forbidden on the bridge and pyrotechnic recognition signals were also banned. Another problem was that the Mediterranean favoured smaller rather than larger submarines, with its clear waters and the lack of great depths, although, of course, these submarines were always too close to the surface anyway.

Typical of the way in which the submarines did all that they could to keep Malta supplies was the case of HMS *Saracen*. The submarine reached Malta via Gibraltar, sailing with a convoy to Malta. Being smaller than the minelaying submarines, *Saracen* had two of her fuel tanks cleared of diesel and filled with aviation fuel instead, while every space aboard was filled with other stores, including food. The priority was to carry medical supplies and powdered or tinned milk for children and babies.

In peacetime, Malta had always been one of the most popular postings for the members of the Royal Navy, and an equally popular place in which to call. In wartime, despite the miserable conditions aboard submarines that had to remain submerged when in harbour during daytime, there was little enthusiasm for a 'run ashore', visiting the bars and other attractions of Valletta, as there was little to eat and not much to drink. Indeed, one army officer recalled his pleasure at being invited with a friend to dinner aboard a submarine.

In addition to flying her 'Jolly Roger' at the end of a successful patrol, HMS *Porpoise* added a second flag flown beneath the Jolly Roger's tally of ships sunk. This was marked 'PCS' for 'Porpoise Carrier Service', with a white bar for each successful supply run; there were at least four for this one boat alone.

The 'Magic Carpet' submarines did not confine themselves to their supply runs. After unloading in Malta, they would take mines from the underground stores and proceeded north to lay them off the main Italian ports, such as Palermo, before returning to Egypt. On a number of occasions, these submarines also found and torpedoed Axis shipping, with one boat torpedoing and sinking an Italian submarine and then torpedoing an Italian merchantman, which stubbornly refused to sink until the submarine surfaced and sank her with gunfire. After arriving in Malta, *Saracen* had gone looking for Axis merchantmen, but instead had found a destroyer and attacked and sank that instead; later, she was to account for an Italian submarine.

Meagre though the capacity of the submarines might have been, compared with that of cargo ships and tankers, the steady trickle of supplies did at least stave off defeat. Arrival of the famous convoy of Operation Pedestal in August 1942 saw increased submarine activity.

Although by October 1942 the situation continued to be difficult, and there was even the renewed German air offensive in that month – a last twitch of a wounded animal – Malta-based units remained on the offensive, with the submarines *Unbending*,

The provision of submarine depot ships, with engineering and other support functions aboard, meant that the operating area for the submarines could be extended. This is HMS *Adamant* at Durban in May 1942. *(IWM A10827)*

Unbroken, United, Utmost and *Safari* attacking a convoy of five merchant ships, including a tanker and escorted by seven destroyers, south of the Italian island of Pantelleria, coordinating the attack with aircraft from Malta.

There were other unusual duties for the submarines, as on 21 April 1941, when the Mediterranean Fleet ventured west for a major attack on the Italian-held port of Tripoli. To ensure accurate shore bombardment, usually a great difficulty when attacking from the sea in the dark, Cunningham had the submarine *Truant* positioned accurately four miles off the harbour, showing a light to seaward as a navigation

mark. Later that same year, in July 1941, two submarines helped to confuse the enemy and assist a convoy making its way to Malta. The convoy was code-named Operation Substance. While the Mediterranean Fleet steamed west towards Malta from Alexandria and Force H escorted a convoy eastwards from Gibraltar, the two submarines were west of Crete making fleet signals to indicate that the Mediterranean Fleet was operating in the area, while the Fleet itself maintained radio silence.

Truant was one of the new T class of submarines, intended for operations in distant waters, and the arrival of the class was indeed timely once Japan entered the

This happy group shows just how cramped the mess of a submarine could be. This is probably aboard HMS *Triumph*. *(Collection of S.V. Wragg)*

war. The T class could handle the long Pacific distances; it displaced 1,571 tons when submerged and had eight bow torpedo tubes, as well as a further two amidships and one aft, as well as a 4in gun and light AA weapons. Surface speed was just over 15 knots; while submerged, the maximum speed was less than 9 knots, although at this speed the batteries would need recharging after an hour.

The original range was 8,000 miles, but this was later extended to 11,000 miles by the use of welding to strengthen the boats during construction and by using some of the ballast tanks to carry fuel, but even the extended range of a T class boat compared badly with the range of more than 32,000 miles of the German Type IXD U boat. However, British naval vessels have generally been short on range, doubtless a result of having a massive empire with frequent opportunities for refuelling and replenishment.

In between the small U class and the large longer-range T class was the S class, such as *Saracen*, a handy intermediate-size submarine for a wide range of duties. The S class had a submerged displacement of between 960 and 999 tons, with six torpedo tubes in the bows and one in the stern; either 3in or 4in guns were fitted. Surface speed was just under 15 knots, while submerged the maximum speed was 9 knots, although again this was a 'one hour dash' and 2 knots was more usual for prolonged patrolling.

The U class had a submerged displacement tonnage of 730 tons; the early boats had six torpedo tubes in the bows, but in later versions this was reduced to four. Guns varied, with some having a 12pdr and others a 3in gun, as well as light AA weapons. Surface speed was just under 12 knots; again, the maximum speed submerged was 9 knots, with the usual limitations.

As the war progressed, British submarines improved, largely as a result of the steady adoption of welding instead of riveting in construction, which produced a stronger craft capable of taking greater punishment and diving safely to greater depths. Nevertheless, the British submarines were reliable and well armed. Armament included 3in or 4in guns, which could be used to good effect against small vessels, and both the T and the U classes had light anti-aircraft weapons. Generally, British and American submarines had far less to fear from attack by aircraft than the submarines of the Axis, whose maritime reconnaissance seems to have been preoccupied with anti-shipping operations.

SUBMARINE STRATEGY

Submarine strategy and tactics modified enormously between the belligerent nations,

and could be varied from time to time. The Admiralty decided in 1939 that the priority target for the Royal Navy's submarines would be enemy warships. The tactics used were to wait within their individual patrol areas, submerged, for enemy warships to appear. Later, in 1941 in the Mediterranean, they were frequently given roving commissions to attack anything that appeared a worthy target, and naturally this included merchant vessels supplying Axis forces in North Africa and Greece. The same approach was later applied in Asian waters. So successful was the work of the 10th Flotilla's U class boats in disrupting the supplies sent to Rommel's *Afrika Korps* during the campaign in the Western Desert that his chief of staff, Lt Gen Fritz Bayerlein admitted that 'We should have taken Alexandria and reached the Suez Canal if it had not been for the work of your submarines.'

The Royal Navy did not neglect specialised craft, including the midget submarine. After experimenting with a one-man submarine based on a design known as the Welman, basically a cross between a midget submarine and a human torpedo, British midget submarines evolved into the X-craft with a four-man crew. One or two members of the crew had to leave the craft in wet-suits and with breathing apparatus to place explosive charges on the target (the Axis used midget submarines carrying torpedoes). The X-craft's finest hour came on 20 September 1943, when a small force of six of these vessels penetrated the defences around the Altenfjord and placed explosive charges on the hull of the German battleship *Tirpitz*. The impact of the charges was such that the ship's machinery and main armament were put out of action for seven months. Earlier, human torpedoes, known to the Royal Navy as 'chariots', had mounted an unsuccessful attempt to sink the ship in October 1942.

Even midget submarines had a depot ship, and one of these diminutive craft can be seen just before the superstructure of HMS *Bonaventure* in late 1944. *(IWM A26927)*

The X-craft midget submarines had a crew of just four men. This picture shows just how small they really were. *(IWM A21698)*

Even smaller and more vulnerable were the two-man human torpedoes, or 'chariots' in naval slang, which was at least kinder than the term used by their inventors the Italians, who called them 'pigs'. *(IWM A22111)*

In April 1944, and again that September other X-craft attacked and damaged a floating dock in Norway after an earlier attack using one-man submarines had failed. In the run-up to the Normandy landings, two X-craft were used by Combined Operations Pilotage Parties to survey the Normandy beaches and then, later, to guide in the invasion forces.

A development of the X-craft was the XE-craft, and these were put to good use in the Far East, when their crews disabled Japanese communications cables and also damaged a cruiser.

All in all, British submarines sank 169 warships (including 35 U boats) and 493 merchant vessels throughout the war years, but this came at an extremely high cost: no less than seventy-four British submarines were sunk, a third of the total number deployed during the war. While just one submarine was lost in the four months of war in 1939, the losses grew to twenty-four boats in 1940, and were almost as high again in 1942, when twenty were lost. A third of British submarine losses were due to enemy minefields. In fact only one submarine survived contact with an enemy mine – HMS *Triumph*, which lost her bows as far aft as frame eight, or in more readily understandable terms, she lost her bows and torpedo tubes, but without incurring any casualties. Her survival is all the more remarkable because she had ten torpedoes loaded at the time.

CHAPTER ELEVEN

COASTAL FORCES

England expects that every man will do his duty.
Horatio, Lord Nelson (1758–1805)

Despite having much success with coastal motor boats, CMBs, during the First World War, the Admiralty largely neglected small craft between the wars. It was not until 1935 that orders were placed with small boatyards that specialised in fast small craft. Initially, the success of the craft introduced to service was hampered by the lack of a fast, light diesel engine, and petrol engines had to be used, with a substantially increased risk of fire and explosion. The first craft were all motor torpedo boats (MTBs), but these were later joined by motor gunboats (MGBs), which were often more than 100ft in length.

The latter also proved very effective in dropping and picking up agents off enemy-held coastlines. By 1944, the Royal Navy was operating a highly effective combination of MTBs and MGBs in the Channel. British experience in such craft was later used by the United States Navy in the Pacific, which had also neglected these small warships completely, although this was because it was felt that they had no role in a Pacific war. When it became apparent that such craft had much to offer, especially in operation among the island groups, British designs were obtained and developed into the famous PT boats.

COASTAL FORCES EXPANDED

Faced with the threat of enemy E-boats, the Royal Navy's coastal forces were expanded. Initially, the Navy depended on slow motor launches, completely incapable of matching the E-boats. Conversion of faster vessels into MGBs was urgently put in hand, although the first of these was not available until March 1941. In the interim, improved MTBs were built and these took the war to the enemy. Under the collective title of Coastal Forces (CF), these small craft soon had special bases built for them around the coasts, and while each base had an experienced RN captain as CO, the flotillas and the individual craft were largely commanded by RNVR officers, and at least one historian has credited the verve of CF to the originality brought to the operation by young people freed from naval tradition.

CF were not confined to home waters, and in the Mediterranean proved especially useful at hit-and-run raids on Axis shipping in the Adriatic and in putting ashore small groups of commandos for attacks alongside partisans in Greece and Yugoslavia. On the other side of the leg of Italy, in the Tyrrhenian Sea, CF attacked German coastal shipping used to keep land forces supplied.

The best defence against German E-boats were the fast motor gunboats or MGBs of Coastal Forces. Here is C class *MGB 328* (closest to the camera) off Dover. *(IWM A7449)*

A Fairmile 'D' motor gunboat at speed. *(IWM HU2087)*

Generally, Coastal Forces were smaller craft intended to operate primarily in off-shore waters both in the defensive and offensive role, which meant that British coastal forces often ventured across the Channel and found themselves doing battle at sea with German E-boats engaged on similar missions. While the most famous types of coastal craft were the MTB, and the larger MGB, coastal forces also embraced both minesweepers, keeping British ports and shipping routes open, and minelayers operating off the enemy coast, although this was also helped by the 'gardening' operations of RAF Bomber Command, aided by shore-based squadrons of the Fleet Air Arm. The availability of these craft also meant that they were able to augment the work of the RAF's air–sea rescue launches.

While much has been written about the importance of the convoy system, initially the biggest threat to merchant shipping came from German mines, laid by aircraft, U-boats and surface vessels. The problems were aggravated once the Germans began using 'influence type' mines. The British had developed and actually laid the first magnetic mines in 1918, but by 1939 had still not developed a satisfactory means of sweeping these; the minesweeping force was completely equipped for, and dedicated to, sweeping moored contact mines. Luck was to play a part in the solution: in November 1939 a German mine dropped on land, and was dissected by Lt Cdr J.G.D. Ouvry in an act of outstanding courage. With the knowledge thus gained, the Royal Navy was able to press ahead with the development and production of an effective magnetic sweep. Yet by November 1939 enemy mines had almost brought the east coast convoys to a halt, with twenty-seven ships totalling 120,958 tons lost during the month. In all, the first seven months of the war saw 128 ships lost, totalling 429, 899 tons, all to mines.

Responsibility for mine disposal and countermeasures lay with HMS *Vernon*, the shore establishment on the old Gunwharf at Portsmouth. One of the peculiarities of what might be described as the division of responsibilities between the armed forces was that the Royal Navy was not simply concerned with clearing mines at sea, it was also responsible for those that landed ashore as well. When the Germans started dropping delayed-action mines, it was the Royal Navy that had to defuse them. An officer, normally a lieutenant, and a rating would set to work, often far from the sea. This was a hazardous work, made even more dangerous when the Germans started to booby-trap their mines. On one occasion, on 6 August 1940, a mine being stripped at *Vernon* exploded, killing an officer and four ratings as well as causing serious injuries to others. Afterwards, mines were stripped and examined in a disused quarry, known as the mine investigation range and accordingly given the service nickname of 'HMS *Mirtle*'!

Elsewhere, the rationale for coastal or light forces was that it was wasteful to deploy seagoing ships for operations in offshore waters. The greater speed and manoeuvrability of such craft was another factor in their success, while the use of wooden hulls in many classes also meant that they provided a poorer radar image and were less susceptible to magnetic mines. With low crewing requirements such craft could be built in considerable numbers and, of course, their small size meant that many small boatyards could be employed in the war effort, rather than place still more pressure on the overburdened and much-bombed shipbuilding industry.

While the advocates of small fast craft maintained that with their torpedoes, the MTBs posed a potent threat to much larger ships, their main use was in hit-and-run raids, especially against small merchant

Coastal Forces not only operated the glamorous MTBs and MGBs, but also carried out the vital task of minesweeping. This is a minesweeping trawler of Dover Command; one source suggests from the identity letters on her bows that her name might be *Botanic*. (IWM A6309)

This ex-Belgian trawler, the *Adronie Camiel*, escaped from the Germans and was taken up by the Admiralty as a coastal patrol boat, based at Milford Haven. (IWM A7907)

ships. MGBs could face considerable dangers if they were confronted by a destroyer, since they lacked weapons of sufficient calibre to fight back and were, of course, small and vulnerable to even a single hit by 4in or 5in ammunition. Nevertheless, there were some notable successes. One of the best was the sinking of the auxiliary cruiser (for which one can read armed merchant raider) *Komet*, in October 1942, by *MTB 236* just as the German vessel was starting her second sortie and attempting to break out into the Atlantic.

The role of Coastal Forces in rescue work should not be underestimated. Perhaps one of the best examples was that of Walter Blount, who having suffered the 'miserable existence' of commanding a converted herring drifter defending the boom at Scapa Flow in Orkney, was posted to Dover in command of a motor anti-submarine boat on the basis that he had completed an Asdic course. This in itself was a disappointment, as he had wanted an MGB or MTB; however, and in fact he did little submarine hunting, but instead was put on search and rescue duties, picking up no less than twenty-seven downed RAF aircrew in the Channel. The drill was that, once rescued and dried off, the airmen were given the key to the gin cupboard on condition that they left their 'wings' pinned to the cupboard door 'for the record'. This work was of such importance that Blount received his first DSC for the rescues.

The Southern Railway ferry *Ryde* worked as a minesweeper during the war, usually close to her normal Portsmouth–Ryde route. *(IWM HU1261)*

The British trawler *Foula*, one of the Isles class, wearing camouflage. *(IWM A12234)*

OFF TO THE MED

British and American coastal forces collaborated in the Mediterranean and the Adriatic, initially attacking Axis convoys supplying the garrison on Corsica. In the Adriatic, the Allies still held the Yugoslav island of Vis, which was used as a base for light forces. Once again Walter Blount was involved, as second-in-command of a flotilla commander's MTB. As in the Mediterranean, the prey for these small, fast craft was the enemy coastal convoys, essential by 1944 since Tito's partisans and the rugged nature of the coastal areas had made road transport hazardous.

During October 1944, in command of *MTB 634*, Blount took part in a night attack against two German coastal convoys as they attempted to retreat northwards. Blount's craft had lost one of its engines, making steering difficult, and this lack of manoeuvrability meant that he ended up in a close-range gun action with a ship carrying a cargo of mines, which caught fire and burnt like a 'gigantic bonfire' rather than exploding – fortunate since the MGB was so close that it would have been caught by the explosion. In the other convoy, many of the ships were the German 'F-lighter' cargo vessels, usually armed with a powerful 88mm gun and excellent night vision equipment, but in a five-hour action four of the F-lighters and another four vessels were either sunk or beached, and a German E-boat was also sunk. One British seaman was killed and another three wounded. Blount received a bar to his DSC for what was described as 'one of the finest Coastal Forces' actions of the war.

A second bar to Blount's DSC came in February 1945 when, leading three MGBs fitted with radar off the Istrian coast, he caught a convoy of three merchant ships, all armed with 88mm guns, and sank all three by gunfire and torpedo.

It fell to Coastal Forces to take the surrender of around forty enemy vessels at the mouth of the River Tagliamento, between Venice and Trieste. This was what amounted to a one-way mission in heavy weather, as the MTB set out from Ancona and could not return without refuelling. Aided by air cover from Spitfires, the craft arrived only to find that the expected surrender was not taking place and that some of the ships had even fired at the Spitfires. Led by Lt Cdr Tim Bligh, Blount and an interpreter boarded what seemed to be the leading enemy vessel and demanded their immediate surrender, to the surprise of the German admiral; but eventually he was persuaded that surrender was the only option. Several E-boats were either scuttled or set on fire, while the rest, together with several merchantmen, were escorted to Ancona.

One role that fell to Coastal Forces was that of infiltrating agents into enemy-held territory and also picking up agents and partisans from enemy coastlines. On one such mission, during the night of 3/4 August 1940, Patrick Whinney, later a commander, Royal Naval Reserve, used a commandeered French motor dispatch vessel to land agents at Ouistreham. Later, Whinney visited Spain from Gibraltar to purchase Spanish fishing vessels to create a flotilla of craft, soon known as the African Coastal Flotilla, that reconnoitred landing sites and future advanced bases in North Africa. Italian-pattern craft were also obtained. In 1944, Whinney established an advanced base of his own at Bastia in Corsica, this time using borrowed British, American and Italian craft. On one occasion, a group of Italians, led by a general, had to be picked up off the Italian coast using an American patrol boat; as Whinney and PO Jim Bates paddled their dinghies ashore through the surf, they were nearly shot by their intended passengers, who thought that it was a German trap!

CHAPTER TWELVE

RECRUITMENT AND TRAINING

*This priceless heritage [of sea power], born out of our insular state,
has been handed down and cultivated through the ages.*
David, Lord Beatty, 28 October 1920

The pre-war Royal Navy was entirely a volunteer navy, and one which was founded on long terms of service. Men joined from the age of 16 years onwards, while officers began training as early as 13, the latter expecting, and expected, to spend their life in the service. The ordinary seaman signed up for an initial twelve years, but not until he was 18 and had completed his shore training. Between the two world wars, in an effort to maintain manpower levels, the terms of service for ratings were amended with a special 'short service' option of seven years, followed by five years in the reserves; but as the recession began to bite, the Admiralty soon found that it had succeeded in meeting its manning levels, and the short service scheme was dropped. At the end of the initial twelve-year engagement, ratings could sign on for a further ten years, on completion of which they were eligible for a pension. Most of those engaged in a second term of service were petty officers or chief petty officers, or at least leading rates.

These circumstances were already coming under pressure from the new branches of the service, including wireless telegraphy and electrical engineering, yet, to the sur-prise of many traditionalists, the 'new' trades were easily assimilated into ships' companies.

Manpower in the pre-war navy amounted to 109,000 men and less than 10,000 officers, plus 12,400 officers and men of the Royal Marines, the latter manning a quarter of the armaments of the larger ships, as well as having a traditional function of providing manpower for landing parties and supplying bands for the larger ships; there were also Royal Marine stewards in many wardrooms.

The regular manpower was adequate for the peacetime complement of the active fleet, but there were also 73,000 men in the reserves. These included the Royal Fleet Reserve, consisting of pensioners or men who had not renewed their initial twelve-year engagement on completion, and the Merchant Navy personnel in the Royal Naval Reserve. The figure also included 6,000 men of the Royal Naval Volunteer Reserve, who were genuine amateurs. A number of reservists had been recalled in 1935 when Italy invaded Abyssinia, provoking an international outcry and a crisis for which the League of Nations had been ill prepared. There was a repeat performance three years later at the time of the Czecho-slovakian crisis. The reserves were recalled again in mid-June 1939, and the reserve fleet, much of it unmodernised, was again manned. Full mobilisation was ordered in August.

The demands of war saw the RNVR grow to 48,000 officers and 5,000 ratings. Many RNVR personnel rose to command cor-vettes, minesweepers and destroyers, others took command of Fleet Air Arm squadrons as that element of the RN expanded rapidly. The RNVR was most heavily represented in those areas of the service that had been neglected in peacetime, so as well as the vastly expanded Fleet Air Arm, which only passed fully to Admiralty control shortly before the outbreak of war, the volunteer reservists also provided many of the officers for the MGBs and MTBs of Coastal Forces. By mid-1944, the RN had reached its peak strength of 863,500 personnel, including 73,500 of the Women's Royal Naval Service, the 'Wrens'. Many of the lower deck person-nel in wartime were conscripts called up under the National Service Acts for 'hostilities only'.

Recruitment in wartime was supported by the introduction of conscription as not only men, but also women without young chil-dren, were all required to register for national service. The bulk of those called up for the armed forces went into the British Army, but others were allocated to the Royal Navy and the Royal Air Force – indeed the wise would volunteer for the service of their choice, especially if, for example, they wanted to fly, so as to exercise some control over their lives. For those interested in flying, the Fleet Air Arm was a wise choice as it avoided the backlog of applicants who had volunteered for the RAF but had been sent home as the service struggled to cope with the training demands of wartime expansion.

OFFICER TRAINING

Under wartime pressures, the traditional means of recruiting naval officers had to change. In peacetime, regular officers had joined as early as the age of 13 years, spend-ing four years at the Royal Naval College at Dartmouth, which operated as a fee-paying public school. Those who had attended other schools joined at 17 or 18 years, and spent a term at Dartmouth. In both cases, after graduating from Dartmouth, they would spend eighteen months as a midship-man. Despite the cap badge, midshipmen were not regarded as being officers in the full sense, being addressed as 'Mr' and not joining their seniors in the wardroom, the naval term for the officers' mess, but instead being confined to the 'gunroom mess'. In peacetime, a midshipman who wanted to fly would undergo most of his training with the RAF, with the Royal Navy providing catapult training so that he could fly seaplanes and amphibians from battleships, battlecruisers and cruisers. Training for pilots and observers that had taken two years in peace-time was compressed into ten wartime months.

While commissioning from the ranks, or in naval parlance the 'lower deck', became significant during and after the Second World War, it had been a rarity in the pre-war Navy. To obtain a sufficient number of experienced officers for the rapid wartime expansion, many senior ratings, normally chief petty officers, the naval equivalent of an Army staff sergeant or an RAF flight sergeant, were commissioned under the 'Upper Yardman Scheme'.

With war looming, another means of increasing the number of young officers was the introduction of a Special Entry Scheme at Dartmouth. In September 1942 the College was bombed, as a result of which it was evacuated to Eaton Hall, Cheshire, until

Young officer candidates early in their training wore white ribbons on their caps to indicate their status. *(Via Mrs M.J. Schupke)*

the end of the war. Later, the site at Dartmouth became a centre for Combined Operations in the preparations for D-Day as the area had become an amphibious base for American troops and ships preparing for the Normandy landings.

Before this, it was already clear that extra training facilities would be needed, especially with the massive increase in the number of volunteer reserve officers that was already foreseen. In 1939 Hove Marina and nearby Lancing College were requisitioned by the government and commissioned as HMS *King Alfred*. The reservists' college later relocated to Exbury House in the New Forest before the Normandy landings in 1944. During the war years, 22,508 RNVR officers passed out from *King Alfred*.

Nevertheless, by 1942 it had become apparent that *King Alfred* alone could not hope to meet the growing demand for officers. The initial reaction was to set up university naval divisions, which would select and train potential officers, but it soon became clear that the way forward was to improve the means of selecting suitable candidates from the lower deck. A trial scheme at HMS *Glendower*, a seaman new-entry training establishment at Pwllheli in north Wales, showed promise and was soon extended to the seamen training establishments at *Collingwood*, *Ganges*, *Raleigh* and *Royal Arthur*, while more specialised candidates were found at the stokers' school at *Duke*, communications specialists at *Excalibur* and naval airmen at *Gosling*.

The peacetime practice of naval officers becoming midshipmen before undertaking aircrew training also underwent change under wartime conditions. In the hurry to get as many pilots and observers as possible and as quickly as possible, not only was training reduced from two years to ten months for the duration, naval airmen were produced who were not strictly speaking 'sailors who could fly', but instead 'fliers who went to sea'. An Air Branch was formed to accommodate both the RNVR pilots and observers and also those members of the Royal Air Force who had volunteered to stay with the Royal Navy when it regained control of its own aviation. Flying training has been covered in detail in the *Fleet Air Arm Handbook*, but it is sufficient to mention here that aspiring pilots and observers were given basic training at HMS *St Vincent*, a stone frigate at Gosport, before being sent to 'start their basic' flying training, initially with the RAF.

As the RAF struggled to cope with its own expanded training needs, many naval airmen received their training with the United States Navy, returning to the Royal Navy for the final stages. They were not commissioned until flying training was completed, and even then had to await the end of their post-training leave of just a week, but started operational conversion courses as naval officers. With a few exceptions, naval pilots and observers were commissioned, in contrast to RAF practice, in which there were a substantial number of non-commissioned

Many recruits passed through HMS *Ganges*, a shore establishment at Shotley, which retained the name of an old training hulk when the function transferred ashore. Here is the preserved figurehead from the original ship. *(HMS* Ganges *Association)*

pilots, usually sergeants. The rank at which one was commissioned was determined by age, with RNVR officers often missing the rank of midshipman altogether. Those over 21 years of age became temporary sub-lieutenants, those under 21, temporary acting sub-lieutenants, and those under 20 became temporary midshipmen. This must have been hard, for two men with exactly the same training and experience could join the fleet with one as a midshipman on five shillings a day and the other as a temporary sub-lieutenant on nine shillings and sixpence a day. The midshipmen were not allowed spirits, even though on aircraft carriers they usually joined the wardroom rather than the gunroom mess. Flying pay was an extra four shillings a day.

TRAINING RATINGS

In the pre-war Royal Navy, personnel could join either as adults or, more usually as boys, being sent to one of the Boys' Training Establishments at HMS *Ganges*, at Shotley, near Ipswich, HMS *St Vincent* at Gosport, or HMS *Caledonia* on the Clyde, while HMS *Impregnable* at Devonport had been closed between the wars. *St Vincent* had been a Royal Marine barracks but, like its officer counterpart at Dartmouth, *Ganges* had started with an old hulk of the same name being moored offshore; as time took its toll on the hulks and as numbers increased, both establishments had moved into purpose-built accommodation ashore. *Ganges* itself was still being developed as war loomed, with a new school block built and opened just before the outbreak of war. Under the pressure of wartime needs, the Admiralty decided in spring 1940 to use the establishment for training adult ratings, including many wartime 'hostilities only' personnel, and for the duration it lost its role as a training establishment for boys. At

first, an entry of 264 HO ratings arrived while *Ganges* was still home to 1,500 boys, but in May 600 boys were transferred to the Isle of Man where they were joined by evacuees from the other two establishments to create a new combined Boys' Training Establishment, HMS *St George*, on the site of a former holiday camp. Then shortly afterwards, the remaining boys left to go to new training establishments at Devonport and Liverpool. New training establishments had been planned before the war, including HMS *Collingwood*, just outside Fareham in Hampshire, and HMS *Raleigh* at Torpoint in Cornwall.

These measures were accompanied in 1940 by a halving of the time allowed to ratings to receive their basic training. While training of specialists such as wireless telegraph ratings had been conducted at *Ganges*, this was also removed to Highnam Court, near Gloucester, in an attempt to speed up the flow of personnel through *Ganges*; this new establishment was commissioned as a satellite of *Ganges*. By this time, the Royal Navy's personnel strength was in excess of 250,000, giving some idea of the pace of wartime expansion. Highnam Court was developed to have accommodation for up to 3,000 personnel, while *Ganges* was expanded to accommodate 17,000. During the war years, from Easter 1940 until October 1945, no fewer than 60,968 HO ratings passed through *Ganges*, including a number from the Empire.

Specialised training such as that for wireless telegraphy followed basic training. One of the new training establishments, *Collingwood*, started to receive wireless telegraph trainees in June 1940, with a thousand trainees joining every three weeks for a ten week course, while a Radio Direction Finding School was also added in 1942. *Collingwood* also trained Wrens as cooks, stewards, messengers and telephonists.

Certificate of Service, with the top right-hand corner intact, indicating that the bearer was not dismissed the service with a 'bad' character. In fact, lower down one can see that he was awarded the Distinguished Service Medal (DSM). *(Collection of S.V. Wragg)*

A passing-out parade of recruits marching through the streets of Ipswich. *(HMS* Ganges *Association)*

Yet, while much had been done between the two wars to improve and reorganise the Royal Navy's specialist training, it was not until 1944 that responsibility for naval diving passed from the Gunnery Branch at HMS *Excellent*, based on Whale Island in Portsmouth Harbour, to HMS *Vernon*, which was based on the old gunwharf on the harbourside and trained personnel in mine recovery and destruction, so that diving, mine warfare and mine countermeasures were all together for the first time.

Unfortunately, Portsmouth was also conveniently placed for German air raids, and one heavy air raid in 1940 demolished one of the main buildings, *Dido* Building, and killed one hundred people in just one night. On 3 May 1941 much of *Vernon* was evacuated to Roedean girls' school at Brighton, becoming *Vernon* (R), where it is claimed the evacuees were delighted to find

bell pushes labelled 'Ring for Mistress'. In fact, the *Vernon* diaspora took in many sites, as far afield as Port Edgar, on the banks of the Firth of Forth, near Queensferry. A new diving school and experimental station was established at Brixham on 27 October 1944 and known as *Vernon* (D), with the 'D' referring to Dartmouth, which handled its administrative support. Much of the work at Brixham centred around clearing mines in harbour waters.

A problem for the Royal Navy during the earlier period of rapid expansion during the First World War had been that far too many young petty officers lacked power of command. Short courses had been introduced in the three main home ports, while a petty officers' school was established at HMS *Royal Arthur*. These lessons were borne in mind as once again the Royal Navy expanded almost eightfold.

CHAPTER THIRTEEN

PERSONAL AND PERSONNEL

Their blood was Stockholm tar, and their every finger a marlinespike.
Early nineteenth-century saying

Life for the Royal Navy during the Second World War had its compensations, of which duty-free alcoholic drinks while at sea, and duty-free tobacco products even while in the UK, were just a part. But naval discipline also imposed restrictions. Only officers were allowed spirits. Every society imposes its rules, and the Royal Navy was no exception.

UNIFORMS

Uniforms were issued free to ratings, while officers had to buy their own. The uniforms for ratings were made from navy-blue serge, while those for officers were the double-breasted navy-blue barathea jacket, of a style and cut copied by many navies and by the British Merchant Navy. At first, there was no naval equivalent of the battledress issued to the Army and the RAF. For aircrew this was a nuisance, because the standard naval uniform, worn under a flying jacket, snagged as they climbed into their cramped cockpits. It was not until the war was well advanced that the pilots of 832 Squadron ordered and paid for their own Royal Navy battledress uniforms in serge. As with the battledress for officers in the British Army, it was still worn with a collar and tie – a privilege enjoyed by all ranks in the RAF. Naval

officers could ask their tailor for a uniform in fine serge, which was lighter in weight than barathea, but this was frowned upon by many senior officers if worn on parade.

The standard naval uniform gave a clear indication of the trade of the rating wearing it, as well as his rank and his length of good conduct. For wartime, the rank, good conduct and trade badges were always red on the standard blue uniform, and blue on white tropical uniforms. The pre-war practice of having these badges in gold on the No 1 blue uniform was not reinstated for many years after the war. Trade badges were worn on the right arm of all ratings with the exception of CPOs, who wore two identical badges on the collars of their blue uniform, or on the right cuff of tropical white uniform, or the right sleeve if a short-sleeved shirt was worn.

The rank of a rating, ordinary seaman, able bodied seaman or airman, leading seaman or airman, or petty officer, was worn on the left arm, above any good conduct stripes for regular personnel, and good service stripes for reservists. One good conduct stripe was awarded for the first three years of good conduct, or good service in the reserves, two for eight years and three for thirteen years. (Good conduct was often referred to as 'undetected crime' by the more experienced, and cynical, naval people.) This meant that an experienced man with good conduct would eventually be a 'three badge . . .'; that is, he would have three stripes and confuse the uninitiated, who might think that he was a sergeant! After the war, this changed, with each stripe denoting a straight four years' good conduct. CPOs did not wear good conduct badges; their badge of rank was the row of brass buttons around the cuffs of the jacket. Young junior ratings were always wary of a 'three badge PO', who would be by definition an old salt with at least thirteen years service, wise in the ways of the world and, more important, those of the Royal Navy.

The penalties for bad conduct varied, but anyone discharged from the service on the grounds of poor conduct would find that the top right corner of the first page of their service record had been cut off. There could be no fooling a future employer.

The cut of the uniform varied with rank. Below the rank of petty officer, ratings wore the traditional 'square rig', a serge jumper with collar and vest, and serge bell-bottom trousers. The vest was usually white, but in northern conditions would be navy blue. The blue collar which hung over the shoulders of the jumper was bordered by three white stripes, one for each of Nelson's great victories at the Nile, Copenhagen and Trafalgar, while there was also a black ribbon, in mourning for Nelson, although this was swapped for white when the rating was being married. On parade and for walking out, a rope lanyard would be added. On his head, the rating wore the standard naval cap without a peak, known as a 'lid'. The peacetime tradition of having the name of his ship in gold on the cap tally was abandoned in favour of the simple letters 'HMS' in gold, partly for security, and partly for economy, as personnel could change

ships very frequently, while naval airmen were constantly switching between ships and shore stations. Petty officers wore a single-breasted pea jacket in fine serge with collar and tie, while CPOs had double-breasted jackets; both wore peaked caps with gold badges, although that for the CPOs was more elaborate. The exceptions to the wearing of the square rig for junior ratings were stewards and sick bay attendants, who also wore a single-breasted serge jacket and tie and ordinary trousers, but with a red cap badge. When marching or on guard duty, khaki webbing and gaiters were worn by ratings.

In tropical kit, which was usually white, the standard issue for junior ratings consisted of white shorts, while the white vest would be worn without the jacket. Stewards, petty officers and chief petty officers wore open-necked tropical white shirts. Ratings up to and including petty officers wore navy-blue knee socks and black shoes; chief petty officers had white knee socks and white shoes. White cap-covers were issued only with tropical kit in wartime and for some years afterwards.

Occasionally, usually for those deployed ashore in the desert or the jungle, often in support of the Army, khaki uniforms were issued, and except for badges of rank, etc., this was similar to the uniform issued to personnel in the other services.

Working clothing for those engaged in messy jobs was a heavy blue cotton overall for ratings, but white for officers. This would be worn, for example, by naval air mechanics, and was expected to be worn with the standard issue hat when working outside.

Warrant officers wore a thin version of the traditional sub-lieutenant's ring and loop, with an officer's cap badge. Midshipmen wore buttons on their cuffs, with two pieces of cloth and brass buttons on their

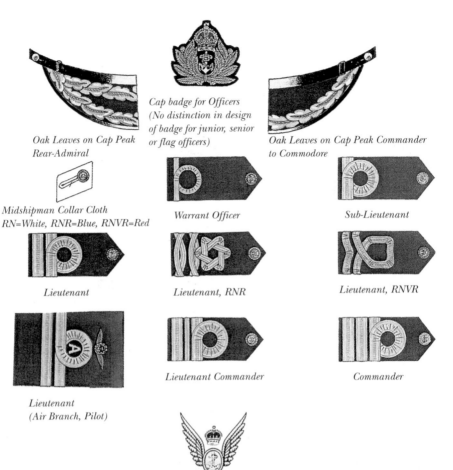

Oak Leaves on Cap Peak
Rear-Admiral

Cap badge for Officers
(No distinction in design
of badge for junior, senior
or flag officers)

Oak Leaves on Cap Peak Commander
to Commodore

Midshipman Collar Cloth
RN=White, RNR=Blue, RNVR=Red

Warrant Officer

Sub-Lieutenant

Lieutenant

Lieutenant, RNR

Lieutenant, RNVR

Lieutenant
(Air Branch, Pilot)

Lieutenant Commander

Commander

Observer Wings

Notice the difference between the wings for pilots and for observers. *(Sources: Various)*

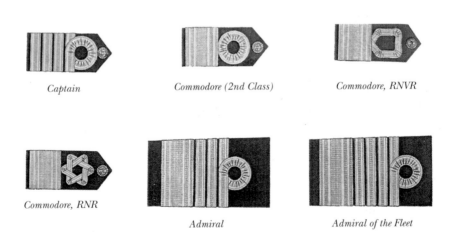

Captain

Commodore (2nd Class)

Commodore, RNVR

Commodore, RNR

Admiral

Admiral of the Fleet

Rings for Rear Admiral are one broad and one narrow with a loop, and for Vice Admiral, one broad and two narrow, the upper having a loop. *(Sources: Various)*

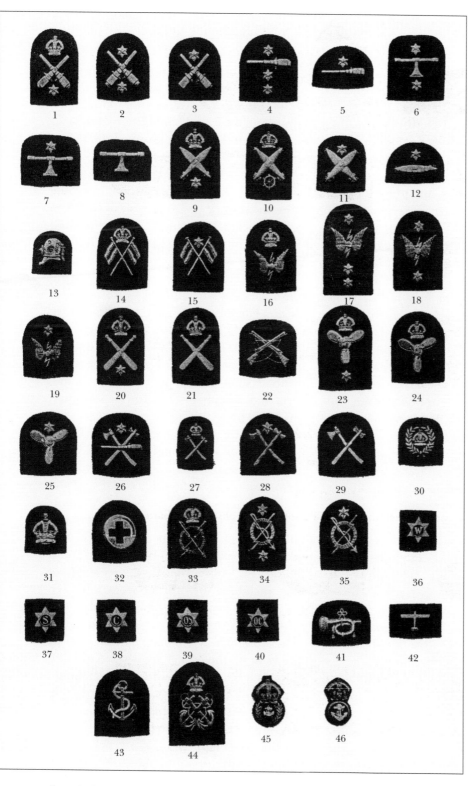

1. Gunner's Mate. 2. Gunlayer, 1st Class. 3. Gun Layer, 2nd Class. 4. Captain of the Gun, 1st Class. 5. Seaman Gunner. 6. Rangetaker, 1st Class. 7. Rangetaker, 2nd Class. 8. Rangetaker, 3rd Class. 9. Torpedo Gunner's Mate. 10. Torpedo Coxswain. 11. Leading Torpedoman. 12. Seaman Torpedoman. 13. Diver. 14. Chief Yeoman of Signals. 15. Leading Signalman and Signalman. 16. Petty Officer Telegraphist. 17 and 18. Leading Telegraphist. 19. Telegraphist. 20. Physical and Recreational Training Instructor, 1st Class. 21. Physical and Recreational Training Instructor, 2nd Class. 22. Good Shooting Badge. 23. Mechanician. 24. Chief Stoker and Stoker Petty Officer. 25. Leading Stoker and Stoker, 1st Class. 26. Chief Armourer. 27. Chief Shipwright. 28. Chief Petty Officer Artisan. 29. Shipwrights and Artisans. 30. Master-at-Arms. 31. Regulating Petty Officer. 32. Sick Berth Rating. 33. Submarine Detector Instructor. 34. Submarine Detector Operator, 1st Class. 35. Submarine Detector Operator, 2nd Class. 36. Writer. 37. Supply Rating. 38. Cook. 39. Officer's Steward. 40. Officer's Cook. 41. Bugler. 42. Telegraphist Air Gunner. 43. Leading Seaman. 44. Petty Officer. 45. Chief Petty Officer Cap Badge. 46. Petty Officer Cap Badge.

Opposite: Naval officers' badges of rank and insignia.   *Above:* Naval ratings' trade badges.

collars; the cloth was white for regulars, blue for the RNR and red for the RNVR. The straight rings and loops were for the regulars, with a complex double ring for RNR officers, and a simple single wavy ring for the 'Wavy Navy' RNVR officers. Certain specialists had coloured cloth between the rings, including red for doctors, always known in the Royal Navy as surgeons, brown for dentists, purple for engineers, green for electrical and electronics, and white for paymasters. Paymasters were general administrators, since secretaries were members of the paymaster branch. Instructors had blue cloth between their rings.

Pilots and observers had their wings, which differed, above the loop on the rings of their cuff. Not all aircrew were recognised as belong to the Air Branch, since many were regarded as general service officers, in effect sailors who flew rather than fliers who went to sea. Those in the Air Branch had a capital letter 'A' within the loop of their rings. All RNVR officer pilots and observers were treated in this way, but there were a number of regular officers as well, usually those who had transferred from the RAF. When wearing tropical kit or battledress, the wings were worn on the left breast above any medals.

The cap badge for warrant officers, midshipmen and officers was more elaborate than that for senior ratings. The use of oak leaves on the peak of the cap differed slightly in the Royal Navy from the practice in the RAF, with commanders, captains and commodores having one row of oak leaves, and two rows for rear admiral and above. As with all other ranks, white cloth covers were not usually issued for wear with blue uniforms during the war years, or for some years afterwards, with an exception being made in the sub-tropical areas, where the armed forces changed into blue uniform for the winter months. Another wartime utility measure was the suspension of the traditional mess kit for formal dining evenings.

In tropical kit, officers usually wore a white shirt and shorts, but in some cases khaki was worn, with white or khaki cap-covers and white or khaki knee socks. Shoes were white unless wearing khaki, when black shoes were worn. Markings of rank were worn on shoulder epaulettes when wearing tropical kit. Some senior officers, including Adm Sir Andrew Cunningham, persisted in wearing peacetime 'Number Ones' as their tropical kit, as a further mark of their authority.

The Royal Marines wore blue uniform, with a jacket that buttoned up to the neck for non-commissioned men, but with a shirt, collar and tie for officers. Wings were worn on the left breast. Officers wore their badges of rank, similar to those of the Army, on their shoulder epaulettes. Tropical uniform was khaki, except for ceremonial, which was white.

The Wrens were re-established in 1939. They did not serve aboard warships. Wren uniforms usually consisted of a navy blue jacket and skirt with white collar and tie. Junior ratings in the Wrens wore hats similar to those of their male counterparts, although senior ratings and officers had more elaborate styles. Trade badges and insignia for rank were in a lighter shade of blue, including the officers' rings, although the curl was replaced by a diamond. While ranks for ratings were modified forms of those for men, such as leading wren or petty officer wren, the officer ranks owed more to Merchant Navy practice, with a commander being a chief officer, a lieutenant-commander a first officer, a lieutenant a second officer and a sub-lieutenant a third officer, but the Wren equivalent of a captain was a commandant. Pay for the Wrens was considerably lower than for their male counterparts, and while Wrens did not go to battle in warships, their work in the main naval ports meant that they were on the receiving end of the Blitz.

FOOD AND ACCOMMODATION

Wartime conditions in the Royal Navy varied. There was the obvious discomfort in being in confined conditions aboard a ship, where even officer accommodation was cramped by the standards of those living ashore, and this situation was worsened by the increased complement of ships in wartime. There was strict segregation between the lower deck (the ratings) and the upper deck (the officers). Aboard a carrier, priority was given to the aircraft, to their munitions, fuel and spares, then to the ship's own armament, leaving the ship's company and the personnel of the embarked squadrons to fit in around it. For the ratings, there were hammocks, often in large messdecks; for the officers, there were cabins, but it was not unusual for these to be shared by two or three officers, sometimes more. Even officers' cabins could be noisy, and usually, being higher up in the hull of the carrier, they would be more likely to be disturbed by flying, and especially the thump of an aircraft landing.

There were few concessions to the Fleet Air Arm at first, and naval aviators, especially the non-commissioned, landing back aboard after a night patrol, could find sleep difficult in the cramped, and often noisy, conditions of a warship messdeck in daytime. Unlike the RAF, where the whole base revolved around the needs of the aircrew, and where in most cases entire squadrons were scrambled or sent on a mission, in the Royal Navy for much of the time, the airmen were seen as a nuisance. It was not just sleep that the returning aviator might find difficult: meal times were at first very

rigid, especially for rating airmen, usually telegraphist air gunners.

Meal times for ratings were breakfast at 07.00, lunch at noon, afternoon tea at 16.00 and supper at 18.00. During the early years, if a telegraphist air gunner, happened to be flying at these times, that was his bad luck. If he was lucky, and someone remembered, a meal would be set aside for his return, by which time it would be a congealed, greasy mess. On one occasion, after a long cross-country flight and several missed meals, one TAG recalled how he had to go to the officers' wardroom to get a chit signed so that the duty cook could prepare some food.

By contrast, mealtimes for those serving aboard a submarine were varied, and of course this was possible because the same times applied to the entire crew. The main meal of the day was at midnight, known to many as 'big eats', with supper at 06.00 and breakfast at 19.00.

There were three different types of messing arrangements for ratings. There was general messing, in which the paymaster or his deputy would draw up a menu for all the lower deck, and each mess sent a duty 'cook', chosen by roster, to collect the meals for the agreed number of men in the mess. The meals would be served and eaten on the mess deck at a wooden table, with the men sitting on wooden stools or benches, and at night the mess became the sleeping accommodation for the men. A variation on this would be canteen messing, in which supplies were drawn, including a ration of meat, potatoes and any other vegetables, from the ship's provision store and prepared in the mess, again by a duty 'cook', and then taken to the galley to be cooked. Once the meals were cooked, they would be collected and served as in general messing. This system was applied in HMS *Argus*, for example. Then, on the later ships, including

Living, sleeping and eating all had to be carried out within the same cramped space on a submarine. A bunk can be seen folded away behind the rating sitting down, while another two have taken to their berths, possibly to find some space. *(Collection of S.V. Wragg)*

the escort carriers, there was cafeteria messing, in which eating and sleeping took place in different areas of the ship, and the ratings had their meals in a self-service cafeteria, as they would ashore.

Most accounts of the war years suggest that the standard of catering was good, and that even for the lower deck, rationing had little impact, and those at sea fared better for food than the civilian population. Nevertheless, there were some hardships. The carriers may have been large ships for the most part, but they also had large complements and soon ran out of potatoes. At a time when the civilian population had very conventional meals with little sign of today's international cuisine, rice was a staple part of the naval diet.

People had their favourites, made even more glamorous by naval slang. A 'cackleberry' was an egg, a 'Spithead pheasant' a kipper, and a 'train smash' tinned herring in tomato source. The rations could be augmented by treats from the NAAFI (the Navy, Army and Air Force Institutes), aboard the larger ships and in every air station and barracks.

Fresh water was another problem, especially on the older ships, such as the converted battlecruiser *Furious*. Never designed for the number of men aboard, and in any case designed to operate with the Home Fleet, she soon ran out of fresh water for washing, shaving or bathing. Salt-water had to be used for these functions, and special salt water soap was issued, which took a long time to lather. Experienced sailors soon adjusted and habitually became very careful in their use of water, even though the newer carriers were much better in this respect, including *Ark Royal*, aboard which fresh water seemed to be plentiful. The escort carriers, with their merchant hulls, also tended to be better able to meet the freshwater needs of their crews. This may well have been because the vast majority of these ships were US conversions, and as befitted a navy with relatively few overseas bases and the vast expanses of the Pacific, American warships had very good freshwater provision.

Accommodation in the escort carriers could be spartan, nevertheless. Even officers sometimes found themselves accommodated next to the inside of the hull. One recalled how they were blown out of their bunks when an escorting destroyer swept past making a depth-charge attack! By contrast, accommodation on the armed merchant cruisers, converted from liners, could be luxurious.

One especially spartan feature on the escort carriers were the ratings' lavatories, which consisted of wooden benches with holes cut in them and water running underneath. The younger members of the crew could be relied upon to put oily rags or screwed-up newspapers into this stream, light them, and then wait for the panic that ensued! Normally, the only real victim was the first to be reached by these improvised fireships.

None of this should disguise the fact that many naval airmen of all ranks were often anxious to return to sea, despite the discomforts and the dangers. The Fleet Air Arm had few bases of its own at the start of the war, and these quickly became overcrowded. Yeovilton was still not complete at the time of the Battle of Britain. As its needs changed, the RAF released some bases to the Admiralty, but much depended on the location. This was part of the problem. The Fleet Air Arm needed air stations close to the ports and anchorages used by the fleet. Aircraft could not be kept on board while in harbour because they were vulnerable and could not be flown from a ship not under way. The Home Fleet was moved forward to Scapa Flow and this meant that an air station had to be quickly improvised at Hatston, just outside Kirkwall, on the mainland of Orkney. A bleak position in winter, it was muddy, wet, windy, and it snowed often, but the men were quartered in bell-tents. A warm climate did not always mean ideal conditions either. Hal Far, then an RAF base, on the southern end of Malta, also provided tented accommodation, through the heat of the Maltese summer.

For officers, it was different. Meals were served in the wardroom, and on the larger ships this usually had an ante-room with a bar. For naval airmen, meals would be provided to match the flying programme, including serving bacon and eggs in the small hours if a major bombing raid required an early start. Most accounts suggest that the effort was probably not worth it, since, understandably, many aircrew had little appetite before a major operation. Wardroom meals were served by stewards, and officers would also have a steward to look after their other needs, such as laundry, although usually it would be a case of one steward to two or three officers in the same cabin. The gunroom mess was also comfortable, a bit like a prefects' common room. On submarines and the smaller ships, however, the wardroom could be cramped, little more than a small dining room, while on submarines the officers' bunk space could also intrude.

On most ships, the wardroom had a hierarchy. Many senior officers would have a distinct corner of their own, and so too would the Royal Marines if there were a substantial number aboard. On all but the smaller warships, the commanding officer was not a member of the wardroom, and would only appear when invited by the wardroom president, usually his second-in-command.

Accounts differ over whether wardroom life was boozy or not. Only a fool would get seriously drunk before flying early the next day, and doubtless some did not drink when flying was possible. Nevertheless, wardroom life was sociable, and when operating with the United States Navy with its 'dry' ships, visits by American officers to the more relaxed Royal Navy must have helped oil the wheels of collaboration. Little money changed hands in the wardroom. Officers had an account, which had to be settled monthly. Senior officers kept an eye on this, and if anyone appeared to be drinking heavily, there would be a quiet word, and if notice wasn't taken, the account could be restricted or even closed altogether. A popular feature of wardroom life was the sing-songs around the piano. This was a time when most well-educated young men could play the piano, and in the Fleet Air Arm there seemed to be many lyricists able to pen a few words to a popular tune; many of these eventually appeared in a *Fleet Air Arm Songbook*.

There was another aspect to life aboard ship. In common with every ship, naval or merchant, aircraft carriers kept a ship's log. There were also squadron logs, and individual pilots and observers also maintained a logbook. In the Fleet Air Arm, colour was added to the dry official accounts of life afloat by the existence in many ships of the 'line book', an informal and sometimes irreverent account of life aboard ship, and the deeds and misdeeds of the ship's officers.

SERVING WITH THE MERCHANT NAVY

While the number of naval personnel serving ashore was around twice that actually at sea, even afloat not all naval personnel served aboard warships. As the war progressed, many found themselves serving on merchant vessels, as distinct from the liners that became armed merchant cruisers, and the trawlers, drifters and occasional paddle steamer that did service as minesweepers or engaged in anti-submarine or even convoy escort work; the men serving aboard these found themselves in the Royal Navy and subject to naval discipline with a temporary rank. There were also the catapult-armed merchant ships (CAM-ships) and the merchant aircraft carriers (MAC-ships), all of which continued to carry cargo while having naval and, in the case of most CAM-ships, RAF personnel, aboard. Naval and, for that matter, Army personnel also served aboard defensively armed merchant ships, and to be fair, many of these ships also had Merchant Navy personnel trained as gunners as the war progressed. There were also the radio operators and other members of

Ratings taking a meal aboard the escort carrier *Avenger*, which clearly has cafeteria messing, marking a welcome change from the practice of eating and sleeping in the same quarters. *(IWM A10960)*

the convoy commodore's staff aboard his ship, usually one of the merchant ships, who would be responsible for controlling the convoy.

The service personnel assigned to a merchant vessel in effect served two masters, since they remained in their own service, and subject to service discipline, pay and conditions, but they also had to sign on as members of the ship's company and come under the authority of the ships' master. One naval officer recalled serving aboard a MAC-ship, where he was told he would receive an additional shilling a week, which was never paid in his experience, and also receive a bottle of beer a day, which was duly provided. Accounts generally seem to agree that the food aboard the merchantmen was good.

Less happily, on some ships at least, no one seemed to have told the Merchant Navy that there was a war on. Mealtimes were dictated by trade union hours, as was other work, so that when an ammunition locker was damaged at the weekend, it had to wait until the Monday morning to be repaired.

No less than 24,000 Royal Navy gunners served aboard Merchant Navy vessels during the war, and of these 3,000 were killed, while another 14,000 gunners came from the Army, of which 1,222 lost their lives. The need for gunners aboard merchantmen was such that another 150,000 Merchant Navy personnel also received gunnery training.

PERKS OF THE JOB

Officially, there were few perks for the Royal Navy. Duty-free drink while at sea, and duty free cigarettes and tobacco even when in the UK, were about it. Cheap drink and tobacco products while stationed abroad were something shared by all three services. Stationed at home or abroad, or serving in a ship at sea, the usual UK income tax was still payable.

Nevertheless, given the visits by many ships, including those on convoy escort duty, to North America, and the austere wartime rationing at home, some smuggling was to be expected. The Fleet Air Arm played its part in this. Ships were met by Customs officers on reaching port, and sometimes just before entering harbour, but by this time the aircraft had flown off. Some accounts suggest that these were sometimes fairly heavily laden, and Customs inspection at the naval air stations receiving these aircraft varied in its intensity and, most important, in how promptly Customs would arrive. In any event, many officers would buy a bottle of spirits before leaving the ship.

But there was another way in which the acquisitive seafarer could improve his lot. When an aircraft or ship was lost, all of its equipment was written off. Some stores officers would work hard to ensure that any shortfall in their stores just happened to be on the most recently lost aircraft. The aircrew could benefit as well. On seeking a fellow member of his squadron who had just been rescued after ditching, one naval officer found him celebrating the acquisition of a fine pair of binoculars which he had managed to save as his aircraft sank beneath the waves, and which, of course, had been written off.

CHAPTER FOURTEEN

WARSHIPS

Priest: Bless our ship.
Men: May God the Father bless her.
P: Bless our ship.
M: May Jesus Christ bless her.
P: Bless our ship.
M: May the Holy Spirit bless her.
P: What do you fear, seeing that God the Father is with you?
M: We fear nothing.
P: What do you fear, seeing that God the Son is with you?
M: We fear nothing.
P: What do you fear, seeing that God the Holy Spirit is with you?
M: We fear nothing.
From the dedication ceremony for HMS Vindex *by the Bishop of Newcastle, 20 November 1943*

The Royal Navy in 1939 was still very much a 'big gun' navy. But only two of the battle-ships *Rodney* and *Nelson*, had been built since the First World War, although by 1939 four new battleships were building – the King George V class. This was partly a result of the restrictions imposed by the Washington Naval Treaty and by other later naval agreements. Nevertheless, belatedly, some of the older ships had been modernised. Realising the importance of the convoy in the war, the Admiralty had ordered the conversion of six old cruisers as anti-aircraft escorts, as well as fifteen destroyers dating from the First World War.

Orders for new ships included sloops, slow but with considerable endurance and ideal as convoy escorts, and these displaced between 1,000 and 1,250 tons, with no less

than fifty-three already in service on the outbreak of war. In addition, a new class of small, but fast, destroyer, the Hunt class, 900 tons and 32 knots, with dual-purpose arma-ment but no torpedo tubes, was ordered. Initially there were twenty on order when war broke out, and another sixty-six were ordered later. These were to prove unsuit-able for much convoy work, lacking endur-ance, but they were ideal for service in the Channel and North Sea, and to protect coastal shipping. Finally, in 1939 and 1940 orders were placed for a new breed of small but long-endurance escort – the famous Flower class corvettes, based on the hull form of a commercial whaler. They were to prove uncomfortable in a seaway, and their top speed of just fifteen knots meant that they could not overtake a U-boat on the surface, but even so, they were to provide invaluable service.

The war years were to reshape the Royal Navy. Learning from American practice, the Royal Navy improved, provision for refuelling at sea and replenishment of ships under way, the American abeam method being far more efficient, and capable of being used in far worse sea states, than the British in-line method of refuelling.

Destroyers were to be seen as being better suited to the offensive than as convoy escorts, with their narrow beam making them unsuitable as escorts while their high speed was unnecessary and their short range a drawback. Realising that something more than a corvette or a sloop was needed for escort duties, the frigate was reinvented, but not as a 'maid of all work' as in Nelson's navy, but to provide enhanced anti-aircraft or anti-submarine support wherever this might be needed. There was also to be an appreciation that submarines of all sizes had a role to play, with smaller submarines proving highly suitable for the Mediterranean.

The financial constraints of the inter-war years had meant that much had been neglected. Despite its success with small craft during the First World War, fast launches had disappeared from the Royal Navy, even though it was clear that the Germans in particular were developing such craft, indeed, advertising these in publications such as *Jane's Fighting Ships*. This neglect could be due to the fact that many believed that any future European war would follow the entrenched positions of the First World War Western Front, with Dutch neutrality respected, but the fall of France allowing German use of her ports was not foreseen.

Equipment in the ships varied. Guns and gunnery were generally good, although the fire and control arrangements, and the anti-aircraft or HA weapons themselves, were inferior, and this was why the wartime Royal Navy became almost completely dependent on Swedish Bofors and Swiss Oerlikon weapons, manufactured under licence. There was also an over-emphasis at first on guns that could be sued against other ships (low angle or LA), at the expense of anti-aircraft weaponry (high angle or HA). Some calibres were available, such as the new 4.5in, that could handle both roles, but most weapons were intended to be one or the other.

Nevertheless, the Royal Navy had two advantages, one of which was the possession of asdic, which was superior to the hydrophone listening aids of the First World War, while another was the steady introduction of radar across the fleet.

THE COST OF THE WAR

The Royal Navy lost, overall throughout the war years, 3 battleships, 2 battlecruisers, 5 aircraft carriers and another 3 escort carriers, 28 cruisers (with another 3 in the Royal Australian Navy), no less than 132 destroyers (plus 4 in the RAN and 6 Royal Canadian Navy), 74 submarines, a monitor, 10 sloops (with another 2 RAN and 1 Royal Indian Navy), 3 cutters, 10 frigates, 22 corvettes, 32 fleet minesweepers, 3 fast minelayers and 5 other minelayers, 15 armed merchant cruisers, 6 AA ships, 2 fighter catapult ships (which were really merchant vessels) and 2 depot ships. A third of submarine losses were due to hitting mines – a bigger hazard for British submarines than for the Germans because of the way in which the two navies were deployed.

In return, the Royal Navy and Commonwealth navies as well as 'free' forces under RN command, accounted for 514 of the 785 German U-boats sunk, with another 166 destroyed by the USN and twelve shared between the RN and USN. The remainder were sunk by RAF Coastal Command.

The Soviet Navy contributed little during the Second World War, largely because many of its ships were obsolete. In May 1944 the Royal Navy handed over the battleship *Royal Sovereign*, seen here after the transfer, as well as four submarines and eight of the former US Navy Town class destroyers. *(IWM A23816)*

U-boat losses can be attributed to the following causes:

Surface ships	246
Shore-based aircraft (other than bombing raids)	245
Bombing raids	61
Accidents and scuttling	57
Shared between surface ships and aircraft	50
Ship-borne aircraft	43
Unknown causes	29
Mines	26
Submarines	21
Russian advance	7

Other German losses included 2 battleships, 2 battlecruisers, 3 'pocket' battleships, 2 old battleships, the single uncompleted aircraft carrier, 8 cruisers, 101 destroyers and torpedo boats, 7 armed merchant cruisers used as commerce raiders, 23 minelayers, 25 smaller escort vessels, 282 minesweepers, 64 mine destructor boats or *sperrbrecher*, 146 E-boats (known to the Germans as S-boats), 860 miscellaneous craft and as many as 600 ferry barges, mainly in the surface follow-up to the invasion of Crete. The Italians lost a battleship, although two more were knocked out at Taranto, 14 cruisers, 85 destroyers and torpedo boats, 3 minelayers, 84 submarines, 35 minesweepers, 72 miscellaneous craft and about 60 barges.

BATTLESHIPS

QUEEN ELIZABETH CLASS

Queen Elizabeth, Warspite, Valiant, Barham, Malaya

Built during the First World War but modernisation started before the Second World War, largely driven by the fact that new capital ships could not be laid down before 1 January 1937. On the outbreak of war, *Warspite* had been completely reconstructed, while work on *Queen Elizabeth* and *Valiant* was in hand, but *Malaya* and *Barham* had been only partly reconstructed. Attention was given to improving underwater protection and AA armament, but the main armament was also improved, using modern shells so that the range of the 15in guns went from 23,400 yards to 32,200 yards. Nevertheless, there were limitations on what could be achieved: while armour plating was improved by laying 2.5in armour on top of the original 1in, but this was, of course, far inferior to a single sheet of 3.5in had it been possible to retrofit this. Over the magazines, doubtless with the lessons of Jutland in mind, armour plating was 4in over the original 1in. *Warspite* was the first to receive attention, with torpedo bulges fitted as early as 1926, while funnels were merged into one to stop back draughts carrying gases to the bridge. There was an almost ten-fold increase in pump capacity to handle fires or flooding. Torpedo tubes were removed as part of the modernisation, which also saw a catapult added, plus accommodation for two Supermarine Walrus aircraft. Machinery was also improved, with the upgrading of the geared turbines, and as a result the maximum range increased from 4,400 miles at 10 knots to 13,500 miles. The number of boilers was reduced from twenty-four to eight of a much-improved design.

Barham torpedoed and sunk off Libya, 25 November 1941.

Displacement: The 1940 standard saw these ships displace 36,450 tons full load.
Armament: 8 × 15in; 20 × 4.5in HA guns; 32 × 2pdr HA guns in four mountings; 16 × 0.5in guns in four mountings.
Maximum speed: 25 knots.

ROYAL SOVEREIGN CLASS

Royal Sovereign, Resolution, Revenge, Royal Oak, Ramillies (all 1916–17)

Built during the First World War, but their smaller size meant that less could be done to update them. *Ramillies* had underwater bulges fitted and in 1917 it was decided to extend this protection to the other four ships of the class. As war approached, efforts were made to keep the AA armament up to date, but while some ships received facilities for aircraft, these were later removed. Fixed underwater torpedo tubes were removed, and although it was planned to provide above-water fixed tubes, only *Royal Oak* was so fitted. In 1942, *Royal Sovereign* was transferred to the USSR on loan. No major reconstruction such as given to the Queen Elizabeth class was accorded any ship of this class.

Royal Oak torpedoed and sunk, Scapa Flow, 14 October 1939.

Displacement: In 1940, these ships displaced 29,150 tons full load.
Armament: 8 × 15in guns; 12 × 6in guns; 4 × 4in HA guns (8 on *Royal Oak*); 2 × torpedo tubes.
Maximum speed: 22 knots.

King George V Class

King George V, Prince of Wales, Duke of York, Anson (ex-*Jellicoe*), *Howe* (ex-*Beatty*)

These ships were affected by the London Naval Treaty 1936, which placed a 14in upper limit on gun size subject to Japanese and Italian agreement. By the time it became clear that this would not be forth-

The battleship HMS *Duke of York* prepares for her sea trials in the Firth of Forth, off Rosyth, 24 October 1941. *(IWM A6029)*

coming, Britain had already laid down the first two ships and so committed herself to the lower-calibre weapons. Their retention avoided any delays to construction, but at a cost of some loss of effectiveness and also in the need to manufacture, store and handle 14in rounds in addition to the already wide variety of shell sizes in service.

Prince of Wales sunk by Japanese aircraft, 10 December 1941.

Displacement: 35,000 tons.
Armament: 10 × 14in, 16 × 5.25in HA/LA
Maximum speed: 28.5 knots

NELSON CLASS
Nelson, Rodney (1927)
Originally intended to be a new class of battlecruisers displacing 48,000 tons, but such plans had to be cancelled when the Washington Naval Treaty limited new capital ships to 35,000 tons. As completed, these ships dismayed the traditionalists and were known to the fleet as 'Rodnol' after a fleet of tankers, but interference between 16in and 6in armament was minimised, while the use of nine 16in guns against eight 15in meant that the total weight of a broadside rose from 15,360lb to 18,432lb.

Displacement: 33,900 tons
Armament: 9 × 16in, 12 × 6in, 6 × 4.7in HA
Maximum speed: 23 knots

Vanguard
A one-off that did not enter service until after the end of the war, but marked a return to eight 15in guns as her main armament. At one stage, consideration was given to converting the ship to an aircraft carrier, but this was rejected on 15 July

The two sisters *Rodney* and *Nelson* were nicknamed 'Rodnol' after some inter-war tankers because of their unusual profile. *Nelson* looks even more unusual here, because of the effect of her camouflage. *(IWM A9280)*

1942. The final displacement of 51,420 tons marked an increase of almost 3,500 tons over the original design. Had she been completed as a carrier, no doubt she would have been available earlier, and would have been of some use during her uneventful service life.

BATTLECRUISERS

Hood (1920)

Intended to be modernised with extensive additional protection before war broke out, but this programme would have taken three years and was abandoned, despite an Admiralty Ship Department report that noted the poor protection over her magazines. She was lost during the battle with the German battleship *Bismarck* on 24 May 1941, supposedly hit by a shell from the heavy cruiser *Prinz Eugen*, blowing up and leaving just three survivors.

Displacement: 42,100 tons.
Armament: 8 × 15in, 12 × 5.5in, 8 × 4in HA.
Maximum speed: 31 knots.

Renown, Repulse (1916)

Renown, extensively modernised 1936–9, with eight boilers replacing the original forty-two and making this one of the fastest capital ships in the RN. *Repulse*, refitted 1918–21, and again 1933–6, with additional armour and protection.

Repulse sunk by Japanese aircraft, 10 December 1941.

Displacement: 32,000 tons
Armament: Renown 8 × 15in; 10 × 4.5in HA/LA; *Repulse* 12 × 15in and 8 × 4in HA
Maximum speed: 29 knots.

FLEET AIRCRAFT CARRIERS

Argus (1918)
Passenger liner for Italy, converted on slipway.

Displacement: 14,000 tons standard; 16,500 tons deep load.
Armament: 6 × single 4in; 4 × single 3pdr; 4 × single machine guns; 1943, 13 × single 20mm Oerlikon added.
Endurance: 5,200 miles at 12 knots.
Complement: 760.
Aircraft: originally 20, 15 in 1941.
Lifts: Originally 2, but aft lift removed in 1941.
Catapults: 1.
Became an accommodation ship, Chatham, August 1944.

Ark Royal (1938)

Displacement: 22,000 tons standard; 27,720 tons deep load.
Armament: 8 × twin 4.5in; 4 × octuple 2pdr pom-pom; 4 × single 3pdr; 8 × single.
Endurance: 11,200 miles at 10 knots.
Complement: 1,580.
Aircraft: originally 60, 54 in 1941.
Lifts: 3.
Catapults: 2.

Torpedoed 13 May 1941; sank 14 May 1941. One crew member lost.

COURAGEOUS CLASS
Courageous (1928), Glorious (1930)
Converted from battlecruisers.

Displacement: 22,500 tons standard; 27,560 tons deep load.
Armament: 16 × single 4.7in; 4 × single 3pdr; 10 × single 0.303in machine guns.
Endurance: 2,920 miles at 24 knots.
Complement: 1,260.
Aircraft: 48.
Lifts: 2.
Catapults: 2.

Courageous torpedoed on 17 September 1939 by *U-29* in SW Approaches, with loss of 518 lives. *Glorious* sunk by gunfire from German battlecruisers *Scharnhorst* and *Gneisenau*, 8 June 1940, withdrawing from Norway. Lost most of her crew.

Eagle (1924)
Converted from battleship *Almirante Cochrane* being built for Chile.

Displacement: 22,600 tons standard, 27,500 tons deep load.
Armament: 9 × single 6in; 5 × single 4in; 2 × octuple 2pdr (1937); 12 × single 20mm Oerlikon (1942); 4 × single 3pdr; 2 × twin 0.303in machine guns.
Endurance: 3,000 miles at 17 knots.
Complement: 988.
Aircraft: 22 in 1942.
Lifts: 2.
Catapults: none.

Ship evaluated concept of starboard island. Hit by four torpedoes from *U73*, 11 August 1942, while on Malta convoy, sank with loss of 160 lives.

Furious (1918)
Converted in stages from battlecruiser as first aircraft carrier.

Displacement: 22,450 tons standard: 27,165 tons deep load.
Armament: 6 × twin 4in; 4 × octuple 2pdr pompom; 4 × twin 20mm Oerlikon; 7 × single 20mm Oerlikon.
Endurance: 3,700 miles at 20 knots.
Complement: 1,218.
Aircraft: 33 in 1939.
Lifts: 2.
Catapults: none.

Hermes (1924)

Displacement: 10,850 tons standard: 13,700 tons deep load.
Armament: 6 × single 5.5in; 3 × single 4in; 2 × quad 0.5in.
Endurance: 2,930 miles at 18 knots.
Complement: 700.
Aircraft: 12 in 1939.
Lifts: 2.
Catapults: none.

Sunk on 9 April 1942 by Japanese aircraft off Ceylon.

ILLUSTRIOUS CLASS
Illustrious (1940), *Formidable* (1940), *Victorious* (1941).

Displacement: 23,207 tons standard: 28, 619 tons deep load.
Armament: 8 × twin 4.5in; 5 × octuple 2pdr pompom; 3 × single 40mm Bofors; 19 × twin 20mm Oerlikon; 14 × single 20mm Oerlikon.
Endurance: 11,000 miles at 12 knots.
Complement: 1,997.
Aircraft: 54.
Lifts: 2.
Catapults: 1.

Victorious extensively rebuilt between 1950 and 1958 to emerge as one of the world's most advanced carriers.

MODIFIED ILLUSTRIOUS CLASS
Indomitable (1941)
Design modified to incorporate a lower hangar. Upper hangar was fitted with rails to increase capacity to three squadrons of Seafires and reduce handling damage to the aircraft, but this had to be abandoned as the system proved cumbersome under intensive combat conditions.

Displacement: 24,680 tons standard; 29,730 tons deep load.
Armament: 8in plus 6 × octuple 2pdr pompom; 2 × quadruple 40mm Bofors; 2 × twin 40mm Bofors; 21 × twin 20mm Oerlikon; 18 × single 20mm Oerlikon.
Complement: 2,100.
Aircraft: 56.
Lifts: 2.
Catapults: 1.

IMPLACABLE CLASS
Implacable, *Indefatigable* (1944)
Modifications included upper and lower hangars, although forward lift only served upper hangar; four propeller shafts instead of three.

Displacement: 23,450 tons standard: 32,110 tons deep load.
Armament: 8 × twin 4.5in; 5 × octuple 2pdr pompom; 3 × quadruple 2pdr pom-pom; 21 × twin 20mm Oerlikon; 19 × single 20mm Oerlikon.
Endurance: 12,000 miles at 10 knots.
Complement: 2,300.
Aircraft: 81.
Lifts: 2.
Catapults: 1.

Unicorn (1943)
Originally intended as a maintenance and support carrier, but deployed operationally on occasion.

Displacement: 16,530 tons standard: 20,300 tons deep load.
Armament: 8 × 4in; 16 × 2pdr pom-pom; 13 × single 20mm Oerlikon.
Endurance: 11,000 miles at 12 knots.
Complement: 1,094.
Aircraft: 36.
Lifts: 2.
Catapults: 1.

LIGHT FLEET CARRIERS

COLOSSUS CLASS

Colossus (1944), *Glory* (1945), *Ocean* (1945), *Pioneer* (1945) (ferry carrier), *Venerable* (1945), *Vengeance* (1945).

Built to merchant standards to permit construction in yards not familiar with warship work. One hangar deck.

Displacement: 13,190 tons standard: 18,040 tons deep load.
Armament: 6 × quadruple 2pdr pom-poms; 11× twin 20mm Oerlikon; 10 × single 20mm Oerlikon.
Endurance: 8,300 miles at 20 knots.
Complement: 1,300.
Aircraft: 42.
Lifts: 2.
Catapults: 1.

*Colossu*s loaned to French navy as *Arromanches*, 6 August 1946, purchased by the French Navy in 1951. *Venerable* sold to Royal Netherlands Navy, 1 April 1948, becoming the new *Karel Doorman* on 28 May 1948. Sold to Argentina as *25 de Mayo*, 1 September 1969. *Vengeance* loaned to Royal Australian Navy on 13 May 1952, in reserve in RN 13 August 1955; sold to Brazilian Navy as *Minas Gerais*, 13 December 1956.

AUXILIARY OR ESCORT CARRIERS

These ships were known to the Admiralty, and at first to the United States Navy, as auxiliary aircraft carriers, but the USN later adopted the term 'escort carrier', and this has passed into popular use. In fact, these ships did very much more than simply act as escorts, becoming anti-submarine carriers,

Carriers often had to help refuel their escorts, especially on anti-submarine hunting groups. This is *Ameer* refuelling her plane-guard destroyer. *(Via C.S. 'Bill' Drake)*

aircraft transports and maintenance carriers, as well as providing flight decks for combat aircraft covering forces ashore. The only thing they did not do was operate in fleet actions because of their low speed.

Activity (1942)
Laid down as refrigerated cargo vessel *Telemachus* for Ocean Steamship, but converted on slipway.

Displacement: 11,800 tons standard; 14,529 tons deep load.
Armament: 1 × twin 4in, 6 × twin 2mm Oerlikon; 8 × single 20mm Oerlikon.
Maximum speed: 18 knots.
Complement: 700.
Aircraft: 10.

Short hangar 100ft long; single lift aft; arrester gear but no catapult.

AMEER OR RULER CLASS
Ameer (1943), *Arbiter* (1943), *Atheling* (1943), *Begum* (1943), *Emperor* (1943), *Empress* (1943), *Khedive* (1943), *Nabob** (1943), *Premier* (1943), *Patroller* (1943), *Puncher** (1944), *Queen* (1943), *Rajah* (1944), *Ranee* (1943), *Reaper* (1944), *Ruler* (1943), *Shah* (1943), *Slinger* (1943), *Smiter* (1944), *Speaker* (1943), *Thane* (1943), *Trumpeter* (1943), *Trouncer* (1944)

Sometimes referred to as the Ruler class. Similar in design to, but larger than, the Avenger class and US Bogue class, these were built as carriers rather than converted, although still using merchantman hulls.

Displacement: 11,400 tons standard; 15,400 tons deep load.

*Crewed by Royal Canadian Navy, but with RN Fleet Air Arm personnel.

Armament: varied according to role, but generally included: 2 × 5in; 8 × twin 40mm Bofors; 20 × 20mm Oerlikon.
Maximum speed: 18 knots.
Complement: 646.
Aircraft: 20.

Arrester gear aft and hangar with two lifts; single accelerator on port side forward, capable of handling heavier aircraft.

Archer (1941)
Laid down as a US merchant vessel, *Mormacland*, using a standard C3 hull, converted at Newport News with a wooden-planked flight deck and a small starboard-side island for navigation and air control, but no smokestack (exhaust fumes were discharged horizontally). Suffered considerable technical problems that delayed entry into service.

Displacement: 10,220 tons standard; 12,860 tons deep load.
Armament: 3 × 4in; 6 × 20mm twin Oerlikon; 7 × 20mm single Oerlikon.
Maximum speed: 16.5 knots.
Complement: 550, aircraft 12–15.

Quarter-length hangar with single lift aft, arrester gear aft and a single hydraulic accelerator.

ATTACKER CLASS
Attacker (1942), *Battler* (1942), *Chaser* (1943), *Fencer* (1943), *Hunter* (1943), *Pursuer* (1943), *Ravager* (1943), *Searcher* (1943), *Stalker* (1942), *Striker* (1943), *Tracker* (1943)
These ships were identical to the USN's Bogue class and transferred to the Royal Navy under lend-lease.

Displacement: 10,200 tons standard, 14,400 tons deep load.

Armament: 2 × 4in, 4 × twin 40mm Bofors, 4 × twin 20mm Oerlikon, 4 × 20mm Oerlikon.
Maximum speed: 18.5 knots.
Complement: 646.
Aircraft: 20.

Arrester wires aft; single hydraulic accelerator forward.

Audacity (1941)
Norddeutscher Line cargo vessel *Hannover*, converted after capture.

Displacement: 10,200 tons standard, 11,000 tons deep load.
Armament: 1 × 4in; 1 × 6pdr; 4 × 2pdr; 4 single 20mm Oerlikon.
Aircraft: 8 fighters.
Maximum speed: 15 knots.

Arrester gear aft but no hangar, lifts or catapults. Torpedoed by *U-751* off Portugal, 20 December 1941.

AVENGER CLASS
Avenger, *Biter*, *Dasher* (all 1942)

Displacement: 12,150 tons standard; 15,700 tons deep load.
Armament: 3 × 4in; 19 × single 20mm Oerlikon.
Maximum speed: 16.5 knots.
Complement: 555.
Aircraft: 15.
Machinery: Single diesel driving one shaft.

Arrester gear aft and hangar with single lift; flight decks were extended to 440ft on arrival in UK.

Avenger torpedoed by *U-155* off Gibraltar on 15 December 1942, exploded and sank. After the war, *Biter* transferred to French Navy as *Dixmude*. *Dasher* exploded as result of an aviation fuel explosion and sank in Firth of Clyde on 27 March 1943. Also *Charger*, Avenger class ship retained by USN for carrier deck landing training for RN pilots trained in the US under the 'Towers Scheme', and not transferred to UK.

Campania (1944)
Riveted construction similar to *Nairana* and *Vindex* (below) but slightly longer and wider. First British escort carrier to have an AIO (Action Information Organisation).

Displacement: 12,450 tons standard; 15,970 tons deep load.
Maximum speed: 16 knots.
Armament: 2 × 4in; 16 × 2pdr, 8 × twin 20mm Oerlikon.
Complement: 700.
Aircraft: 18.

Arrester gear aft but no catapults and just one lift.

NAIRANA CLASS
Nairana, *Vindex* (1943)
Used a refrigerated-cargo-ship hull design with riveted construction.

Displacement: 13, 825 tons standard; 16,980 tons deep load.
Armament: 2 × 4in; 16 × 2pdr.
Maximum speed: 16 knots.
Complement: 700.
Aircraft: 21.

Arrester gear aft but no catapults and just one lift. *Vindex* slightly smaller. *Nairana* transferred to the Royal Netherlands Navy on 23 March 1946 as the first *Karel Doorman*.

Pretoria Castle (1943)
Conversion of the armed merchant cruiser and formerly Union Castle passenger liner of the same name. Officially an escort

carrier – by far the largest auxiliary or escort carrier operated by the RN – she was used solely for trials and training.

Displacement: 19,650 tons standard; 23,450 tons deep load.
Armament: 4 × 4in; 16 × 2pdr; 20 × single 20mm Oerlikon.
Complement: 580.
Aircraft: 21.

Arrester gear aft, accelerator and hangar with one lift forward.

SEAPLANE CARRIER

Albatross
Transferred from the Royal Australian Navy in 1938.

Displacement: 4,800 tons standard; 6,000 tons deep load.
Armament: 4 × 4.7in; 4 × 2pdr.
Speed: 20 knots.

Complement: 450.
Aircraft: 9.
Catapults: 1.

By wartime, the ship was mainly used for training Walrus pilots for shipboard flights, but she provided fleet spotting for the landings at Madagascar. After being hit by a torpedo in August 1944, she was not repaired and was later converted into a merchantman.

HEAVY CRUISERS

KENT CLASS
Kent (54), **Suffolk** (55), **Berwick** (65), **Cumberland** (57), **Cornwall** (56), **Australia*** and **Canberra*** (all 1928)
(*Royal Australian Navy)
Limited to 10,000 tons by the Washington Naval Treaty, ordered in 1923–4. Modified during construction with a revolving catapult for aircraft. Distinctive three smokestack design. In 1935, improvements started

A heavy cruiser, HMS *Berwick*, in the North Sea, 1941. *(IWM 6169)*

The heavy cruiser HMS *Kent* at speed near Scapa Flow in 1941. *(IWM 6164)*

to be made to armour and the single 4in HA replaced by twin mountings and 2pdr 4 barrelled pom-poms added, the torpedo tubes removed and the catapult replaced by a fixed catapult with hangar and crane for two aircraft. Later, Oerlikons and radar also added.

Displacement: 10,000 tons.
Armament: 8 × 8in, 6 or 8 × 4in HA.
Maximum speed: 31.5 knots.

Canberra sunk off Solomon Islands, 9 August 1942; *Cornwall* sunk Indian Ocean, 5 April 1942.

LONDON CLASS
London (69), **Devonshire** (39), **Shropshire*** (83), **Sussex** (96) (all 1929)

* Later transferred to the Royal Australian Navy.

Four ships ordered 1925–6 as modified Kents, but *London* was refitted in 1938–9 with her three raked funnels replaced by two vertical. *Devonshire*, *Sussex* and *Shropshire* later had their armament altered. In 1942, *Shropshire* transferred to RAN, *Devonshire* and *Sussex* lost X turret so that additional AA and fire control equipment could be fitted.

Displacement: 9,850 tons.
Armament: 8 × 8in; 8 × 4in HA.
Maximum speed: 32 knots.

NORFOLK CLASS
Dorsetshire (40), **Norfolk** (78) (both 1930)
Meant to be similar to London class, but more modern 8in guns were fitted. From 1937 onwards, armament improved. X turret removed 1944.

Displacement: 9,950 tons.
Armament: 8 × 8in; 8 × 4in HA.
Maximum speed: 32 knots.

Dorsetshire sunk Indian Ocean, 5 April 1942.

YORK CLASS

Exeter (68), 1931; *York* (90), 1930
Intended to be 8,000 tons rather than the higher displacement of the earlier classes, but due to shorter length, same power required for same speed. Two smokestacks.

Displacement: 8,300 tons.
Armament: 6 × 8in; 4 × 4in HA; 2 × multiple pom-pom; 2 × triple torpedo tubes; revolving catapult for seaplane.
Maximum speed: 32 knots.

York lost off Crete 1941; *Exeter* sunk in Battle of Java Sea, 1 March 1942.

SOUTHAMPTON OR TOWN CLASS

The following ships would have been classed as light cruisers under the Washington Naval Treaty definitions, which stated that heavy cruisers had guns of 8in and light cruisers guns of 6in calibre, but have generally been regarded as 'heavy' cruisers due to their tonnage and large number of guns fitted.
Southampton (83), *Newcastle* (76), *Sheffield* (24), *Birmingham* (19), *Glasgow* (21), *Gloucester* (62), *Liverpool* (11), *Manchester* (15) (all 1937–9)

Displacement: 9,100–9,400 tons.
Armament: 12 × 6in, 18 × 4in HA.
Maximum speed: 32 knots.

Southampton abandoned after being heavily damaged, 11 January 1941.
Gloucester sunk on 22 May 1941 by air attack during German invasion of Crete.
Manchester sunk on 12 August 1942 during Operation Pedestal.

EDINBURGH OR IMPROVED SOUTHAMPTON CLASS

Edinburgh (16), *Belfast* (35) (both 1939)

Displacement: 10,000 tons.
Armament: 12 × 6in; 12 × 4in HA.
Maximum speed: 32.5 knots.

Edinburgh sunk on Arctic convoy duty.

FIJI CLASS

Bermuda (52), *Ceylon* (30), *Fiji* (58), *Kenya* (14), *Mauritius* (80), *Newfoundland* (59), *Nigeria* (60), *Trinidad* (46), *Gambia** (48), *Jamaica* (44), *Uganda* (66)†.
*Transferred to the Royal New Zealand Navy.
†Transferred to the Royal Canadian Navy.
Intended to follow on from the Southampton class, but with a lower displacement to keep within treaty commitments.

Displacement: 8,000 tons.
Armament: 12 × 6in, 8 × 4in HA.
Maximum speed: 31.5 knots.

Fiji sunk on 22 May 1941 during German invasion of Crete.
Trinidad sunk on Russian convoy duty.

LIGHT CRUISERS

LEANDER CLASS

Leander (75), *Achilles** (70), *Ajax* (22), *Neptune* (20), *Orion* (85) (all 1933–5)
Conceived as destroyer support/leader and anti-destroyer class with 1 heavy catapult and 2 seaplanes. These ships had a single funnel which gave them an odd appearance, and in 1937, the single 4in mountings were replaced by double mountings. Bofors/ Oerlikons ordered later. Ships sometimes mistaken for destroyers, which helps to explain the tactics of the *Graf Spee*'s CO when attacked.
*Transferred to the Royal New Zealand Navy.

Displacement: 7,154 tons.

Armament: 8 × 6in in 4 turrets; 4 × 4in HA; 4 × 0.5 mgs; 2 × quadruple torpedo tubes.

Maximum speed: 32 knots.

Neptune lost in Mediterranean on 18 December 1941.

In 1937, several ships had single 4in HA mountings replaced by twin mountings. Catapults and aircraft removed 1942 and replaced by radar. *Achilles* re-armed 1943–4 when X turret removed for additional AA weapons.

ARETHUSA CLASS

Arethusa (26), *Galatea* (71), *Penelope* (97), *Aurora* (12) (all 1935–7)

The RN wanted 50 cruisers by the end of 1936, but to keep within the London Naval Treaty of 1930, it meant that displacement of the new class had to be reduced towards 5,000 tons. Weight was saved by having three turrets rather than four, and by carrying just one aircraft with a single lightweight catapult.

Displacement: 5,220 tons.

Armament: 6 × 6in; 4 or 6 × 4in HA; 2 × 0.5in mg; 2 × triple torpedo tubes.

Maximum speed: 32 knots.

Galatea sunk by torpedo on 15 December 1941; *Penelope* torpedoed off Anzio on 18 December 1944.

MODIFIED LEANDER OR AMPHION CLASS

Amphion, *Apollo*, *Phaeton*, transferred to RAN as *Perth*, *Hobart* and *Sydney* respectively before outbreak of war.

Similar to Leander, but with twin funnels.

Displacement: 7,197 tons.

Armament: 8 × 6in; 4 × 4in HA.

Maximum speed: 32.5 knots.

E CLASS

Emerald (D66), *Enterprise* (D52) (both 1926)

Intended to be three vessels but only two were completed. Refitted between 1934 and 1936 with the addition of catapults and cranes for aircraft. Modified during war to improve working conditions on deck, and AA armament improved.

Displacement: 7,550 tons.

Armament: 7 × 6in; 3 × 4in HA.

Maximum speed: 32 knots.

RALEIGH CLASS

Effingham (D98), *Frobisher* (D81), *Hawkins* (D86) (1914–16)

Originally five vessels, but one converted into a seaplane carrier during First World War and another, *Raleigh*, ran aground in 1922. *Frobisher* converted into a cadet training ship in 1932 and in 1936 had all of her armament removed. Re-armed 1939–42 with 7 × 7.5in guns, but reconverted to the training role in 1944–5. *Hawkins* also reappeared as a 7.5in cruiser, but with the addition of four × 4in HA guns. *Effingham* became a 6in cruiser in 1936 as below.

Displacement: 9,500–9,850 tons.

Armament: 9 × 6in; 4 × 4in HA; 2 × 8 barrelled pom-pom, plus aircraft and catapult in place of one funnel, but lost when she struck a reef off Norway.

Maximum speed: 30.5 knots.

C CLASS

Coventry (D43), *Curlew* (D42), *Cairo* (D87), *Calcutta* (D82), *Carlisle* (D67), *Curacoa* (D41), *Colombo* (D89), *Caledon* (D53), *Capetown* (D88), *Cardiff* (D58), *Ceres* (D59), *Caradoc* (D60), *Calypso* (D61) (all 1917–19)

Built during First World War and originally intended to be scrapped under the London Naval Treaty of 1930, but retained. In 1935, it was decided to convert these ships to AA ships with HA guns only, with *Coventry* and *Curlew* first to be treated in this way. All 6in and 3in armament and torpedo tubes replaced by ten 4in HA guns in single mountings, with two 8 barrelled pom-poms in *Coventry* and two 4 barrelled pom-poms in *Curlew*. Removing the heavier calibre weapons meant that ballast had to be added to maintain stability.

Later conversions used an amended specification, with 8 × 4in HA and a single 4 barrelled pom-pom.

Curlew was sunk by aircraft off Norway on 26 May 1940. *Calypso* was torpedoed in the Mediterranean on 12 June 1940. *Calcutta* was sunk by aircraft north-west of Alexandria on 1 June 1941. *Cairo* was sunk on 12 August 1942 on Malta convoy (Operation Pedestal). *Coventry* was sunk by aircraft off Tobruk on 14 September 1942.

Displacement: 4,290 tons.
Original armament: 5 × 6in; 2 × 3in HA.
Maximum speed: 29 knots.

D CLASS

Danae (D44), *Dauntless* (D45), *Dragon* (D46), *Delhi* (D47), *Durban* (D99), *Dunedin* (D93), *Despatch* (D30), *Diomede* (D92) (all 1918–22) Intended to be a class of eleven ships, but only eight were built. At one time it was intended that these should follow the C class into conversion as AA cruisers, but this only proceeded piecemeal. In 1940, *Delhi* re-armed with American-built 5in HA guns in the US following favourable reports on these weapons.

Displacement: 4,900 tons.
Armament: 6 × 6in; 3 × 4in; 4 × triple torpedo tubes.
Maximum speed: 29 knots.

Dragon was loaned to the Free Polish Navy in 1942, but suffered severe damage in 1944 and was replaced by *Danae*, which had earlier been converted to an AA cruiser with the removal of a 6in turret and its replacement by two 4in HA/LA guns.
Dunedin sunk in the South Atlantic on 24 November 1941.
Durban used as block ship at Normandy, June 1944.

DIDO CLASS

Dido (61), *Euryalus* (42), *Naiad* (93), *Phoebe* (43), *Sirius* (82), *Bonaventure* (31), *Hermione* (74), *Cleopatra* (33), *Scylla* (98), *Charybdis* (88), *Argonaut* (61), *Spartan* (95), *Royalist* (89), *Bellona* (63), *Black Prince* (81), *Diadem* (84).

Originally intended as destroyer-leader evolved from the Arethusa class, and at 5,000 tons freeing up tonnage for the Belfast class. Armament was originally planned to consist of five twin 5.25in turrets able to be LA or HA, so that separate HA armament was not needed, but supply problems meant that some ships received destroyer 4.5in calibre guns instead.

Displacement: 5,450 tons.
Armament: Either 8 or 10 × 5.25in HA/LA or 8 × 4.5in HA/LA; 2 × 4-barrelled pom-pom; 2 × 0.5in machine guns; 2 × triple torpedo tubes; 6 × depth charges.
Maximum speed: 33 knots.

Naiad, Hermione, Bonaventure, Charybdis, torpedoed.
Spartan sunk by glider bomb off Anzio in January 1944.
Argonaut was struck by torpedoes at both bow and stern in late 1942, but survived and after temporary repairs was taken to the USA to be rebuilt, and remained out of action for 10 months.

ARMED MERCHANT CRUISERS

Armed merchant cruisers were liners and cruise ships taken up from trade and equipped with six, seven or eight elderly 6in guns and some anti-aircraft armament, in which state they were supposed to be the escort for the convoys that were to keep Britain's merchant fleet safe. Most retained their merchant-shipping names and often many of their crew as well, signed on as naval personnel under special articles. The concept had first been used during the late nineteenth century, but had been resurrected during the First World War, although in that conflict attacks on enemy shipping were much in mind. The rationale behind the concept was that such ships had the size to maintain a good speed in the open sea and the deck space and accommodation to take cruiser-calibre guns. The weakness in the argument

was that they lacked the armour to withstand heavy punishment from a German light cruiser, let alone anything heavier, and given the primitive weapons with hand-loading, they could not maintain an adequate rate of fire. The ships that survived the first year or two of convoy escort duties were generally converted into anti-aircraft cruisers, in which role they were much more successful. The exception was the *Pretoria Castle*, which was converted into an auxiliary aircraft carrier.

It is impossible to give the details of all of the armed merchant cruisers as these varied so much, but altogether fifty-six ships were requisitioned, and of these no less than fifteen were sunk, mainly during the first two years of war. Among the most notable of these were the ex-P&O liner *Rawalpindi*, sunk by the German battlecruisers *Gneisenau* and *Scharnhorst* off Iceland, and the *Jervis Bay*, sunk by the heavy cruiser *Admiral Scheer*.

The armed merchant cruiser *Pretoria Castle*, later converted into the Royal Navy's largest auxiliary or escort carrier. *(IWM 5189)*

The fast mine-layer HMS *Abdiel* at Colombo in Ceylon, now Sri Lanka, in February 1942. *(IWM A9688)*

But in both cases their sacrifice, which earned their commanding officers the Victoria Cross, reduced the toll among the merchantmen. The lesson that was learnt was that these ships were better used as auxiliary anti-aircraft cruisers.

MINELAYERS

Adventure (M23) (1927)

Displacement: 6,740 tons.
Armament: 4 × 4.7in HA; 340 mines.
Maximum speed: 28 knots.

ABDIEL CLASS
Abdiel (M39), *Latona* (M76), *Manxman* (M70), *Welshman* (M84), *Ariadne* (M65), *Apollo* (M01) (all 1940–3)
Six vessels were built of the Abdiel class, intended to be seaworthy and fast vessels able to lay as many mines as possible, with *Abdiel,*

Latona, Manxman in the 1938 programme and *Welshman* in 1939, with *Ariadne* and *Apollo* in the 1941 programme with modifications as a result of service experience.

Displacement: 2,640 tons.
Armament: First four ships, 2 × twin 4in; 3 × twin Bofors; 5 × twin Oerlikons.
Repeat Abdiel class had 6 × 4in HA/LA; single 4 barrelled 2pdr pom-pom; 2 × 0.5in machine guns. All ships 150 mines.
Maximum speed: 9.75 knots.

Abdiel sunk by mine entering Taranto on 10 September 1943.
Latona sunk by bomb on 25 October 1941.
Welshman sunk by torpedo in Mediterranean on 1 February 1943.
Manxman survived being torpedoed on 1 December 1942, because blast blew machinery across the engine room causing her to heel away from the damage.

DESTROYERS

V AND W CLASSES

Vimiera (L29), *Vanity* (L38), *Vanessa* (D29), *Vanoc* (H33), *Versatile* (D32), *Vimy* (D33), *Velox* (D34), *Vivacious* (D36), *Vortigen* (D37), *Vidette* (D48), *Valentine* (L69), *Vega* (L41), *Venetia* (D53), *Vanquisher* (D54), *Vesper* (D55), *Violent*, *Verity* (D63), *Vansittart* (D64), *Volunteer* (D71), *Veteran* (D72), *Vivien* (L23), *Venomous* (D75), *Valorious* (L00), *Viceroy* (L21), *Viscount* (D92), *Verdun* (L93) (1917–24)

Wallace, *Wryneck* (D21), *Warwick* (D25), *Watchman* (D26), *Walker* (D27), *Whirlwind* (D30), *Wrestler** (D35), *Wakeful* (H88), *Walpole* (D41), *Windsor* (D42), *Wessex* (D43), *Westminster* (L40), *Winchelsea* (D46), *Westcott* (D47), *Winchester* (L55), *Wolfhound* (L56), *Wild Swan* (D62), *Wivern* (D66), *Wishhart* (D67), *Wanderer* (D74), *Witherington* (D76), *Whitshed* (D77), *Wolverine* (D78), *Wren*, *Witch* (D89), *Whitehall* (D94), *Woolston* (L49), *Worcester*, *Whitley* (L23), *Wolsey* (L02) (1917–24)

*Transferred to Royal Australian Navy.

Displacement: 1,090–1,120 tons.
Armament: 4 × 4in; 6 × torpedo tubes.
Maximum speed: 34/35 knots.

SHAKESPEARE CLASS

HMS **B**roke (D83), HMS *Keppel* (D84), HMS *Wallace* (L64) (all 1914–18)
Built as leaders for the V and W classes, most ships of this class were decommissioned between the wars.

Displacement: 1,554 tons.
Armament: 4 × 4in; 1 × 4 barrel 2pdr; 2 × 20mm; 8 × 0.5in(*Wallace*); 5 × 4.7in; 1 × 3in (*Broke* and *Bruce*); all had 6 torpedo tubes.
Maximum speed: 34/35 knots.

S CLASS

Sabre (H18), *Scimitar* (H21), *Sardonyx* (H26), *Sturdy* (H28), *Stronghold* (H50), *Scout* (H51), *Saladin* (all 1917–24)

Displacement: 905 tons.
Armament: 3 × 4in; 3 × torpedo tubes.
Maximum speed: 34.5–36 knots.

Between the wars, two private designs entered service, both ordered in 1925. *Amazon*, 1,350 tons, built by Thorneycroft, and *Ambuscade*, 1,170 tons, built by Yarrow. Both had 4 × 4.7in guns, 2 × single 2pdr and two sets of triple torpedo tubes.

A CLASS

Codrington (leader) (D65), *Acasta* (H09), *Achates* (H12), *Acheron* (H45), *Active* (H14), *Antelope* (H36), *Anthony* (H40), *Ardent* (H41), *Arrow* (H42) (all 1930)
Ordered in 1927, the class consisted of a destroyer leader, *Codrington*, and eight standard vessels.

Displacement: *Codrington* 1,738 tons, others 1,330 tons.
Armament: 4 × 4.7in; 2 × 2pdr pom-pom; 4 × Lewis guns; 2 × quadruple torpedo tubes.

B CLASS

Keith (leader) (D06), *Basilisk* (H11), *Beagle* (H30), *Blanche* (H47), *Boadicea* (H65), *Boreas* (H77), *Brazen* (H80), *Brilliant* (H84), *Bulldog* (H91) (all 1931)
This was a 1928 repeat order of the A class ships, but fitted with Asdic. The leader, *Keith*, was the same size as the standard ships, causing one gun to be removed to accommodate the captain's staff.

C AND D CLASSES

Kempenfelt (I18) (i) was transferred to the Royal Canadian Navy in 1939, following four

The destroyer HMS *Echo* leads her sister HMS *Eclipse* at speed out of an Icelandic anchorage in March 1942. *(IWM A8089)*

other ships transferred pre-war. All built 1931.

Duncan (D99), *Defender* (H07), *Diamond* (H22), *Daring* (H16), *Decoy* (H75), *Dainty* (H53), *Delight* (H38), *Diana* (H49), *Duchess* (H64) (1932)

Again developments of the A class for the 1929 and 1930 programmes, but slightly longer for greater endurance and speed, with a 3in HA gun in place of the 2pdr. Leaders were *Kempenfelt* and *Duncan*.

E AND F CLASSES

Exmouth (leader (H02), *Echo* (H23), *Eclipse* (H08), *Escapade* (H17), *Escort* (H65), *Esk* (H15), *Express* (H61), *Electra* (H27), *Encounter* (H10) (all 1934)
Faulknor (leader) (H62), *Fearless* (H67), *Foresight* (H68), *Foxhound* (H69), *Fortune* (H70), *Forester* (H74), *Fury* (H76), *Fame* (H78), *Firedrake* (1935)

G, H AND I CLASSES

Grenville (leader) (H03), *Gallant* (H59), *Grenade* (H86), *Garland* (H37), *Gipsy* (H63), *Glowworm* (H92), *Grafton* (H89), *Greyhound* (H05), *Griffin* (H31) (1936)

HERO CLASS

Hardy (leader) (H87) (i), *Harvester* (H19), *Hasty* (H24), *Havant* (H32), *Havoc* (H43), *Hereward* (H93), *Hero* (H99), *Hostile* (H55), *Hotspur* (H01), *Hunter* (H35), *Hyperion* (H97) (1937)

HAVANT CLASS

Similar to H Class above, building for Brazil and taken over by the Royal Navy after the outbreak of war.

The destroyer flotilla leader HMS *Kelly* passing a message to HMS *Kelvin*, another K class destroyer. *(IWM A4081)*

Havant (H32), *Harvester* (H19), *Havelock* (H88), *Hesperus* (H57), *Highlander* (H44), *Hurricane* (H06).

INTREPID CLASS
Inglefield (leader) (D02), *Icarus* (D03), *Ilex* (D61), *Imogen* (D44), *Imperial* (D09), *Impulsive* (D11), *Inconstant* (H49), *Intrepid* (D10), *Isis* (D87), *Ivanhoe* (H05) (1938)

Displacement: leader 1,530 tons, other ships 1,370 tons.
Armament: 8 × 4.7in; 10 × torpedo tubes.
Maximum speed: 36.5 knots.

TRIBAL CLASS
Afridi (F07), *Cossack* (F51), *Eskimo* (F75), *Mashona* (F59), *Gurkha* (F20), *Maori* (F24), *Mohawk* (F31), *Nubian* (F36), *Sikh* (F82), *Zulu* (F18), *Matabele* (F26), *Punjabi* (F21), *Ashanti* (F51), *Bedouin* (F67), *Somali* (F33), *Tartar* (F43) (all 1938/1939)
Two leaders and standard vessels marking significant improvement in armament.

Displacement: 1,870 tons.
Armament: 8 × 4.7in; 4 × torpedo tubes.
Maximum speed: 36.5 knots.

J OR JAVELIN AND K OR KELLY CLASSES
Jervis (F00), *Jackal* (F22), *Javelin* (F61), *Jaguar* (F34), *Juno* (F46), *Janus* (F53), *Jersey* (F72), *Jupiter* (F85), *Kelly*, *Kandahar* (F28), *Kelvin* (F37), *Khartoum* (F45), *Kashmir* (F12), *Kimberley* (F50), *Kingston* (F64), *Kipling* (F91) (all 1939)

Displacement: leaders 1,695 tons, others 1,690 tons.
Armament: 6 × 4.7in; 10 × torpedo tubes.
Maximum speed: 36 knots.

L OR LAFOREY AND M OR MILNE CLASSES
Laforey (G99), *Lance* (G87), *Lively* (G40), *Legion* (G74), *Lightning* (G55), *Lookout* (G32), *Loyal* (G15), *Mahratta* (G23), *Milne* (G14), *Musketeer* (G86), *Myrmidon* (G90), *Matchless* (G52), *Meteor* (G74), *Marne* (G35), *Martin* (G44) (1941/1942)

Displacement: leaders 1,935 tons; other ships 1,920 tons.
Armament: 6 × 4.7in; 8 × torpedo tubes.
Maximum speed: 36 knots.

N CLASS
Nerissa (G65), *Nizam*, *Noble* (G84), *Nonpareil* (G16), *Napier*, *Nester*, *Norman*, *Norseman* (1942)
Similar to above.

HUNT CLASS
Type I: *Atherstone* (L05), *Fernie* (L11), *Berkeley* (L17), *Hambledon* (L37), *Garth* (L20), *Cattistock* (L35), *Cottesmore* (L78), *Holderness* (L48), *Eglinton* (L87), *Cleveland* (L46), *Quorn* (L66), *Mendip* (L60), *Tynedale* (L96), *Pytchley* (L92), *Exmoor* (L61) (i), *Southdown* (L25), *Cotswold* (L54), *Meynell* (L82), *Quantock* (L58), *Whaddon* (L45), *Brocklesby* (L42) (all 1940–41)
Type II: *Avondale* (L06), *Eridge* (L68), *Liddesdale* (L100), *Blankney* (L30), *Farndale* (L70), *Silverton* (L115), *Oakley* (L72) (i), *Heythrop* (L85), *Croome* (L62), *Puckeridge* (L108), *Lamerton* (L88), *Badsworth* (L03), *Dulverton* (L63), *Hurworth* (L28), *Southwold* (L10), *Chiddingfold* (L31), *Exmoor* (ex-*Burton*) (L08) (ii), *Wheatland* (L122), *Beaufort* (L14), *Tetcott* (L99), *Calpe* (L71), *Lauderdale* (L95), *Middleton* (L74), *Grove* (L77), *Ledbury* (L90), *Wilton* (L128), *Hursley*

(L84), *Blackmore* (L43), *Oakley* (ex-*Tickhan*) (L98) (ii), *Bedale* (L26), *Bramham* (L51), *Bicester* (L34), *Zetland* (L59), *Cowdray* (L52) (1941–2)
Type III: *Airedale* (L07), *Aldenham* (L22), *Albrighton* (L12), *Belvoir* (L32), *Bleasdale* (L50), *Derwent* (L83), *Catterick* (L81), *Bolebroke* (L65), *Eskdale*, *Border* (L67), *Hatherleigh* (L53), *Blean* (L50), *Penyland* (L89), *Tanatside* (L69), *Holcombe* (L56), *Melbreak* (L73), *Limbourne* (L57), *Haydon* (L75), *Wensleydale* (L86), *Rockwood* (L39), *Goathland* (L27), *Modbury* (L91), *Easton* (L09), *Haldon* (L19), *Eggesford* (L15), *Stevenstone* (L16), *Talybont* (L18) (1942–3)
Type IV: *Brecon* (L76), *Brissenden* (L79) (1942 and 1943)
This was the final pre-war design.

Displacement: 1,000–1,430 tons.
Armament: 4 or 6 × 4in HA/LA in twin turrets; 1 × 2pdr 4 barrelled pom-pom; 2 × Lewis guns; 50 × depth charges with one rail and two throwers. Type III and IV had torpedo tubes instead of a turret.

WAR EMERGENCY DESTROYERS

The need to increase the number of ships dramatically led to emergency measures, while experience gained at some cost in the Norwegian and French campaigns led to an increase in armament, with strong emphasis on HA. These ships had the lower weight 50pdr 4.7in gun as the 62pdr was still under development. The Q-C classes had substantially increased endurance of 3,850 miles with 20 knots seen as patrol speed rather than the 15 knots of the earlier ships. The ships were built as emergency flotillas. As older ships were either withdrawn or lost in action, names were recycled, which must have taken some of the pressure off the ship naming committee members! The 5th emergency flotilla and later had the Tribal class bow, while the 4th emergency flotilla onward had officer accommodation forward with crew accommodation forward and aft depending on armaments. The final emergency flotillas, the 12th and 13th, did not enter service until after the war ended.

1st Emergency Flotilla: **Oribi** (G66), **Offa** (G29), **Onslow** (G17), **Onslaught** (G04), **Opportune** (G80), **Obdurate** (G39), **Orwell** (G98), **Obedient** (G48) (1941–2)

2nd Emergency Flotilla: **Panther** (G41), **Paladin** (G69), **Pakenham** (G06), **Penn** (G77), **Partridge** (G30), **Pathfinder** (G10), **Petard** (G56), **Porcupine** (G93) (1941–2)

3rd Emergency Flotilla: **Quentin** (G78), **Quiberon***(G81), **Quality***(G62), **Quickmatch*** (G92), **Quilliam** (G09), **Quadrant*** (G11), **Queenborough***(G30), **Quail** (G45) (1943)

*Transferred to the Royal Australian Navy.

4th Emergency Flotilla: **Rotherham** (H09), **Redoubt** (H41), **Racehorse** (H11), **Raider** (H15), **Relentless** (H85), **Rapid** (H32), **Roebuck** (H95), **Rocket** (H92) (1942–3)

5th Emergency Flotilla: **Scorpion** (G72), **Savage** (G20), **Saumarez** (G12), **Scourge** (G01), **Success** (G26), **Swift** (G46), **Serapis** (G94), **Shark** (G03) (1943)

6th Emergency Flotilla: **Troubridge** (R00), **Tuscan** (R56), **Tumult** (R11), **Tyrian** (R67), **Teazer** (R23), **Termagant** (R89), **Tenacious** (R45), **Terpsichore** (R33) (1943–4)

7th Emergency Flotilla: **Grenville** (R97), **Ulster** (R83), **Urchin**, **Ulysses** (R69), **Undine** (R42), **Urania** (R05), **Ursa** (R22), **Undaunted** (R53) (ii) (1943–4)

8th Emergency Flotilla: **Hardy** (R08) (ii), **Venus** (R50), **Vigilant** (R93), **Virago** (R75), **Verulam** (R28), **Valentine** (R17) (ii), **Vixen** (R64), **Volage** (R41) (1943–4)

9th Emergency Flotilla: **Kempenfelt** (R03) (ii), **Wakeful** (R59) (ii), **Wizard** (R72), **Wager** (R98), **Whelp** (R37), Wessex (R78) (ii), **Wrangler** (R48), **Whirlwind** (R87) (1943–4)

10th Emergency Flotilla: **Myngs** (R06), **Zambesi** (R66), **Zest** (R02), **Zephyr** (R19), **Zealous** (R39), **Zebra** (R81), **Zodiac** (R54), **Zenith** (R95) (1944)

11th Emergency Flotilla: **Caprice** (R01), **Cambrian** (R85), **Cassandra** (R62), **Caesar** (R07), **Carron** (R30), **Cavalier** (R73), **Cavendish** (R15), **Carysfort** (R25) (1944)

Displacement: 1,570/2,175 tons.

Armament: 5 × single HA 4.7in; 1 × quadruple torpedo tubes; up to 70 depth charges with two rails and four throwers. Later vessels included some with 4in guns and minelaying equipment, or 4 × 4.7in; 1 × 4 barrelled pom-pom; 2 × 0.5in machine gun; 2 × quadruple torpedo tubes.

BATTLE CLASS

1st Destroyer Flotilla: **Barfleur** (R80), **Camperdown** (R32), **Trafalgar** (R77), **Hogue** (R74), **Finisterre** (R55), **Lagos** (R44), **St Kitts** (R18), **Gabbard** (R47) (1944–6)

Following on from the War Emergency ships, the Battle class evolved, ordered in 1942. Only *Armada* (R14) of the 2nd Flotilla was completed before the war ended. Originally, stabilisers were intended to be fitted, but feedback from earlier experience was that these induced a 'jerky' motion and increased sea-sickness while the space could be used for extra fuel. Range at 20 knots was 4,400 nautical miles.

Displacement: 2,332–3,153 tons.

Armament: 2 × twin 4.5in HA/LA; 4 × twin Bofors; 4 × 20mm single Oerlikon; 1 × 4in star shell gun.

Maximum speed: 32 knots.

TOWN CLASS

Annapolis*, **Bath** (I17), **Belmont** (H46), **Beverley** (H64), **Bradford** (H72), **Brighton****

(I08), *Broadwater* (H81), *Broadway* (H90), *Burnham* (H82), *Burwell* (H94), *Buxton** (H96), *Caldwell* (I20), *Cameron* (I05), *Campbeltown* (I42), *Castleton* (I23), *Charlestown* (I21), *Chelsea*** (I35), *Chesterfield* (I28), *Churchill*** (I45), *Clare* (I14), *Georgetown*** (I40), *Hamilton* (I24), *Lancaster* (G05), *Leamington** (G19), *Leeds* (G27), *Lewis* (G68), *Lincoln*** (G42), *Ludlow* (G57), *Mansfield*†* (G76), *Montgomery* (G95), *Newark* (G08), *Newmarket* (G47), *Newport†* (G54), *Ramsay* (G60), *Reading* (G71), *Richmond*** (G88), *Ripley* (G79), *Rockingham* (G58), *Roxburgh*** (I07), *St Albans*** (I15), *St Clare**, *St Croix**, *St Francis*, *St Mary's* (I12), *Salisbury** (I52), *Sherwood* (I80), *Stanley* (I73), *Wells* (I95).

*RCN for all or part of the period on lease.

**Later transferred to the Soviet Navy.

†Norwegian Navy for all or part of the time on lease.

These were fifty ex-US destroyers, provided from the United States Navy in exchange for the right to use British naval bases in the Caribbean. All of First World War vintage, they were modified after delivery to meet the Royal Navy's specifications, with armament modified with ballasting to enhance sea-keeping, as

The Town class destroyers were First World War veterans provided by the United States Navy in return for the use of British bases in the Caribbean, and easily recognisable by their four smokestacks. This is HMS *Brighton*. *(IWM A9221)*

well as deeper bilge keels. Ten ships were manned by the Royal Canadian Navy and another two by the Free Norwegian Navy. The ships were known as the A, B, C and D-Type Town classes, or sometimes otherwise known as the Burnham, Montgomery, Newport or Leeds classes respectively.

Displacement: 1,190–1,725 tons.

Armament: 4 × 4in LA guns; 1 × 3in LA; 12 × 18in torpedo tubes in triple mountings; 8 × depth charges; 2 × 0.5in machine guns. Many ships had 1 × 4in LA gun; 1 × 12pdr HA/LA; 3 × 20mm Oerlikon; 2 × 0.5in Browning machine gun: 2 × Lewis guns; 1 × set of triple torpedo tubes; 1 × hedgehog thrower with 60 depth charges.

In 1944, nine were loaned to the Soviet Navy. Several of these ships were lost on war service, with the most famous being that of *Campbeltown*, sacrificed on the famous St Nazaire raid.

SUBMARINES

Submarines were assigned to flotillas, the size of which could vary and were under local command, although overall there was an Admiral (Submarines), A(S), whose role included overall supervision of training and the specification of new craft. The most famous flotilla was the 10th based in Malta and which proved right the Admiralty's contention pre-war that Malta could be a base for offensive operations. Unlike the German Navy, the Royal Navy did not have tanker (milch cow) or supply submarines, but such was considered in February 1942 by A(S), who feared that the existing S and T classes would not be adequate for the war in the Far East. He would have also been aware of the importance of the submarines in keeping Malta supplied, and wished to have a vessel that could carry 600 tons of fuel and 36 torpedoes on an external canister. An acute shortage of design personnel meant that there were delays in

The submarine HMS *Satyr* at Greenock on 20 January 1943. (*IWM A14072*)

designing such a craft, then the existing submarine construction programme could not be interrupted, and while conversion of an existing craft was seen as a means of by-passing these problems, but once again the disruption to existing programmes meant that the project had to be abandoned in July 1943.

The London Naval Conferences of 1930 and 1936 had limited submarines to 2,000 tons standard displacement and gun armament to a maximum 5.1in calibre weapon, while each power could retain or build three vessels of 2,800 tons carrying a 6.1in gun, although the United Kingdom never made use of this allowance. Under wartime pressures, AA armament with Oerlikon guns was introduced on all except the U class, while stern firing tubes were also added in 1940 and 1941 to the S and T classes, with both having a stern tube and the T having two aft-facing tubes amidships. Air conditioning was gradually introduced because the dehumidifiers in the T and S classes were inadequate for tropical operations. These became increasingly important as the Royal Navy moved back into the Far East. Freon air conditioning allowed patrols of up to 45 days, sometimes longer.

At the end of the First World War, the Grand Fleet was retitled as the Atlantic Fleet. Planners wanted a distant patrol submarine with a surface displacement of 1,200 tons, and a maximum speed on the surface of 15 knots, a cruising speed of 12 knots, and endurance of 10,000 miles, with habitability suitable for the tropics. In the end, the result was the Oberon class.

H CLASS

H31, H4 (all 1918–20)
Based on First World War designs, these were reputedly among 'the most popular boats in the service' according to a 1939 publication.

Displacement, surface/submerged: 400/500 tons.
Armament: Four torpedo tubes.
Maximum speed: surface 13 knots, submerged, 10 knots.

OBERON CLASS

Oberon (N21), *Otway* (N51), *Oxley* (55 P) (all 1927–9)

Displacement, surface/submerged: 1,311/ 1,831 tons.
Armament: 6 × bow tubes, 2 × stern; 1 × 4in gun; 2 × Lewis guns.
Range of 11,400 miles at 8 knots, with a maximum submerged speed of 9 knots for two hours.

ODIN CLASS

Odin (N84), *Otus* (N92), *Oswald* (N58), *Osiris* (N67), *Olympus* (N35), *Orpheus* (N46). Overseas Patrol Type submarines, but larger than the Oberon class.

Displacement, surface/submerged: 1,781/ 2, 038 tons.
Range: 11,400 miles at 8 knots, with a surface speed of 17.5 knots and diving depth of 500 feet.

PARTHIAN CLASS

Parthian (N75), *Proteus* (N29), *Perseus* (N36), *Pandora* (N42), *Phoenix* (N96). Similar to the Odin class.

Displacement, surface/submerged: 1,760/ 2,040 tons.
Range: 10,750 miles, at 8.5 knots.

RAINBOW CLASS

Rainbow (N16), *Regent* (N41), *Regulus* (N88), *Rover* (N62).
Again similar to the Odin class, but with increased use of welding.

Seen from the depot ship HMS *Forth*, and over the conning towers of the submarines *Sturgeon* (left) and *Tigris* (right), is HMS *Graph*, the former *U-570*, captured by the Royal Navy. The location is Holy Loch, a submarine base on the Firth of Clyde, with good access to the Atlantic. *(IWM A9873)*

The small size of the U class submarines is clearly shown here. HMS *Unshaken* is leaving the harbour at Algiers on patrol, February 1943. *(IWM A14985)*

The minelaying submarine HMS *Rorqual* arriving at Malta, with Valletta in the background. She is clearly on her way to the base at Manoel Island. *(IWM A14680)*

Displacement, surface/submerged: 1,763/ 2,030 tons.

Range: 10,900 miles at 8 knots, with a maximum surface speed of 18 knots.

S OR SWORDFISH CLASS

Swordfish (N61), *Sturgeon* (N73), *Seahorse* (96 S), *Starfish* (19 S) (all 1933–4)
Salmon (N65), *Shark* (N54), *Sealion* (N72), *Snapper* (N39), *Seawolf* (N47), *Sunfish* (N81), *Spearfish* (N69), *Sterlet* (N22) (all improved Swordfish class, 1934–6)

Attention turned to operations in narrow waters with the S class first ordered in 1929.

Displacement: surface/submerged: 760 tons/ 935 tons.

Armament: 3in HA gun; 2 × machine guns; 6 × torpedo tubes with 12 torpedoes.

Range: 4,700 miles at 14 knots, submerged speed 10 knots.

PORPOISE CLASS

Cachalot (N83), *Grampus* (N56), *Narwhal* (N45), *Porpoise* (N14), *Rorqual* (N74), *Seal* (37M) (all 1933–7)

Designed as minelayers after trials at HMS *Vernon* showed that mines remained efficient for a month if exposed to alternate wetting and drying as the submarine dived and surfaced. One problem with mine-laying submarines was the time taken to flood the mine-casing, so that diving took longer, but with a special Q-tank fitted, diving time went from 92 to 74 seconds, about the same as for the Odin class. These submarines also proved their worth as cargo carriers on the 'Magic Carpet' runs to besieged Malta.

Displacement, surface/submerged: 1,520– 2,157 tons.

Armament: 1 × 4in; 8 × torpedo tubes; up to 50 mines.

Maximum speed: 16 knots (surfaced), 8.75 knots (submerged).

THAMES CLASS

Clyde (N12), *Severn* (N57), *Thames* (N71) (all 1932–5)

A larger and faster ocean patrol class, being the first British submarines capable of more than 20 knots and intended to be able to keep pace with a battle fleet.

Displacement: surface/submerged: 1,800–2,700 tons.
Armament: 1 × 4in; 6 × torpedo tubes.
Maximum speed: 22.5 knots (surfaced), 10 knots (submerged).

T CLASS

Taku (N38), *Talisman* (N78), *Tarpon* (N17), *Tetrarch* (N77), *Thistle* (N24), *Thunderbolt* (ex-*Thetis*) (N25), *Tigris* (N63), *Torbay* (N79), *Triad* (N53), *Tribune* (N76), *Trident* (N52), *Triton* (N15), *Triumph* (N18), *Truant* (N68), *Tuna* (N94), *Tempest* (N86), *Thorn* (N11), *Thrasher* (N37), *Traveller* (N48), *Trooper* (N91), *Trusty* (N45), *Turbulent* (N98), *Tabard* (P342), *Taciturn* (P334), *Tactician* (P314), *Talent* (P333) (i), *Talent* (P337) (iii), *Tally-Ho* (P317), *Tantalus* (P318), *Tantivy* (P319), *Tapir* (P325), *Tarn* (P336), *Taurus* (P339), *Telemachus* (P3221), *Templar* (P316), *Teredo* (P338), *Terrapin* (P323), *Thermopylae* (P355), *Thorough* (P324), *Thule* (P325), *Tiptoe* (P332), *Tireless* (P327), *Token* (P328), *Totem* (P352), *Tradewind* (P329), *Trenchant* (P331), *Trespasser* (P312), *Truculent* (P315), *Trump* (P333), *Truncheon* (P353), *Tudor* (P326), *Turpin* (P354), *P311* (all 1938 onwards)

The first eight of this class were operational on the outbreak of war, but another eleven were under construction. *Thetis* had sunk in Liverpool Bay on 1 June 1939, but was later refloated and reconditioned before being recommissioned as *Thunderbolt*. The type was intended to replace the P and R classes in the Far East. Three boats, *Tetrarch*, *Talisman* and *Torbay*, were modified to carry six mines, but this was not successful and they were re-converted. The increased used of welded construction and better steel allowed the second batch to provide improved diving depth of 350 feet, although

the first craft achieved 400 feet safely on trials.

Displacement, surface/submerged: 1,300/1,595 tons.
Armament: 1 × 4in; 2 × Lewis guns; 8 × torpedo tubes.
Maximum speed: 15.75 knots (surfaced), 9 knots (submerged).
Endurance: 4,500 miles at 11 knots (surfaced), 55 hrs at 2.5 knots (submerged).

Many of the surviving submarines were rebuilt post-war.

UNITY CLASS

Undine (N48), *Unity* (N66), *Ursula* (N59), *Umpire* (N82), *Una* (N87), *Unbeaten* (N93), *Undaunted* (N55) (ii), *Union* (N56), *Unique* (N95), *Upholder* (N99), *Upright* (N89), *Urchin* (N97), *Urge* (N17), *Usk* (N65), *Utmost* (N19), *P32, P33, P36, P38, P39, P41, P47, P48, P52, Ultimatum* (P34), *Ultor* (P53), *Umbra* (P35), *Unbending* (P37), *Unbroken* (P42), *Unison* (P43), *United* (P44), *Universal* (P57), *Unrivalled* (P45), *Unruffled* (P46), *Unruly* (P49), *Unseen* (P51), *Unshaken* (P54), *Unsparing* (P55), *Unswerving* (P63), *Untamed* (P58), *Untiring* (P59), *Uproar* (ex-*Ullswater*) (P31), *Upstart* (P65), *Usurper* (P56), *Uther* (P62), *Vandal* (P64), *Varangian* (P61), *Varne* (P81), *Vox*, *Upshot* (P93), *Urtica* (P83), *Vagabond* (P18), *Vampire* (P72), *Variance*, *Varne*, *Veldt*, *Vengeful* (P86), *Venturer* (P68), *Vigorous* (P74), *Viking* (P69), *Vineyard*, *Virtue* (P75), *Virulent* (P95), *Visigoth* (P76), *Vivid* (P77), *Volatile* (P96), *Voracious* (P78), *Vortex*, *Votary* (P29), *Vox* (P73), *Vulpine* (P79) (all 1938 onwards.)

Undine, *Unity* and *Ursula* were ordered in 1936 and completed in late 1938 as training submarines. Nevertheless, experience in the Mediterranean soon showed that there was a need for smaller submarines as larger boats proved to be vulnerable in the clear and relatively shallow waters. Diving depth was 200ft. Later vessels had the two bow external tubes omitted in favour of a 3in gun, later changed to a 12pdr, although the modification also improved sea-keeping. The later V class boats had superior welded pressure hulls.

Displacement, surface/submerged: 600/700 tons.

Armament: 6 × torpedo tubes or 4 × torpedo tubes and either 1 × 3in or 1 × 12pdr gun.

Maximum speed: 12.5 knots (surfaced), 8 knots (submerged).

NEW S OR SAFARI CLASS

P222, *Safari* (P211), *Saga* (P257), *Sahib* (P212), *Sanguine* (P266), *Saracen* (P247), *Satyr* (P214), *Sceptre* (P215), *Scorcher* (P258), *Scotsman* (P243), *Scythian* (P237), *Sea Devil* (P244), *Sea Dog* (P216), *Sea Nymph* (P223), *Sea Rover* (P218), *Sea Scout* (P253), *Selene* (P254), *Seneschal* (P255), *Sentinel* (P256), *Seraph* (P219) *Shakespeare* (P221), *Shalimar* (P242), *Sibyl* (P217), *Sickle* (P224), *Sidon* (P259), *Simoom* (P225), *Sirdar* (P226), *Sleuth* (P261), *Solent* (P262), *Spark* (P236), *Spearhead* (P263), *Spirit* (P245), *Spiteful* (P227), *Splendid* (P228), *Sportsman* (P229), *Sprightly*, *Springer* (P265), *Spur* (P266), *Statesman* (P246), *Stoic* (P231), *Stonehenge* (P232), *Storm* (P233), *Stratagem* (P234), *Strongbow* (P235), *Stubborn* (P238), *Sturdy* (P248) (ii), *Stygian* (P249), *Subtle* (P251), *Supreme* (P252), *Surf* (P239), *Syrtis* (P241) (all 1942 onwards)

In January 1940, Admiral (Submarines) decided that additional submarines were required for operations in the North Sea, for which the U class was considered too small and the T class too big. Essentially the new submarines were to be an updated S class with improvements incorporated in the light of experience, including increased

diving depth and measures taken to reduce noise. The first vessel of this class was *Safari*, which was test-dived to 350ft. Later versions had increased fuel provision created by using part of the ballast tanks, with operations in the Far East in mind, for which Freon air conditioning units were also specified. As with the T class, from 1940 onwards, the internal torpedo tubes could be used to lay mines, with eight mines carried in place of four re-load torpedoes.

Displacement, surface/submerged: 805/995 tons.

Armament: 1 × 3in or 4in; 6 × torpedo tubes.

Endurance: 3,800 miles, or at 3 knots.

HMS *GRAPH* (P715)

The former German U-boat *U-570*, captured by a British escort vessel south of Iceland in August 1941, gave the Royal Navy access to the German Enigma codes. The capture was kept secret and the U-boat was commissioned into the Royal Navy as HMS *Graph*.

A CLASS

In June 1941, the PM demanded a new class of submarine that could be built quickly and cheaply, but with long range and high surface speed, although initially it would be used close to home to resist invasion and enforce a blockade of German ports. This was the A class, intended to have a maximum speed of 17 knots, but also to be able to cruise at 15 knots so as to be able to overtake surface vessels. As completed, these were 1,360/1,590-ton vessels capable of 19 knots or 12,200 miles at 10 knots, which could be increased to 15,200 miles with an additional 48 tons of fuel stored in no. 4 main tank. Engine supply problems meant that four of the class were limited to 18 knots using a six-cylinder engine rather than the standard eight-cylinder version.

The initial order was for 46 vessels, 21 from Vickers Armstrongs at Barrow-in-Furness, 6 each from Cammell Laird and Vickers Armstrongs, High Walker, 5 from Scotts S & E Co., and 2 each from Portsmouth, Devonport and Chatham dockyards. Later, a further 20 were planned, but never ordered, while 30 of the original vessels were cancelled. The first to be completed, *Amphion*, was delivered from Barrow on 27 March 1945. Trials showed that 18.5 knots could be achieved on the surface, 8 knots submerged, and diving time was much improved. Diving depth was 500ft, but on trials 600ft was achieved. Nevertheless, despite the brilliance of the design, the A class boats were completed too late for service in the Second World War.

MIDGET SUBMARINES

X-craft, XE-craft, from 1943 onwards.

The Royal Navy came late to the concept of midget submarines or X-craft, on which the pioneering work, as with human torpedoes, was largely conducted in Italy. After experiments with the one-man Welman, which was effectively a cross between a human torpedo and a submarine, the Royal Navy developed the 35-ton X-craft, which was deployed against the German battleship *Tirpitz* with considerable success. There were two types, the original X series and the developed XE series for operations in the Far East against Japan. Both types had a four-man crew, one of whom had to be a diver, and carried two large explosive charges which had to be laid under the target, while the diver could also add limpet mines to the target's hull. The midget submarines had to be taken fairly close to the target by a mother ship, ideally a larger submarine, but in the case of the attack on Japanese shipping at Singapore, the XE craft managed a trip of forty miles each way.

ESCORTS

Experience during the First World War had shown that the Flower class sloops, originally designed for minesweeping, were invaluable on many other tasks, expecially escort duties, once the Admiralty introduced a convoy system. After the First World War, no new sloops were constructed until 1927, when two were ordered, *Bridgewater* and *Sandwich*, incorporating improvements, and small numbers of sloops were also ordered in the years that followed. *Bridgewater* displaced 1,045 tons, and continued the tradition of being equipped for minesweeping. In the Second World War, Captain F.J. 'Johnnie' Walker's 2nd Support Group was to account for no less than twenty-three U-boats, led by his own ship, *Starling*.

In 1931, renewed interest in sloops saw the decision to build two new classes: the Halcyon class, a simple and cheap sloop–minesweeper, and the Grimsby class, an improved sloop, still with minesweeping capability but also suitable for tropical service. The Halcyon class totalled eighteen ships, although three were completed as survey ships that could be easily reconverted for minesweeping duties. The larger Grimsby class totalled just eight vessels, and also had a longer endurance than the Halcyon class. Under wartime conditions, both classes had their minesweeping gear removed and then were used exclusively as escorts, while minesweeping needs were met by a combination of new construction and converted fishing vessels.

An indication of what the future held for the sloop came as early as 1933, when plans were laid for a new sloop to be known as the ocean convoy, without minesweeping gear but with increased armament and anti-submarine abilities. The first was laid down as *Bittern*, but renamed *Enchantress* before launch, and was used as an Admiralty yacht. This was a larger vessel than any before, at 1,520 tons, with almost 19 knots maximum speed and a useful endurance of 6,400 miles. At the same time, a coastal convoy sloop was also designed primarily for anti-submarine warfare, and the first of these was *Kingfisher*. By contrast with the larger sloop, this displaced 742 tons, although speed was 20 knots and range was 4,050 miles. Six vessels of the Kingfisher class were built between 1934 and 1936, with three of the improved Guillemot class. During the Second World War, these were reclassified as corvettes. An improved ocean convoy design was the *Egret* class of three ships, of 1,768 tons displacement and endurance of 6,200 miles. This class included improvements tried in some of the later ocean convoy type, with the 4 × 4.7in guns replaced by 4 × twin 4in HA and also improved short-range armament.

An improvement over the Egret class was the Black Swan class, first ordered in 1937, with 1,960 tons deep displacement, capable of 19.25 knots and with a range of 6,100 miles. These continued the pattern for HA armament, but 3 × twin 4in, while minesweeping and anti-submarine warfare gear was also fitted. Four ships of this class were built before war broke out, although the last two were without minesweeping gear. In 1940–2, additional vessels were ordered with a wider beam to allow for improved armament and better stability, known as the Modified Black Swan class. As the war progressed, these ships changed from being riveted to having as much as 30 per cent of the structure welded, while stabilisers were fitted to both the Black Swan and Modified Black Swan classes.

SLOOPS AND SLOOP/MINESWEEPERS

BRIDGEWATER CLASS (later vessels also known as **HASTINGS AND SHOREHAM CLASSES**)
Bridgewater (L01/U01), *Sandwich* (L12/U12), *Hastings* (L27/U27), *Folkestone* (L22/U22), *Scarborough* (L25/U25), *Penzance* (L28/U28), *Shoreham* (L32/U32), *Bideford* (L43/U43), *Fowey* (L15/U15), *Rochester* (L50/U50), *Falmouth* (L34/U34), *Milford* (L51/U51), *Weston* (L72/U72), *Dundee* (L84/U84) (all 1928–33)

Displacement: 1,025 tons–1,105 tons (leaders).
Armament: 2 × 4in HA or 1 × 4in HA and 1 × 4in LA.
Maximum speed: 16.5 knots.

HALCYON CLASS
Halcyon (J42), *Skipjack* (J38), *Harrier* (J71), *Hussar* (J82), *Speedwell* (J87), *Niger* (J73) (i), *Scott* (J79, *Salamander* (J86), *Hebe* (J24), *Hazard* (J02), *Sharpshooter* (J68), *Gleaner** (J83), *Gossamer** (J63), *Sphinx* (J69), *Jason** (J99), *Leda* (J93), *Seagull* (J85), *Bramble* (J11) (i), *Britomart* (J22), *Speedy* (J17) (1933–7)
*Used as survey ships.
Ordered in 1931. Although classified as sloops, many of these ships took over the minesweeping role late in the war.

Displacement: 800 tons.
Armament: 1 × 4in LA; 1 × 3in HA.
Maximum speed: 16.5 knots.
Endurance: 4,200 miles at 15 knots.

GRIMSBY CLASS
Grimsby (L16/U16), *Leith* (L36/U36), *Lowestoft* (L59/U59), *Wellington* (L65/U65), *Deptford* (L53/U53), *Londonderry* (L76/U76), *Aberdeen* (L97/U97), *Fleetwood* (L47/U47) (all 1933–6)

Displacement: 990 tons.
Armament: 2 × 4.7in LA; 1 3in HA.
Maximum speed: 16.5 knots.

Originally classified as a sloop, HMS *Guillemot* was reclassified as a corvette later in the war. *(IWM A21008)*

BITTERN CLASS
Bittern (L07/U07), *Enchantress* (originally named *Bittern*) (L56/U56), *Stork* (L81/U81), *Pelican*. 1937–8.
Enchantress became Admiralty yacht.

Displacement: 1,520 tons.
Armament: 4 × 4.7in HA/LA.
Maximum speed: 18.5 knots.
Endurance: 6,400 miles.

EGRET CLASS
Egret (L75/U75), *Auckland* (L61/U61), *Pelican* (L86/U86) (all 1937)

Displacement: 1,768 tons.
Armament: 4 × twin 4in HA plus short-range weapons.

KINGFISHER CLASS
Kingfisher (L70/K70), *Mallard* (L42/K42), *Puffin* (L52/K52), *Kittiwake* (L30/K30), *Sheldrake* (L06/K06), *Widgeon* (L62/K62),

Guillemot (L89/K89), *Shearwater* (L39/U39), *Pintail* (L21/U21) (all 1936–7, with last three ships essentially improved versions of Kingfisher class)

Displacement: 742 tons.
Armament: 1 4in HA.
Maximum speed: 20 knots, range 4,050 miles.

BLACK SWAN CLASS
Black Swan (L57/U57), *Flamingo* (L18/U18), *Erne* (U03), *Ibis* (U99) (all 1939)
These were among the first warships to be fitted with stabilisers.

Displacement: 1,960 tons.
Armament: 3 × twin 4in.
Maximum speed: 19.25 knots.
Endurance: 6,100 miles.

MODIFIED BLACK SWAN CLASS
Cygnet (U38), *Woodpecker* (U08), *Whimbrel* (U29), *Wren* (U28) (ii), *Kite* (U87), *Wild*

Goose (U45), *Chanticleer* (U05), *Starling* (U66), *Crane* (U23), *Pheasant* (U49), *Woodcock* (U90), *Redpole* (U69), *Magpie* (U82), *Amethyst* (U16), *Hart* (U58), *Lapwing* (U62), *Lark* (U11), *Hind* (U39), *Peacock* (U96), *Mermaid* (U30), *Alacrity* (U60), *Opossum* (U33) (all 1940–5, plus five completed post-war)

These incorporated many Black Swan class features, including stabilisers, and as the ships of the class were delivered, they showed increasing use of welded construction.

Displacement: 1,881 tons.

Armament: 3 × twin 4in HA/LA; 2 × twin Bofors; 2 × twin Oerlikons, later replaced by 2 × single Bofors; 100 × depth charges, 4 × throwers, 2 × rails; some had a split hedgehog mounting.

EX-UNITED STATES COAST GUARD CUTTERS

Tahoe class: *Lulworth, Hartland, Fishguard, Sennen, Culver.*

Saranac class: *Gorleston, Walney, Banff, Landguard, Totland.*

Ten ex-USCG cutters were also provided under lend-lease, five of the Tahoe class and five of Saranac class. These owed much to merchant ship practice in design and construction.

Displacement: 2,116 tons, Tahoe; 2,117 tons, Saranac.

Armament: 1 × 4in HA/LA; 2 × 2pdr pom-pom; 1 × Bofors; 7 × Oerlikons, hedgehog with 100 depth charges and 4 throwers.

Maximum speed: 16 knots.

Endurance: 8,000 miles at 8 knots.

CORVETTES AND FRIGATES

It was decided that the trawlers that conducted so much anti-submarine work during the First World War were no longer suitable, and something faster was needed. Four classes were finally selected:

Flower Class Corvettes, based on a whaler design and originally termed 'patrol vessels, whaler type').

River Class Frigates, originally described as twin-screw corvettes (until February 1943).

Castle Class Corvettes, later classed as frigates.

Loch Class Frigates.

FLOWER CLASS CORVETTES

Gladiolus (K34), *Gardenia* (K99), *Geranium* (K16), *Godetia* (K72)(i), *Primrose* (K91), *Bluebell* (K80), *Clematis* (K36), *Anemone* (K48), *Coreopsis* (K32), *Primula* (K14), *Campanula* (K18), *Asphodel* (K56), *Heliotrope** (K03), *Honeysuckle* (K27), *Salvia* (K97), *Cyclamen* (K83), *Arbutus* (K86), *Candytuft** (K09), *Crocus* (K49), *Jonquil* (K68), *Snapdragon* (K10), *Columbine* (K94), *Delphinium* (K77), *Tulip* (K29), *Hollyhock* (K64), *Marguerite* (K54), *Verbena* (K85), *Aubretia* (K96), *Hydrangea* (K39), *Larkspur** (K82), *Daniella* (K07), *Petunia* (K79), *Snowdrop* (K67), *Azalea* (K25), *Sunflower* (K41), *Veronica** (K37), *Carnation* (K00), *Nigella* (K19), *Convolvulus* (K45), *Marigold* (K87), *Begonia** (K66), *Auricula* (K12), *Wallflower* (K44), *Dianthus* (K95), *Dahlia* (K59), *Zinnia* (K98), *Polyanthus* (K47), *Celandine* (K75), *Mignonette* (K38), *Mimosa* (K11), *Lavender* (K60), *Jasmine* (K23), *Myositis* (K65), *Lobelia* (K05), *Narcissus* (K74), *Penstemon* (K61), *Arabis** (K73), *Periwinkle** (K55), *Clarkia** (K88), *Calendula** (K28), *Hibiscus** (K24), *Camellia** (K31), *Mallow* (K81), *Peony* (K40), *Erica* (K50), *Gloxinia* (K22), *Picotee* (K63), *Gentian* (K90), *Hyacinth* (K84), *Rhododendron* (K78), *Heather* (K69), *Freesia* (K43), *Orchis* (K76), *Kingcup* (K33), *Pimpernel* (K71), *Violet* (K35), *Amaranthus* (K17), *Spiraea* (K08), *Burdock* (K126), *Woodruff* (K53), *Starwort* (K20), *Clover*

The Flower class corvette HMS *Bluebell* at Tyne Dock in June 1942. No doubt to the relief of all concerned, there never was an HMS *Pansy*. (*IWM A28377*)

(K134), **Alyssum** (K100), **Samphire** (K128), **Campion** (K108), **Aconite** (K58), **Ranunculus** (K117), **Stonecrop** (K142), **Vetch** (K132), **Coriander** (K183), **Sundew** (K57), **Coltsfoot** (K140), **Acanthus** (K01), **Rose** (K102), **Rockrose** (K51), **Loosestrife** (K105), **Bellwort** (K114), **Oxlip** (K123), **Saxifrage** (K04), **Pennywort** (K111), **Borage** (K120), **Lotus** (K93)(i), **Pink** (K137), **Meadowsweet** (K144), **Abelia** (K184), **Alisma** (K185), **Anchusa** (K186), **Armeria** (K187), **Aster** (K188), **Bergamot** (K189), **Vervain** (K190), **Monkshood** (K207), **Cowslip** (K196), **Eglantine** (K197), **Sweetbriar** (K209), **Montbretia** (K192), **Thyme** (K210), **Fritillary** (K199), **Snowflake** (originally **Zenobia**) (K211), **Genista** (K200), **Tamarisk** (K216), **Chrysanthemum** (K195), **Potentilla** (K214), **Hyderabad** (originally **Nettle**) (K212), **Lotus** (K130)(ii), **Godetia** (K226)(ii), **Buttercup** (K193), **Poppy** (K208), **Bryony**, **Balsam** (K72), **Heartsease*** (K15), **Nasturtium** (K107) (plus ex-French vessels acquired after the fall of France and while under construction, including **La Maloine** (K46), while a number of ships were transferred to the Royal Canadian Navy or the free navies).

* Transferred to the United States Navy.

Flower class corvettes were 30ft longer than the whaler design on which they were based, giving better sea-keeping, higher speed and better watertight provision. While diesel propulsion would have given a better endurance, a shortage of diesel engines meant that triple expansion steam engines were used. HMS *Gladiolus* was ready for trials in April 1940, and was the first of 145 ships built in the UK, with another 23 built in Canada for the Admiralty and 70 for the RCN itself.

Iceland was one of the departure points for convoys to the Soviet Union. Here is the Free French corvette *Aconit*, one of the Flower class, leaving the Havalfjord in January 1942. *(IWM A7310)*

Displacement: 1,170 tons.
Armament: 1 × 4in gun; 1 × 2pdr; 1 × Lewis gun; 40 × depth charges with 2 rails and 2 throwers.
Maximum speed: 16.5 knots.
Endurance: 4,000 miles at 12 knots.

RIVER CLASS FRIGATES
Adur* (K269), **Rother** (K224), **Spey** (K246), **Swale** (K217), **Tay** (K232), **Exe** (K92), **Waveney** (K248), **Test** (K239), **Wear** (K230), **Jed** (K235), **Lagan** (K259), **Kale** (K241), **Ness** (K219), **Itchen** (K227), **Moyola** (K260), **Teviot** (K222), **Nith** (K215), **Cuckmere** (K299), **Trent** (K243), **Tweed** (K250), **Mourne** (K261), **Bann** (K256), **Dart** (K21), **Derg** (K257), **Ribble** (K525), **Ettrick** (K254), **Strule** (originally **Glenarm**) (K258), **Ballinderry** (K255), **Chelmer** (K221), **Deveron** (K265), **Nene** (K270), **Plym** (K271), **Towey** (K294), **Helford** (K252), **Fal** (K266), **Tavy** (K272), **Usk** (K295) (ii), **Aire** (K262), **Tees** (K293), **Helmsdale** (K253), **Windrush** (K370), **Meon** (K269), **Braid** (K263), **Cam** (K264), **Wye** (K371), **Dovey** (K523), **Torridge** (K292), **Odzani** (K356), **Avon** (K97), **Taff** (K637), **Nadder** (K392), **Lochy** (K365), **Monnow** (K441), **Teme** (K458), **Awe** (K526), **Halladale** (K471), **Annan** (K404).
*Transferred immediately to the United States Navy and did not enter service.

River class frigates were first mooted in late 1940 when it was realised that something larger would be better suited for the Atlantic convoys – and a higher speed of 22 knots was also considered desirable. The River class were built to merchant ship practice, and like the Flower class used triple expansion steam engines, although with two rather than the single engine of the Flowers. Minesweeping gear was usually fitted.

Displacement: 1, 855 tons deep load.
Armament: 2 × 4in HA/LA guns; 2 × 2pdr singles or 2 × twin Oerlikons; 2 × 20mm Oerlikons on bridge wings; 100 × depth charges, 8 × throwers, 2 rails of 15 depth charges each.
Maximum speed: about 19.5 knots, with 5,000 miles range at 15 knots.

CASTLE CLASS CORVETTES

Hadleigh Castle (K355), *Kenilworth Castle* (K420), *Bramborough Castle* (K412), *Allington Castle* (K689), *Pembroke Castle* (K496), *Lancaster Castle* (K691), *Norham Castle* (K497), *Caistor Castle* (K690), *Oakham Castle* (K530), *Denbigh Castle* (K696), *Farnham Castle* (K413), *Hedingham Castle* (originally *Gorey Castle*) (K491) (i), *Portchester Castle* (K362), *Carisbrooke Castle* (K379), *Berkeley Castle* (K387), *Flint Castle* (K383), *Leeds Castle* (K384), *Rushden Castle* (K372), *Dumbarton Castle* (K388), *Oxford Castle* (K392), Guildford Castle (K389), *Knaresborough Castle* (K389), *Tintagel Castle* (K399), *Tunsberg Castle* (originally *Shrewsbury Castle*), *Hedingham Castle* (originally *Changeville Castle*) (K529) (ii), *Sandgate Castle* (K488), *Hurst Castle* (K416), *Pevensey Castle* (K449), *Wolesey Castle* (K499), *Launceston Castle* (K387), *Rising Castle* (K494), *Tamworth Castle* (K490), *Morpeth Castle* (K693), *Sherbourne Castle* (K498), *Hever Castle* (K495), *Walmer Castle* (K492), *Nunney Castle* (K493); *Alnwick Castle* (K405), *Amberley Castle* (K386).

Nevertheless, the Flowers had impressed, and in 1942 it was decided to build a larger version better suited for ocean convoys and with more space for anti-submarine equipment than on the River class. The increase in length from 205ft to 252ft also meant that they would be more comfortable in a seaway.

Displacement: 1,580 tons.
Armament: 1 × 4in, 2 × twin Oerlikon amidships; 2 × single Oerlikon on bridge wings; 1 × Squid anti-submarine weapon forward with 81 projectiles; 125 × depth charges, 1 rail, 2 throwers.
Maximum speed: about 16.5 knots, with 6,200 miles range at 15 knots.

LOCH CLASS FRIGATES

Loch Fada (K390), *Loch Eck* (K422), *Loch Killin* (K391), *Loch Ruthven* (K645), *Loch Shin* (K421), *Loch Insh* (K433), *Loch Craggie* (K609), *Loch Fyne* (K429), *Loch Lomond* (K437), *Loch Gorm* (K620), *Loch Scavaig* (K648), *Loch Katrine* (K625), *Loch Quoich* (K434), *Loch Achray* (K426), *Loch Tarbert* (K431), *Loch Glendhu* (K619), *Loch More* (K639), *Loch Tralaig* (K655), *Loch Killisport* (K628), *Loch Arkraig** (K603), *Loch Veyatie** (K658).
* Completed post-war.

Loch class frigates were designed to be built using prefabricated construction.

Displacement: 2,260 tons.
Armament: 1 × 4in, 1 × 2pdr; 2 × twin and 2 × single Oerlikons; 2 × Squid mtgs with 150 projectiles; 15 × depth charges and 1 dc rail.
Maximum speed: about 18.5 knots and 7,000 miles range.

CAPTAIN CLASS FRIGATES

These were lend-lease ships of the USN's Evarts and Buckley class destroyer escorts. Their armament differed from their USN sisters.

The Loch class frigate *Loch Killisport*. (IWM A30288)

Affleck (K362), *Aylmer* (K463), *Balfour* (K464), *Bayntun* (K310), *Bazely* (K311), *Bentinck* (K314), *Bentley* (K465), *Berry* (K312), *Bickerton* (K466), *Blackwood* (K313), *Bligh* (K467), *Braithwaite* (K468), *Bullen* (K469), *Burges* (K347), *Byard* (K315), *Byron* (K508), *Calder* (K349), *Capel* (K470), *Conn* (K509), *Cooke* (K471), *Cosby* (K559), *Cotton* (K510), *Cranstoun* (K511), *Cubitt* (K512), *Curzon* (K513), *Dacres* (K472), *Dakins* (K550), *Deane* (K551), *Dolmett* (K473), *Drury** (K316), *Duckworth* (K351), *Duff* (K352), *Ekins* (K552), *Essington* (K353), *Fitzroy* (ii) (K553), *Foley* (K474), *Gardiner* (K478), *Garlies* (K475), *Goodall* (K479), *Goodson* (K480), *Gore* (K481), *Gould* (K476), *Grindall* (K477), *Halstead* (K556), *Hargood* (K582), *Holmes* (K581), *Hoste* (K566), *Hotham* (K583), *Inglis* (K570), *Inman* (K571), *Keats* (K482), *Kempthorne* (K483), *Kingsmill* (K484), *Lawford* (K514), *Lawson* (K516), *Loring* (K565), *Louis* (K515), *Manners* (K568), *Moorsom* (K567), *Mounsey* (K569), *Narborough* (K578), *Pasley* (K564), *Redmill* (K554), *Retalick* (K555), *Riou* (K557), *Rowley* (K560), *Rupert* (K561), *Rutherford* (K558), *Seymour* (K563), *Spragge* (K572), *Stayner* (K573), *Stockham* (K562), *Thornborough* (K574), *Torrington* (K577), *Trollope* (K575), *Tyler* (K576), *Waldegrave* (K579), *Whitaker* (K580).

*Returned to the United States Navy and re-named USS *Drury*.

Displacement: 1,140 tons.
Armament: 3 × 3in HA/LA guns; 9 × 20mm guns; 4 × depth charge projectors, 2 depth charge rails, 1 hedgehog.
Maximum speed: 21 knots.

BAY CLASS FRIGATES

Widemouth Bay (K615), *Veryan Bay* (K651), *St Austell Bay* (K634), *St Brides Bay* (K600), *Cardigan Bay* (K630), *Bigbury Bay* (K606), *Whitesand Bay* (K633) (plus a further 18 built post-war)

The Bay Class was a development of the Loch with extensive AA armament for the war against Japan.

Most details were similar to those for the Loch class, but armament included: 2 × 4in HA/LA; 2 × 40mm twin power-worked Bofors; 4 × 40mm single Bofors or 20mm single Oerlikon; 1 × 24 depth charge Hedgehog projector, 2 depth charge rails, 4 depth charge throwers.

FLEET MINESWEEPERS

ALGERINE CLASS

Algerine (J213), *Alarm* (J140), *Albacore* (J101), *Acute* (J106), *Cadmus* (J230), *Circe* (J214), *Espiegle* (J216), *Fantome* (J224), *Felicity* (J369), *Mutine* (J227), *Onyx* (J221), *Loyalty* (J317), *Ready* (J223), *Rinaldo* (J225), *Rosario* (J219), *Spanker* (J226), *Vestal* (J215), *Cockatrice* (J229), *Rattlesnake* (J297), *Waterwitch* (J304), *Fly* (J306), *Hound* (J307), *Hydra* (J275), *Orestes* (J277), *Aries* (J284), *Brave* (J305), *Antares* (J282), *Clinton* (J286), *Friendship* (J398), *Gozo* (J287), *Pelorus* (J291), *Pickle* (J293), *Lightfoot* (J288), *Acturus* (J283), *Pincher* (J294), *Persian* (J347), *Fancy* (J308), *Larne* (J274), *Melita* (J289), *Postillion* (J296), *Plucky* (J295), *Recruit* (J298), *Lennox* (J276), *Rifleman* (J299), *Octavia* (J290), *Truelove* (J303), *Welfare* (J356), *Mary Rose* (J360), *Skipjack* (J300), *Providence* (J325), *Regulus* (J327), *Thisbe* (J302), *Seabear* (J333), *Moon* (J329) (ii), *Coquette* (J350), *Felicity* (J369), *Golden Fleece* (J376), *Courier* (J349), *Serene* (J354), *Prompt* (J378), *Flying Fish* (J370), *Lysander* (J379), *Lioness* (J377), *Mariner* (J380), *Marmion* (J381) (ii), *Storm Cloud* (J369), *Sylvia* (J382), *Tanganyika* (J383), *Squirrel* (J301), *Rowena* (J384), *Chameleon* (J387), *Cheerful* (J388), *Hare* (J389), *Wave* (J385), *Jewel* (J390), *Liberty* (J391), *Welcome* (J386), *Jaseur* (J428), *Maenad* (J335), *Laertes* (J433) (ii), *Mameluke* (J437), *Mandate* (J438), *Marvel* (J443), *Romola* (J449), *Magicienne* (J436), *Michael* (J444), *Minstrel* (J445), *Bramble* (J273) (ii), *Myrmidon* (J454), *Rosamund* (J439), *Mystic* (J455), *Orcadia* (J462), *Nerissa* (J456), *Niger* (J442) (iii), *Ossary* (J463), *Pluto* (J446), *Polaris* (J447), *Pyrrhus* (J448), *Fierce* (J453) (1942–5)

This class had better deep sea capabilities, and with the ability to double up as escort vessels should the need arise. Again displacement and range varied according to the machinery fitted: The initial order was for ships with twin turbine machinery, but later orders were for ships with slow and then fast reciprocating engines, the latter being particularly successful.

Displacement: 1,122 tons turbine; 1,162 tons reciprocating.
Armament: 1 4in; 4 × 20mm Oerlikon; 2 × Lewis gun; 80 × depth charges, 4 × throwers, 2 rails.
Range: 6,000 miles.

ABERDARE CLASS

Aberdare (J49), *Abingdon* (J23), *Albury* (J41), *Alresford* (J06), *Bagshot* (J57), *Derby* (J90), *Dundalk* (J60), *Dunoon* (J52), *Elgin* (J39), *Fareham* (J89), *Fermoy* (J40), *Fitzroy* (J03) (i), *Forres*, *Harrow* (J61), *Huntley* (J56), *Kellett* (J05), *Lydd* (J44), *Pangbourne* (J37), *Ross* (J45), *Saltash* (J62), *Saltburn* (J58), *Selkirk* (J18), *Stoke* (J33), *Sutton* (J78), *Tedworth* (J32), *Tiverton*, *Widnes* (J55) (1917–19)

Classified as sloop minesweepers until 1937.

Displacement: 700 tons.
Armament: 1 × 4in.
Maximum speed: 16 knots.

One of the small fast vessels used to move vital war materials from Sweden. *(MH23863)*

BANGOR CLASS

No less than 128 ships of this class were built for the Royal Navy, plus another twelve for the Royal Canadian Navy and nine for the Royal Indian Navy, all during 1940–3.

These ships were built with a mixture of turbine or diesel machinery, with some having reciprocating machinery; displacement varied according to machinery type.

Displacement: 578 tons, diesel; 687 tons, turbine; 725 tons reciprocating.
Armament: Initially 1 × 4in HA; 1 × 2pdr pom-pom, 2 × 0.5in machine gun or Oerlikons; initially just 4 × depth charges were provided, but later increased to 40 depth charges with double chutes and 2 throwers.
Maximum speed: 16.5 knots, but endurance varied between 4,000 miles for steam and 5,900 miles for diesel.

The fleet minesweepers were complemented by motor minesweepers which were responsible for the coastal minesweeping around Britain, just 105 feet in length. No less than 278 were built in the UK and many parts of the Empire, which resulted in many falling into enemy hands when the Japanese took Hong Kong and Singapore. The urgency with which these vessels were built meant that unseasoned timber had to be used, while the quality was further affected by the use of unskilled labour during construction. The unseasoned timber created problems as it seasoned and adjusted its shape! Larger wooden minesweepers, the 126ft motor minesweeper, followed and eighty-five were built, proving very satisfactory even in open water. In addition, under the US lend-lease programme about 150 130ft minesweepers were also provided, sometimes described as a cross between a trawler and a large motor launch.

Minesweeping and anti-submarine work was also helped by the use of many converted fishing vessels, while even some paddle steamer ferries were pressed into service.

MONITORS

Roberts, Abercrombie

Monitors emerged during the First World War expressly designed to bombard enemy-held Belgian ports, and none were built between the wars. An elderly monitor, *Marshal Soult*, was considered for refit, but it was decided instead to build a new ship, *Roberts*, but to use the 15in guns from the older vessel, after these had been extensively reconditioned. Black Swan class machinery was also used to cut costs and speed development. The performance was largely dictated by that of the elderly First World War-vintage *Erebus*, but as it became clear that *Erebus* was difficult to handle in a rough sea, modifications were made, including the fitting of twin rudders. *Roberts* completed in October 1941. *Abercrombie* was the second and last monitor built during the war years, completing in May 1943. She was generally similar to the design of *Roberts*.

Displacement: 8,123 tons.
Armament: 2 × 15in; 8 × 4in; number of multi-barrelled 2pdr pom-poms.
Maximum speed: 12.5 knots.

Erebus, Terror (1916)

Displacement: 7,200 tons.
Armament: 2 × 15in; 8 × 4in HA.
Maximum speed: 12 knots.

SMALL CRAFT

Even a blue-water navy such as the Royal Navy has a shoreline to protect, and during the First World War the Navy received 600 motor launches from the USA for anti-submarine duties. These were based on an American design of leisure craft and, at just 80ft in length, soon proved inadequate for work in the open seas around the coastline of the United Kingdom. Between the two world wars, the Admiralty received many unsolicited proposals for small, fast marine craft from boatbuilders, doubtless anxious to free themselves from the famine of orders during the years of recession, but the Admiralty was also short of funds and no orders were placed. It was not until 1938 that Swan Hunter produced an experimental fast launch, *Tarret*, of 110ft length with an all-welded steel hull with two lightweight Paxman diesel engines of an entirely new design. Displacement was just 80 tons, and while speed was intended to be 30 knots, only 23.5 knots could be achieved on trials in 1940. Although eventually taken over by the Admiralty, *Tarret* was soon scrapped and never saw operational service.

Far more successful was the Fairmile series of motor launches, already under construction on the outbreak of war in Europe. Fairmile had created a shadow production organisation using small boatyards, which assembled the boats from waterproof bonded plywood prefabricated in London. At first, no armament was specified, but the initial craft known as the Type A, 110ft in length and powered by three 600 bhp engines, entered service armed with a 3pdr gun aft, two Lewis guns and twelve depth charges; equipped with Asdic, it had a crew of two officers, two petty officers and twelve junior ratings. Trials gave a speed of 25 knots, and displacement was 50 tons. Twelve Type As were built, although the later craft had just two engines and were converted to fast minelayers.

Although the prefabrication scheme worked well, experience in service with the Fairmile A showed many shortcomings,

Black Ranger, an Admiralty tanker, at Scapa Flow, possibly either just before or after refuelling the aircraft carrier HMS *Victorious* in March 1942. *(IWM A8153)*

highlighting the need to double fuel capacity and improve seakeeping, as well as change the awkward layout of the accommodation. The Type B was intended to resolve these problems, and was also planned to return to the three-engined configuration; but the supply of engines from the US was insufficient for this and instead just two engines were used, allowing 50 per cent more boats to be built. By this time, no less than thirty-eight boatyards were involved in the assembly of these craft, at some sacrifice, since many of their facilities such as sawmills and joiners' shops could not be used. The Fairmile B was 112ft in length and displaced 67 tons; 388 were built in the UK, with another 264 in the Dominions, many of them funded locally. Armament varied, but a typical arrangement was a single 3pdr forward, an Oerlikon amidships and another aft, while on each side of the bridge were twin Vickers 0.303in machine guns. Rockets were used to illuminate targets, and fourteen depth

charges were carried. Displacement was just over 87 tons. A major weakness was the use of petrol engines, and many vessels were lost in accidental explosions; toxic gases in the fire extinguishers used added to the problems, leading to a number of lives lost.

For harbour defence, the Fairmile B series was complemented by 72ft harbour launches, built of wood both to economise on strategic materials and utilise the resources of the yachtbuilders. These had diesel engines of various makes, including the dependable Gardner 150hp design. Some 200 were built in the UK and another 56 in the Dominions, as well as a number under lend–lease. In the Mediterranean, these craft also undertook open-water duties, including escorting convoys off the North African coast.

While motor torpedo boats had been used by the RN during the First World War, the Admiralty did not order any further craft until 1935, although British boat builders provided a number of craft for overseas navies. A number of fast, planing craft were built as ships' boats, and from these in 1935 the British Powerboat Company offered a 60ft MTB with three Napier aviation-derived petrol engines, capable of launching two torpedoes from the engine room through ports in the transom. Armament also included quadruple 0.303 in machine-gun mountings forward and aft. The 18-ton displacement and the power available meant that speeds of up to 37 knots were achieved. The first of six was delivered in March 1937, and later the order was increased to nineteen, sufficient for three flotillas, making them the Royal Navy's sole MTBs in 1939.

Vosper, the leading builder of fast motor launches, built a competing design, 68ft in length but known variously as the 70ft and as *MTB102*, which gave a better performance, reaching 43.7 knots, but suffering from structural weakness. It was finally damaged in a heavy sea off the Needles.

Next, the British Powerboat Company produced its own private-venture MTB, known appropriately as the private venture (PV) boat, again using marinised aircraft engines, this time the Rolls-Royce Merlin, the start of that company's long connection with marine engines. The 30-ton boat could carry four torpedoes on the deck, and on trials reached 44.4 knots. Despite some shortcomings, in 1938 four boats based on the Vosper design but with additional strengthening in the hull were ordered, with another two ordered from Thorneycroft.

On the outbreak of war, orders were placed with a number of builders for additional MTBs, but production was slow because of shortages of both engines and armament. In fact, the strategic situation was severely compromised by even using some engines from Italy, which source promptly dried up when that country entered the war in June 1940. Armament was poor, although twin 0.5in machine guns replaced the quadruple 0.303s later. Eventually, the supply of US Packard engines helped to boost production. It was not until 1940 that a single hull form was standardised – the Vosper design – to enable a standard set of docking chocks to be used. Subcontracting of orders was attempted in 1940, but this proved unsatisfactory.

One project that kept surfacing between the wars and during the Second World War was for a small 45ft MTB that could be carried aboard warships and released to make hit-and-run attacks on enemy shipping or shore installations; this was attempted but with little success. There were also experiments with hydrofoil and semi-hydrofoil boats, again with little success.

Motor gun boats were not available at the outbreak of war, but their use became an urgent necessity after the fall of France and the Low Countries enabled German E-boats to raid British ports and coastal convoys, and commence minelaying in British coastal waters. In haste, whatever came to hand was armed and pressed into service, with *MGB50–67* being Vosper 70ft MTBs originally intended for the French Navy, while a number of boats intended for export to Sweden were also found and their export stopped. Armament varied widely with whatever came to hand being utilised, and even included an electrically operated turret recovered from an aircraft due to be scrapped. Some had 2pdr guns, hand-operated, which could throw a gunner off his feet in the open sea. Later, two 0.5in twin machine guns abreast the bridge were fitted, while Oerlikon Mk IVs provided the main armament.

The first attempt at a standardised MGB came with another British Power Boat Company design, which was 71.5ft long.

Even herring drifters were called up for war service. This is *Fisher Boy* in dry dock. *(IWM A26025)*

This mounted a 2pdr automatic gun forward and a twin Oerlikon aft. Fortunately, at the right time, the building jigs for the Fairmile A were available and not being used, and the Fairmile A design was adapted to become the Fairmile C, with increased speed from three supercharged Hall Scott engines. A power-operated 2pdr gun was mounted forward and a hand-operated 2pdr aft, while two 0.5in machine guns were positioned either side of the bridge; the armament was changed later. The craft generally gave good service, apart from weaknesses such as an over-large turning circle.

The next stage was to order steam-turbine MGBs, a necessity forced on the Admiralty as a result of the absence of any satisfactory British high-speed, lightweight diesel engine. The Admiralty had estimated that on a 50-ton displacement, steam-turbine machinery could be found to give 8,000hp. Nine boats were ordered from five shipbuilders, but only seven were delivered, as enemy action prevented production at one yard. Design started in October 1940 and the first boat was ready in November 1941. These craft were 135ft in length, while displacement had grown to 165 tons. Once again, armament varied, but a typical example had a 2pdr gun power-operated forward and a hand-operated 2pdr aft, with two twin 0.5in machine guns abreast the bridge; two 21in lightweight torpedo tubes could be fitted. These armaments were frequently increased, so that the complement of three officers and twenty-four men was often increased to forty-four men. Typical of a later example was two power-operated 6pdr guns, one forward and one amidships, a 3in hand-operated gun aft, 2 twin Oerlikons abreast the bridge, and two 21in torpedoes. In action, these craft were extremely successful and feared by E-boat commanders.

The next stage was the Fairmile D MGB, first introduced in February 1942. These eventually had a similar armament to the steam gunboats, but the use of plywood continued to be less satisfactory than steel, as it was prone to break when moving at high speed through heavy seas, while the hull-form created difficulties when work had to be done on the boats out of water, as excessive pressure was experienced on one section of the hull, which further added to damage. Nevertheless, these craft took on the main part of the war against the E-boats, with 288 built.

Camper and Nicholson produced a combined large MTB and fast anti-submarine boat, 110ft in length and powered initially by three Packard engines on the first example, MGB *501*; MGBs *502–509* that followed used Paxman diesel engines. These had a similar armament to the steam MGBs, but were mainly completed as cargo carriers, bringing small consignments of vital items, notably ball-bearings, from neutral Sweden and disguised to look like small coasters. Further craft included MGB *511–518*, with a heavier armament including two 6pdr guns and four 18in torpedoes.

Small anti-submarine boats were also built, for example a 60ft craft from the British Power Boat Company, of which five were ordered initially. Before deliveries of this were completed, another 70ft boat was ordered, but found to be unsatisfactory; however, a 63ft design built for South Africa was found to have good seakeeping qualities, and eighteen were ordered. Nevertheless, despite this effort, the motor anti-submarine boats were found to be poor sub-hunters and most were converted either for air-sea rescue work or to MGBs.

CHAPTER 15

NAVAL BASES

When thou givest to thy servants
to endeavour any great matter
Grant us also to know that it is not the beginning
but the continuing of the same unto the end.
Sir Francis Drake

The three main naval bases for the Royal Navy in 1939 were the historic ones of Devonport, Portsmouth and Chatham, which as part of the Nore Command also embraced Sheerness. Each of these was more than simply a port and a dockyard, but also included a number of shore stations for training and specialised aspects of the work of the fleet. Augmenting these bases were those at Rosyth, Pembroke Dock, and Gibraltar and Malta. During the Second World War, the Royal dockyards laid down over thirty new ships and carried out more than 97,000 refits.

CHATHAM

Chatham was the last of the three great naval ports and dockyards to be built, dating from 1613. Often associated with Sheerness, Chatham was the main base, with Sheerness providing support facilities. The rationale for building a naval base at Chatham was the need to defend London, and other dockyards built in the early days with the same objective included Harwich, Woolwich and Deptford. Nevertheless, as wars with the

Dutch passed and France became the main enemy, the importance of these ports declined, and only Chatham survived.

While Portsmouth built the first modern battleship, Chatham found itself at the same time engaged on the construction of the naval vessel of the future, the submarine, launching its first 'boat' in 1908. T class submarines such as HMS *Torbay* were among those Second World War boats built here. Despite the proxity of Chatham to Eastchurch on the Isle of Sheppey, as near a birthplace for British naval aviation as could be found, during the Second World War the port was probably the least involved of any with naval aviation.

DEVONPORT

Although Plymouth was a naval base from the time of Edward I and used in wars with the French, it is perhaps best known for its connection with Sir Francis Drake and the defeat of the Spanish Armada in 1588, although Drake's early naval reputation was gained as a privateer. In 1824 the dockyard area became independent of Plymouth

HMS *Sceptre*, one of the medium-sized S class boats, leaving harbour through an open defence boom. *(RN Submarine Museum, Neg.1237)*

Off Devonport in May 1943 is the motor fishing vessel *MFV60*, one of just fifteen vessels that still used sail, as well as a petrol engine, during the Second World War. *(IWM A16905)*

itself, as Devonport. During the eighteenth and nineteenth centuries Plymouth, or more precisely Devonport, became the second-largest base for the Royal Navy.

During the Second World War, Devonport was ideally situated for protection of the Western Approaches, but it also meant that it was within easy reach of German bombers, and much of its command work was relocated to Liverpool.

PORTSMOUTH

Portsmouth, on Portsea Island, was strategically well placed to become the Royal Navy's main port and dockyard, and as early as 1194 King Richard I had ordered the construction of a dockyard. Henry VII had the world's first dry dock completed there in 1496. The large size of Portsmouth harbour

meant that there was considerable space for mooring in reserve during times of peace. The Solent and Spithead provided a sheltered anchorage which, during the eighteenth and nineteenth centuries, was also a well protected assembly point for convoys.

Over the years, almost 300 warships were built at Portsmouth, perhaps the most notable being the first battleship of the modern era, HMS *Dreadnought*. Lack of space meant that when submarines arrived, they were based across the harbour at Haslar, HMS *Dolphin*, at Gosport.

Nevertheless, the advantages of Portsmouth, such as proximity to the English Channel, also worked against it during the Second World War, since the approaches were easily mined and the dockyard was within easy reach of German bombers.

Boom defence vessels played an unglamorous but important role in maintaining the booms that were set up to protect wartime harbours. This is HMS *Barberry*, a Barricade class boom defence vessel. *(IWM A27642)*

A boom defence vessel at Rosyth. These laid and raised protective net booms to prevent enemy submarines entering harbours and anchorages. *(IWM A6052)*

ROSYTH

While for most of British history, the threat had come from the south, with France, Spain, the Netherlands and then France again being seen as the most likely enemy, by the early twentieth century it was clear that a newly united and ambitious Germany posed the biggest threat. This led to the search for a convenient dockyard on the east coast of Scotland, an area notably lacking in sheltered anchorages. The choice fell on Rosyth on the north bank of the Firth of Forth and not too far from Edinburgh.

Construction work began in 1909, although by the time the dockyard was completed, in 1916, the nation was already at war with Germany. Unlike Chatham, Devonport and Portsmouth, Rosyth was not a manning port, and did not undertake construction of warships but concentrated instead on refitting and repair work. Although it was a naval base, the forward base for the Royal Navy in two world wars was at Scapa Flow in Orkney, simply an anchorage without major repair facilities. In fact, after the First World War, Rosyth was closed until war broke out in 1939.

OVERSEAS BASES

The three main overseas bases for the Royal Navy in 1939 were Gibraltar, Malta and Singapore, but preoccupation with the war in Europe meant that the last of these was neglected, despite promises made to Australia and New Zealand between the wars. The fall of Singapore to Japanese forces in 1942 meant that this major base was lost. Other bases became important, but these, such as Trincomalee in Ceylon, now Sri Lanka, were effectively anchorages rather than main bases, although 'Trinco' did have the advantage of nearby airfields for the Fleet Air Arm and the Royal Air Force.

GIBRALTAR

The only one of the overseas bases to remain fully operational throughout the war, Gibraltar provided refit and repair facilities and its security was enhanced when a runway was built on the site of the racecourse. It was used as a base by Force H and provided easy access to the Mediterranean and the Atlantic. Had Spain entered the war on the side of the Axis, with whom the Spanish dictator Franco had much in common, the base would have become untenable, and as it was, Spanish workers were sent home at nightfall to ensure security.

MALTA

Malta's connection with the British came in 1799, when a delegation reached one of Nelson's ships to seek help in evicting the French, who had occupied the island. The island, despite its excellent Grand Harbour, remained something of a backwater until the opening of the Suez Canal in 1869 put it on the main shipping routes to India and Australia. Despite the excellence of the dockyard facilities, heavy Axis air attack from June 1940 onwards made use of the base difficult, although it did sterling work in January 1941 in making emergency repairs to the stricken aircraft carrier *Illustrious*.

During the height of the war in the Mediterranean, Malta remained a base for light forces and also for submarines, which, with aircraft based at Hal Far (then an RAF station) and a small resident force of light cruisers and destroyers (Force K), harried the convoy routes that supplied Axis ground and air forces in North Africa.

CHAPTER SIXTEEN

NAVAL AIR SQUADRONS

After the formation of the Fleet Air Arm in 1924 as a part of the Royal Air Force, separate blocks of squadron numbers were allocated. Numbers 401–439 were fleet spotter flights, assigned to battleships and cruisers; 440–459 were fleet reconnaissance flights, and 460 onwards were fleet torpedo flights.

Many of these squadrons and flights were renumbered in the 700 series in 1936, a system that was retained when the Admiralty regained full control of the Fleet Air Arm. Under this scheme, 700–749 were catapult flights and squadrons, but eventually these merged into 700 Squadron, with a suffix for each flight. This left the numbers 701–710 for amphibian and floatplane squadrons from 1943 onwards. Numbers 750–799 were assigned for training and ancillary squadrons, in contrast to the RAF practice of not assigning squadron numbers to training units. Combat squadrons were 800–809 for fighter squadrons and 810–819 for torpedo bomber squadrons, later torpedo spotter reconnaissance (TSR) and torpedo bomber reconnaissance (TBR) squadrons; 820–859 were initially spotter reconnaissance squadrons, later becoming TSR and, finally, TBR squadrons. Originally, the latter included 860–869, but these were assigned to Dutch-manned and then Royal Netherlands Navy squadrons. Numbers 870–899 were initially for single-seat fighter squadrons, but 870–879 were assigned to Royal Canadian Navy squadrons. As numbers ran out, new series prefixed by '1' were assigned for the many squadrons manned by members of the Royal Navy Volunteer Reserve. Leaving aside unused blocks, 1700–1749 became torpedo bomber reconnaissance squadrons; 1770–1799 two-seat fighter squadrons; 1810–1829 dive-bomber squadrons; and 1830–1899 were initially assigned to single-seat fighter squadrons.

In June 1943 embarked squadrons were grouped into numbered wings, given the title 'naval' to avoid confusion with RAF wings, followed by a suffix to designate its purpose, either fighter or torpedo bomber reconnaissance. This took effect on 25 October 1943. In contrast to RAF practice, in which a wing usually meant three squadrons, the number of squadrons in a naval wing varied, and in one case a wing amounted to a solitary squadron. In most cases, wing leaders were lieutenant commanders, or Royal Marine majors, equivalent to the RAF rank of squadron leader, rather than the more senior ranks of commander or lieutenant colonel, the equivalent of the RAF rank of wing commander. From 30 June 1945 the naval wings of the British Pacific Fleet were

A Grumman Martlet (the Royal Navy's name for the Wildcat) from HMS *Formidable*'s 888 Squadron flies over the battleship HMS *Warspite* during the landings at Diego Suarez. *(IWM A9713)*

merged into carrier air groups, often headed by a commander.

The advent of carrier air groups reflected the close coordination with the United States Navy as the war in the Pacific reached its climax. With the war in Europe over, and resources concentrated on the Far East, it made sense for the navy to align with American practice. Anticipating heavy losses, it was planned to have spare groups, so that the fleet carriers would have a 100 per cent reserve, and the light fleet carriers 50 per cent.

THE SQUADRONS

700: Re-formed Hatston 21 January 1940, as the HQ unit for all battleship and cruiser flights, with an initial strength of 42 Walruses, 11 Seafoxes and 12 Swordfish floatplanes. Reached strength of 63 Walruses in June 1942. Disbanded on 24 March 1944. Re-formed on 11 October 1944 as Maintenance Test Pilot Training Squadron at Donibristle.

701: Re-formed on 7 May 1940 at Donibristle, to provide for temporary units formed ashore. Disbanded 8 June 1941. Re-formed on 1 October 1942, to take over the 700 Squadron flight at Beirut. Disbanded 15 August 1943. Re-formed at Heston on 18 April 1945, for communication duties, flying a number of types.

702: Merged into 700, 21 January 1940. Re-formed 27 December 1940, operating Seafoxes from armed merchant cruisers. Shore-base was Lee-on-Solent. Sea Hurricane flight formed 10 May 1942, to operate two catapult aircraft from CAM-ship *Maplin,* only example of FAA-catapult fighters. Disbanded July 1943. Re-formed 1 June 1945 at Hinstock as Instrument Flying and Checking Unit.

703: Took over armed merchant cruiser flights from 702 Squadron when formed on 3 June 1942, equipping with Vought Kingfishers. Shore base Lee-on-Solent, but three Walruses based at Walvis Bay in South Africa. Disbanded 1 May 1944, to be reformed 19 April 1945, at RAF Thorney Island, Naval Air-Sea Warfare Development Unit, NASWDU, to evaluate new aircraft.

704: Formed at Zeals on 11 April 1945, as an OTU for the de Havilland Mosquito, with four aircraft detached to join 703 in June on NASWDU work.

705: On outbreak of war, Mediterranean Fleet catapult squadron. Absorbed into 700 Squadron, 21 January 1940. Re-formed at Ronaldsway, IoM, on 7 March 1945, as a Replacement Crew Training Unit with Swordfish IIIs. Disbanded, 24 June 1945.

706: Formed 10 April 1945, as a pool squadron at Schofields, Australia, for the British Pacific Fleet.

707: Formed 2 February 1945 as a Radar Trials Unit at Burscough, the Naval School of Airborne Radar. Swordfish, Ansons, Avengers and Barracudas operated. Merged into 778 Squadron, October 1945.

708: Formed at Lee-on-Solent, 1 October 1944, as the Firebrand Tactical Trials Unit, Aircraft used on rocket-firing trials with deck landing trials aboard *Glory* in May 1945. Disbanded post-war.

709: Formed at St Merryn, Cornwall, on 15 September 1944, as part of the School of Naval Air Warfare's Ground Attack School. Seafire L.IIIs operated, later joined by Hellcats. Disbanded post-war.

710: Formed as a seaplane squadron for *Albatross* at Lee-on-Solent on 23 August 1939, with six Walruses. Took part in the Madagascar Campaign in 1942. Disbanded at Lee-on-Solent on 14 October 1943. Re-formed at Ronaldsway, 7 October 1944, with Barracudas and Swordfish for torpedo training. Disbanded post-war.

711: Mediterranean Fleet catapult squadron, absorbed into 700 Squadron in 1940. Re-formed on 9 September 1944, as a torpedo training squadron, based at Crail, Fife, operating Barracudas. Disbanded post-war.

712: Assigned to 18th Cruiser Squadron on the outbreak of war, nine ships with eighteen Walrus aircraft, then merged into 700 Squadron, January 1940. Re-formed at Hatston, 2 August 1944, as a communications squadron. Disbanded 23 August 1945.

713: Merged into 700 Squadron, January 1940. Re-formed at Ronaldsway, IoM, 12 August 1944, as a TBR Training Squadron, operating Barracudas. Disbanded late 1945.

714: Merged into 700 Squadron, 1940. Re-formed at Fearn as a TBR Training

Squadron, 1 August 1944, equipped with Barracudas. Moved to Rattray on 30 October 1944. Disbanded late 1945.

715: Merged into 700 Squadron, 1940. Re-formed 17 August 1944, at St Merryn, from part of 736 squadron as part of the School of Air Combat, with Seafires and Corsairs. Reabsorbed by 736, post-war.

716: Merged into 700 Squadron, 1940. Re-formed at Eastleigh, near Southampton, on 28 June 1944, as the School of Safety Equipment, with Sea Otters to provide instruction on search and rescue operations. Disbanded post-war.

717: Formed at Fearn as a TBR training squadron on 1 July 1944, 717 operated Barracudas. Moved to Rattray, 30 October 1944. Disbanded post-war.

718: Merged into 700 Squadron, January 1940. Re-formed at Henstridge as an army cooperation training unit, 5 June 1944, with Seafires and Spitfires. Became the School of Naval Air Reconnaissance in April 1945.

719: Formed on 15 June 1944 at St Merryn, as a School of Air Combat air firing training squadron, with Seafires and Corsairs. Disbanded 2 January 1945.

720: Merged into 700 Squadron, January 1940. Re-formed 1 August 1945, operating four Avro Ansons.

721: Formed at Belfast on 1 March 1945, as a fleet requirements unit for the Pacific Fleet, operating Vengeance target tugs. The squadron disbanded in August 1945.

722: Formed at Tambaram on 1 September 1944, as a fleet requirements unit with Miles Martinets for target drogue towing.

Swordfish and Wildcats were added. It disbanded in October 1945.

723: Formed at Bankstown, New South Wales, 28 February 1945, as a fleet requirements unit with eight Martinets and eight Corsairs, and Hellcats later. After the war ended, moved to Schofields and later disbanded.

724: Formed as a naval air communications squadron at Bankstown, NSW. Disbanded post-war.

725: Formed at Eglinton, 27 August 1943, as a fleet requirements unit with three Blackburn Rocs, to provide target-towing. Disbanded post-war.

726: Formed at Durban, 7 July 1943, and eventually operated a variety of aircraft. Disbanded post-war.

727: Fleet requirements unit formed at Gibraltar on 26 May 1943. Unusually, target towing was provided for all three services. The squadron moved to RAF Ta Kali in Malta before disbanding on 7 December 1944.

728: Fleet requirements unit formed at Gibraltar, 1 May 1943. Defiants were deployed to Oujda in French Morocco to provide towing for an American AA battery firing range. Merged into 775 Squadron on 4 July 1943. Re-formed 14 August 1943, moving to Ta Kali as a fleet requirements unit, providing target towing for Mediterranean Fleet and the British Army, then the US Navy at Naples. Moved to Luqa post-war.

728B: Formed as a fleet requirements unit at Ta Kali in January 1945, with five Martinets and Seafires, and disbanded in July.

729: Began operations on 15 May 1945, Coimbatore with Oxfords and Harvards. Moved to Tambaram in June and Puttalam in July, and then to Ceylon in late August. Disbanded post-war.

730: Formed at Abbotsinch, 17 April 1944, for communications duties. A variety of aircraft operated, including Reliants. Disbanded, 1 August 1945.

731: Formed at East Haven, 5 December 1943, to provide training for deck landing control officers. Pilots nicknamed 'Clockwork Mice'. Absorbed into other squadrons post-war.

732: An OTU formed at Brunswick on 23 November 1943, using Corsairs, to provide aerodrome dummy deck landing (ADDL) training. Disbanded, 1 July 1944. Re-formed at Drem, 15 May 1945, as a Night Fighter Training School. Disbanded post-war.

733: Formed as a fleet requirements unit for the British Eastern Fleet at Minneriya, on 1 January 1944. Varied equipment. Tasks included radar calibration.

734: Formed at Worthy Down, near Winchester, 14 February 1944, as an engine handling unit with Merlin-engined Whitley 'flying classrooms'. Moved to Hinstock post-war and disbanded.

735: Formed at Inskip on 1 August 1943, as an ASV, air-to-surface vessel radar, raining unit, at first operating Swordfish. Ansons were also used as flying classrooms. Moved to Burscough in March 1944. Disbanded post-war.

736: Formed at Yeovilton, 24 May 1943, as the School of Air Combat, equipped with Seafires. Later became the Fighter Combat School, part of the School of Naval Air Warfare. Disbanded September 1945.

737: Formed at Dunino on 22 February 1943, as an amphibious bomber reconnaissance training squadron using Walruses, but soon disbanded. Re-formed at Inskip on 15 March 1944, as an air-to-surface vessel, ASV radar training unit using Swordfish and Anson flying classrooms. Disbanded post-war.

738: Pilot training squadron formed at Quonset Point, Rhode Island, on 1 February 1943; moved to Lewiston on 31 July 1943 where advanced carrier training was provided for American-trained RNVR pilots. Disbanded on 31 July 1945.

739: Formed as the Blind Approach Development Unit at Lee-on-Solent, 15 December 1942, with a Swordfish and a Fulmar. Moved to Worthy Down, 1 September 1943, and to Donibristle, October 1944. Disbanded 7 March 1945.

740: Formed 4 May 1943, at Arbroath as part of No. 2 Observer School, using Walruses plus a handful of Swordfish and Kingfishers. Disbanded 5 August 1943. Re-formed 30 December 1943, at Machrihanish as a communications squadron from a flight in 772 Squadron. A wide variety of aircraft operated. Disbanded on 1 September 1945.

741: Observer training squadron formed 1 March 1943 at Arbroath, as part of no. 2 Observer Training School. Operated Swordfish. Disbanded, 19 March 1945.

742: Communications squadron formed Colombo, 6 December 1943, operating Beech Expeditors. Operations included many regular services. Moved to

Coimbatore on 15 September 1944, later becoming the Naval Air Transport Squadron. The squadron flew many millions of miles with just one fatal accident. It disbanded in August 1946.

743: Formed on 1 March 1943 as part of No. 2 Telegraphist/Air Gunners School at Yarmouth, Nova Scotia, with a mixture of RCAF and RN personnel. Training ended on 19 March 1945, and the squadron disbanded on 30 March 1945.

744: First squadron redesignated as 754 in June 1944, due to the appearance of another 744 squadron in the UK, also a training squadron, formed at Maydown, 6 March 1944, to train crews for operations from MAC-ships.

745: Formed on 1 March 1943, with Swordfish, Seamews and Ansons. Disbanded, 3 March 1945.

746: Formed as the Naval Night Fighter Interception Unit, 23 November 1942, at Lee-on-Solent. In May 1943, it came under the control of the Naval Fighter Direction Centre at Yeovilton, developing tactics and analysing the experiences of pilots from the carrier squadrons. Its Firefly night fighters operated against the V-1 flying bombs. Became the Naval Night Fighter Development Squadron in March 1945, evaluating aircraft and their equipment.

747: Part of the TBR Pool, formed at Fearn, 22 March 1943, it evolved into an OTU. Disbanded post-war.

748: Formed as part of the fighter pool, St Merryn, 12 October 1942, it provided refresher flying. It became No. 1 Naval OTU in March 1943. A series of moves occurred

during 1944, returned to St Merryn in August 1945, and later disbanded.

749: Formed at Piarco, Trinidad, on 1 January 1941, as part of No. 1 Observers School, it used Walrus aircraft at first, but in 1942 these were joined by the Grumman Goose. During that year, operational anti-submarine patrols were also undertaken. Disbanded post-war.

750: Formed Ford, 24 May 1939, as part of No. 1 Observers School, operating Sharks and Ospreys. Moved to Piarco in Trinidad, where the school reopened on 5 November 1940. At its peak, up to 40 Sharks and 70 Albacores were operated. Barracudas were introduced before the squadron disbanded post-war.

751: Formed at Ford, 24 May 1939, for the new No. 1 Observers School, initially equipped with Walruses. Moved to Arbroath on 19 August 1940, after the German air raid on Ford, to become part of No. 2 Observers School. Disbanded, 2 May 1944.

752: Formed in May 1939, at Ford, as part of No. 1 Observers School, with Proctors and a few Albacores. Moved to Piarco, Trinidad, and regrouped there on 5 November 1940. Disbanded, 9 October 1945.

753: Formed at Lee-on-Solent, 24 May 1939, as part of No. 2 Observers School, operating Sharks and Seals. Moved to Arbroath on 23 August 1940, where the Seals were replaced by Swordfish. Disbanded post-war at Rattray.

754: Formed at Lee-on-Solent, 24 May 1939, as part of No. 2 Observers School, initially with Walruses plus some Seafoxes and Vega Gulls. A change of role came in June 1941, with the arrival of eighteen Lysander target tugs. Disbanded, 27 March 1944. Re-formed at Yarmouth, Nova Scotia, as No. 1 Naval Air Gunners School by renumbering 744 Squadron. Disbanded, 12 March 1945.

755: Formed at Worthy Down, 24 May 1939, to train TAGs within No. 1 Air Gunners School. Moved to Jersey, 11 March 1940, but was evacuated on the fall of France. On 1 December 1942, took over 756 and 757 NAS. Disbanded, 31 October 1944. Re-formed as a communications squadron, Colombo, 24 March 1945, operating Expeditors. Disbanded post-war.

756: Became operational on 6 March 1941 at Worthy Down, where it provided the advanced element of the TAG course using Proctors. Merged into 755 and disbanded on 1 December 1942. Re-formed on 1 October 1943, at Katukurunda, Ceylon, providing refresher flying and deck landing training, with a mixture of aircraft. Disbanded post-war.

757: Formed, 24 May 1939, but disbanded 15 August 1939. Re-formed 6 March 1941, with Skuas and Nimrods, as part of No. 1 Air Gunners school, but disbanded into 755 Squadron, 1 December 1942. Re-formed at Puttalam as a fighter pool squadron on 2 October 1943. Used Corsairs, Hellcats, Seafires and Wildcats to train pilots in landing on escort carriers. Moved post-war to Katukurunda, where it disbanded.

758: Formed at Eastleigh, 1 July 1939, from renumbered 759 Squadron as part of No. 2 Air Gunners School, operating Sharks and Ospreys, and then Skuas and Proctors. Moved to Arbroath on 14 October 1940. Disbanded, 1 February 1941. Re-formed at Donibristle, 25 May 1942, as the Beam Approach School, using Airspeed Oxfords, then to Hinstock, 15 August 1942, to become the Blind Approach School. Became

the Naval Advanced Instrument Flying School in April 1943, using more than 100 Oxfords, and small numbers of other types. Disbanded post-war into 780 Squadron.

759: Re-formed at Eastleigh on 1 November 1939, as a fighter school and pool squadron, operating Skuas, Rocs and Sea Gladiators. Absorbed 769 Squadron on 1 December 1939. In April 1943, it became the Advanced Flying School of No. 1 Naval Air Fighter School, with Sea Hurricanes, Spitfires, Fulmars and Masters, with Seafires arriving in August. In November 1944, it became a mainly Corsair unit. Disbanded, 1946.

760: Formed as Fleet Fighter Pool No. 1 at Eastleigh on 1 April 1940, it moved to Yeovilton on 16 September 1940 as the Fighter Pool. In August 1941, it became part of the Fleet Fighter School operating Sea Hurricanes. Disbanded, 31 December 1942. Re-formed at Inskip as an anti-submarine operational training squadron, 1 May 1944, to train pilots on rocket projectile attacks and anti-flak cannon fire. Disbanded, 1 November 1944. Re-formed at Zeals on 10 April 1945 as part of No. 1 Naval Air Fighter School. Disbanded, 1946.

761: Formed at Yeovilton, 1 August 1941, as the advanced training squadron of the Fleet Fighter School. Moving to Henstridge as No. 2 Naval Air Fighter School on 10 April 1943, the squadron provided deck landing training on *Argus* and later the escort carrier *Ravager*. Disbanded post-war.

762: Formed as an advanced flying training school squadron at Yeovilton, 23 March 1942. Disbanded into 761 Squadron, 9 June 1943. Re-formed, 19 March 1944, from part of 798 Squadron at Lee-on-Solent as the Two Engine Conversion Unit, using Oxfords and Beauforts.

763: First formed as Torpedo Reconnaissance Pool No. 1 at Worthy Down, 15 December 1939. Disbanded, 8 July 1940. Re-formed on 20 April 1942, as a seaplane training squadron equipped with Walruses aboard the seaplane carrier *Albatross*, preparing crews for battleship and cruiser flights. Disbanded, 13 February 1944. Re-formed again, 14 April 1944, Inskip, as an anti-submarine operational training squadron equipped with Avengers. Disbanded on 31 July 1945, and absorbed into 785 Squadron at Crail.

764: Formed at Lee-on-Solent, 8 April 1940, as a seaplane training squadron, equipped mainly with Walruses, with some Seafoxes and Swordfish. Disbanded on 7 November 1943. Re-formed on 19 February 1944, at Gosport, as the User Trials Unit, initially with Barracudas and Avengers for torpedo trials. Disbanded, 1 September 1945.

765: Formed, 24 May 1939, Lee-on-Solent, as a seaplane school and pool squadron, with Walruses, Swordfish and Seafoxes. Disbanded on 25 October 1943, with the fall in demand for seaplane training. Re-formed on 10 February 1944, with Wellingtons at Charleton Horethorne as a travelling recording unit, to monitor the efficiency of radar units. Disbanded post-war in Malta.

766: Formed at Machrihanish, 15 April 1942, to provide a night torpedo attack course using Swordfish. Post-war, the squadron moved to Rattray and Lossiemouth.

767: A redesignation of 811 Squadron, formed as a deck landing training squadron at Donibristle on 24 May 1939, initially operating a mixture of Moths, Sharks and Swordfish. In November 1939, a detachment was sent to Hyères de la Palyvestre, near Toulon in the South of France, to use *Argus* for training. Deck landing training continued right up to the fall of France, while nine of its aircraft bombed Genoa on 13 June 1940, after Italy entered the war. Afterwards, the squadron had to be evacuated, with twelve aircraft eventually reaching Malta, where they formed the basis of 830 Squadron on 1 July 1940. On 8 July 1940, the old squadron regrouped, still as a deck landing training squadron, at Arbroath. The squadron was equipped with Barracudas in June 1944, and provided a TBR course for the rest of the war.

768: Part of the Deck Landing Training School at Arbroath, formed 13 January 1941, using Swordfish. Disbanded post-war at East Haven.

769: Formed at Donibristle, 24 May 1939. A fighter deck landing training squadron equipped with Rocs, Sea Gladiators and Skuas. Disbanded, 1 December 1939. Re-formed, 29 November 1941, as a unit within the Deck Landing Training School at Arbroath, using Swordfish and Albacores. Changed to TBR training in 1944, before moving to Rattray on 28 July 1945. Merged with 717 Squadron post-war.

770: Formed as a deck landing training squadron, Lee-on-Solent, 7 November 1939, until disbanding on 1 May 1940. Re-formed at Donibristle, 1 January 1941, as a fleet requirements unit for target towing and marking the fall of shot. During 1945, a wide assortment of aircraft was operated, including Beaufighters, Mosquitoes and Spitfires. Disbanded shortly after the war ended.

771: Formed 24 May 1939, at Portland. Initially fourteen Swordfish and some Walruses were operated. First to discover that the *Bismarck* had put to sea from her Norwegian fjord on 22 May 1941, spotted by one of her Marylands. Early in 1945, the squadron became one of the first to operate Hoverfly helicopters.

772: Formed Lee-on-Solent, 28 September 1939, as a fleet requirements unit. Duties included SAR, target-towing, radar calibration, height finding and photography, and in addition, on 27 May 1944, squadron carried out a dummy attack on the Fleet in an exercise to prepare for the Normandy landings. Became the Fleet Requirements Unit School on moving to Ayr on 2 July 1944.

773: Formed 3 June 1940, as a fleet requirements unit in Bermuda for ships on the West Indies Station. Disbanded at Bermuda, 25 April 1944. Re-formed, 1 June 1945, Lee-on-Solent. Moved to Brawdy post-war.

774: Formed at Worthy Down, 10 November 1939, as an armament training squadron for observers and TAGs, with a mixed strength of three Rocs, three Skuas, four Swordfish and four Shark target tugs. On 24 October 1944, the squadron moved to Rattray; disbanded there, 1 August 1945.

775: Formed Dekheila, November 1940, as a fleet requirements unit for the Mediterranean Fleet. Disbanded post-war.

776: Fleet requirements unit formed Lee-on-Solent, 1 January 1941. Disbanded Burscough, October 1945.

777: Formed at Hastings, Sierra Leone, 1 August 1941, as a fleet requirements unit, with a small number of Rocs and Swordfish. Throughout most of 1943, the squadron was responsible for the air defence of Sierra Leone. It disbanded at Hastings on 25 December 1944. Re-formed on 23 May 1945, as a trials unit operating aboard *Pretoria Castle*, using a number of different aircraft. Merged into 778 Squadron post-war.

778: Formed Lee-on-Solent, 28 September 1939, as a Service Trials Unit squadron, testing and evaluating tactics, aircraft types, armament and equipment. The squadron moved to Gosport in August 1945, and in the immediate post-war period absorbed several other squadrons.

779: Formed as a fleet requirements unit on 1 October 1941 at Gibraltar where it disbanded, 5 August 1945.

780: Conversion course unit formed at Eastleigh, 2 October 1939, to train experienced civilian pilots in naval flying. By August 1943, its role had changed to converting Swordfish and Albacore pilots to the monoplane Barracuda. Disbanded, 2 January 1945.

781: Formed, 20 March 1940, as a communications unit at Lee-on-Solent. Disbanded, Lee-on-Solent, 31 July 1945, into 782 and 799 squadrons.

782: Established 1 December 1940, as the Northern Communications Squadron. Origins lay in an unnumbered communications flight at Donibristle, formed July 1940, using former Jersey Airways crews commissioned into the Royal Navy. Operated for the most part almost as an airline, linking isolated naval air stations in Scotland and Northern Ireland, the Northern Isles, and also flying from these to Lee-on-Solent. The squadron survived for some years after the war.

783: An air-to-surface vessel radar training squadron formed Arbroath, 9 January 1941.

Operated in conjunction with the Naval Air Signals School from March 1943, when Barracudas, Fireflies and Avengers were introduced. The squadron survived for some years after the war.

784: A night fighter training squadron formed at Lee-on-Solent, 1 June 1942, using two Chesapeakes and six Fulmars, with additional Fulmars and Ansons following as the squadron moved to Drem, 18 October 1942. Disbanded 1946, at Dale.

785: Formed as a TBR training squadron, Crail, 4 November 1940. Initial equipment comprised thirteen Sharks and five Swordfish. The squadron became part of No. 1 Naval Operational Training Unit in late 1944. Disbanded early 1946.

786: Formed, Crail, 4 November 1940, as a TBR squadron with nine Albacores. Disbanded into 785 Squadron, late 1945.

787: Formed on 5 March 1941, Yeovilton, as a Fleet Fighter Development Unit. Almost every type of fighter was received by the squadron for testing and evaluation for naval use, including comparative testing of captured aircraft. Early work on the use of rocket projectiles by naval aircraft followed in January 1943. Moved to Westhampnett, July 1945, and survived for some years after the war.

788: Formed at China Bay in Ceylon (now Sri Lanka), 18 January 1942, as British Eastern Fleet's TBR pool, with an initial strength of just six Swordfish. All aircraft were destroyed during the heavy raids by Japanese carrier-borne aircraft on 5 April 1942. Surviving personnel were sent to East Africa, regrouping at Tanga on 20 May 1942, then becoming a fleet requirements unit at Mombasa on 24 June 1942. Disbanded on 11 June 1945.

789: Formed as a fleet requirements unit at Wingfield, South Africa, 1 July 1942. Disbanded, November 1945.

790: Originally formed at Machrihanish, 15 June 1941, as an air target towing squadron operating Swordfish and Rocs until being disbanded into 772 Squadron on 30 September 1941. Re-formed, 27 July 1942, at Charlton Horethorne, attached to the Fighter Direction School, for which the squadron's Oxfords acted as bombers and its Fulmars as fighters, training fighter direction officers. Remained operational until late 1949.

791: Formed as an air target towing squadron at Arbroath, 15 October 1940, initially operating two Rocs, but soon joined by Defiants, Swordfish and Skuas. Disbanded on 10 December 1944.

792: Formed as an air target towing unit at St Merryn, 15 August 1940, initially operating a small number of Masters, Rocs and Skuas. Disbanded, 2 January 1945, into 794 Squadron.

793: Formed as an air target towing squadron at Ford on 25 October 1939, equipped with Rocs. Reassembled on 18 November 1940, at Piarco, Trinidad, attached to No. 1 Observer School, initially using Rocs. Disbanded shortly after the war ended.

794: Formed as an air target towing squadron at Yeovilton on 1 August 1940, operating Rocs and Swordfish. On 1 July 1943, the entire squadron became the Naval Air Firing Unit at Angle. Disbanded at Charlton Horethorne, 30 June 1944. Re-formed at St Merryn, 2 January 1945, as the School of Air Firing, using Harvards, Martinets, Corsairs, Fireflies, Seafires and Wildcats. Role expanded in June 1945, to support the newly formed Ground Attack

School. Post-war, the squadron did not disband until 1947.

795: Originally formed as the Eastern Fleet Fighter Pool at Tanga, Tanganyika, on 24 June 1942, early equipment consisted of Martlets and Fulmars. Six Fulmars embarked in *Illustrious* to support the invasion of Madagascar, before being detached ashore at Majunga on 11 September 1942, to maintain anti-submarine patrols as part of the RAF's 207 Group. Disbanded, 11 August 1943.

796: Formed as the Eastern Fleet TBR Pool at Port Reitz, Mombasa, 25 July 1942, with Albacores and Swordfish. Detachment embarked in *Indomitable* on 29 August 1942, to support the invasion of Madagascar, then disembarked to Majunga on 10 September 1942, to join the RAF's 207 Group. Reassembled at Tanga on 17 November 1942. Became an operational training unit until disbanding on 28 April 1944.

797: A fleet requirements unit formed at Katukurunda, Ceylon, in July 1942 with two Skuas. Disbanded, 24 October 1945.

798: Formed at Lee-on-Solent on 11 October 1943 to provide advanced conversion courses. Twin-engined aircraft broke away to become 762 Squadron, March 1944. Role changed slightly during 1945, providing refresher training, including Fleet Air Arm ex-PoWs.

799: Formed as a pool squadron at Wingfield on 10 September 1943, equipped with Albacores. Disbanded, 20 June 1944. Re-formed, 30 July 1945, Lee-on-Solent, as a flying check and conversion refresher squadron operating Seafires.

800: In 1939, operating Skuas and Rocs aboard *Ark Royal* hunting German shipping in the South Atlantic. During the Norwegian campaign, 800 helped sink the cruiser *Konigsberg* at Bergen, and later shot down six He111 bombers, but the attack on *Scharnhorst* resulted in the loss of four aircraft. In July 1940, the squadron provided fighter cover for the attack on the French fleet at Oran. A year later, took part in the raid on Petsamo. In 1942, took part in the invasion of Madagascar. Embarked in *Biter* for the North African landings, Operation Torch, in November 1942. First to receive the Hellcat, and became part of 7 Naval Fighter Wing. On 3 April 1944 the squadron provided the escort for an attack on the battleship *Tirpitz*. Took part in the invasion of the south of France in August 1944. Ended the war attacking Japanese shipping. Disbanded, December 1945.

801: Re-formed at Donibristle on 15 January 1940, with six Skuas, and in April was operating against German forces in Norway from *Ark Royal*. Later disbanded.

Re-forming at Yeovilton on 1 August 1941 with twelve Sea Hurricanes the squadron moved to Hatston to defend Scapa Flow. Aboard *Eagle* when she was torpedoed on 11 August 1942. Re-formed at Stretton, 7 September 1942, later equipping with Seafires and present at the North African landings. In spring 1944, provided fighter escorts for attacks on the *Tirpitz*. Later embarked in *Implacable* as part of the British Pacific Fleet in May, escorting attacks on Truk, and then targets on and around the Japanese home islands. Disbanded 1946.

802: In 1939, operating from *Glorious* with Sea Gladiators, and still aboard when she was sunk on 8 June 1940, by *Scharnhorst* and *Gneisenau*. Re-formed on 21 November 1940, at Hatston. The squadron was aboard *Audacity* when she was sunk by *U-741* on 21 December 1941. Re-formed at Yeovilton on 1 February 1942, with Sea Hurricanes and in September embarked aboard *Avenger* to provide fighter escorts for the Arctic convoy, PQ18. Remained with *Avenger* for the North African invasion, and still aboard when she was torpedoed by *U-155* on 15 November 1942. Re-formed 1 May 1945, at Arbroath, and remained operational for some years after the war.

803: In 1939, embarked in *Ark Royal* with Skuas and Rocs and recorded the first 'kill' of any British fighter squadron, shooting down a Do18 on 26 September 1939. Took part in the sinking of the cruiser *Konigsberg* in April 1940. Lost all but two of its aircraft in an attack on the *Scharnhorst* on 6 June 1940. Re-equipped with Fulmars in October 1940, before embarking in *Formidable* to cover Malta convoys. Present at the Battle of Cape Matapan on 28 March 1941. In August 1941, it became the RN Fighter Squadron in the Western Desert. In April 1942, embarked in *Formidable*, carrying out long-range reconnaissance in the Indian Ocean. Provided army cooperation before disbanding at Tanga, 12 August 1943. Re-formed at Arbroath on 15 June 1945, with Seafires. Post-war, transferred to the Royal Canadian Navy.

804: Formed, 30 November 1939, Hatston, with four Sea Gladiator fighters. Embarked in *Glorious* in April 1940, providing fighter cover while the ship ferried aircraft to Norway. Operated Sea Hurricanes from catapult-armed merchant ships until this role passed to the RAF. In October 1942, joined *Dasher* with Sea Hurricanes to provide air cover for the North African landings. Equipped with Hellcats, it became part of 7 Naval Fighter Wing in October 1943, and embarked in *Emperor* in December, providing fighter cover for North Atlantic convoys and for raids on the

Tirpitz. Disbanded into 800 Squadron, 18 June 1944. Re-formed at Wingfield, 24 September 1944, with Hellcats. Embarked in *Ameer*, January 1945, to provide air cover for the landings on Ramree Island. Disbanded in November 1945.

805: Formed at Donibristle, 4 May 1940, as a Roc seaplane fighter squadron for operations in Norway, but plan abandoned. Disbanded on 13 May 1940. Re-formed, 1 January 1941, at Akrotiri in Cyprus, operating Fulmars and Buffaloes. Re-equipped with Martlets in July 1941, operated with the RAF as a joint unit over the Western Desert. Disbanded, 10 January 1943. Re-formed at Machrihanish, 1 July 1945, with Seafires. Disbanded 1948.

806: Formed 1 February 1940, as a fighter squadron at Worthy Down, with Skuas and Rocs. Moved to Hatston on 28 March 1940, and took part in attacks on shipping and shore installations at Bergen, before returning south to cover the evacuation from Dunkirk. In June 1940, equipped with Fulmars and embarked in *Illustrious* before she sailed for the Mediterranean. In the Mediterranean, the squadron accounted for more than twenty enemy aircraft. Provided air cover for the withdrawal from Crete. Hurricanes were flown throughout the summer of 1941, operating as part of the RN Fighter Squadron in North Africa. Disbanded into 803 Squadron while in East Africa on 18 January 1943. Re-formed at Machrihanish, 1 August 1945, with Seafires. Disbanded, 1947.

807: Formed on 15 September 1940 as a fighter squadron at Worthy Down, with Fulmars. Later embarked in *Ark Royal* to cover Malta convoys, and with another squadron accounted for fifteen enemy aircraft, as well as a number of probables.

When the carrier was torpedoed, four aircraft reached Gibraltar.

Re-equipped with Fulmars and Sea Hurricanes, embarked in *Argus*, providing cover for convoys. First squadron to receive Seafires, joining *Furious* for the North African landings in November, then embarked in *Indomitable* at the end of May 1943, for the landings on Sicily. Squadron later transferred to *Battler*, and provided air cover for the Salerno landings. In April 1944, some aircraft were detached to operate with the Desert Air Force in Italy, before regrouping aboard *Hunter* for the invasion of the South of France in August. Provided fighter support for the liberation of Rangoon in April and May 1945, followed by air cover for anti-shipping strikes.

808: Formed as a fleet fighter squadron, Worthy Down, 1 July 1940, with Fulmars. Moved to Castletown, in September, patrolling the Irish Sea and Western Approaches. August 1940, aboard *Ark Royal*, it joined Force H in the Mediterranean, and with 807 Squadron accounted for nineteen enemy aircraft over a period of ten months in operations against Sicily and in defence of Malta convoys. Absorbed into 807 Squadron when *Ark Royal* sank on 13 November 1941.

Re-formed at Donibristle on 1 January 1942, with Fulmars. Seafires introduced in December 1942. Squadron operated briefly from *Battler* in April 1943, but was back with the carrier in July 1943, to cover the Salerno landings. Trained in close support operations, and in May 1944, operated from Lee-on-Solent with the 2nd Tactical Air Force to support the Normandy landings. Equipped with Hellcats in October 1944. Embarked in *Khedive*, January 1945, operated off Malaya and Sumatra maintaining air patrols and anti-shipping strikes, and provided air cover for the

liberation of Rangoon, before returning to anti-shipping strikes. It struck against airfields on Sumatra and was present for the Japanese surrender in Malaya. Disbanded, December 1945.

809: Formed Lee-on-Solent, 15 January 1941, as a fleet fighter squadron with Fulmars, it embarked in *Victorious* in July for the raid on Kirkenes, shooting down four Bf109s and Me110s for the loss of three aircraft. Later, on 9 March 1942, provided fighter escorts for an attack on the German battleship *Tirpitz*. Took part in the Malta convoy, Operation Pedestal. After tactical reconnaissance for the North African landings, it re-equipped with Seafires, and then provided air cover for the Salerno landings.

During 1944, it operated briefly with the Desert Air Force, then covered the landings in the South of France in August. Fighter cover was provided for the liberation of Rangoon, and reconnaissance over Malaya and Sumatra. It was present for the surrender of Japanese forces in Malaya. Disbanded, early 1946.

810: In 1939, the squadron was operating Swordfish from *Ark Royal*, making one of the first attacks on a U-boat on 14 September 1939. During the Norwegian Campaign in April 1940, it attacked the airfield at Vaernes. Attacked French battleship *Strasbourg* on 3 July 1940, and four days later *Dunkerque*. Operations in the Mediterrean followed, bombing Cagliari, interrupted by renewed attacks on the French Fleet, this time at Dakar in West Africa, in September, with an attack on the battleship *Richelieu*. Flew against the Italian Fleet at Cape Spartivento, and bombed the Tirso Dam in Sardinia on 2 February 1941, then operated against the naval bases at Leghorn and La Spezia.

Aboard *Ark Royal* in May 1941, took part in the search for the German battleship

Bismarck, later crippled in a torpedo attack by the carrier's Swordfish. Embarked in *Illustrious* for the Madagascar operation in May 1942. Re-equipped with Barracudas at Lee-on-Solent, April 1943, was aboard *Illustrious* for operations off Norway in July, returning to the Mediterranean for the Salerno landings. The following year, bombed the oil facilities and docks at Sabang in Sumatra, and raided the Andaman Islands. Back in the UK in 1945, undertook anti-shipping operations with RAF Coastal Command. At the end of the war, the squadron disbanded.

811: Formed May 1939, but lost its aircraft when *Courageous* was torpedoed on 17 September 1939. Re-formed at Lee-on-Solent, 15 July 1941. After operations with RAF Coastal Command, the squadron embarked in *Biter*, in February 1943, for convoy escort duties. In spring 1943, two U-boats were damaged, leaving them to be destroyed by surface vessels. Under Coastal Command control for most of 1944, in September, it embarked in Vindex, with Swordfish and Wildcats, for an Arctic convoy. Disbanded, 9 December 1944.

812: In 1939, operated Swordfish from *Glorious*. Carrier recalled to the Home Fleet for the Norwegian campaign, but squadron assigned to Coastal Command for minelaying off the Dutch coast. July 1941, embarked in *Furious* for attack on the Arctic port of Petsamo. Transferred to *Ark Royal*, September 1941, but most aircraft airborne when the ship was torpedoed. Using air-to-surface vessel radar, made the first night sinking of a U-boat, *U-451*, on 21 December 1941. Merged into 811 on 18 December 1942. Re-formed at Stretton with Barracudas, on 1 June 1944, 812 embarked in one of the new light fleet carriers, *Vengeance*, in January 1945, joining the British Pacific Fleet. Remained in the Far East after the war. Disbanded, Lee-on-Solent, August 1946.

813: Embarked in *Eagle* at Singapore in 1939, operating Swordfish. In spring 1940, the carrier sailed to the Mediterranean, where 813 acquired four Sea Gladiators that shot down several Italian bombers. The Swordfish sank merchant ships and a destroyer in a raid on Tobruk, and another destroyer in a raid on Sicily. Four of its aircraft joined *Illustrious* for the attack on the Italian Fleet at Taranto. Later, operating from a shore base near Port Sudan, the squadron accounted for five Italian destroyers before re-embarking in *Eagle* and sailing for the Atlantic, where the U-boat support ship *Elbe* was sunk and a tanker forced to surrender. Its aircraft were ashore at Gibraltar when *Eagle* was sunk on 11 August 1942. The squadron was able to support the North African landings. It disbanded in the UK on 18 October 1943.

Re-formed at Donibristle on 1 November 1943, with Swordfish for operations from *Campania*. Operating in the North Atlantic and on Arctic convoys, the Swordfish sank U-921 on 30 September 1943, and U-365 on 13 December. In April 1945, the squadron operated its final Arctic convoy aboard *Vindex*, and disbanded on 15 May 1945.

814: In 1939, it was operating Swordfish from *Hermes*. With the fall of France, the squadron attacked the French fleet, damaging the *Richelieu* on 8 July 1940, at Dakar. *Hermes* sailed for the Indian Ocean in December 1940, hunting for enemy vessels. After operating with the RAF during May 1941, the squadron re-embarked in *Hermes* and sailed for Ceylon, and was ashore when *Hermes* was sunk by Japanese aircraft on 9 April 1942. Disbanded, 31 December 1942, at Katukurunda. Re-formed at Stretton as a torpedo bomber reconnaissance unit, 1 July 1944, with Barracudas, the squadron embarked in *Venerable* in March 1944, for the Far East, but saw no further action before the war ended.

815: Formed on 9 October 1939 at Worthy Down, equipped with Swordfish but soon disbanded into 774 Squadron. Re-formed on 23 November 1939, as a spare squadron. On detachment to RAF Coastal Command, provided cover for the Dunkirk evacuation. Embarked aboard *Illustrious* in June, it formed the mainstay of the successful raid on Taranto on the night of 11–12 November 1940. When *Illustrious* was badly damaged by bombing off Malta on 10 January 1941, five aircraft in the air flew to Malta, where the squadron absorbed the survivors of another *Illustrious* squadron, 819. At the end of January 1941, it moved to Crete for attacks on enemy shipping and mine-laying. The squadron evacuated to Dekheila in April, and then posted to Cyprus to attack Vichy French shipping in Syria, sinking a destroyer and damaging another. Returning to Dekheila in August 1941, the squadron operated in support of the British 8th Army in the Western Desert. The squadron disbanded on 24 July 1943, at Mersa Matruh.

Re-formed at Lee-on-Solent, 1 October 1943, with Barracudas, the squadron embarked in *Begum* in February 1944. Embarked aboard *Indomitable* in July, to become part of the British Eastern Fleet. In August 1944, it joined an attack on the port of Emmahaven in Sumatra, followed by attacks on Sigli and on the Nicobar Islands. Returned to the UK in *Activity* during November 1944. The war ended before it could re-equip with Avengers. Disbanded Rattray, January 1946.

816: Formed 3 October 1939, aboard *Furious*, with Swordfish, it made the first aerial torpedo attack of the Second World War during the Norwegian Campaign in April 1940. Attempted to attack the *Scharnhorst* in September, and on 22 September 1940, five aircraft were lost during an attack on shipping at Trondheim. The squadron joined RAF Coastal Command in March 1941, for operations off the Dutch and French coasts. The squadron re-embarked in *Furious* in June to provide anti-submarine cover while RAF aircraft were ferried to Malta. Transferred to *Ark Royal*, and remained with her until she was sunk on 13 November 1941, then merged into 812 Squadron.

Re-formed 1 February 1942, at Palisadoes, Jamaica, with Swordfish and embarked in *Avenger* to cover a convoy from the USA to the UK. On arrival, operations were undertaken under Coastal Command control. It joined *Dasher* in February 1943, for Arctic convoy escort duties, but suffered severe casualties when the ship blew up on 27 March 1943. Regrouped at Machrihanish. Later, six Seafires were received and the squadron embarked in *Tracker* for the North Atlantic convoys. In January 1944, the squadron transferred to *Chaser* for service with the Arctic convoys. On 4 March 1944, an aircraft helped the destroyer *Onslaught* sink a German U-boat, and then on the following days, *U-366* and *U-973* were sunk by the squadron's aircraft. The squadron returned to operations over the English Channel in support of the Normandy landings. Disbanded at Perranporth, 1 August 1944. Re-formed at Lee-on-Solent on 1 February 1945, with Barracudas for duties aboard a light fleet carrier, but in July, it re-equipped with Firefly FR1s. It remained operational until 1948.

817: Formed at Crail, 15 March 1941, with Albacores, it embarked in *Furious* in July for the attack on Petsamo, before transferring to *Victorious* in August for operations in the Barents Sea. A torpedo attack on the German battleship *Tirpitz* on 9 March 1942, was unsuccessful. The squadron supported the North African landings, while on 21 November 1942, one of its aircraft sank *U-517* in the North Atlantic.

Back in the UK, transferred to *Indomitable* in March, and 817 covered the landings at Sicily. After the ship was badly damaged the squadron was put ashore at Gibraltar, and disbanded on 1 September 1943.

Re-formed at Lee-on-Solent on 1 December 1943, with new Barracudas. It embarked in *Begum* for the voyage to Ceylon, where the Wing operated from shore bases before rejoining *Indomitable* on 23 July 1944. Operations were carried out over Sumatra and the Nicobar Islands. On 13 January 1945, lost its aircraft in a tropical storm. The squadron disbanded, 21 February 1945. Re-formed at Rattray on 1 April 1945, with Barracudas, moved to Fearn later that month. Disbanded, 23 August 1945.

818: Formed Evanton, 24 August 1939, with Swordfish, and embarked on 25 August in *Ark Royal* at Scapa Flow. The Norwegian Campaign in April 1940, saw the entire squadron embarked in *Furious*, and on 11 April 1940, they attacked two German destroyers in Trondheim Fjord.

On 30 May 1940, the squadron moved to Thorney Island, to operate with Coastal Command, before joining *Ark Royal* for the Mediterranean. It took part in the attacks on the Vichy French Fleet at Oran, including the battleship *Strasbourg*. In May 1941, the squadron joined the hunt for the battleship *Bismarck*, and two of its aircraft scored the torpedo hits that disabled the ship. Re-equipped with Albacores on 1 November 1941. Embarked in *Formidable* on

4 February 1942, to join the Eastern Fleet. Disbanded, 24 June 1942. Re-formed at Lee-on-Solent, 19 October 1942, with Swordfish before joining *Unicorn* in March 1943. Later sailed to Ceylon, arriving in February 1944. Disbanded at Cochin on 14 October 1944.

Re-forming, 1 May 1945, at Rattray, with Barracudas, the squadron moved to Fearn in June. Moved back to Rattray, to disband on 15 August 1945.

819: Originally formed at Ford, 15 January 1940, with Swordfish. Part of the squadron detached to Coastal Command at Detling to protect the Dunkirk evacuation. In June, the squadron embarked in *Illustrious*, operating in the North Atlantic before joining the Mediterranean Fleet in August. Aircraft from the squadron took part in the attack on Taranto. When *Illustrious* was attacked on 10 January 1941, those aircraft in the air flew to Hal Far, where the squadron disbanded into 815 Squadron.

Re-formed at Lee-on-Solent, 1 October 1941, with Swordfish, the squadron took part in trials in *Avenger* in June 1942, before being seconded to Coastal Command for three months. Moved to Machrihanish on 16 April 1943, prior to joining *Archer*, for North Atlantic convoys. On 23 May 1943, one of the squadron's aircraft was the first to sink a U-boat, *U-752*, using rocket projectiles.

Three Wildcats were transferred from 892 Squadron during August 1943, before the squadron embarked in the escort carrier, *Activity*, and the following month the Swordfish received anti-shipping ASV radar. Further Wildcats were received in March 1944. On the next Arctic convoy, one of the squadron's Swordfish shared the destruction of *U-288* with an aircraft from 846 Squadron on 3 April 1944, while the Wildcats shot down four enemy aircraft. After this, the Swordfish were based ashore with Coastal Command, operating from East Coast

A Fairey Swordfish of No. 836 Squadron lands aboard the MAC-ship *Adula* after an anti-submarine patrol in late 1944. *(Via Lord Kilbracken)*

airfields prior to the Normandy landings, and then later with flights detached to airfields in Belgium.

Returning to the UK, the squadron disbanded at Bircham Newton, 10 March 1945.

820: In 1939, embarked in *Ark Royal* operating Swordfish, having earlier that year been the first to land aboard the carrier. Recalled for the Norwegian campaign. Following the fall of France, *Ark Royal* was sent to North Africa, with 820 Squadron mining the French naval base at Oran and sending torpedo attacks against French warships. An attack on Cagliari followed, before the French naval base at Dakar in West Africa was attacked in September 1940. Took part in the operation against the German battleship *Bismarck*.

Transferred to *Victorious* on 17 June 1941, re-equipped with Albacores. In February 1942, transferred to *Formidable*, for the Indian Ocean, where it was present at the landings on Madagascar, returning to the UK in time for the landings in North Africa. During this operation, a squadron aircraft sank *U-331*. The squadron supported the landings at Sicily and then at Salerno. Disbanded at Donibristle, 13 November 1943. Re-formed at Lee-on-Solent, 1 January 1944, operating Barracudas, embarking in *Indefatigable* on 10 June 1944 for an attack on the German battleship *Tirpitz* in a Norwegian Fjord. In September, the squadron re-equipped with Avengers before re-embarking for passage to Ceylon. During the first half of 1945, the squadron was involved in bombing the oil refineries at

Palembang on Sumatra, followed by raids against the airfields of the Sakashima Gunto islands during the spring. The squadron attacked targets in the Japanese home islands, including many in the Tokyo area, right up to VJ-Day. Disbanded, March 1946.

821: In 1939, it was operating twelve Swordfish from *Ark Royal*, being recalled in April, 1940, for the Norwegian campaign. On 21 June 1940, was involved in the unsuccessful attack on the *Scharnhorst*. Disbanded on 2 December 1940.

Re-forming at Detling on 1 July 1941, the squadron transferred to Egypt in January 1942. Re-equipped with Albacores in March, it briefly operated from Cyprus to attack enemy targets in Rhodes. In November, the squadron moved to Malta to attack enemy convoys from Italy to North Africa. Returned to the UK without its aircraft and disbanded on 10 October 1943. Re-formed on 1 May 1944, with Barracudas, it embarked in *Puncher* in November 1944. In February, 1945, began mine-laying off the Norwegian coast. Embarked in *Trumpeter* on 3 July 1945, for the Far East, reaching Cochin in southern India on 26 July, but returned home without seeing further action. Disbanded early 1946.

822: In 1939, it was operating Swordfish aboard *Courageous*, and ceased to exist after the carrier was torpedoed and sunk on 17 September 1939. Re-formed at Lee-on-Solent, 15 October 1941 with Swordfish, which were replaced by Albacores in March 1942, before the squadron embarked aboard *Furious* on 17 July 1942, for convoy escort duty, followed by support for the North African landings. Took part in an attack on La Senia airfield on 10 November 1942, in which forty-seven enemy aircraft were destroyed. Re-equipped with Barracudas in July 1943, at Lee-on-Solent.

The squadron arrived in southern India, in April 1944. Squadron joined *Victorious* for dive bombing operations over Sumatra, but the aircraft proved ill-suited to tropical operations, and the squadron's personnel were shipped home in October.

Regrouping at Lee-on-Solent on 18 November 1944, the squadron was equipped with Barracudas, for operations over the English Channel under the control of RAF Coastal Command. Disbanded, February 1946.

823: Aboard *Glorious*, in the Mediterranean in 1939, operating Swordfish. The carrier was sent to the Red Sea and Indian Ocean, both to protect trade routes and to find German shipping. Recalled to home waters on the invasion of Norway in April 1940. Withdrawing from Norway, she was sunk with half of 823's aircraft and personnel aboard. On 21 June 1940, took part in an unsuccessful attack on the *Scharnhorst*. Disbanded at Hatstopn, 3 December 1940.

Re-formed at Crail on 1 November 1941, with Swordfish that were later replaced by Albacores. Joined *Furious* in August, disembarking in September to operate with Coastal Command on English Channel anti-submarine patrols. Re-equipped in June 1943, with Barracudas. Reached India aboard *Atheling*, but on 6 July 1943, was merged into 822 Squadron.

824: In 1939, it was aboard *Eagle* at Singapore, operating Swordfish. The carrier was ordered to the Mediterranean in May, 1940. Two aircraft were detached to *Illustrious* for the raid on Taranto on 11–12 November 1940. Arriving at Port Sudan in March 1941, the squadron sunk Italian destroyers off Eritrea on 3 April 1941, and damaged two others so badly that they had to be beached. Rejoined *Eagle* on 19 April 1941 to search for the battleship *Bismarck* in the South Atlantic, but instead sunk the U-boat support vessel *Elbe* on 6 June 1941, and forced the tanker *Lothringen* to surrender on 15 June 1940. Most of the aircraft were aboard *Eagle* when she sank on 11 August 1942. The few aircraft ashore in Gibraltar merged into 813 Squadron.

Re-formed on 1 October 1942, at Lee-on-Solent, with Swordfish Is, then embarked in *Unicorn* in March 1943. In August, six Sea Hurricanes provided a fighter element, before the squadron transferred to *Striker* on 27 October 1943. Wildcats replaced the Sea Hurricanes in June 1944, ready for Arctic convoy escort. Disbanded, 16 October 1944, at Abbotsinch. Re-formed at Katukurunda, Ceylon, on 2 July 1945, with Barracudas, but the war ended and the squadron eventually disbanded in January 1946.

825: Embarked in *Glorious*, in the Mediterranean in 1939, operating Swordfish. The carrier was deployed to the Red Sea and Indian Ocean, and returned to the Mediterranean in January 1940, but was recalled to home waters on the invasion of Norway in April. The squadron disembarked during the evacuation from Dunkirk, losing eight aircraft. Embarked in *Furious* in July. During September 1940, the squadron was involved in night bombing operations against Norwegian ports. Regrouped aboard *Victorious* on 19 May 1941, to take part in the *Bismarck* operation. The squadron transferred to *Ark Royal* and some of its aircraft were airborne when the carrier was torpedoed on 13 November 1941; these landed at Gibraltar to be absorbed by 812 Squadron.

Re-formed on 1 January 1942, at Lee-on-Solent with Swordfish. On 12 February 1942, without fighter cover, six aircraft pressed home an attack on the *Scharnhorst* and *Gneisenau* in poor weather and failing light, with the loss of all six aircraft and

thirteen out of the eighteen personnel aboard, for which the CO, Lt Cdr Esmonde, received a posthumous VC.

Regrouped on 2 March 1942, still at Lee-on-Solent, with Swordfish IIs, later moving to Machrihanish. After working with Coastal Command direction throughout the winter on operations over and around the English Channel, on the Arctic convoys, on 22 August 1944, *U-354* was sunk, and over the next couple of weeks, two more U-boats were shared with surface vessels. Disbanded into 815 Squadron on 3 April 1945.

Re-formed with RCN personnel at Rattray on 1 July 1945, and formally transferred to the Royal Canadian Navy on 24 January 1946.

826: Formed 15 March 1940, at Ford, with Albacores. Covered the Dunkirk evacuation, flying from Detling, before operating with Coastal Command until November 1940, based at Bircham Newton, making twenty-two night attacks against coastal targets and escorting more than ninety convoys. Embarked in *Formidable* in November 1940. Anti-submarine and reconnaissance cover was provided for a Malta convoy before the Battle of Matapan at the end of March 1941, when the squadron's aircraft participated in a torpedo attack, damaging the battleship *Vittorio Veneto*. Raids followed on Axis bases in North Africa before the squadron covered the evacuation of Crete. After a spell at Dekheila, the squadron moved to Nicosia on 1 July 1941, for attacks on Vichy French shipping at Beirut. In June 1943, it covered the invasion of Sicily. Disbanded at Ta Kali, 16 October 1943.

Re-formed at Lee-on-Solent on 1 December 1943, with Barracudas before embarking in *Indefatigable* in June 1944. Took part in an attack on the battleship *Tirpitz*, lying in a Norwegian fjord, followed by anti-submarine and anti-shipping patrols off Norway. A further attack on *Tirpitz* followed. Disbanded into 820 Squadron at Machrihanish on 23 October 1944.

Re-forming at East Haven on 15 August 1945, manned by the Royal Canadian Navy. Disbanded in February 1946.

827: Formed with Albacores, 15 September 1940, at Yeovilton, before operating under Coastal Command. In June 1941, was involved in attacks on the battlecruisers, *Scharnhorst* and *Gneisenau*. During the raid on Kirkenes on 30 July 1941, it lost half of its aircraft, although one Albacore shot down a Ju87.

In October joined *Indomitable*, sailing to Aden, where it arrived in January 1942, for anti-submarine patrols in the Red Sea and Indian Ocean. Joined the invasion of Madagascar in May 1942. Joined the Malta convoy, Operation Pedestal, in August.

Re-equipped with Barracudas at Stretton in January 1943. On 30 March 1943, the squadron transferred to *Victorious*, and on 3 April 1943, it shared with 830 Squadron ten hits during a dive bombing attack on the *Tirpitz* in Norway. Another attempt was made on *Tirpitz* in July, from *Formidable*, when a smokescreen saved the ship, but two hits were made while flying from *Furious* in August.

Absorbed 830 Squadron in October, 1944. Embarked in *Colossus* in January 1945, to join the British Pacific Fleet. On arrival in Ceylon disembarked, and did not re-embark until after the war had ended.

828: Formed at Lee-on-Solent, 15 September 1940, with Albacores. After work up it operated under Coastal Command. Embarked in *Victorious* on 2 July 1941, and took part in the raid on Kirkenes, losing five aircraft. From 18 September 1941, it operated from Malta, attacking enemy convoys between Sicily and North Africa. In March 1942, the squadron operated jointly with 830 Squadron as the Naval Air Squadron Malta. Between them, these squadrons sank thirty ships and damaged another fifty. Disbanded at Hal Far on 1 September 1943.

Re-formed at Lee-on-Solent, 1 March 1944, with Barracudas, it embarked in *Implacable* in August. Deployed to *Formidable* later that month to take part in Operation Goodwood, a strike against the battleship *Tirpitz*. Avengers replaced the Barracudas in January, 1945. On 13 March 1945, the squadron re-embarked in *Implacable* to join the British Pacific Fleet, and undertook raids on Truk and later on the Japanese home islands. Disbanded in June 1946.

829: Formed at Ford, 15 June 1940 with Albacores. On 7 October 1940, it moved to St Eval, operating under Coastal Command. On 15 November 1940, it embarked aboard *Formidable* to provide cover for a convoy to West Africa and Cape Town. The squadron took part in the Battle of Matapan, when an Albacore scored a direct hit on the battleship *Vittorio Veneto*. Re-equipped with Swordfish it embarked in *Illustrious* on 7 March 1942, taking part in the invasion of Madagascar. Disbanded into 810 Squadron in South Africa on 7 October 1942.

Re-formed at Lee-on-Solent on 1 October 1943, with Barracudas. Embarking in *Victorious* on 12 February 1944, the squadron took part in an attack on the battleship *Tirpitz* on 3 April 1944, losing two aircraft. On 9 July 1944, it merged into 831 squadron, also aboard the carrier.

830: Formed out of 767 Squadron, Hal Far, 1 July 1940, operating Swordfish, the squadron carried out bombing raids against Sicily and Libya, including a dive-bombing raid on oil storage tanks in Sicily, and on 19 July, bombed a U-boat. On a number of operations, the squadron operated with 828, combining in March 1942 as the Naval Air Squadron Malta. On 31 March 1943, it disbanded.

Re-formed at Lee-on-Solent on 15 May 1943, with Barracudas, most of which were flown by members of the RNZNVR. In October, it joined *Furious* for operations off Norway. On 3 April 1944, it shared with 827 Squadron ten hits during a dive bombing attack on the *Tirpitz* in Norway. On 3 October 1944, the squadron was disbanded at Hatston into 827.

831: Formed on 1 April 1941, at Crail operating Albacores. Embarked in *Indomitable* in October and arrived at Cape Town at the end of December. Spent time with the carrier in the Indian Ocean and at shore bases, including Aden. Re-embarked for the invasion of Madagascar in June 1942. Returned to the UK after *Indomitable* damaged on Malta convoy, and the squadron was reinforced by a small number of Barracudas.

The squadron re-embarked in *Indomitable* in March 1943, and in May became a Barracuda squadron. Transferred to *Furious* in March 1944, for an attack on the battleship *Tirpitz*. Further attempts were made using *Victorious* in May, but bad weather intervened and instead attacks were made on convoys off Norway. The squadron returned to the Far East aboard the carrier, and attacked shore installations and oil storage facilities in Sabang Harbour on Sumatra, and attacked nearby airfields. The squadron moved home to disband at Lee-on-Solent on 6 December 1944.

832: Formed at Lee-on-Solent on 1 April 1941, operating Albacores, it embarked in *Victorious* in August, for operations off Norway. Aircrew are credited with 'inventing' the naval version of British battledress at their own expense, as a practical solution to the wear and tear on traditional uniform for the rough conditions of open cockpit flying. The carrier operated off Iceland in November 1941, and February 1942, anti-shipping sorties off Norway, before escorting Arctic convoys, broken only by a raid on the battleship *Tirpitz*. After a spell ashore, re-embarked in October 1942, for the North African landings, after which it carried out attacks on shore targets as well as maintaining anti-submarine patrols off the coast of North Africa.

The squadron re-equipped with Avengers in January 1943, while visiting the USA aboard *Victorious*, en route to the Pacific. Operations were conducted from *Victorious* in the Coral Sea in May 1943, before it joined the USS *Saratoga* to support landings in the Solomons. The squadron re-embarked in *Victorious* in July to return home.

In February 1944, embarked aboard *Athene* and *Engadine* for Ceylon, disembarking at Katukurunda on 15 April 1944. Operating from *Illustrious*, it took part in a bombing raid on Sourabaya on 17 May 1944, after which it transferred to *Begum* on 26 May 1944, for six months. It returned home aboard *Begum*, and disbanded on 21 February 1945.

833: A Swordfish squadron formed on 8 December 1941. Joined *Biter* in September 1942, assigned to cover the North African landings. It embarked in *Argus* on 25 December 1942, to return home to Stretton. From 1 February 1943, the squadron operated with Coastal Command, for mine-laying, anti-shipping and anti-submarine patrols over the English Channel. After a spell operating from *Stalker*, with a number of Seafires added to the squadron, it merged into 836 Squadron on 7 January 1944.

Re-formed on 26 April 1944, with Swordfish and Wildcats aboard the escort carrier *Activity*, it provided cover for an Arctic convoy, and afterwards for two North Atlantic convoys, before covering a Gibraltar convoy and then disbanding at Eglinton, on 13 September 1944.

834: Formed in Jamaica at Palisadoes on 10 December 1941, as a Swordfish squadron, then embarked in the first American-supplied escort carrier, *Archer*, in March 1942, to sail to Cape Town. After providing cover for convoys, it moved ashore, eventually under Coastal Command at Exeter. Moved to Machrihanish in April 1943. In June, six Seafires were added to form a fighter flight, and on 8 July 1943 it embarked in *Hunter*, to escort a Gibraltar convoy, where the Seafires were transferred to cover the Salerno landings. The Swordfish and Seafires

regrouped aboard *Battler* on 7 September 1943, and sailed to Aden to provide anti-submarine patrols, rejoining *Battler* on 17 October 1943, to provide convoy protection in the Indian Ocean. In March 1944, one of the squadron's aircraft spotted the German tanker *Brake*, which was then sunk by a destroyer. Seafires were replaced by Wildcats in April 1944, and continued with convoy protection before disembarking at Trincomalee, Ceylon, on 7 October 1944. The personnel took passage back to the UK in November, disbanding on 6 December 1944.

835: Formed at Palisadoes, Jamaica, 15 February 1942, as a Swordfish squadron, it flew to Norfolk, Virginia, ready to embark in *Furious* on 3 April 1942, reaching Lee-on-Solent on 15 April 1942. Operated from

A predominantly white Fairey Swordfish of no. 860 Squadron manned by members of the Royal Netherlands Navy. White was regarded as the best colour for anti-submarine aircraft in the North Atlantic. *(Royal Netherlands Maritime Institute)*

Scotland and Northern Ireland, between periods of deck landing training aboard the escort carrier *Activity*. Embarked in *Battler* on 10 April 1943, for convoy escort duties, gaining a fighter flight of six Sea Hurricanes. Transferred to *Chaser* on 6 November 1943, and then to *Nairana* on 30 December. The squadron's fighters accounted for two Ju290s in May and June 1944. The squadron's aircraft attacked two U-boats and shot down four enemy aircraft while on the Arctic convoys. No. 835 Squadron disbanded at Hatston on 31 March 1945.

836: Formed at Palisadoes, Jamaica, 1 March 1942 as a Swordfish squadron. Moved to New York before joining *Biter* on 2 June 1942, for the UK. Operated from a number of bases in Scotland, before passing to Coastal Command at Thorney Island on 30 December 1942. On 5 July 1943, the squadron moved to Maydown, and became the parent squadron for MAC-ship flights. The squadron's strength was reduced with the decline of the U-boat menace and the growing use of escort carriers, so it disbanded at Maydown on 29 July 1945.

837: Formed 1 May 1942, Palisadoes, as a Swordfish squadron. Embarked in *Dasher* on 25 July 1942, covering a North Atlantic convoy. When *Dasher* blew up in the Firth of Clyde on 27 March 1943, it was ashore, but disbanded on 15 June 1943.

Re-formed at Stretton, 1 August 1944, as a Barracuda squadron but did not receive the first of these aircraft until 4 September 1944. Embarked in *Glory* on 4 April 1945, to join the British Pacific Fleet in May, but the war ended before the Squadron could see action, although it covered the Japanese surrender at Rabaul.

838: Formed Dartmouth, Nova Scotia, on 15 May 1942, as a Swordfish squadron.

Embarked aboard *Attacker* on 12 December 1942, but did not start its move to the UK until 2 March 1943, accompanying a convoy from the Caribbean to the UK. It was assigned to MAC-ship duties, moving to Maydown on 13 June 1943, but merged into 836 Squadron on 13 August 1943.

Re-formed at Belfast on 1 November 1943, as a Swordfish squadron, it. Eventually moved to Harrowbeer on 20 April 1944, operating with Coastal Command on anti-submarine duties in the English Channel, in the period immediately before and during the Normandy Landings. Later, it moved to operate from Coastal Command's Scottish bases. Later, it was moved to Thorney Island, disbanding on 3 February 1945.

840: Formed at Palisadoes on 1 June 1942, as a Swordfish squadron. Joined *Battler* on 12 December 1942, later transferring to *Attacker* to provide anti-submarine cover for UK-bound convoy. At Hatston in May, the squadron was assigned to MAC-ship duties, but merged into 836 squadron on 13 August 1943.

841: Formed at Lee-on-Solent, 1 July 1942, as a special duty unit with two Albacores, later increased to four. Operated as part of the RAF, it made ninety-nine night attacks against enemy shipping and E-boats. Disbanded at Manston, 1 December 1943.

Re-formed at Lee-on-Solent, 1 February 1944, as a Barracuda squadron. In August, it joined *Implacable* for anti-submarine and anti-shipping strikes off Norway before disbanding into 828 Squadron at Hatston, 28 November 1944.

842: Formed at Lee-on-Solent as a Swordfish squadron, 1 March 1943, it moved to to Hatston in May; acquiring a fighter flight of Seafires. On 5 August 1943, the squadron embarked in *Fencer*, and provided anti-submarine cover for the occupation of the

Azores during October and November. On 10 February 1944, a Swordfish sank *U-666*. When *Fencer* escorted an Arctic convoy, 842 attacked eleven German U-boats and sank three, *U-277* on 1 May 1944, and the following day, *U-674* and *U-959*. After operations from other carriers, the squadron moved to Thorney Island, and disbanded, 15 January 1945.

845: Formed at Quonset Point, 1 February 1943, as an Avenger squadron. Embarked aboard *Chaser* from Norfolk, Virginia, on 1 June 1943, to cover a convoy to the UK. Boosted by a fighter flight of Wildcats, it was shipped aboard *Atheling*, *Engadine* and the SS *Strathnaver* to Katukurunda in Ceylon, arriving on 5 April 1944, when the fighter flight transferred to 890 Squadron.

Embarking in *Illustrious* in May, it mounted a dive bombing raid on the oil refinery and harbour at Sourabaya, Java, before transferring to *Ameer* in July for convoy protection in the Indian Ocean, gaining a fighter flight of Wildcats, which it kept until February 1945. Embarked aboard *Empress* to provide anti-submarine cover during operations against Malaya and Sumatra. *Shah* brought the squadron's personnel back to the UK in September. Disbanded at Gourock on 7 October 1945.

846: Formed at Quonset Point as an Avenger squadron on 1 April 1943. Joined *Ravager* on 2 July 1943, providing anti-submarine cover for an eastbound convoy. The squadron spent the rest of the year at Scottish air stations, acquiring a Wildcat flight on 20 December 1943, before embarking aboard *Tracker* on 4 January 1944, to provide cover for Gibraltar convoys. In March and April, the escort carrier covered Arctic convoys, and on one the squadron's aircraft attacked six U-boats outward, and another two on the return.

The squadron embarked in *Trumpeter* on 5 July 1944, for anti-shipping and mine-laying operations off Norway. An Arctic convoy was escorted in March 1945. After VE-day, the squadron lost its fighter flight and plans to join the British Pacific Fleet were abandoned. Renumbered as 751 Squadron, 22 September 1945.

847: Formed as a Barracuda squadron at Lee-on-Solent on 1 June 1943, it embarked in *Illustrious* on 28 November 1943, for the Indian Ocean. In April 1945, the squadron dive-bombed the oil storage tanks and harbour installations at Sabang, and later on the Andaman Islands. Merged into 810 Squadron at Trincomalee on 30 June 1944.

848: Formed, 1 June 1943, as an Avenger squadron at Quonset Point, embarked in *Trumpeter* on 4 September 1943, providing anti-submarine cover for an eastbound convoy. Posted to Manston on 20 April 1944, and then to Thorney Island, it operated as part of Coastal Command, and providing anti-shipping and anti-submarine support for the Normandy landings.

It returned to Fleet Air Arm control to embark in *Formidable*, providing anti-submarine cover on the way to Gibraltar, from where the squadron flew to Dekheila, not re-embarking until 27 January 1945. Arriving in the Far East, the squadron attacked airfields in the Sakishima Gunto during April, following this by attacks on Formosa. A number of aircraft were lost during kamikaze attacks on the carrier, which also suffered damage from a serious hangar fire. VJ-day intervened and the carrier and her squadrons returned to Australia. The squadron left its aircraft in Australia and its personnel returned home. Disbanded at Devonport on 31 October 1945.

849: Formed at Quonset Point on 1 August 1943, as an Avenger squadron, it joined *Khedive* on 1 November 1943. The squadron was deployed to Perranporth on 20 April 1944 to operate under Coastal Command during the Normandy landings.

Returning to Fleet Air Arm control, it embarked aboard *Rajah* on 9 August 1944, sailing to Ceylon. The squadron transferred to *Victorious*, from which bombing raids were carried out against the oil refineries at Pangkalan Brandon and Palembang in Sumatra during January 1945. In March it mounted strikes against the Sakishima Gunto, and, later, Formosa was attacked, before the carrier withdrew to Australia. Returning aboard *Victorious*, the squadron attacked the Japanese home islands, hitting targets in and around Tokyo. Disbanded on the return of the personnel to the UK, 31 October 1945.

850: Formed at Quonset Point on 1 January 1943, but disbanded at the end of the month, to reform as an Avenger squadron on 1 September 1943, at Squantum. Embarked in *Empress* in February 1944, providing anti-submarine patrols for a UK convoy. Moved to Perranporth to operate under Coastal Command for the Normandy landings, sinking one enemy merchant vessel and damaging another off the Channel Islands on 24 July 1944. Disbanded on 24 December 1944, after further operations with Coastal Command.

851: An Avenger unit formed at Squantum, 1 October 1943, and embarked in *Shah* in January 1944, and sailed for the Indian Ocean, where a flight of four Wildcats was added. Three U-boats were attacked during August. Early in 1945, the Wildcat flight was disbanded. The squadron's aircraft raided targets in Burma during April and May, and attacked a Japanese cruiser. Disbanded at Gourock on 7 October 1945.

852: Formed as an Avenger squadron at Squantum, 1 November 1943, and embarked in *Nabob* on 11 February 1944. A Wildcat flight of was added in May 1944, and the squadron re-embarked for mine-laying and anti-shipping strikes off Norway. After *Nabob* was torpedoed by *U-354* in August, the squadron transferred to *Trumpeter* on 10 September, before disbanding on 17 October 1944.

853: An Avenger squadron formed at Squantum, 1 December 1943, and joined *Arbiter* on 31 May 1944, to sail for the UK. A Wildcat flight formed in September, ready for the squadron to join *Tracker* on 12 September 1944, to escort an Arctic convoy. Transferred to *Queen* on 27 January 1945, for operations off Norway, followed by further Arctic convoy duty. Disbanded on 30 May 1945.

854: An Avenger squadron formed at Squantum on 1 January 1944, and embarked in *Indomitable* on 10 April 1944. On 23 May 1944, the squadron was assigned to Coastal Command at Hawkinge and then at Thorney Island during the Normandy landings. Squadron personnel embarked in *Activity* on 7 September 1944, for Ceylon. The squadron joined *Illustrious* on 1 December 1944, bombing targets in Sumatra throughout December and January, with attacks on the Sakishima Gunto during March and April 1945. Disbanded on its return to the UK, on 8 December 1945.

855: An Avenger squadron formed at Squantum, 1 February 1944, and embarked on 6 May 1944, aboard *Queen* for the UK. Disembarking. It was immediately assigned to Coastal Command, to cover the Normandy landings. Disbanded on 19 October 1944 at Machrihanish.

856: Forming at Squantum as an Avenger squadron, 1 March 1944, it embarked in *Smiter* in June. Embarked aboard *Premier* on 13 September 1944, with a Wildcat flight, for operations off Norway. During April and May 1945, *Premier* escorted Arctic convoys, returning after VE-day. Disbanded Hatston, 15 June 1945.

857: Avenger squadron formed at Squantum, 1 April 1944, and embarked aboard Rajah on 29 June 1944. It re-embarked on 9 September 1944, for Ceylon, where it transferred to *Indomitable* on 27 November. Through the rest of the winter, it attacked targets in Sumatra, before moving to targets in the Sakashima Gunto and Formosa in the spring. Remained in the Far East after VJ-day to operate against Japanese suicide boats off Hong Kong on 31 August 1945 and 1 September. Disbanded 30 November 1945.

860: A Royal Netherlands Navy-manned squadron formed 15 June 1943, at Donibristle with Swordfish, to become part of the MAC-ship wing. VE-Day meant the end of the squadron's MAC-ship role. Post-war, the squadron became an integral part of the Royal Netherlands Navy.

877: Hurricane unit formed 1 April 1943, at Tanga, Tanganiyka, it moved to Port Reitz in Kenya in July, but plans to move to Ceylon were abandoned and it disbanded on 30 December 1943.

878: A Martlet squadron formed, 1 March 1943, it embarked in *Illustrious* on 8 June 1943. Operated from the carrier off Iceland, before providing fighter cover at Salerno. Disbanded at Eglinton, 25 January 1944.

879: Formed St Merryn, 1 October 1942, as a Fulmar squadron, it moved to Old Sarum on 18 November 1942, to train in army support. A move to Stretton on 22 March 1943, saw it equipped with Seafires. The squadron embarked in *Attacker* on 29 July 1943, sailing to the Mediterranean where it flew seventy-five patrols covering the Salerno landings. It returned to the UK on 6 October 1943. Returning to the Mediterranean, spring, 1944, it was split into flights, some of which operated with the Desert Air Force in Italy. Re-united aboard *Attacker* on 23 July, to provide cover for the landings in the south of France, after which it undertook operations in the Aegean. On 11 December 1944, it disembarked to Dekheila, before re-embarking on 14 April 1945, for Ceylon.

At the end of the war, the squadron operated over Malaya and Singapore, before returning to disband at Nutts Corner, 7 January 1946.

880: Formed at Arbroath on 15 January 1941, as a fighter squadron with a mixture of aircraft, including Martlets, some borrowed Sea Gladiators and then Sea Hurricanes, some of its aircraft provided air cover for the raid on Petsamo, when a Do18 was shot down. Reunited, the squadron joined *Indomitable* on 10 October 1941, and sailed to join the British Eastern Fleet. In May 1942, the squadron supported the landings in Madagascar.

Air cover was provided for the major Malta convoy, Operation Pedestal, in August 1942, when eight enemy aircraft were shot down and three damaged for the loss of three Sea Hurricanes. Returning home to Stretton, the squadron re-equipped with Seafire in September, before joining *Argus* on 16 October 1942, to provide support for the North African landings in November, and later for the landings in Sicily in July 1943, and, after transferring to *Indomitable*, for the Salerno landings in September.

The squadron transferred to *Furious* in February 1944, for operations off Norway, including attacks on the battleship *Tirpitz*. Four aircraft were detached in June 1944. In January 1945, the squadron moved to *Implacable* on 15 March 1945 to join the British Pacific Fleet. It provided patrols and fighter escorts for attacks on the island of Truk, and dive-bombed oil storage tanks. Later, the squadron attacked the Japanese home islands, inflicting heavy losses on Japanese aircraft. After the war ended, merged into 801 Squadron at Schofields, 11 September 1945.

881: Formed as a Martlet squadron at Lee-on-Solent on 1 June 1941, the squadron embarked in *Illustrious* on 15 March 1942 for the Indian Ocean to take part in the invasion of Madagascar in May. With 882 Squadron, it shot down seven enemy aircraft. It returned to the UK on 4 February 1943. A flight embarked briefly aboard *Furious* in July for operations off Norway, accounting for one German aircraft. Re-equipping with Wildcats in August while at Eglinton, the squadron joined *Pursuer* on 26 November 1943. Covering a Gibraltar convoy during February 1944, its aircraft shot down two enemy aircraft and damaged another. Fighter cover was provided for attacks on the German battleship *Tirpitz* in April and June, accounting for another German aircraft. Later, the squadron spent three days aboard *Fencer* covering an anti-shipping operation off Norway.

The squadron re-embarked in *Pursuer* on 4 July 1944, for the Mediterranean, and flew almost 200 sorties during the landings in the South of France in August, before moving to the Aegean in September. Returning to the UK, the squadron spent the winter months operating from a number of carriers, before re-embarking in *Pursuer*

for Cape Town on 23 March 1945, where it re-equipped with Hellcats. Meant to join the British Pacific Fleet, VJ-Day intervened, and the personnel returned to the UK, disbanding on arrival, 27 October 1945.

882: A Martlet squadron formed at Donibristle, 15 July 1941, the squadron joined *Illustrious* on 22 February 1942, to support the landings in Madagascar, when, with 881 Squadron, they shot down seven enemy aircraft. On 19 May 1942, the two squadrons were merged. Re-formed at Donibristle on 7 September 1942, it joined *Victorious* on 6 October 1942, for the North African landings the following month, returning to the UK before sailing to the Pacific for operations in the Coral Sea in May 1943, followed by support for the American landings in the Solomon Islands in June. The carrier returned to the UK and the squadron disembarked to Eglinton on 26 September 1943. In December, it joined *Searcher*, covering a convoy to the United States, and after returning in February 1944, the squadron covered attacks on the *Tirpitz*.

On 5 July 1944, 898 Squadron was absorbed. Re-embarked in *Searcher*, it covered the landing in the south of France, during which 167 sorties were flown, operating in support of US Army units. On 9 February 1945, augmented by two Firefly night-fighters from 746 Squadron, the squadron operated off Norway, including a successful attack on the U-boat base at Kilbotn. In June, *Searcher* sailed for Ceylon, but on arrival the war had ended. Disbanded, 9 October 1945.

883: Formed as a Sea Hurricane squadron on 10 October 1941 at Yeovilton, on 28 January 1942, the squadron moved to Scotland to operate as part of RAF Fighter Command. After returning to the Fleet Air Arm, the squadron embarked in the escort carrier

Avenger on 16 June 1942, for Arctic convoy duties, starting with PQ18, in September, the first Arctic convoy to have a carrier in the close escort, and with 802 shot down five German aircraft, damaging another seventeen. During the North African landings, *Avenger* was torpedoed on 15 November 1942, and blew up, with the squadron aboard.

884: A Fulmar squadron formed at Donibristle, 1 November 1941, the aircraft were replaced by hooked Spitfires, in December. After working up the squadron joined Fighter Command in Scotland on 22 March 1942. Rejoining the Fleet Air Arm on 21 July 1942, the squadron embarked in *Victorious* two days later, giving fighter cover to the Malta convoy, Operation Pedestal. After returning to the UK, and the RAF, the squadron re-embarked to provide fighter cover during the landings in North Africa. It returned to Fighter Command, operating from several Scottish bases before disbanding on 20 July 1943, at Machrihanish.

885: Formed at Dekheila on 1 March 1941, with Sea Gladiators and Buffaloes, it embarked in *Eagle* on 3 March 1941 for a week, returning as a shore-based squadron. It disbanded on 1 May 1941. Re-formed on 1 December 1941, at Yeovilton as a Sea Hurricane squadron, it eventually joined *Victorious* on 29 June 1942, and provided distant fighter cover for two Arctic convoys, PQ17 and QP13, the following month. Afterwards, it took part in Operation Pedestal, the Malta convoy of August 1942. On returning, it received Seafires. It joined *Formidable* on 28 October 1942, providing fighter cover for the North African landings, and remained with the carrier for the invasion of Sicily and the Salerno landings. Returned to the UK on 18 October 1943, and disbanded at Lee-on-Solent on 15 November.

Re-formed at Lee-on-Solent on 15 February 1944, it operated with Seafires as part of 2nd Tactical Air Force, after D-Day. In July, at Lee-on-Solent, it absorbed 886 and 887 squadrons, before replacing its Seafires in November with Hellcats. Embarked in *Ruler* on 16 December 1944, and early in 1945, sailed to join the British Pacific Fleet, initially to provide fighter cover over the fleet replenishment area. Time was spent ashore at Ponam, in the Admiralty Islands, when a TBR flight was formed first with Corsairs and then with Avengers. The squadron disbanded at Schofields on 27 September 1944.

886: A Fulmar squadron formed at Donibristle, 15 March 1942, it joined Fighter Command on 11 August 1942. Returned to the Fleet Air Arm on 7 October 1942, at Stretton, spending the next nine months in Scotland and Northern Ireland. It re-equipped with Seafires in March 1943, and acquired a Swordfish flight aircraft in June. The squadron embarked in *Attacker* on 19 June 1943, providing fighter and anti-submarine cover for the Salerno landings.

Returning to the UK at Burscough on 7 October 1943, the squadron lost its Swordfish. After D-Day, it joined the 2nd Tactical Air Force. On 19 July 1944, it merged into 885 Squadron.

887: Fulmar squadron formed at Lee-on-Solent, 1 May 1942, but re-equipped in December with Spitfires while awaiting Seafires. Embarked aboard *Unicorn* on 19 April 1943, and in May covered a Malta convoy. After returning to the UK, it went back to provide fighter cover for the Salerno landings in September. On 6 July 1944, embarked in *Indefatigable* and saw action off Norway, covering strikes against the battleship *Tirpitz*.

The squadron joined *Implacable* in mid-October, before returning to *Indefatigable* on 21 November 1944, and sailing to join the British Pacific Fleet. In January 1945, it covered attacks on Sumatra, followed by the Sakishima Gunto in March and April, and then on Formosa, before seeing action over the Japanese home islands. Disbanded post-war.

888: Martlet squadron formed at Lee-on-Solent, 1 November 1941. Embarked in *Formidable* on 4 February 1942, sailing to the Indian Ocean for the invasion of Madagascar. Briefly at Donibristle from 21 September 1942, on 20 October, the squadron re-embarked for the North African landings, when it accounted for two enemy aircraft. In the Mediterranean for most of 1943, it covered the landings in Sicily and at Salerno. It disbanded at Yeovilton on 16 November 1943.

Re-formed at Burscough with Hellcats on 10 June 1944. On 9 September 1944, the squadron joined *Rajah* for Ceylon, to be based ashore as a PR squadron. Joining *Indefatigable* on 24 December 1944, it operated over Sumatra, moving to *Empress* on 7 February 1945 for PR operations over the Kra Isthmus, Penang, Phuket and Sumatra. Until the end of the war, the squadron conducted similar duties operating from other carriers. Post-war, the squadron engaged in aerial surveys. Disbanded in the UK in August 1946.

889: Formed on 16 March 1942, with Fulmars for the fighter defence of the Suez Canal, with early night fighter operations as part of the RAF in Egypt and Syria. By the end of the year, it partially re-equipped with Hurricanes for operations over the Western Desert. Disbanded on 28 February 1943.

Re-formed at Colombo Racecourse on 1 April 1944, with Seafires, it joined *Atheling* on 13 May 1944, for operations over the Bay of Bengal. Heavy losses due to accidents saw the squadron disband at Puttalam on 11 July 1944. Re-formed again on 1 June 1945, at Woodvale with Hellcats, it disbanded on 11 September 1945.

890: Formed on 15 June 1942 at Dartmouth, Nova Scotia, without aircraft until it reached Norfolk, Virginia, on 26 June, when ex-USN Wildcats were obtained. It received Martlets in September, and joined *Battler* on 8 September 1942, for the UK. It joined *Illustrious* on 14 June 1943 for operations off Iceland and Norway, before joining Force H in the Mediterranean, providing support for the Salerno landings in September. On returning to the UK, its personnel embarked in *London* for Ceylon, where it disbanded at Puttalam on 1 August 1944.

891: Formed, 1 July 1942, at Lee-on-Solent as a Sea Hurricane squadron. Embarked aboard *Dasher* on 15 October 1942, to provide fighter cover over the North African invasion beaches. In December, back with the Home Fleet in northern waters, the squadron rejoined the ship to provide fighter cover for a convoy to Iceland, and a flight was aboard when she blew up in the Firth of Clyde on 27 March 1943. Disbanded on 5 April 1943. Re-formed, 1 June 1945, at Eglinton, as a Hellcat night fighter squadron, it disbanded at Nutts Corner on 24 September 1945.

892: Formed on 15 July 1942, as a Martlet squadron at Norfolk, Virginia, it embarked in *Battler* on 8 December 1942, sailing to the UK. On 19 February 1943, the squadron joined *Archer* to provide fighter cover for Atlantic convoys, but it disbanded aboard the ship on 11 August 1943. Re-formed as a night fighter squadron with Hellcats at Eglinton on 1 April 1945, it later embarked in *Ocean*. Disbanded in spring 1946.

893: Formed as a Martlet and Fulmar squadron, Donibristle, 15 June 1942, it was operating only Martlets when it joined *Formidable* on 21 October 1942, and provided fighter cover for the North African landings. It was at the invasion of Sicily in July, and the Salerno landings in September, 1943. Returning to the UK on 18 October 1943, it covered an Arctic convoy before disbanding on 16 November 1943.

894: Formed at Norfolk, Virginia, 15 August 1942, as a Martlet squadron, it was one of the few FAA units to use USS *Wolverine*, a converted river steamer, for deck landing training. On 8 December 1942, it joined *Battler* for the UK, where it re-equipped with Seafires. A detachment joined *Illustrious* on 2 July 1943, to be followed by the rest of the squadron, sailing with the ship to Malta in August to provide fighter cover for the Salerno landings in September. The squadron returned home and on 24 July 1944, embarked aboard *Indefatigable*, covering operations over and off Norway, including two attacks on the battleship *Tirpitz*, shooting down two German aircraft on 22 August 1944.

Joining *Implacable* for Ceylon on 21 November 1944, later transferring to *Indefatigable*, it covered attacks on Sumatra in January 1945, and the Sakishima Gunto in March and April, followed by the Japanese home islands as the war ended. Disbanded at Gosport on 15 March 1946.

895: Formed at Stretton as a Sea Hurricane squadron on 15 November 1942, it operated Seafires before disbanding at Turnhouse, on 30 June 1943.

896: Formed as a Martlet squadron on 15 September 1942, at Norfolk, Virginia, then joining *Victorious* en route to the Pacific on 1 February 1943. Helped to provide air cover for landings by the US Marines in the Solomons during June. Returning to the UK at Eglinton on 26 September 1943, the squadron re-equipped with. Embarked in *Pursuer* on 26 November 1943, and provided air cover for a Gibraltar convoy in February 1944. In April, the squadron provided air cover for an attack on the battleship *Tirpitz*. Merged into 881 Squadron on 12 June 1944.

Re-formed on 9 January 1945, at Wingfield, as a Hellcat squadron, it joined *Ameer* on 24 April 1945, for Ceylon. Fighter-bomber sorties were mounted over the Nicobar Islands during July, before transferring to *Empress* on 17 July, to cover minesweeping operations off Phuket. Disbanded in the UK on 19 December 1945.

897: Formed as a Seafire and Fulmar fighter squadron, Stretton, 1 August 1942, it disbanded into 801 and 880 squadrons on 3 September 1942. Re-formed at Stretton as a Sea Hurricane squadron, 1 December 1942, it received Seafires in March 1943. On 4 August 1943, the squadron joined *Unicorn*, and sailed to provide fighter cover for the Salerno landings in September. It later provided cover for the Normandy landings, during which it accounted for a Bf109 and damaged a midget submarine. On 15 July 1944, it merged into 885 Squadron at Lee-on-Solent.

898: Formed as a Martlet squadron at Norfolk, Virginia, on 15 October 1942, it joined *Victorious* on 3 February 1943, on her way to the Pacific, and in June helped cover the US Marines landing on the Solomons. On its return to the UK, the squadron re-equipped with Wildcats. On 9 December 1943, it embarked in *Searcher* to support North Atlantic convoys. In April 1944, fighter cover was provided for an attack on the battleship *Tirpitz*, and then for anti-shipping strikes off Norway, accounting for four Bv138s and a Fw200. Merged into 882 Squadron on 5 July 1944.

Re-formed at Wingfield, as a Hellcat squadron, 1 January 1945. Joining *Attacker* on 23 June, it sailed for Ceylon, too late for further action. Returned home and disbanded on 12 December 1945.

899: Formed at Hatston, 15 December 1942, with Seafires, it joined *Indomitable* on 11 March 1943. The squadron covered the invasion of Sicily, and then moved to *Hunter* to cover the landings at Salerno. Returned to the UK, 13 October 1943. Joined *Khedive* on 1 April 1944, and in July sailed to cover the Allied landings in the South of France during August, when more than two hundred sorties were flown. In September, shore targets and shipping were attacked at Crete and Rhodes. Embarked in *Chaser* on 25 January 1945, and sailed to Ceylon in February. Saw no further action, but became an OTU for RAAF personnel who had volunteered to transfer to become the nucleus of an Australian FAA, it disbanded on 18 September 1945.

1700: Formed as a Sea Otter squadron on 1 November 1944, at Lee-on-Solent, it joined *Khedive* on 8 January 1945, sailing to southern India. On 8 February 1945, the squadron added some Walruses. Moving to Ceylon, its aircraft embarked in a number of escort carriers for mine sweeping and search and rescue duties. The squadron moved ashore once the war ended, and merged into 733 Squadron on 3 June 1946.

1701: Sea Otter squadron formed at Lee-on-Solent, 1 February 1945, it joined *Begum* on 17 April 1945, for the Far East, becoming the mother squadron for search and rescue units attached to Mobile Naval Air Bases, or MONABs. Disbanded in 1946.

1702: Sea Otter squadron, formed at Lee-on-Solent, 1 June 1945. Deployed to the Mediterranean. Disbanded, late 1946.

1703: Formed on 1 August 1945, with Sea Otters at Lee-on-Solent. Suffered technical problems and disbanded, 18 September 1945.

1770: Firefly squadron formed Yeovilton, 10 September 1943. Joined *Indefatigable*, 18 May 1944, to take part in operations off Norway, including attacks on *Tirpitz*, before *Indefatigable* sailed to the Far East. The squadron joined attacks on the oil and port installations on Sumatra in January 1945, then over the Sakishima Gunto and later against Formosa. Disbanded on 30 September 1945.

1771: Firefly squadron, formed at Yeovilton, 1 February 1944, before joining *Implacable* on 22 September 1944. In October, the squadron flew reconnaissance over Norway, including the *Tirpitz* anchorage, followed by strike sorties, sinking a troopship and damaging four other ships. *Implacable* sailed for the Far East in March 1945, with the squadron joining attacks on Truk, in the Caroline Islands, during June, and then the Japanese home islands. Disbanded at Nowra on 16 October 1945.

1772: Firefly squadron formed at Burscough 1 May 1944. Joined *Ruler*, 20 January 1945. Embarked in *Indefatigable* on 7 July 1945, joining the British Pacific Fleet for attacks against the Japanese home islands. The squadron dropped supplies on PoW camps once the war ended. Disbanded at Portsmouth on 10 March 1946.

1790: Formed with Firefly night fighters at Burscough on 1 January 1945. Joined *Vindex*, 24 June 1945, for Australia, arriving as the war ended. Disbanded at Devonport on 3 June 1946.

1791: Formed, 15 March 1945, with Firefly night fighters at Lee-on-Solent, intended for Pacific theatre, but VJ-Day intervened. Disbanded at Burscough, 23 September 1945.

1792: Firefly night fighter squadron formed at Lee-on-Solent, 15 May 1945. Joined *Ocean* post-war for the Mediterranean.

1820: Formed on 1 April 1944, at Brunswick with Helldivers. Joined *Arbiter* for passage to the UK on 5 July 1944. After several aircraft were lost in accidents, disbanded at Burscough, 16 December 1944.

1830: Formed at Quonset Point, 1 June 1943, with Corsairs. On 9 October 1943, embarked in *Slinger* for passage to the UK. Embarked in *Illustrious* on 9 December 1943, and in early January 1944, the ship sailed for Ceylon to join the Eastern Fleet. Fighter sweeps over the Bay of Bengal followed by attacks on shore installations and shipping at Sabang in April, and in May at Sourabaya, and the Andaman Islands in June, before returning to Sabang in July. Returning to Ceylon on 2 November 1944, it covered attacks on oil refineries and harbours on Sumatra during December 1944, and January 1945. During March and April, operations were carried out against airfields in the Sakishima Gunto. Squadron disbanded on 28 July 1945, on return to the UK.

1831: Formed at Quonset Point on 1 July 1943, with Corsairs. Embarked in *Trumpeter* on 6 October 1943. Disbanded, 10 December 1943. Re-formed at Brunswick, 1 November 1944, it joined *Pursuer* on 1 February 1945. Joined *Glory* on 11 May 1945. The ship sailed to the Far East. The

squadron saw no action before the war ended. Disbanded in 1946.

1832: Wildcat squadron, formed 15 August 1943, at Eglinton. Intended to provide four aircraft fighter flights that could be attached to TBR squadrons embarked in escort carriers. The first of ten such flights embarked in *Fencer* on 20 November 1943, after which the flights were absorbed into TBR squadrons. Disbanded on 1 June 1944.

1833: Corsair squadron formed at Quonset Point on 15 June 1943. On 17 October 1943, it embarked in *Trumpeter*. Moved to *Illustrious* on 22 December 1943. Fighter sweeps over the Bay of Bengal were followed by attacks on shore installations and shipping at Sabang in April, and in May at Sourabaya, and the Andaman Islands in June, before returning to Sabang in July. In November, the squadron covered attacks on oil refineries and harbours on Sumatra during December 1944, and January 1945. During March and April, operations were carried out against airfields in the Sakishima Gunto. Personnel returned to the UK, where the squadron disbanded on 28 July 1945.

1834: Corsair squadron formed 15 July 1943, at Quonset Point. Joined *Khedive*, 1 November 1943. Joined *Victorious*, 12 February 1944. Provided fighter cover for attacks on *Tirpitz*, then headed for the Far East in June. Between July 1944, and January 1945, it covered attacks against Sumatra, followed by operations against the Sakishima Gunto between March and May. Later flew against targets in the Tokyo area. Post-war, the squadron left its aircraft at Nowra. Returned home, disbanding on arrival, on 31 October 1945.

1835: Corsair squadron formed at Quonset Point on 15 August 1943. Disbanded on

Maintainers, mainly petty officers, with a Supermarine Seafire of No. 897 Squadron aboard HMS *Stalker*. The overalls would have been blue. *(Via S.H. Wragg)*

23 November 1943, at Brunswick, Maine. Re-formed at Brunswick, 1 December 1944. Earmarked for the British Pacific Fleet, but the war ended. Disbanded, Nutts Corner, 3 September 1945.

1836: Corsair squadron formed at Quonset Point on 15 August 1943. Joined *Atheling* on 18 December 1943. Transferred to *Victorious*, 8 March 1944. Provided fighter cover for attacks on *Tirpitz* during April, the squadron headed the Far East in June. Between July 1944, and January 1945, the squadron covered attacks against Sumatra, before becoming involved in operations against the Sakishima Gunto between March and May, and later flew against targets in the Tokyo area. Post-war, aircraft abandoned at Nowra. Disbanded in the UK, 31 October 1945.

1837: Corsair squadron formed at Quonset Point on 1 September 1943. Embarked in *Begum* on 19 January 1944. Joined *Atheling* on 26 February 1944, sailing for Ceylon, where it went ashore to the RAF station at Minneriya, 13 April 1944. Joined *Illustrious* on 19 June 1944, seeing action over the Andaman Islands and providing fighter cover for a raid on Sabang. On 14 August 1944, transferred to *Victorious*, but merged into 1834 and 1836 squadrons, 9 September 1944. Re-formed on 1 July 1945 at Eglinton. Disbanded on 18 August 1945 at Nutts Corner.

1838: Formed as a Corsair squadron at Brunswick on 1 October 1943, it joined *Begum* on 19 January 1944. Embarked in *Atheling*, 26 February 1944, for Ceylon. Joined *Victorious* on 23 July 1944, for the raid on Sabang, returning ashore on 27 July, to Colombo Racecourse. The squadron re-embarked in *Atheling* on 25 August 1944 for South Africa, and merged into 1830 and 1833 squadrons, 13 September 1944.

1839: Formed as a Hellcat squadron at Eglinton, 15 November 1943, it embarked in *Begum* on 26 February 1944, and sailed for India. On 25 July 1944, embarked in *Indomitable*. During July, covered attacks on Sumatra, and also undertook photographic reconnaissance. It returned to operations over Sumatra in December 1944, and January 1945, and later was in action over the Sakashima Gunto. Absorbed 1840 Squadron on 27 April 1945. Post-war, disbanded 30 November 1945, on return to the UK.

1840: Hellcat squadron formed at Burscough on 1 March 1944, joining *Indefatigable* on 25 June 1944. It operated in turn from *Furious* on 9 July 1944, *Formidable* on 31 July, and *Indefatigable* on 7 and 15 August 1944, covering attacks on *Tirpitz*. Joined *Speaker* on 16 December 1944, later sailing to provide cover for the British Pacific Fleet's auxiliaries. Merged into 1839 Squadron on 27 April 1945.

1841: Formed as a Corsair squadron at Brunswick on 1 March 1944, before joining *Smiter* on 5 June 1944. Embarked aboard *Formidable* on 26 June 1944. During July and August, the squadron joined the fighter escort for attacks on *Tirpitz*. Sailed with the carrier to the Far East. Saw action over the Sakishima Gunto in April and May 1945. Towards the end of the war, the squadron saw action around Tokyo, with one of its pilots, Lt R.H. Gray DSC, RCNVR, being awarded a posthumous Victoria Cross. After VJ-Day, the personnel returned to the UK, disbanding on arrival, 31 October 1945.

1842: Corsair squadron formed at Brunswick on 1 April 1944, reaching the UK aboard *Rajah* on 13 July 1944. Embarked in *Formidable* on 7 August 1944. Covered attacks on the *Tirpitz* during August. The ship sailed to the Far East, where the squadron flew operations over the Sakishima Gunto, and later in the Tokyo area. After VJ-Day, its personnel returned to the UK. Disbanded on arrival, 31 October 1945.

1843: Corsair squadron formed at Brunswick on 1 May 1944. Arrived in the UK aboard *Trouncer* on 24 August, joining *Arbiter* on 14 February 1945. Sailed to Australia, the but saw no action before the war ended. Disbanded on arrival in UK, 10 December 1945.

1844: Hellcat squadron formed at Eglinton, 15 December 1943. Embarked in *Begum* on 26 February 1944, for the Far East, where it joined *Indomitable* on 25 July 1944, and provided fighter cover for attacks on Indaroeng and Emma Haven in Sumatra, as well as photographic reconnaissance. Attacks followed on Sigli in September and the Nicobar Islands in October. In December, it attacked oil installations in Sumatra. During January 1945, the squadron attacked airfields at Pangkalan Brandan, and oil refineries at Palembang. In March, it joined raids on the Sakashima Gunto and Formosa. Disbanded on return to UK, 30 November 1945.

1845: Corsair squadron formed at Brunswick on 1 June 1944. Joined *Puncher* on 30 August 1944. Later embarked in *Slinger* on 19 December 1944, to join the British Pacific Fleet, but disbanded on 5 April 1945.

1846: Corsair squadron formed at Brunswick, 1 July 1944. Joined *Ranee* on 18 October 1944. On 2 January 1945, it joined

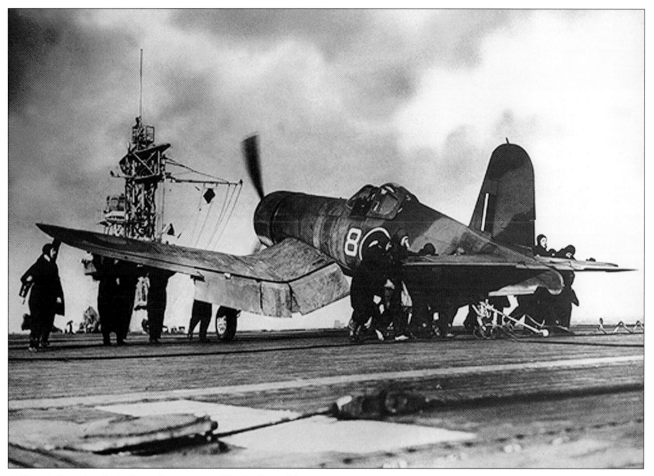

A Corsair is unhooked aboard a carrier. *(Vought Aircraft)*

Colossus. The carrier sailed to the Far East in February, but the squadron was too late for action. Disbanded at Gosport on 23 July 1946.

1847: Hellcat squadron formed on 1 February 1944 at Eglinton, with two-thirds of its twelve pilots from the Royal Netherlands Navy. Absorbed into 1840 Squadron at Eglinton on 20 May 1944.

1848: Corsair squadron formed at Brunswick, 1 July 1944. Joined *Ranee* on 18 October 1944, for the UK. Disbanded on 21 November 1944 at Machrihanish.

1849: Corsair squadron formed at Brunswick on 1 August 1944. Joined *Reaper* on 22 November 1944. Suffered from a high accident rate and disbanded on arrival in the UK on 6 December.

1850: Corsair squadron formed at Brunswick on 1 August 1944. Joined *Reaper* on 23 November 1944. Embarked in *Vengeance* on 25 February 1945, and sailed for the Far East, but too late for the war. Disbanded at Gosport on 12 August 1946.

1851: Corsair squadron formed at Brunswick on 1 September 1944. Joined *Thane* on

28 December 1944. Embarked in *Venerable* on 6 March 1945, it reached Tambaram in southern India on 7 June 1945, but too late to see action. Disbanded post-war.

1852: Corsair squadron formed at Brunswick on 1 February 1945. Joined *Patroller* on 4 May 1945 for the UK. After VJ-Day, the squadron disbanded at Nutts Corner on 29 August 1945.

1853: Corsair squadron formed at Brunswick on 1 April 1945. Joined *Rajah* for the UK on 24 July 1945. Disembarked to Machrihanish on 6 August 1945, to disband on 15 August, VJ-Day.

APPENDIX I

THE BOARD OF ADMIRALTY IN 1940

First Lord – Rt Hon. Albert V. Alexander took over from Winston Churchill on 12 May 1940

First Lord and Chief of Naval Staff

Second Sea Lord and Chief of Naval Personnel

Third Sea Lord and Controller

Fourth Sea Lord and Chief of Supplies and Transport

Fifth Sea Lord and Chief of Naval Air Services

Deputy Chief of Naval Staff – retitled Vice-Chief of Naval Staff on 22 April 1940

Assistant Chief of Naval Staff – retitled Assistant Chief of Naval Staff (Trade) on 27 May 1940

Assistant Chief of Naval Staff (Foreign)

Assistant Chief of Naval Staff (Home)

Parliamentary and Financial Secretary

Civil Lord

Controller of Merchant Shipbuilding and Repairs

Permanent Secretary

APPENDIX II

BATTLE AND CAMPAIGN HONOURS

The Royal Navy was involved from the start of the Second World War until the very end, although for a period in the Far East, Australian and New Zealand naval units held the line, usually under US command, until the Royal Navy was able to return.

Adriatic 1944
Some forty warships entered the Adriatic to hinder the convoys carrying supplies along the coast for Axis forces, which were forced to resort to sea transport because of the difficult terrain of Yugoslavia and Albania and the activities of partisan forces. Later, the evacuation of German troops was hindered.

Aegean 1943–4
Operations in the Aegean occupied more than a hundred warships and six Fleet Air Arm squadrons, attacking German evacuation routes from Greece and also the remaining German naval units in the area. The naval air squadrons operated from escort carriers.

Anzio 1944 – Operation Shingle
In an attempt to bypass the stalemate preventing Allied forces advancing on Rome, Allied forces landed at Anzio on 22 January 1944. Almost sixty warships were involved, including fourteen minelayers, although there was no Fleet Air Arm involvement. Good natural defensive positions and appalling weather helped the German resistance, and even supplying forces ashore proved difficult; this was solved by using amphibious DUKWs and lorries, which were loaded in Naples and then driven ashore at Anzio. Many warships were lost, including the cruisers *Penelope* and *Spartan*, and the destroyers *Inglefield* and *Janus*, as well as a dozen or so minor warships.

Arctic 1941–5
The Russian convoys presented one of the most difficult tasks for the Royal Navy during the Second World War, with the extreme weather being as big an enemy as the German naval and air forces operating from bases in Norway. The almost constant daylight during the summer months meant that convoys had to be suspended at the height of the summer, but in winter the extreme cold and severe storms also seriously affected the convoys. The cold was so intense that metal became brittle and aircraft tailwheels could break off, while aircrew in Swordfish with open cockpits wore as much clothing as possible, and had difficulty getting in and out of cockpits. Forty convoys with a total of 720 ships were escorted to the Soviet Union, and thirty-five

escorted back with a total of 680 ships. One hundred merchant ships were lost, amounting to 605,837 gross tons, while the Royal Navy lost the cruisers *Edinburgh* and *Trinidad*, six destroyers and eleven other warships, including the submarine *P551*. Around 360 warships were involved overall and twenty naval air squadrons.

Atlantic 1939–45

The longest-running campaign of the war, and covered in Chapter 3, the Battle of the Atlantic started on the first day of the war, 3 September 1939, with the torpedoing of the liner *Athenia*, loaded with civilians including many evacuees. Nevertheless, it really started in earnest after the fall of France gave the Germans naval bases with easy access to the Atlantic, and air bases to match. No less than 1,400 British warships took part in the battle, and around thirty naval air squadrons. In addition to the convoy war and the campaign against the German U-boats, major events in the battle included the hunt for and the sinking of the German battleship *Bismarck*.

Barents Sea December 1942

This is covered in Appendix III in the account of Capt R. Sherbrooke's Victoria Cross for his gallant defence of Russian convoy JW51B on 31 December 1942, when the convoy was threatened by the German heavy cruiser *Hipper*. Ten Royal Navy warships were involved.

Biscay 1940–5

The Bay of Biscay was the vital route for convoys to and from the Mediterranean and Africa, which included ships heading for destinations east of Suez. The Bay was within easy reach of German air and naval bases in France from June 1940 onwards. It was not until 1942–3 that improved anti-submarine warfare equipment aboard RAF

Coastal Command reconnaissance aircraft and the arrival of escort carriers started to affect the U-boat menace. In one week in July 1943, the Royal Navy's 2nd Support Group with USN and RAF aircraft accounted for nine U-boats, leading to the suspension by the German naval chief, Adm Dönitz, of U-boat activity from the Biscay ports. It is surprising that only seventy-six warships are accorded this battle honour.

Bismarck May 1941

The hunt for and the eventual sinking of the German battleship *Bismarck* started with the detection of the ship leaving a Norwegian port and included the gunnery battle in the Denmark Strait that led to the loss of the battlecruiser HMS *Hood*. It also involved aircraft from the carriers *Ark Royal* and *Victorious*. It is covered more fully in Chapter 3. Thirty-six ships were involved, and six naval air squadrons.

Burma 1944–5

From October 1944 until the end of the war with Japan, the Royal Navy, with support from the Royal Indian Navy, attacked Japanese bases in Burma in support of the British offensive aimed at removing Japanese forces from that country. This was the furthest extent of Japanese domination of the Far East, with British and Indian forces successfully fending off Japanese attempts to invade India. To support the assault on Ramree Island in January 1945, the battleship *Queen Elizabeth* and cruiser *Phoebe* bombarded Japanese guns sited in caves overlooking the beaches, supported by aircraft from the escort carrier *Ameer*. More than 120 British and Indian warships were involved, and nine naval air squadrons. Latterly the campaign was conducted at a time when the main British involvement was increasingly with the United States Navy taking the war to Japan.

Calabria 1940

Also known as the Battle of Punto Stilo. While protecting two Mediterranean convoys, Adm Sir Andrew Cunningham in *Warspite* led his three British battleships and the aircraft carrier *Eagle* against Italian ships led by Adm Campioni. On 9 July 1940 the Italians managed to fight off an air strike from *Eagle*, but when shells from *Warspite* hit the battleship *Cesare* and the cruiser *Bolzano*, the Italians broke off the engagement. Had Cunningham's other battleships been able to keep pace with *Warspite*, this could have proved a significant British victory early in the war with Italy. Twenty-five British warships were involved.

Cape Bon 1941

On 13 December three British and one Dutch destroyer engaged Italian ships off Cape Bon in Tunisia, sinking two Italian light cruisers.

Cape Matapan 1941

See Matapan.

Crete 1941

While the main German assault on Crete came from the air, with paratroops followed by glider-borne and air-landed troops, the Mediterranean Fleet successfully warded off the seaborne element of the invasion and then, under heavy German air attack, evacuated British, Empire and Greek troops from the island, losing three cruisers and eight destroyers in the process, while the aircraft carrier *Formidable* was damaged beyond local repair. The Royal Navy also lost 2,261 men, 750 of them in the cruiser *Gloucester*. Almost seventy ships were involved, with five naval air squadrons.

Diego Suarez 1942

Operation Ironclad, the invasion of Madagascar, may seem like a sideshow during a global war, but it was occupied by the Vichy French and available to Axis forces, while well positioned to block British convoys to Egypt, which by this stage of the war had to steam past the Cape of Good Hope north towards the Suez Canal. On 5 May, British forces invaded, taking the Vichy French by surprise. An advance party of just fifty Royal Marines were embarrassed by the number of prisoners taken. Just over thirty ships were involved, including two aircraft carriers and the elderly battleship *Ramillies*, as well as eight naval air squadrons.

Dieppe 1942

Operation Jubilee, the assault on the beaches and the harbour at Dieppe on 19 August 1942, was partly a rehearsal for a later invasion of France. The assault, mainly by Canadian troops, was detected by the Germans while it was getting under way and was a failure, with many of the troops taken prisoner.

Dunkirk 1940

Operation Dynamo, the evacuation of the British Expeditionary Force from Dunkirk, took from 28 May to 4 June and saved 338,266 men for the continued fight against the Axis powers. Nine destroyers were lost, although one was later salvaged, and another nineteen of more than fifty destroyers involved were damaged. Of the 848 vessels of widely varied types that took part, most were merchantmen, fishing vessels and pleasure craft requisitioned at short notice. The entire operation took place under heavy German aerial attack.

English Channel 1939–45

The area covered by this campaign ranged from Southend to the Scilly Isles and then round to Bristol – hazardous waters during the Second World War, being within easy reach of German air and light naval forces, augmented by shore-based heavy artillery. A defensive barrage of mines was sown at Dover, while the Germans also laid mines, which were of the magnetic type, against which the British initially had no defensive measures. One convoy in July 1940 lost five out of its twenty-one ships with others damaged, so that only eleven ships reached their destination. Eventually, convoys stopped running down the east coast and through the Straits of Dover. More than 400 ships were involved in this campaign, with five naval air squadrons, usually operating under RAF Coastal Command control.

Greece 1941
During April 1941 the German invasion of Greece reached its climax, and on 24/25 April, British and Empire troops started to be evacuated, mainly to Crete since Egypt was some 500 miles away, in Operation Demon. In seven nights, 50,732 troops were evacuated, at the cost of two destroyers and four transports. More than thirty ships were involved.

Japan 1945
From 16 July until 11 August 1945, the Royal Navy took part in the final air assault on Japan using its, by this time, formidable air power, but just four of the fast armoured aircraft carriers received this campaign award.

Kula Gulf 1943
One of the battles during the Guadalcanal campaign. Just one British ship, *Leander*, took part, under US command.

Libya 1940–2
Not only did the Mediterranean Fleet carry out a series of hit-and-run raids against Axis forces, but it was also concerned with safeguarding supplies to British forces; the Fleet Air Arm was active in providing close air support for the British units fighting in the desert. More than a hundred warships were involved, and nine naval air squadrons.

Lingayen Gulf 1945
Following the US invasion of the Philippines, Japanese forces mounted desperate counter-attacks including the Battle of Lingayen Gulf, which ran from 5–9 January 1945. Most of the ships involved were American, but they were supported by a small number of Australian warships and the British cruiser *Shropshire*.

Madagascar 1942
See Diego Suarez above.

Malaya 1942–5
Malaya, with its tin and rubber, was important to the Japanese, and British naval operations in the area gained in intensity as the war drew to an end, with the 26th Flotilla's five destroyers engaged in the discovery and sinking of the Japanese heavy cruiser *Haguro* in 1945, with help from no. 851 Naval Air Squadron. No less than twenty-four ships share this campaign honour.

Malta Convoys 1941–2
No convoys were as dangerous as those to Malta, which often required the combined resources of the Mediterranean Fleet and Force H, and while escort carriers or even MAC-ships were adequate elsewhere, the Malta convoys required fleet carriers and battleships. It was not unknown for convoys to be aborted or wiped out, and even the most famous of them all, Operation Pedestal in August 1942, which lifted the siege of the Maltese islands, lost all but five of the fourteen merchantmen, as well as the aircraft carrier *Eagle* and two cruisers, *Manchester* and *Cairo*. Almost 200 ships share this campaign honour, and eighteen naval air squadrons.

Matapan 1941

This night action is fully covered in Chapter 4. The Italians lost three cruisers and two destroyers. Twenty-four British warships were involved, including the battleships *Warspite* and *Barham*, and the aircraft carrier *Formidable*, with aircraft from six naval air squadrons flying from the carrier, the battleships and a base in Crete.

Mediterranean 1940–5

Italian entry into the Second World War in June 1940 made the 'Med' a major theatre of war, and threatened the survival of the Maltese islands and the security of the Suez Canal. Chapter 4 covers this theatre in greater detail. Almost 250 ships were included in this campaign, and nineteen naval air squadrons.

Narvik 1940

Two battles were fought at Narvik on 10 and 13 April 1940, as part of the Norwegian campaign as British and French forces attempted to stop the German invasion of Norway. The action is covered in Chapter 2, and in Appendix III with an account of Capt Warburton-Lee's posthumous Victoria Cross. The action was an outstanding success for the Royal Navy, despite losing two destroyers, as ten German destroyers and a U-boat were destroyed. Sixteen ships were involved, including the battleship *Warspite* and the aircraft carrier *Furious*.

Normandy 1944

Out of 1,212 warships deployed in support of the Normandy landings on 6 June 1944, 78 per cent were British, ranging from drifters to battleships, and greater detail is given in Chapter 7.

North Africa 1942–3

Operation Torch saw the Allies invade North Africa on 8 November 1942, the first assault on Axis-held territory. The operation is dealt with in greater detail in Chapter 7. The campaign continued until May 1943 as German forces in Tunisia mounted a strong defence. Well over 200 British naval vessels were involved, as well as Free Dutch ships, and sixteen Fleet Air Arm squadrons.

North Cape 1943

The Battle of the North Cape came about as a result of an attack on Arctic convoys by the German battlecruiser *Scharnhorst*, which was sunk with heavy loss of life. In addition to gunfire from the cruisers *Belfast* and *Jamaica*, then joined by the battleship *Duke of York*, a feature of the operation was a daring torpedo attack under heavy fire by four destroyers – *Savage*, *Saumarez* and *Scorpion*, with the Norwegian *Stord* at 3,000 yards in the early evening, while later four more destroyers – *Musketeer*, *Opportune*, *Virago* and *Matchless* – attacked at even closer range. In all, twelve British ships were involved.

North Sea 1939–45

Inevitably, the North Sea saw action early in the war, with no less than seventy-nine merchant ships totalling 260,000 tons lost in the first four months of the war, mainly as a result of the German minefields that almost closed the Port of London. A convoy system was quickly introduced and losses fell, but after the fall of Denmark, the Low Countries and France, German domination of the eastern side of the North Sea meant that coastal convoys were much reduced. Fleet Air Arm squadrons operating under RAF Coastal Command control helped protect shipping and mounted operations against German shipping, including minelaying near enemy-held ports.

Norway 1940–5

The failure of the Norwegian campaign did not end the Royal Navy's involvement, and the rest of the war saw attacks on the

German battleship *Tirpitz* hiding in Norwegian fjords (in which case the battle honours mention only the carriers and the embarked naval air squadrons, not the escorts for the carriers), and on coastal convoys supplying German forces in Norway and also bringing Swedish iron ore down the coast from Norwegian ports to Germany. More than 200 ships received the honour, and forty-three naval air squadrons.

Okinawa 1945

This was the last great combined operation and battle of the Pacific war, and in March 1945 Task Force 57, the British Pacific Fleet under Vice Adm Sir Bernard Rawlings sent aircraft to strike at Japanese bases in the Sakishima Gunto group of islands, flying 5,335 sorties from the aircraft carriers *Illustrious*, *Indomitable*, *Indefatigable* and *Victorious*, supported by the battleships *Howe* and *King George V*, escorted by five cruisers and fourteen destroyers, of which three accompanied the supply ships and tankers of the Royal Fleet Auxiliary. After the landings on 1 April, the warships were subjected to kamikaze attack over a six-week period, when the heavily armoured flight decks of the British carriers proved their worth. All in all, seventy ships received this honour, with nineteen naval air squadrons.

Pacific 1939–45

After Japan entered the war, there was little involvement by the Royal Navy in the Pacific until 1945, when ships and aircraft could be released from the war in Europe, including the Arctic convoys. In the meantime, most of the effort in the area was made by the United States Navy, with some Australian and New Zealand assistance.

Palembang 1945

The second major effort by the Royal Navy in the Far East was the attack on Japanese

airfields and oil installations on the island of Sumatra, with the most significant raids at Palembang on 24 and 29 January 1945. The Fleet Air Arm mounted no less than 378 sorties, with forty-one aircrew and thirty aircraft lost. Once again, only the carriers and naval air squadrons gained this honour, with four carriers and thirteen squadrons.

Punto Stilo 1940

See Calabria above.

River Plate 1939

This was the first significant British naval victory of the Second World War and has been covered in Chapter 2. The three British cruisers *Achilles* (manned by the Royal New Zealand Navy), *Ajax* and *Exeter* so damaged the German pocket battleship *Graf Spee* that she was eventually scuttled; they share this award with no. 700 Naval Air Squadron.

Sabang 1944

The first major effort by the Royal Navy in the Far East was the attack on Japanese airfields and oil installations at Sabang on the island of Sumatra on 25 July 1944. In addition to an air attack, heavy units of the British Eastern Fleet bombarded Japanese shore installations, including exchanging fire with shore batteries. Twenty-two warships, including the battleship *Queen Elizabeth* and battlecruiser *Renown*, and the aircraft carriers *Illustrious* and *Victorious*, share this honour with seven naval air squadrons.

St Nazaire 1942

The daring action at St Nazaire on the night of 28 March 1942 is covered fully in Appendix III, as two naval officers received the Victoria Cross for their part in this operation. Sixteen out of the nineteen naval vessels involved belonged to Coastal Forces, while the Town class destroyer *Campbeltown*, which also won the honour, was loaded with explosives and played a sacrificial role in the operation.

Salerno 1943

The Allied landings at Salerno, covered in Chapter 7, on 9 September 1943, were accompanied both by heavy naval bombardment, and air cover by the Fleet Air Arm operating from escort carriers and the supposed maintenance carrier *Unicorn* operating in the combat role. More than 150 ships share this honour with fifteen Fleet Air Arm squadrons.

Sfax 1941

The 14th Destroyer Flotilla attacked an Italian convoy consisting of one large and two small destroyers escorting five merchantmen off the Tunisian coast on the night of 15/16 April 1941. Starting at 02.20, a furious night action ensued, at the end of which all the enemy ships were destroyed. The battle honour goes to the four British destroyers *Janus*, *Jervis*, *Mohawk* and *Nubian*.

Sicily 1943

Operation Husky, the Allied invasion of Sicily, started on 10 July 1943 and was the first invasion of Axis territory. It is covered in Chapter 7. Almost 200 British warships were involved, with another sixty-eight from the US Navy and twelve from 'free' navies. The close proximity of Sicily to British airfields in Malta meant that the carrier force was not heavily involved, but eight naval air squadrons also carry this honour.

Sirte 1942

As with many Second World War naval engagements involving ship-to-ship fighting, as opposed to carrier-borne aircraft, the Battle of Sirte on 22 March 1942 arose from an attack on a convoy. Rear Adm Philip Vian was escorting a convoy of four merchantmen from Alexandria to Malta with four light cruisers and ten destroyers, joined later by another cruiser and a destroyer from Malta and a destroyer on anti-submarine operations. This force was confronted by Admiral Iachino with the battleship *Littorio*, cruisers and destroyers. Heavily outgunned, the British force laid a thick smokescreen through which repeated torpedo attacks were launched, with three destroyers surviving direct hits by 15in shells from the *Littorio*. The Italians withdrew, but two of the four merchantmen were sunk in a later air attack, and the two that reached Malta were sunk before they could be completely unloaded. Nineteen ships carry this honour.

South of France 1944

Although the main landings in the south of France on 15 August 1944 were by American and French troops, heavy support was provided by the Royal Navy, including the Fleet Air Arm operating from escort carriers. The operation was far less intensely fought than the Salerno landings; nevertheless, more than a hundred Royal Navy ships were involved, with seven naval air squadrons.

Spada 1940

The action off Spada in Crete on 19 July 1940 involved the light cruiser HMAS *Sydney*, with five destroyers, facing two Italian cruisers. Despite being outnumbered, *Sydney* sank one Italian cruiser and damaged the other, which was driven off.

Spartivento 1940

Force H, with the battlecruiser *Renown* and aircraft carrier *Ark Royal*, from Gibraltar, was escorting a convoy to Alexandria on 27 November 1940, when it was engaged by two

Italian battleships and seven cruisers. The gunnery exchange lasted an hour and saw the British heavy cruiser *Berwick* and an Italian destroyer damaged, after which the Italians withdrew. Somerville decided not to pursue, favouring protection of the convoy, and his action prompted an Admiralty enquiry, which found in his favour. Thirty warships and six naval air squadrons have this honour.

Taranto 1940

This action on the night of 11/12 November 1940 was one of the most brilliant of the Second World War and is covered in Chapter 4. Twenty-one Swordfish biplanes from the aircraft carrier *Illustrious* attacked the Italian fleet. Just two aircraft were shot down, while three enemy battleships were put out of action. Only the aircraft carrier and the four naval air squadrons involved carry this award.

Walcheren 1944

On 1 November 1944 the Royal Navy supported landings on the island of Walcheren intended to give access to the Scheldt estuary and the major port of Antwerp. The planned heavy-bomber support was grounded by fog, and the assault force had to face heavy German fire, but the landings proceeded at a cost of nine vessels sunk and 372 men killed. There were 180 landing craft, but the honour is carried by the monitors *Erebus*, *Roberts* and *Kingsmill* and the battleship *Warspite*, as well as two minelayers.

APPENDIX III

VICTORIA CROSS AWARDS

The first decorations for the Royal Navy during the Second World War were presented on 19 December 1939 by King George VI at HMS *Vernon*, the Royal Navy's mine clearing centre on Portsmouth harbour. Lt Cdr John Ouvry received the Distinguished Service Order for dismantling an air-dropped German magnetic mine at Shoeburyness on 24 November 1939. This courageous act enabled effective countermeasures to be developed. Ouvry was accompanied on the parade ground by several other members of the service, receiving decorations for either assisting him in his dangerous task or other tasks where mines were rendered safe for recovery and examination, including Lt Cdr Roger Lewis (DSO), Lt J.E.M. Glenny (DSC), CPO C.E. Baldwin (DSM) and AB A.L. Vearncombe (DSM). Ouvry's DSO seems scant recognition for his work, but then too, the daring air attacks on Taranto and on the *Bismarck* also received scant recognition. As the intensity of the war increased, many more medals were awarded and these are described and listed, but it is simply impossible to record all of the names of those awarded medals in a book of this size. Nevertheless, it is important that those awarded the highest decoration, the Victoria Cross, be duly recognised.

RN VC HOLDERS, SECOND WORLD WAR

Captain Bernard Warburton-Lee RN, on 10 April 1940 at Narvik, Norway, killed in action.

Capt Bernard Warburton-Lee, aged 45 years, was in command of the flotilla leader HMS *Hardy*, leading a flotilla that included *Hotspur*, *Havock* and *Hunter*, which were joined shortly afterwards by *Hostile*. On 9 April 1940 he was ordered to take his flotilla to Narvik to prevent the Germans from landing there. He was informed by the pilot station at Ofotfjord that at least six large destroyers and a U-boat had passed, but in fact the flotilla was heading towards ten German ships. He signalled the Admiralty that he intended to attack at high water, but the Admiralty cautioned him as further intelligence reports came in, telling him that only he could judge whether an attack should be made but: 'We shall support whatever decision you take.'

The attack took the Germans by surprise, with *Hardy* torpedoing the destroyer *Schmidt*, blowing the stern off a second and also sinking or badly damaging several transports, while gunnery wrecked the destroyer *Roeder*. *Hardy* then withdrew to give *Havock* and *Hotspur* an opportunity to

Victoria Cross (VC).

wounded Warburton-Lee was floated ashore, but died before he could reach hospital. The Norwegians looked after the survivors until they could be picked up by a British destroyer. The Germans also sank *Hunter* and so seriously damaged *Hotspur* that *Hostile* and *Havock* had to take her in tow.

Lt Cdr Gerard Roope RN, on 8 April 1940 at West Fjord, Norwegian Sea, killed in action aboard HMS *Glowworm*.

Lt Cdr Gerard Roope was just 35 years old, but he was known to his men as 'Old Ardover' because of his tendency to order a violent change of course when necessary, without regard to the safety or comfort of those aboard. On 8 April 1940, *Glowworm* was heading towards the West Fjord in heavy weather when she was confronted by two German destroyers. *Glowworm* managed to score at least one hit on the German ships, which withdrew northwards, leading her towards the heavy cruiser *Admiral Hipper*. Although Roope realised what was happening, he gave chase. When he spotted *Admiral Hipper*, he signalled HMS *Renown*. Ideally, he should then have shadowed the German ship, but this was impossible because of the heavy seas, and so he decided on a torpedo attack. Five torpedoes were fired, followed later by another five, but no damage was done. By this time, *Glowworm* was badly damaged, with one turret out of action, although the other three remained firing. Roope decided to ram the German heavy cruiser, after which *Glowworm* pulled away, only to be hit by a shell from the *Admiral Hipper* at a range of 400 yards, causing severe damage forward, and the British destroyer started to heel over. Roope gave the order to abandon ship, and before long she rolled over and sank. Only thirty-one out of her ship's company of 149 were saved, despite the best efforts of the Germans.

Roope's heroism remained unreported for some years until the survivors were

attack, after which the flotilla shelled shore positions before deciding to withdraw. As they headed for the open sea, three German destroyers emerged out of the mist coming from another fjord, and were then joined by two others. A running battle then developed with the British ships steaming in line ahead at 30 knots. 'Keep on engaging the enemy,' signalled Warburton-Lee.

The withdrawal was too late, as a shell exploded on *Hardy*'s bridge, killing or wounding every man there. Briefly, the ship was not under command until the badly wounded Lt G.H. Stanning managed to scramble to his feet and take control. Further shells hit the ship and Stanning had no alternative but to beach her. The mortally

released from German POW camps, and so it was that this, the first VC to be won by the Royal Navy during the Second World War, was among the last to be gazetted.

Lieutenant Richard Stannard RNR, later Captain, on 28 April–2 May 1940 at Namsos Wharf, Norway, aboard HMS *Arab*.

On 14 April 1940 Operation Maurice saw the British attempt landings at Namsos, a timber port to the north-east of Trondheim with a good anchorage and a railhead. The naval force included two flotillas each with four armed trawlers, manned almost entirely by the Royal Naval Reserve. They were to patrol for German submarines, but soon became heavily preoccupied with the continuous attacks of Stuka dive-bombers. On the wharf at Namsos were large quantities of hand grenades that had been set on fire during German bombing raids. With no water available ashore, Stannard ran *Arab*'s bows into the wharf and, sending all but two of his crew aft, he then attempted to quench the flames with hoses aimed from the forecastle. After two hours, he had to accept that the task was hopeless. He then joined other ships in warding off enemy air attacks, before putting his vessel under the shelter of a cliff and sending his off-duty watch ashore to establish an armed camp in which they could rest, while those on duty fought off air attacks by day and hunted for submarines at night. When another trawler close by was set on fire by a bomb, with just two crew members he moved *Arab* to safety before the other trawler blew up. Next, a German bomber threatened to attack unless he steered east, but Stannard maintained his course, holding his fire until the enemy was just 800 yards away, before blowing the German aircraft out of the sky. The citation recalls that *Arab* was subjected to thirty-one bombing attacks over a period of five days.

Captain Edward Fegen RN, on 5 November 1940, in mid-Atlantic when HMS *Jervis Bay* was sunk.

Acting Capt Edward Fegen, 49 years old, was in command of His Majesty's Armed Merchant Cruiser *Jervis Bay*, which was a former Shaw Saville & Albion Line passenger liner, completed in 1922, displacing 14,000 tons and with a crew of 254. In 1939, with the Navy desperate for convoy escorts, she was armed with eight elderly, hand-operated 6in guns and two 3in anti-aircraft guns. In November 1940 this ship was in sole charge of a convoy of thirty-eight ships westbound across the North Atlantic to Canada and the United States.

On 5 November in heavy seas, as darkness fell, Fegen spotted the German pocket battleship *Admiral Scheer*. He immediately placed his ship between the German vessel and the convoy, ordering the merchantmen to scatter in the hope that some of them at least might escape. Despite the overwhelming odds, badly wounded with one arm smashed, facing the heavily armoured *Scheer*'s 11in guns and with his ship on fire after taking successive hits, Fegen managed to hold off the Germans for an hour, before the *Jervis Bay* sank, allowing all but four or five of the merchantmen to escape. When the *Jervis Bay* had her ensign shot away, a rating found another and nailed it to the jackstaff as high as possible. The AMC sank at 20.00. Just three officers and sixty-eight men survived to be rescued by a Swedish cargo vessel after the crew voted to go to their aid despite Swedish neutrality. They were taken to a British port.

Temporary Lt Thomas Wilkinson RNR, on 14 February 1942, Malaya Straits, Java Sea, who went down with HMS *Li Wo*.

HMS *Li Wo* was also a ship taken up from trade for the duration of the war, but somewhat unpromising as a warship, being a three-deck, flat-bottomed Yangtze river boat displacing 1,000 tons, which had never been to sea. Thomas Wilkinson, 42 years old, had been her master in peacetime, and remained with her with the rank of temporary lieutenant when she was taken over by the Royal Navy. The Royal Navy gave *Li Wo* a single 4in gun, two machine guns and a depth-charge thrower. Wilkinson had a scratch crew of eighty-two, many of them survivors of ships already sunk by the Japanese, but also including some soldiers and airmen. Merchant ships with British crews usually retained these for the duration of the war, with temporary ranks allocated to them, but *Li Wo*'s Chinese crewmen would not have been allowed to remain.

Wilkinson was ordered to take *Li Wo* to Singapore with HMS *Fuk Wo*, and succeeded in reaching the port, where they were bombed by Japanese aircraft and were then ordered to proceed to Batavia. However, the two ships faced four air attacks and were forced to separate, with the badly damaged *Li Wo* seeking shelter by an island.

On 14 February 1942, late in the afternoon, Wilkinson spotted two enemy convoys, with the larger being escorted by a Japanese heavy cruiser and a number of destroyers. Rather than try to escape, he decided that they should try to inflict some damage on the enemy, and his crew agreed. Hoisting the battle ensign, *Li Wo* was sent straight towards the enemy, guns firing so that the 4in gun set an enemy transport on fire . The battle raged for an hour, by which time *Li Wo* was badly damaged and taking on water, but Wilkinson decided to finish the job, ramming the burning transport, which had been abandoned by her crew. He then ordered his crew to abandon ship before going down with his command but only ten survivors remained to become Japanese POWs.

Once again the VC was not gazetted until returning POWs could bear testimony to the battle, the report eventually appearing on 17 December 1946, some fifteen months after the war had ended.

Capt Frederick Peters RN, on 8 November 1942, Oran Harbour, Algeria, but killed in plane crash on 13 November.

Acting Capt Frederick Peters had received the DSO and DSC during the First World War, and had been out of the RN between 1919 and 1939, when he rejoined. He received a bar to his DSO for his conduct while commanding a destroyer flotilla on convoy escort duty. As Operation Torch got under way, Peters was asked to take two ex-USCG cutters, HMS *Walney* and *Hartland*, into Oran Harbour and capture it. They faced Vichy French shore batteries, cruisers, destroyers and submarines. Aboard the two ships were US Rangers. Peters aboard *Walney* led the force through heavy close-range fire from the shore batteries and the Vichy surface vessels. The *Walney* was taken alongside a French warship and the Rangers threw grappling lines to hold the two ships together while they stormed aboard, but the *Walney* was hit repeatedly until her boilers exploded. In the heavy fire, Peters was blinded in one eye, but he was the sole survivor of the seventeen officers and men on the *Walney*'s bridge. His ship reached the jetty burning and disabled, before sinking. *Hartland* also blew up. Peters and ten of his men reached shore on a Carley float, where they were interrogated and thrown into prison, but later released by the advancing Allied troops. On 13 November a special aircraft was readied at Gibraltar to take Peters to the UK, where it was reported that Churchill wanted to see him about another mission, but the aircraft crashed on take-off and Peters was killed.

Capt, later Rear Adm, Robert Sherbrooke RN, on 31 December 1942, off the North Cape, aboard HMS *Onslow*.

On 22 December 1942 convoy JW51B left Loch Ewe for Russia, with fourteen ships carrying 200 tanks, 2,000 vehicles and 120 warplanes, as well as other cargo. Although at the outset the escort was relatively weak, on 25 December this duty was taken over by the 17th Destroyer Flotilla under Capt Robert Sherbrooke, aged 42 years, in *Onslow*, accompanied by *Obedient*, *Orwell*, *Obdurate* and *Achates*. The convoy was spotted by a U-boat, which reported it to the heavy cruiser *Admiral Hipper*. The pocket battleship *Lützow*, *Admiral Hipper* and six destroyers sailed from the Altenfjord on 31 December to intercept, with *Obdurate* being the first of the escorts to come under German fire. Sherbrooke's plan in such circumstances was to send the merchantmen at full speed away from the convoy while his destroyers would head straight at the enemy as if to make a torpedo attack. Four times the Germans attempted to attack the convoy, but

Depot ships HMS *Tyne* and *Maidstone* post-war, with six unidentified submarines alongside. *(RN Submarine Museum, Neg. 8849)*

on each occasion they were forced to withdraw under cover of a smokescreen as the destroyers raced in, threatening a torpedo attack, driving the Germans beyond range of the convoy and towards a British covering force. This series of actions lasted about two hours, but after forty minutes, Sherbrooke had been seriously wounded and lost the sight of one eye. Eventually, he was forced to disengage as his ship suffered further hits, handing over command to the next most senior officer and only then leaving the bridge to seek medical attention.

Meanwhile, the battle continued, with Lt Cdr Kinloch in *Obedient* mounting a fifth feint towards the enemy, finally turning the heavy cruiser *Admiral Hipper* away, but not before she had hit *Achates* and killed her commanding officer. By this time, the cruisers *Sheffield* and *Jamaica* had arrived and their shells started hitting *Hipper*. The German destroyer *Friedrich Eckholdt* raced towards *Hipper* to offer assistance, but found that she was approaching *Sheffield* instead, which quickly sank the destroyer.

The British tactics had saved the day, but partly because of a lack of determination on the part of the Germans, for when he heard the account of the action, Hitler demanded that the German surface fleet be scrapped, and the German Navy's C-in-C, Raeder, was forced to resign.

Cdr (later Capt) Robert Edward Ryder RN, on 27 March 1942, at St Nazaire.
Lt Cdr (later Captain) Stephen Beattie RN, on 27 March 1942, at St Nazaire aboard HMS *Campbeltown*.
AB William Savage RN, on 27 March 1942, at St Nazaire aboard *MGB314*, died the following day.
Much effort was expended by both the Royal Navy and the Royal Air Force in containing the surviving German battleship, *Tirpitz*. While this ship spent almost its

entire operational life hiding in Norwegian fjords, the threat that she represented should she break out into the Atlantic was real. The only dock on the French Atlantic coast capable of accommodating the *Tirpitz* was the Normandie Dock at St Nazaire. The plan that unfolded was intended to destroy the dock and thus make it more difficult for the Germans to consider sending her into the Atlantic. In an operation code named 'Chariot', a destroyer loaded with three tons of explosives was to ram the dock gates. The destroyer selected was *Campbeltown*, one of the fifty destroyers supplied by the United States in 1940 in return for the use of British bases in the Caribbean. *Campbeltown* was to be escorted by an MGB, an MTB and sixteen motor launches, carrying Army commandos led by Lt Col Charles Newman of the Essex Regiment, who were to land and blow up the dock and other shore installations. In overall command was Cdr Robert Ryder, aged 34 years, with Lt Cdr Stephen Beattie, also 34 years, in command of *Campbeltown*. The task force left Falmouth before dawn on 27 March 1942, the timing dictated by the high spring tides, to cover the 410 miles of open sea and then five miles of the Loire estuary before they could reach St Nazaire. The small force was escorted by the destroyers *Atherstone* and *Tynedale*, who would also pick up the raiders as they withdrew after the attack. Because surprise was important, *Campbeltown* was remodelled to look like a German destroyer and was wearing the German naval ensign. Ryder was in *MGB314*, commanded by Lt Curtis RNVR, with AB William Savage as the gun-layer.

Although they were spotted by a U-boat, the small force was within two miles of the target before German searchlights opened up, but Ryder gained an extra three minutes by offering German identification signals. After this, the small force was intensively illuminated and came under heavy fire. Beattie continued undeterred at a stately 20 knots, full speed for his elderly destroyer, and at 01.34 on 28 March the *Campbeltown* rammed the dock gates, just four minutes later than scheduled, penetrating the caisson to a depth of 36ft. The explosives were set to go off 150 minutes later. Ryder, landing under heavy fire, found that the destroyer had been placed in exactly the correct position; he then ordered *MTB74* to fire her torpedoes, also set to go off later, at the lock gates. The commandos from *Campbeltown* ran ashore to destroy the pumping house, AA positions and a fuel tank, while soldiers from the launches set up a diversionary raid on the Old Mole and the Old Entrance. In all, there were forty-four Army officers and 224 other ranks, as well as sixty-two naval officers and 291 ratings. The commandos were also to take the Ile de St Nazaire, from which the withdrawal was to be made. The commandos suffered heavy casualties as German fire caught their frail launches, and by the time Ryder ordered a withdrawal, just seven out of the sixteen launches were available. As they withdrew, heavily laden with wounded, they were intercepted by E-boats, and one of the rescuing MTBs was sunk and another three damaged before the destroyers *Atherstone* and *Tynedale* were able to pick up the survivors and speed them to Falmouth. At the end of the operation, 144 men had been killed, 23 per cent of the raiding force, with another 215 captured; 271 were brought back to the UK.

Given the immense shock of the ramming, it is not surprising that *Campbeltown*'s explosives did not go off on time, and as the charge was not discovered, many Germans visited the ship, some even taking their wives and mistresses. Then, around noon on 29 May, the ship finally blew up, killing 380 Germans. This death toll was increased the following day when the torpedoes finally blew up. French dockyard workers, feeling that the time had come to attack the Germans, attempted to take over the dock, causing panic among the German guncrews who, in addition to killing eighty French dockyard workers, also killed many of their own men. In addition to the three naval VCs, two were awarded to the Army commandos – Lt Col Newman and, posthumously, Sgt T.F. Durrant.

Ryder's VC was awarded for commanding the attack under heavy fire and ensuring that its objectives were met before ordering and organising the withdrawal, while his MGB was severely damaged. Beattie was awarded the VC for his coolness under fire and determination in ensuring that the *Campbeltown* fulfilled her mission, while AB William Savage, aboard *MGB314*, showed great skill and determination and devotion to duty, maintaining fire while exposed to heavy fire himself, until fatally wounded as his MGB attempted to withdraw. He died the following day.

Acting LS Jack Mantle RN, killed in action on 4 July 1940, in Portland Harbour, aboard HMS *Foylebank*.
Acting LS Jack Mantle, just 23 years old, was a gunner on a 20mm, rapid-fire pom-pom aboard the anti-aircraft armed merchant cruiser *Foylebank*, which was in Portland Harbour in Dorset waiting for a convoy to assemble. Harbours along the south coast were often attacked by German bombers. Mantle had already been mentioned in despatches for shooting down a German aircraft while on convoy duty aboard a French ship. On 4 July 1940 he faced twenty Ju82 Stuka dive-bombers, plunging out of the sky towards him, firing their machine guns and dropping bombs. Early in the action, his left leg was shattered by a bomb, but he continued firing, using hand-gear once the ship's power supply failed. He was

almost immediately wounded again, but he continued firing until he fell at his post. The *Foylebank* sank shortly afterwards.

PO Alfred Sephton RN, on 18 May 1941, off Crete, died the following day aboard HMS *Coventry* near Alexandria.

HMS *Coventry* was sent to protect the hospital ship *Aba*, which was being bombed by Stuka dive-bombers off Crete on 18 May 1941. PO Sephton, aged 30 years, was a director-layer in a direction tower, which was machined-gunned by a Stuka. One bullet passed through Sephton's body and wounded the man behind him. In severe pain and increasingly faint from loss of blood, he remained at his post until the last of the German attackers was driven off. He then insisted that his wounded crewmate, AB Fisher, be taken from the director-tower first. Sephton died from his wounds that night, and was buried at sea the next day, but his coolness in remaining at his post despite his injuries meant that both ships survived (a point made by none other than the C-in-C Mediterranean Fleet, Adm Cunningham) and *Coventry* was not hit by a bomb.

Lt Cdr Eugene Esmonde RN, on 12 February 1942, in the Straits of Dover, 825 NAS, body recovered 26 April.

A major threat to British shipping in the Atlantic and the Bay of Biscay were the fast battlecruisers *Scharnhorst* and *Gneisenau*, which in 1940 had accounted for twenty-two ships, totalling 116,000 tons. The Royal Navy had forced them to take refuge, with the heavy cruiser *Prinz Eugen*, at Brest, in occupied France where the RAF had repeatedly bombed them, causing some damage but unable to ensure their destruction. The Germans decided to return the three ships to northern waters, where they would be safer and could be used against the Arctic convoys. Instead of taking the long route around the west of Ireland, on Hitler's orders the ships were sent through the Straits of Dover. Delays in detecting the ships and communications difficulties over mounting an attack meant that a force of just six Swordfish from no. 825 Squadron was all that was available to attack the three ships, which were escorted by a combat air patrol of thirty Luftwaffe fighters.

In the gloom of a late winter afternoon, Lt Cdr Eugene Esmonde took his six aircraft into the air, but instead of the escort of sixty Spitfire fighters that he had been promised, just ten Spitfires turned up. In poor light, they found the three warships and their escort of ten destroyers. The lumbering Swordfish were caught in a hail of fire from the fighters above and the warships below, but they pressed home a torpedo attack. His aircraft badly damaged as pieces were knocked off it in the heavy fire, Esmonde managed to keep the aircraft airborne long enough to launch its torpedo before it crashed into the sea. His target, the *Prinz Eugen*, managed to avoid the torpedo. All six Swordfish were shot down, with the loss of Esmonde and twelve others out of the eighteen naval airmen involved in the attack. Esmonde was awarded a posthumous VC.

Lt Cdr Malcolm Wanklyn RN, on 24 May 1941, off Sicily aboard HMS *Upholder*, but killed in action 14 April 1942, in Gulf of Tripoli.

Malta during the Second World War became a base for offensive operations even while being starved to death by what amounted to an Axis blockade, with few ships getting through. The most effective submarines for operations in the Mediterranean soon transpired to be the U class, smaller than the other classes and originally intended to be training submarines. The most successful of the submarine commanders based on

Malta was Lt Cdr Malcolm Wanklyn of *Upholder*, which sank almost 140,000 tons of enemy shipping, including a destroyer and troopships.

During the evening of 24 May 1941, while on patrol off the coast of Sicily, *Upholder*'s officer of the watch saw a convoy of Italian troopships escorted by four Italian destroyers. The submarine's listening gear was not working at the time, and she was nearly rammed by a destroyer that had not seen her. Wanklyn manoeuvred *Upholder* into position and fired his torpedoes at the largest Italian troopship, sinking her, before facing an hour of depth-charging, with thirty-seven depth charges dropped.

Sadly, Wanklyn, the first submarine VC of the Second World War, was not to enjoy his success. He refused offers of home leave, despite showing signs of stress, until the entire ship's company qualified, that is, at the end of twenty-five patrols. On 6 April 1942 *Upholder* left Malta on her twenty-fifth patrol to keep a rendezvous with *Unbeaten*. On 14 April two other British submarines close to her area of operations heard heavy depth-charging, and on 18 April the Italian navy claimed that it had sunk a submarine. Whether this was the end for *Upholder* or, as other accounts suggest, she ran into an enemy minefield remains a mystery. Wanklyn's investiture on 3 March 1943 saw his widow and 3-year-old son receive not only his VC, but three DSOs as well.

Cdr (later Rear Adm) Anthony Miers RN, on 4 March 1942, in Corfu Harbour.

Cdr Anthony Miers was one of the RN's most experienced submarine commanders when war broke out, winning two DSOs while in command of HMS *Torbay*. Miers was a great believer in following up an attack if the target did not sink immediately, and on one occasion in the Mediterranean he sent a scuttling party aboard a stricken merchant vessel while his boat's cooks went aboard to raid the ship's supplies to augment their own rations. On 4 March 1942 Miers followed three Italian destroyers and a convoy of merchantmen into a harbour at Corfu. It was a difficult manoeuvre at the best of times, but he was unable to attack until the following morning, and meanwhile had to recharge *Torbay*'s batteries. *Torbay* spent seventeen hours in the harbour, and part of the time lay on the surface in full moonlight recharging the batteries. At daylight, when he could see his targets, he submerged and fired all of his torpedoes, before escaping through a narrow channel, running the gauntlet of around fifty depth charges.

Cdr John Linton RN, on 23 March 1943, aboard HMS *Turbulent* when the submarine hit a mine.

Another of the Royal Navy's submariners to make a reputation for himself in the Mediterranean, Cdr John Linton of HMS *Turbulent* not only sought out shipping targets, but also surfaced and attacked shore targets after careful periscope observation on at least three occasions, shooting up road convoys and trains. On one occasion, he spotted two destroyers escorting two merchantmen in moonlight, although with some mist. He managed to get his submarine ahead of the convoy, and dived to attack it. Finding himself ahead of a destroyer, he waited until it was almost on top of him before firing. As well as the destroyer, he sank one merchantman and set the other on fire so that she blew up. He also landed agents on enemy-held coastlines, and on one occasion sank a German U-boat an operation requiring great skill. He received his VC for sinking 100,000 tons of enemy shipping, including a cruiser, a destroyer, a U-boat, and some twenty-eight supply ships, as well as three trains, having also survived 250 depth charges. Unfortunately, all this came to an end on 23 March 1943, when *Turbulent* hit a mine in Maddelena Harbour in Sardinia.

Lt Cdr Ian Fraser RN, on 31 July 1945, in the Jahore Strait, Singapore, aboard HM midget submarine XE3.
LS James Magennis RN, on 31 July 1945, in the Jahore Strait, Singapore, aboard HM midget submarine XE3.
Lt Cdr Ian Fraser had volunteered to serve in submarines after war broke out, and had narrowly missed being on the submarine *Sahib* when she was sunk and her crew taken prisoner, after being kept ashore in hospital with a broken foot. In March 1944 he answered the call for volunteers for 'special and hazardous service in submarines', and soon found himself in command of the midget submarine XE-3, one of six such boats built and sent to Australia for service against the Japanese navy. The XE series were 50ft long and had a crew of four. They carried two detachable explosive charges as well as a number of limpet mines.

In May 1945, XE3 and XE1 were asked to cut underwater communications cables used by the Japanese, as well as attaching mines to the two cruisers *Takao* and *Mikyo*, anchored in the Jahore Straits, Singapore. Getting to the target was difficult, as the two midget submarines had to travel forty miles underwater past minefields, listening posts, a buoyed boom and the inevitable surface patrols. *Takao*, Fraser's target, was just seventy-five feet from the shore and had only fifteen feet of water under her keel; yet to attack, the submarine had to be under the ship. In fact, on arrival, Fraser found that the ship was aground at the bows and the stern, and only the midship position offered him any space in which to insert his craft, drop the explosive charges and attach the limpet mines. It fell to the sub's diver, LS James Magennis, to attach the limpet

mines to the *Takao*, but he had great difficulty in getting out of the diver's hatch because of the lack of space between the midget submarine and the cruiser. The foul state of the warship's bottom meant that it was extremely difficult to attach the limpet mines, and he was able to do it only after scraping off a number of barnacles. Throughout this effort, which was exhausting, Magennis had problems with his air supply leaking and sending a stream of telltale bubbles to the surface. Fraser then had to extricate the craft and get her out to sea using the same dangerous route that he had taken to the target. Even so, he failed to jettison a limpet carrier, and once again Magennis had to leave the XE-craft and dislodge the carrier. Nevertheless, the attack was successful and the *Takao* finally rested fully on the seabed.

Lt Basil Place RN, on 22 September 1943, Kaafjord, Norway, aboard HM midget submarine X7.
Lt (later Cdr) Donald Cameron RNR, on 22 September 1943, Kaafjord, Norway, aboard HM midget submarine X6.
Once again the need to destroy or at least cripple the battleship *Tirpitz* led to actions that justified the award of the Victoria Cross. In this case, midget submarines, the original X-craft rather than the improved XE-craft, were used. After an earlier attempt using human torpedoes, or 'chariots', had failed because these could not cope with bad weather, an attack using midget submarines was planned.

In September 1943 six X-craft were deployed in an attempt to attack the *Tirpitz* and some of her escorts in the Kaafjord. The operation got off to an inauspicious start, with X9 lost on the outward voyage after breaking her tow from a full-sized submarine, while X8 was damaged and had to be scuttled.

Even once the run in to the target area started, problems emerged. X7, commanded by Lt Basil Place, snagged a mine hawser and Place had to leave the submarine and crawl along the casing, before using his feet to disentangle the hawser; he then had to push the mine away with his feet several times before the submarine was free.

On the morning of 22 September X6, with Lt Donald Cameron in command, ran aground in the Kaafjord, then broke free and surfaced after hitting a rock; but although she dived again, her gyro was out of action and the periscope barely usable. She then ran into a net, surfaced, and was fired at and had hand grenades thrown at her by members of the battleship's crew before she could escape. X6 then went astern, and in doing so her hydroplanes struck the side of *Tirpitz* and dropped her charges. Cameron then scuttled X6 and ordered his crew into the water, where they were picked up by one of the battleship's picket boats.

It was then X7's turn to get caught in a torpedo net surrounding *Tirpitz*, and in attempting to go astern to escape, Place also surfaced, but diving quickly he then found that X7 was stuck at 95ft. Further manoeuvring allowed the X-craft to rise, but this time inside the net less than a hundred feet from *Tirpitz*. He placed his charges but continually became stuck in nets as he attempted to escape.

At 08.12, three minutes early, the charges exploded, knocking Cameron, who was aboard awaiting interrogation, off his feet. The explosions also blew X7 clear of the nets, but by this time she was uncontrollable and surfaced, where she came under heavy fire from the Germans. Place ordered abandon ship, but only he

and one other survived, with two of his crew killed. The heaviest casualties from the gunfire were German, however, as panic swept the ship's gunners and they fired indiscriminately, killing 120 of their own men, many of them in other ships and at shore installations.

Unusually, Place and Cameron were awarded their VCs while still prisoners of war of the Germans. The damage to the *Tirpitz* was considerable, and she was out of action for several months, later being moved to Tromsø, where she came within range of the RAF's heavy bombers.

Lt Peter Roberts RN, on 16 February 1942, Sea of Crete, aboard HMS *Thrasher*.
PO Thomas Gould RN, on 16 February 1942, Sea of Crete, aboard HMS *Thrasher*.
The submarine *Thrasher* in the Mediterranean found and sank a heavily escorted merchantman in broad daylight on 16 February 1942. Afterwards, the submarine was attacked by depth charges, before being bombed by aircraft. It was not until the submarine surfaced and began to roll that it was discovered that there were two unexploded bombs stuck in the casing. Roberts and Gould both volunteered to deal with them. The main problem came with the second bomb, stuck in the casing, which was so low that they had to move sprawled at full length. Working in this confined space in complete darkness, they had to push and drag the bomb for some twenty feet before it could be pushed over the side. Worse still, the submarine was still in waters patrolled by the enemy, and had a ship or aircraft approached, the submarine's commanding officer would have had no option but to crash-dive, unable to give either man time to escape from the casing, in which case both would have drowned.

APPENDIX IV

MEDALS AND DECORATIONS

Naval personnel were eligible for many of the medals and other awards available to all of the armed forces, but they also had their own, peculiar to the Royal Navy. Members of the Fleet Air Arm were also eligible for many of the medals awarded to RAF personnel, including the Distinguished Flying Cross, to the dismay and sometimes outright hostility of many senior naval officers of the old school. It took nerve to wear the DFC ribbon, even if the wearer had earned it during the Battle of Britain!

As with all three services, the full medal and ribbon were worn only on ceremonial occasions, and smaller versions were available to wear with mess kit. On ordinary uniforms, the everyday practice was to wear ribbons only.

In addition to medals, members of all three services were also eligible for the full range of honours, traditionally awarded on the King's birthday and at the New Year and, in theory, since there were no general elections until after the war in Europe ended, on the dissolution of Parliament. Several of these, including the Order of the Bath and the Order of the British Empire, had a military division, and holders would wear the ribbon of the order with their medal ribbons. Knighthoods were usually reserved for senior officers.

AWARDS FOR GALLANTRY

Victoria Cross

The highest award for the British armed services, open to all services and all ranks. A crimson–maroon ribbon, with a bronze cross depicting a lion standing upon the royal crown, below which a semi-circular scroll carries the inscription 'For Valour' on the obverse, and the date of the act of valour on the reverse. The recipient's details were recorded on the reverse of the suspender clasp.

Distinguished Service Order

Normally awarded for outstanding command and leadership under fire and available only to officers, but also available to all three services. A red ribbon with dark blue edges, and a gold or silver-gilt, white- enamelled cross with curved arms. The monarch's crown within a laurel wreath is on the obverse, while the reverse has the royal cypher surmounted by a crown. The year of award appears on the reverse of the suspender clasp.

Distinguished Service Cross

Available to RN, Merchant Navy and RAF officers serving with the fleet, for 'meritorious or distinguished services in action'. Ribbon

Distinguished Service Order (DSO).

Distinguished Service Cross (DSC).

Distinguished Flying Cross (DFC).

had equal widths of dark blue, white and dark blue, and a silver cross with curved arms. The obverse shows the monarch's cypher surmounted by a royal crown within a circle, while the reverse shows the year of award in the lower arm of the cross.

Distinguished Flying Cross

Available only to commissioned officers of the RAF and RN. Ribbon had violet and white diagonal stripes with a silver cross 'flory', into which feathered wings, an aeroplane propeller and bombs are incorporated on the obverse, with the entwined cypher 'RAF' in the centre, while on the reverse there is the royal cypher, and the year of award is engraved on the lower arm.

Distinguished Conduct Medal

Available to personnel of the rank of warrant officer and below in all services for 'distinguished conduct in the field', and this stamped on the reverse side. Ribbon had equal widths of crimson, dark blue and crimson, while the round silver medal carries King George VI's head.

Conspicuous Gallantry Medal

For Royal Navy and Royal Marines personnel of warrant officer rank and below who 'distinguish themselves by acts of conspicuous gallantry in action with the enemy'. Ribbon was white with narrow blue edges with a round silver medal with the

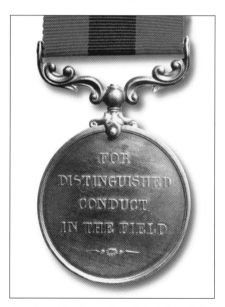

Distinguished Conduct Medal (DCM).

Conspicuous Gallantry Medal (CGM).

Distinguished Service Medal (DSM).

Distinguished Flying Medal (DFM).

King's head and title on the obverse, and on the reverse, 'For Conspicuous Gallantry' surrounded by a wreath of two laurel branches, surmounted by a crown. A variation, the **Conspicuous Gallantry Medal (Flying)**, was created on 10 November 1942 for personnel of warrant officer rank and below of any of the armed services flying in active operations against the enemy. Ribbon was pale blue with narrow, dark-blue edges.

Distinguished Service Medal

For Royal Navy and Royal Marines personnel of warrant officer rank and below who 'show themselves to the fore in action and set an example of bravery and resource under fire'. Ribbon was dark blue with two white central stripes, while the round silver medal showed King George's head on the obverse, and the reverse was similar to the style of the CGM above, but with the words 'For Distinguished Service'.

Distinguished Flying Medal

For Royal Navy and Royal Marines personnel of warrant officer rank and below who show 'valour, courage or devotion to duty performed while flying in active operations against the enemy'. Ribbon had narrow violet and white diagonal stripes, with a silver opal medal carrying King George's head on the obverse, while the reverse shows Athena Nike seated upon an aeroplane with a hawk rising from her hand and below this the words 'For Courage', as well as the date '1918'.

Mention in Despatches Emblem

Available to all ranks and all services for those mentioned in despatches but not receiving a higher award. For the Second World War, a bronze oakleaf emblem was worn on the War Medal ribbon at an angle of 60 degrees from the inside edge of the ribbon, or as a smaller emblem worn horizontally when only the medal ribbon was worn.

War Medal, 1939–45, obverse and reverse.

1939–45 Star.

CAMPAIGN MEDALS AND STARS

War Medal, 1939–45

All members of the armed forces received this providing they completed twenty-eight days' service between 3 September 1939 and 2 September 1945. Ribbon had five equal stripes of red, blue, white, blue and red, with a narrow red stripe in the centre of the white. The obverse of the medal had the crowned head of King George VI, while the reverse shows a lion standing on a fallen dragon, with the dates '1939, 1945' at the top.

All stars were six-pointed, made of copper–zinc alloy, with the royal cypher, 'GRI', in script and with 'VI' below. The surrounding circlet, with a crown at the top, carries the name of the star. The reverse is plain.

In the following, the qualifying time periods were ignored when service was ended by death, when the recipient was evacuated due to wounds or serious illness, or when the recipient was decorated or mentioned in despatches. Time spent as a POW also counted. No more than five stars could be held by any one recipient.

1939–45 Star

Authorised in 1943 and originally known as the 1939–1943 Star, it was amended twice, first to May 1945, and then to 2 September 1945. Awarded for six months' operational service to all services and all ranks. Ribbon had equal stripes of dark blue, red and pale blue (for RN, Army and RAF). A 'Battle of Britain' bar was authorised for fighter aircrew engaged in the battle between 10 July and 31 October 1940, and this was represented by a gilt heraldic rose when ribbons only were worn.

Campaign stars were six-pointed and made of copper–zinc alloy, with a plain reverse. Bars were represented by a silver heraldic rose when only ribbons were worn. From left to right: the Atlantic Star, the Air Crew Europe Star, the Africa Star.

Atlantic Star

Commemorating the Battle of the Atlantic, and available to anyone serving at sea, including Merchant Navy, RAF and Army personnel. Unusual watered ribbon, so that the equal stripes are blue merging into white, merging into sea green.

Air Crew Europe Star

Awarded for two months' operational flying from UK bases over Europe up to 5 June 1944, providing that the recipient had already qualified for the 1939–45 Star. The ribbon had pale-blue centre bordered narrow yellow stripes with slightly wider black edges for day and night operations. Two bars were authorised, 'Atlantic' and 'France and Germany', but only one could be worn, and the bar was represented by a silver heraldic rose when ribbons only were worn.

Africa Star

Awarded to anyone, including Merchant Navy, in the operational area between 10 June 1940 and 12 May 1943. Ribbon was pale buff, for the desert sand, with a central red stripe, with narrow dark-blue left edge and light-blue right edge stripes, for the three services. Naval personnel had a bar, 'North Africa 1942–43', represented by a silver rose when ribbons only were worn.

Pacific Star

Awarded to anyone in the operational area between 8 December 1941 and 2 September 1945, but RN and Merchant Navy personnel had to have qualified for the 1939–45 Star

From left to right: the Pacific Star, the Burma Star, the Italy Star.

first, even though this restriction was removed for the Army and RAF after the war. Ribbon had dark-green centre with a narrow yellow central stripe, for the forests and beaches of the Pacific, with red edges with narrower dark-blue left and light-blue right stripes between the edges and the green. Because of the limitation on the number of stars that could be awarded, those who qualified for the Burma Star after first receiving the Pacific Star usually used the bar, 'Burma', which was represented by a silver heraldic rose when ribbons only were worn.

Burma Star

Awarded to anyone within the operational area, which included part of India, between 11 December 1941 and 2 September 1945; the qualifying conditions were similar to those for the Pacific Star. Ribbon had a red centre with slightly wider edges of dark blue,

orange–yellow, dark blue, equally divided. Again, there was a bar, 'Pacific', for those qualifying for the Pacific Star after first receiving a Burma Star.

Italy Star

Awarded to anyone in the operational area between 11 June 1943 and 8 May 1945, with no preconditions. The ribbon had five equal stripes, appropriately red, white, green, white, red.

France and Germany Star

Awarded for operational service on land from 6 June 1944 in France, the Low Countries and Germany, with no preconditions. Ribbon had five equal strips, blue, white, red, blue, white, for the colours of the Dutch and French flags. Those eligible for the Atlantic Star afterwards could wear the bar, 'Atlantic'.

The France and Germany Star.

The Atlantic Star.

In addition to the above, personnel from Canada, New Zealand, South Africa and Australia could qualify for their own national wartime medals, such as the New Zealand War Service Medal.

APPENDIX V

COMPARISON OF RANKS: ROYAL NAVY AND ARMY OFFICERS

RN	ARMY
Admiral of the Fleet	Field Marshal
Admiral	General
Vice Adm	Lieutenant-General
Rear Admiral	Major-General
Commodore 2nd Class	Brigadier
Captain	Colonel
Commander	Lieutenant-Colonel
Lieutenant-Commander	Major
Lieutenant	Captain
Sub-Lieutenant	First Lieutenant
Temporary Sub-Lieutenant	Second Lieutenant
Midshipman	No equivalent
Warrant Officer	No equivalent
No equivalent	Sergeant Major (RSM and CSM)

RATINGS (RN) AND NON-COMMISSIONED RANKS

RN	ARMY
Chief Petty Officer	Colour Sergeant
Petty Officer	Sergeant
Leading Seaman (Leading Hand)	Corporal
AB	No equivalent
Ordinary Seaman	Private

RM ranks were similar to those of the Army, but with a senior rank of Commandant General.

(*Source*: Imperial War Museum.)

APPENDIX VI

PORTSMOUTH, GOSPORT, YEOVILTON, CHATHAM

While both the Imperial War Museum and the National Maritime Museum have collections and exhibits relating to the Royal Navy and war at sea, there is no substitute for the museums that are directly linked with the history of the Royal Navy. The Royal Naval Museum at Portsmouth is a 'cover all' museum for the Royal Navy, and also has HMS *Victory* and HMS *Warrior* to give visitors a feel for life aboard a warship in the past. However, those with specialised interests will be better served by visits to the Fleet Air Arm Museum at Yeovilton or the Submarine Museum at Gosport, and for an idea of a working dockyard of the past, a visit to Chatham is a must.

PORTSMOUTH

One of Britain's oldest maritime museums, dating to the founding of a Dockyard Museum in 1911, the Royal Naval Museum is in Portsmouth's dockyard. It has permanent exhibitions open to the public as well as being home to Nelson's flagship *Victory* and HMS *Warrior*. Visitors can buy tickets to the museum itself or either of the two ships, or

the *Mary Rose*, whose salvaged remains are on show. Alternatively, there is a comprehensive ticket that allows visitors to return over a twelve-month period, so that they can take in each of these features in turn – there is a great deal to see in just one day! For further information, visit www.royalnavalmuseum.org

GOSPORT

Gosport, on the other side of Portsmouth Harbour, hosts the Royal Naval Submarine Museum. In addition to the displays, the museum is also home to preserved submarines, including HMS *Alliance*, *Holland 1*, the Royal Navy's first submarine, and a midget submarine. For up-to-date information, visit www.rnsubmus.co.uk

YEOVILTON

Home to the Fleet Air Arm Museum, which was founded in 1964, Yeovilton has grown from its original collection of just six aircraft to more than forty, representing one of the largest collections devoted to naval aviation in the world. In addition to the aircraft, a wide range of displays deals with every aspect of naval air power, and includes one on the history of V/STOL, so vital to modern naval aviation, and there are around 250 models of aircraft and ships.

The museum is based near Ilchester in Somerset, on the B3151, just off the A303, and is situated on land that was part of RNAS Yeovilton. Because the museum is constantly adding to its collection of restored aircraft and displays, and has some on loan to other collections, up-to-date information on the current collection is best found by accessing the museum's website, www.fleetairarm.com

CHATHAM

Claimed to be the 'most complete dockyard of the age of sail to survive in the world', the former Royal Dockyard at Chatham covers some 80 acres, and has about a hundred buildings and structures. In use as a Royal Dockyard from 1613 to 1984, it is the location of other historic sites, including its defences at the Chatham Lines and Upnor Castle, and HMS *Pembroke*, the Edwardian naval barracks, as well as the Georgian military barracks at Brompton. For up-to-date information, visit www.chdt.org.uk

ABBREVIATIONS

(A)	Air Branch of the RN or RNVR		DLP	deck landing practice
AA	anti-aircraft		DLT	deck landing training
AB	able-bodied seaman		DSC	Distinguished Service Cross
ADDL	aerodrome dummy deck landing		DSO	Distinguished Service Order
AFC	Air Force Cross		Dt	detachment
ASH	air-to-surface-vessel radar (US-built)		E-boat	German MTBs or MGBs (enemy boat)
ASV	air-to-surface-vessel radar (British-built)		FAA	Fleet Air Arm
			Flt	Flight
BPF	British Pacific Fleet		HMAS	His Majesty's Australian Ship
CAG	carrier air group		HMCS	His Majesty's Canadian Ship
CAM-ship	catapult-armed merchant vessel		HMNZS	His Majesty's New Zealand Ship
Capt	Captain		HMS	His Majesty's Ship
CAP	combat air patrol		KCB	Knight Commander of the Bath
CB	Commander of the Order of the Bath		Lt	Lieutenant
			Lt Cdr	Lieutenant-Commander
CCA	carrier-controlled approach		MAC ship	merchant aircraft carrier (a merchant vessel with a flight deck)
Cdr	Commander			
C-in-C	Commander-in-Chief			
CMG	Companion of the Order of St Michael and St George		MBE	Member of the British Empire
			MONAB	mobile naval air base
CO	commanding officer		MGB	motor gunboat
CPO	chief petty officer		MTB	motor torpedo boat
CVE	escort carrier, more usually known to the RN as auxiliary carriers		MV	motor vessel
			OBE	Officer of the British Empire
			PO	petty officer
CVO	Commander of the Royal Victorian Order		PR	photo reconnaissance
			RAAF	Royal Australian Air Force
DFC	Distinguished Flying Cross		RAF	Royal Air Force
DLCO	deck landing control officer, more usually known as the 'batsman'		RAN	Royal Australian Navy
			RANVR	Royal Australian Naval Volunteer Reserve

RCAF	Royal Canadian Air Force	SAAF	South African Air Force
RCN	Royal Canadian Navy	SANF(V)	South African Naval Force
RCNVR	Royal Canadian Naval Volunteer		(Volunteer), equivalent of RNVR
	Reserve	TAG	telegraphist air gunner
RM	Royal Marines	TBR	torpedo bomber reconnaissance
RN	Royal Navy	TF	task force
RNethN	Royal Netherlands Navy	TSR	torpedo spotter reconnaissance
RNR	Royal Naval Reserve	U-boat	German submarine
RNVR	Royal Naval Volunteer Reserve		(*Unterseeboot*)
RNZNVR	Royal New Zealand Naval	USN	United States Navy
	Volunteer Reserve	USS	United States Ship
RP	rocket projectile	VC	Victoria Cross

CHRONOLOGY

The term 'total war' was an accurate description of the situation faced by the Royal Navy throughout the war years. There has since been much written about the so-called 'phoney war' between the outbreak of war in September 1939 and the German invasion of Denmark and Norway in April 1940, but for the Royal Navy there was no such period. In addition to the major battles, there was the unglamorous and demanding role of minesweeping and convoy protection, and space here permits mention of only the most significant convoy events – mainly those that turned into major sea battles.

1939

3 September
Britain and France declare war on Germany after an ultimatum expires.

17 September
Aircraft carrier HMS *Courageous* torpedoed by *U-29* and sunk.

26 September
Dornier Do18 flying-boat shot down by Blackburn Skua from *Ark Royal*, the first German aircraft to be shot down in the war.

14 October
Battleship *Royal Oak* torpedoed by *U-47* at Scapa Flow and sunk.

23 November
Armed merchant cruiser *Rawalpindi* sunk by German battlecruisers *Gneisenau* and *Scharnhorst* while protecting convoy off Iceland.

13 December
Battle of the River Plate, in which cruisers *Ajax*, *Achilles* and *Exeter* inflict serious damage on the 'pocket' battleship *Admiral Graf Spee*, which seeks refuge in Montevideo, but returns to sea and is scuttled on 17 December.

1940

In this year, as the full pressure of total war became apparent, a massive expansion and relocation of training establishments was undertaken, while the length of shore-based courses was cut in half.

14 February
Destroyer HMS *Cossack* sends boarding party on to German supply ship *Altmark* within Norwegian territorial waters and releases 303 British prisoners from merchant ships sunk by the *Graf Spee*.

8 April
Britain begins to mine Norwegian waters.

9 April
Germany occupies Denmark and begins invasion of Norway. British submarine

Truant torpedoes and sinks light cruiser *Karlsrühe* off Norway.

Mid-April

British and French troops land in Norway; HMS *Furious* covers the landings and afterwards acts as an aircraft transport; *Ark Royal* joins her. HMS *Glorious* recalled from Mediterranean.

10 April

Luftwaffe attacks Home Fleet south-west of Bergen, sinking a destroyer and causing minor damage to the battleship *Rodney* and the cruisers *Devonshire*, *Glasgow* and *Southampton*.

First destroyer action in Narvik Fjord, with British destroyers sinking two German destroyers and several merchantmen, but two British destroyers are also sunk.

Skuas of nos 800 and 803 Naval Air Squadrons flying from HMS *Sparrowhawk*, RNAS Hatston in Orkney attack and sink the German light cruiser *Kønigsberg* at Bergen, the first major warship to be sunk by naval aircraft.

13 April

Second destroyer action at Narvik, often referred to as the 'Second Battle of Narvik', with the battleship *Warspite* and nine destroyers sinking the remaining eight German destroyers.

26 May

Operation Dynamo, the evacuation of the British Expeditionary Force from Dunkirk, begins under the command of Adm Ramsay at Dover.

8 June

Aircraft carrier *Glorious* caught and shelled by *Gneisenau* and *Scharnhorst* during withdrawal from Norway. Carrier and two escorting destroyers *Acasta* and *Ardent* sunk, although *Acasta* scores torpedo hit on *Scharnhorst*.

13 June

Aircraft from *Ark Royal* attack *Scharnhorst* at Trondheim, but only one bomb hits the ship and this fails to explode.

Aircraft of no. 767 Squadron flown by instructors from base in south of France bomb Genoa.

17 June

French seek armistice, meaning that the Royal Navy is entirely on its own in the Mediterranean.

30 June

Aircraft from 830 Squadron based in Malta attack Augusta in Sicily.

3 July

Battle of Mers El-Kebir, attacking Vichy French warships near Oran after French admiral refuses to surrender. French battleship *Bretagne* blows up, while battleship *Provence* and battlecruiser *Dunkerque* crippled.

5 July

Fairey Swordfish from *Eagle* sink an Italian destroyer and a freighter at Tobruk.

8 July

Aircraft from *Hermes* accompanied by two heavy cruisers attack Vichy French fleet at Dakar, damaging the battleship *Richelieu*.

9 July

Battle of Punta Stilo/Calabria sees British and Italian battleships clash, with *Giulio Cesare* badly damaged by shell from *Warspite*, forcing Italians to withdraw. This was the only action during the war when two full battlefleets engaged. Near misses from Italian bombers damage the carrier's fuel system.

19 July

Action off Cape Spada, with light cruiser *Sydney* and five destroyers meeting two Italian light cruisers off Crete. *Sydney* damaged but sinks *Bartolomeo Colleoni* and damages *Giovanni delle Bande Nere*.

U-boat sunk by 830 Squadron aircraft.

20 July

Swordfish from *Eagle* sink two Italian destroyers and a freighter off Tobruk.

15 August

Mediterranean Fleet battleships and cruiser *Kent* bombard Italian positions around Bardia and Fort Capuzzo, with *Eagle*'s Swordfish operating from a shorebase.

22/23 August

Destroyers bombard seaplane base at Bomba, west of Tobruk, joined by three of *Eagle*'s Swordfish operating from a shorebase, and sink two Italian submarines, a depot ship and a destroyer with three torpedoes.

16 September

Swordfish from *Illustrious* sink two Italian destroyers at Benghazi.

23–5 September

Second attack on Dakar, with heavy damage suffered by both navies. Submarines *Persée* and *Ajax* sunk by British, and destroyer *Audacieux* put out of action by cruiser HMAS *Australia*, but submarine *Beveziers* torpedoes *Resolution* while battleship *Barham* and cruiser *Cumberland* both damaged by shellfire, as are two destroyers.

11/12 October

Ajax attacks four Italian destroyers and three MTBs off coast of Tunisia, and in a moonlight battle sinks a destroyer and two MTBs.

17–20 October

Nine U-boats attack convoys SC7 and HX79 with a total of seventy-nine ships. This develops into a four-day battle in which thirty-two ships are lost without any losses by the U-boats, who simply expend all of their torpedoes.

5 November

Armed merchant cruiser *Jervis Bay* sunk by heavy cruiser *Admiral Scheer*, but her sacrifice limits the losses in the convoy she is escorting to five ships, and earns her CO, Capt E.S.F. Fegen, RN, a posthumous VC.

11/12 November

Twenty-one aircraft fly from *Illustrious* to attack the Italian fleet at Taranto, putting three battleships out of action and damaging several other ships and shore installations for the loss of two aircraft. Meanwhile, the Mediterranean Fleet cruisers carry out a diversionary operation in the Straits of Otranto.

17 November

Fourteen Hawker Hurricanes flown off *Argus* for Malta, but only four reach the island. as the others run out of fuel.

27 November

Battle of Cape Teulada between Force H, escorting three fast freighters, and two Italian battleships, *Vittorio Veneto* and *Giulio Cesare*. The cruiser *Berwick* and an Italian destroyer were badly damaged.

17 December

Illustrious sends her aircraft to attack airfields on Rhodes.

18 December

Warspite and *Valiant* bombard the port of Valona in Albania.

20 December

Adm Sir Andrew Cunningham visits Malta aboard *Warspite*, the battleship's first visit since Italy entered the war, and the last for some time.

1941

10 January

Illustrious attacked by Luftwaffe and badly damaged during Operation Excess, the handover of a convoy from Gibraltar to Alexandria off Malta. Ship puts into Malta for emergency repairs.

11 January

Luftwaffe attacks cruisers *Gloucester* and *Southampton* escorting four merchantmen, with *Southampton* having to be abandoned.

16 January

Illustrious provokes an intensified blitz during her stay in Malta for emergency repairs, reaching a peak on this day.

23 January

Illustrious leaves Malta for the United States via the Suez Canal for permanent repairs.

February

U class submarines deployed to Malta for the first time, as well as four J class destroyers.

8–11 February

Convoy battle off Cape St Vincent after *U-37* sinks two ships in convoy HG53 and also alerts the Luftwaffe, which sends five aircraft which each sink a ship. *U-37* then sinks another ship, and guides in the cruiser *Hipper* to sink a number of stragglers before moving on to convoy SLS64 and sinking seven ships.

9 February

Force H in the western Mediterranean, including the battleship *Malaya* and the battlecruiser *Renown* and carrier *Ark Royal*, with a cruiser and ten escorts, attacks targets in the Gulf of Genoa, with the battleships bombarding Genoa, and aircraft bombing Leghorn and mining the port of La Spezia.

25 March

Italian two-man torpedo boats sink a tanker in the anchorage at Suda Bay, and the cruiser *York* is so badly damaged that she has to be run aground, but she is later sunk by the Luftwaffe.

28 March

Battle of Cape Matapan. The Mediterranean Fleet, with battleships *Warspite*, *Valiant* and *Malaya*, the carrier *Formidable* and four cruisers, as well as aircraft based ashore in Crete, engage the Italians battleship *Vittorio Veneto* and eight cruisers. *Vittorio Veneto* badly damaged and stopped at one stage, while three Italian cruisers and two destroyers are sunk.

6/7 April

German troops attack both Yugoslavia and Greece, while the Luftwaffe bombs Piraeus, blowing up a British ammunition ship, which takes ten other ships with her and damages many more, putting the port out of action.

12 April

Twenty Hurricanes flown off *Ark Royal* to Malta.

13 April

British submarine *Spearfish* cripples German pocket battleship *Lützow* in the Baltic.

15/16 April

Four destroyers are sent from Malta to attack an Italian convoy of five ships escorted by three destroyers. They put the three destroyers out of action and sink all five merchant ships, but lose one destroyer.

21 April
Mediterranean Fleet bombards Tripoli supported by aircraft from *Formidable* and Malta, inflicting serious damage.

23 April
Greek army surrenders, and Mediterranean Fleet helps in the evacuation of British forces to Crete.

8 May
Cornwall sinks armed merchant cruiser *Pinguin*.

18–27 May
Battleship *Bismarck*, escorted by the heavy cruiser *Prinz Eugen*, makes her maiden sortie, causing the battlecruiser *Hood* and the new battleship *Prince of Wales* to intercept. They are soon followed by the battleship *King George V*, the battlecruiser *Repulse* and the aircraft carrier *Victorious*. The cruisers *Suffolk* and *Norfolk* sight the German ships and proceed to track them on radar. *Hood* and *Prince of Wales* engage the German ships, but after five minutes *Hood* blows up. *Prince of Wales* is badly damaged and breaks off the fight, but *Bismarck* is also damaged with a fuel leak, and has to divert to Brest. Late on 24 May Swordfish from *Victorious* attack *Bismarck*. On 25 May Force H with *Renown*, *Ark Royal* and two cruisers leaves Gibraltar. The following day, Swordfish from *Ark Royal* score two torpedo hits, while that night destroyers make an unsuccessful torpedo attack. The next day, *King George V* and *Rodney* plus two cruisers engage *Bismarck*, and after ninety minutes she is dead in the water and on fire, later sinking.

20 May
German airborne landings on Crete leave the Royal Navy to disrupt the follow-up seaborne invasion.

21/22 May
The cruisers *Ajax*, *Dido* and *Orion* with four destroyers destroy a German convoy carrying troops and munitions to Crete.

22 May
Luftwaffe attacks Mediterranean Fleet, sinking cruisers *Fiji* and *Gloucester* as well as a destroyer, damaging *Warspite* and cruisers *Carlisle* and *Naiad*.

26 May
Battleships *Queen Elizabeth* and *Barham* with carrier *Formidable* and nine destroyers attack Axis airfields in the Dodecanese, but shortage of aircraft limits the effect and the Luftwaffe seriously damages the carrier. This leaves the Royal Navy with the task of evacuating 17,000 British, Commonwealth and Greek troops from Crete.

22–25 July
To help the USSR, invaded by Germany in June, aircraft from *Victorious* and *Furious* attack Petsamo and Kirkenes north of the Arctic Circle with little success, losing fifteen aircraft.

September
The United States Navy starts to escort convoys as far as the mid-ocean meeting point, easing the pressure on the Royal Navy.

October
Axis losing more than 60 per cent of supplies sent from Italy to North Africa. Two light cruisers and two destroyers based at Malta as Force K.

November
Axis Mediterranean convoy losses reach 77 per cent.

9 November
Force K from Malta, two cruisers and two destroyers, follows aerial reconnaissance

report of an Italian convoy and, using radar, makes a surprise attack, sinking all seven merchantmen in the convoy and one out of the six escorting destroyers. By this time, the flow of men and materiel between Italy and North Africa is effectively stopped.

13 November
U-81 torpedoes *Ark Royal*, crippling the ship, and she sinks on the following day.

22 November
Devonshire sinks German armed merchant cruiser *Atlantis*.

25 November
U-331 torpedoes the battleship *Barham* off the coast of Libya, and as *Barham* rolls over and sinks, she blows up.

29 November
HMAS *Sydney* sinks German armed merchant cruiser *Kormoran*.

7 December
The Japanese carriers *Akagi*, *Kaga*, *Shokaku*, *Zuikaku*, *Hiryu* and *Soryu* send 353 aircraft in two waves to attack the US Pacific Fleet in its forward base at Pearl Harbor in Hawaii, bringing the United States into the war.

10 December
Battleship *Prince of Wales* and battlecruiser *Repulse*, with four destroyers, attacked by Japanese aircraft as they steam for Singapore, with both ships sunk.

12/13 December
Action off Cape Bon, Tunisia, sees two Italian light cruisers, *Alberico da Barbiano* and *Alberto di Giussano*, caught by three British destroyers and a Dutch destroyer, and in a night action both Italian ships are torpedoed and sunk.

14–23 December
A convoy battle develops off Portugal as convoy HG76 on passage from Gibraltar to the UK is attacked by twelve U-boats. The thirty-two merchantmen have Britain's first escort carrier, HMS *Audacity*, three destroyers and nine smaller warships, but the carrier's aircraft and the escorts together manage to sink five U-boats for the cost of three merchantmen, a destroyer and the carrier herself.

17 December
First Battle of Sirte sees the Italian battleships *Littorio*, *Caio Duilio*, *Andrea Doria* and *Giulio Cesare*, escorted by five cruisers and twenty destroyers, accompanying a convoy to Tripoli, encountered by five British cruisers and twenty destroyers escorting a merchantman to Malta. A brief artillery duel is inconclusive, but despite overwhelming superiority, the Italians break off the action as night falls.

18 December
Force K enters an Italian minefield off Tripoli, which sinks the cruiser *Neptune* and a destroyer, while the cruisers *Aurora* and *Penelope* are damaged.

19 December
Three two-man human torpedoes, or *maiales*, enter Alexandria harbour and place explosive charges under the battleships *Queen Elizabeth* and *Valiant* and a tanker. All three ships are damaged, with the battleships out of action for several months.

1942

7–15 February
Japanese forces take Singapore, with its major naval base.

12 February
Gneisenau, *Scharnhorst* and *Prinz Eugen* leave Brest for the 'Channel Dash', but are

detected by the British too late because of technical and organisational failures. Attacks by MTBs and destroyers are beaten off, while all six Swordfish sent to attack are shot down, for which Lt Cdr Eugene Esmonde receives the Fleet Air Arm's first VC posthumously.

23 February

Submarine *Trident* torpedoes *Prinz Eugen*, putting her out of service for the rest of the year.

27 February

Battle of the Java Sea sees an Allied force under the Dutch Rear Adm Karel Doorman with two heavy and three light cruisers and nine destroyers, including the British *Exeter* and Australian *Perth*, encounter two heavy and two light Japanese cruisers and fourteen destroyers as the Allies attempt to attack the Java invasion fleet. Two British destroyers are among the ships lost as well as two Dutch cruisers, while the remaining ships are badly damaged and withdraw.

28 February

HMAS *Perth* and the USS *Houston*, escaping from the Battle of the Java Sea, are caught by the Japanese after sinking four transports, and themselves sunk.

1 March

Exeter and two destroyers are caught by four Japanese cruisers and carrier-borne aircraft, and are attacked and sunk.

6 March

German attempt to attack convoy PQ12 to the USSR using the battleship *Tirpitz* and three destroyers is foiled by bad weather. Later, an attack by aircraft from *Victorious* is beaten off.

22 March

Second Battle of Sirte occurs when the Royal Navy tries to get a convoy of four merchantmen from Alexandria to Malta with an escort of four cruisers and ten destroyers, plus a cruiser and a destroyer from Malta, but are confronted by the Italian battleship *Littorio*, three cruisers and ten destroyers. Sending the convoy on with a small escort, Rear Adm Vian lays a smokescreen and starts a torpedo attack, and in the ensuing battle, which takes three hours, two Italian destroyers are damaged so badly that they later sink, but two British destroyers are also damaged. The delayed convoy approaches Malta after dawn the following day, to have one ship sunk offshore, a tanker badly damaged so that she has to be towed into a harbour, and the final two ships sunk in Grand Harbour before they can be completely unloaded.

April

Heavy attacks by the Luftwaffe throughout the month see three destroyers and three submarines sunk, as well as a number of smaller vessels.

5 April

Japanese carrier-borne aircraft attack Colombo Harbour in Ceylon, damaging the harbour and merchant shipping. At sea, the cruisers *Cornwall* and *Dorsetshire* are attacked by fifty carrier-borne aircraft and sunk within minutes.

8 April

The cruiser HMS *Penelope* escapes from Malta to receive repairs; she has been so badly damaged by shrapnel that she is nicknamed 'HMS *Pepperpot*'.

9 April

The carrier *Hermes*, escorted by an Australian destroyer, is caught by Japanese carrier-borne aircraft and both are sunk off the coast of Ceylon. Meanwhile, Japanese aircraft attack Trincomalee on Ceylon, and cruisers raid merchant shipping in the Bay of Bengal.

20 April
USS *Wasp* flies off forty-eight Spitfires to Malta, of which forty-seven arrive, but twenty destroyed and twelve badly damaged by air attack within minutes of landing.

3–8 May
Battle of the Coral Sea, the first major carrier-to-carrier battle, includes three British cruisers and two destroyers as part of the US Task Force 17.

5–8 May
British forces invade Madagascar with an initial landing at Diego Suarez, supported by the battleship *Ramillies*, aircraft carriers *Illustrious* and *Indomitable*, cruisers and eleven destroyers, finding weak opposition.

9 May
HMS *Eagle* and USS *Wasp* fly off sixty-four Spitfires to Malta, of which sixty-one arrive.

11 May
The Luftwaffe sinks three out of four destroyers attempting to attack an Axis convoy to Benghazi.

30 May
Ramillies is attacked by Japanese midget submarines at Diego Suarez, putting her out of action for some months.

31 May
Japanese midget submarine attack on Sydney Harbour fails.

12–16 June
Convoy Operations Harpoon and Vigorous attempt to lift the siege on Malta, sailing from Gibraltar and Alexandria respectively. Heavy attacks are mounted by E-boats, U-boats and aircraft, so that after the loss of two merchantmen the Alexandria convoy is recalled. Four out of the six merchantmen on the Gibraltar convoy are sunk, but two get through to Malta at a cost of the cruiser *Hermione* and five destroyers, while another three cruisers are damaged. The Italians lose a cruiser, *Trento*, and the battleship *Littorio* is hit by bombs and torpedoes.

2–13 July
Convoy PQ17 to the Soviet Union includes thirty-four merchantmen, thirteen escorts and three rescue ships, plus a close-support force of four cruisers and three destroyers, while the Home Fleet is at some distance on long-range protection with two battleships, an aircraft carrier, two cruisers and fourteen destroyers. After a Luftwaffe attack sinks three ships on 2 July, the Admiralty learns that the North Sea Combat Group with the *Tirpitz* and the cruisers *Hipper*, *Lützow* and *Scheer* is at sea and orders the convoy to scatter. The Home Fleet prepares to intervene, but the German ships turn back. Over the next few days, heavy submarine and air attack develops, with twenty-three merchantmen and one rescue ship lost for five aircraft.

10–15 August
Convoy Operation Pedestal sees a fourteen-ship convoy from Gibraltar to Malta with a heavy escort including the aircraft carriers *Eagle*, *Furious*, *Indomitable* and *Victorious* and the battleships *Nelson* and *Rodney*, seven cruisers and twenty-seven destroyers. Shortage of fuel keeps the Italian fleet in harbour, but E-boats, U-boats and the Luftwaffe attack continuously. *Eagle* is sunk by *U-73*, while the cruisers *Manchester* and *Cairo* and a destroyer are also lost, along with nine merchantmen. The cruisers *Nigeria* and *Kenya* are badly damaged. The convoy effectively lifts the siege of Malta.

12–18 September

Convoy PQ18 to the Soviet Union is the first Arctic convoy to have an escort carrier, *Avenger*, with another twenty warships, to escort forty-one merchantmen. Ten merchantmen are lost to aerial attack, another three to U-boats, but the Germans lose three U-boats and forty aircraft.

8 November

Operation Torch, as the Allied landings in North Africa were designated, supported by the United States Navy and Royal Navy. Overall command of naval forces is with Adm Sir Andrew Cunningham, and the Royal Navy covers two of the three task forces. Centre Task Force has two escort carriers, three cruisers and thirteen destroyers, while Eastern Task Force has the carrier HMS *Argus*, an escort carrier, three cruisers and sixteen destroyers. The eastern flank of the invasion forces is covered by a reinforced Force H, which is deployed in the western Mediterranean with the battleships *Duke of York*, *Nelson* and *Rodney*, the aircraft carriers *Formidable*, *Furious* and *Victorious*, plus three cruisers and seventeen destroyers.

2 December

Force Q, with three cruisers and two destroyers, sinks all four merchantmen and a destroyer escort in an Italian convoy bound for Tunis.

31 December

Action off Bear Island as German heavy cruisers *Hipper* and *Lützow*, each with an escort of three destroyers, attacks Arctic convoy JW51B. The five escorting destroyers mount a determined resistance until reinforced by cruisers *Jamaica* and *Sheffield*, forcing the Germans to break off. *Hipper* hit three times and both navies lose a destroyer.

1943

1 February

Fast minelayer *Welshman* lost off Tobruk with half of her ship's company.

16–20 March

Atlantic convoys HX229 and SC122, with more than ninety ships between them, become involved in a major convoy battle with forty U-boats. Over four days, twenty-one ships are lost for the cost of one U-boat.

May

Resupply of Axis forces in North Africa has become impossible by this stage, forcing them to surrender shortly afterwards.

11/12 June

Operation Corkscrew results in the capitulation of the Italian islands of Lampedusa and Pantelleria under British naval and air attack.

10 July

Operation Husky, the Allied landings in Sicily, with Adm Sir Andrew Cunningham once again in command of the naval forces. The USN provides the Western Naval Task Force, the RN the Eastern. No less than 580 warships and 2,000 landing craft are used, covered by Force H and the Mediterranean Fleet with the battleships *King George V*, *Howe*, *Nelson*, *Rodney*, *Warspite* and *Valiant*, the carriers *Formidable* and *Indomitable*, six cruisers and twenty-four destroyers. Naval firepower breaks up a German armoured division making a counter attack.

3 September

Allied forces cross the Straits of Messina to land at Calabria.

9 September

Operation Avalanche, the Allied landings at Salerno, is covered by Force H with the battleships *Nelson* and *Rodney* and the carriers *Formidable* and *Illustrious*, while Force V under the command of Rear Adm Sir Philip Vian with *Unicorn* and four escort carriers – *Attacker, Battler, Hunter* and *Stalker* covering ground forces ashore.

Following Italian surrender, the Italian fleet sails for Malta and is escorted by the battleships *Howe, King George V, Valiant* and *Warspite*, which also cover a landing at the major Italian naval base of Taranto. German air attack sees *Warspite* and the cruiser *Uganda* damaged, as well as two American cruisers.

22 September

British midget submarines attack *Tirpitz* in the Altenfjord and put her out of action for six months.

4 October

British carrier-borne aircraft attack German convoys around Narvik, sinking 40,000 tons of shipping.

26 December

Battle of the North Cape occurs after battlecruiser *Scharnhorst* with five destroyers attempts to attack Arctic convoy JW55B. The convoy is escorted by fourteen destroyers but with a close-support cruiser squadron including *Belfast, Norfolk* and *Sheffield*, while a long-range protection group includes the battleship *Duke of York* with the cruiser *Jamaica* and four destroyers. The convoy is missed in bad weather which also separates *Scharnhorst* from her escorts, after which the German ship is confronted by the British cruisers, and after a second attempt a twenty-minute battle breaks out, with each side scoring two hits. *Scharnhorst* attempts to withdraw but runs into the *Duke of York* and *Jamaica*, ending up bracketed by the two British support groups. *Duke of York* scores several

hits, and British destroyers mount a torpedo attack, after which British gunfire resumes as the battlecruiser loses way and eventually capsizes.

1944

22 January

Operation Shingle, Allied landing at Anzio, involves four cruisers and a number of destroyers. Cruiser *Spartan* sunk by air attack on 29 January. The cruiser *Penelope* is torpedoed by a U-boat and sunk on 18 February.

3 April

Operation Tungsten, carrier-borne bombers from *Furious* and *Victorious* and three escort carriers – *Emperor, Pursuer* and *Searcher* attack *Tirpitz* and put her out of action for a further three months.

19 April

Aircraft from *Illustrious* and the USS *Saratoga* attack Sabang on Sumatra.

6 June

Operation Overlord, the Allied invasion of Normandy, sees naval forces commanded by Adm Ramsay. In addition to manning many of the landing craft, the Royal Navy provides a bombardment group with the battleships *Warspite* and *Ramillies*, twelve cruisers and twenty destroyers, with a reserve force including *Nelson* and *Rodney* and three cruisers. Attacks by German destroyers and E-boats result in a British destroyer sunk, as well as two German ships. Other Allied destroyers are sunk by mines, as are a number of landing craft.

25 July

Aircraft from *Illustrious* and *Victorious* in the Indian Ocean attack Sabang on Sumatra, while their escorts shell the dock areas.

15 August
Operation Dragoon, the Allied landing in south of France, with battleship *Ramillies* among the five Allied battleships providing covering fire. Fleet of nine escort carriers includes five British ships – *Attacker, Emperor, Khedive, Searcher* and *Stalker.*

24 August
Aircraft from *Indomitable* and *Victorious* attack Padang on Sumatra and later the airfield at Sabang, which is also bombarded by surface vessels of the British Eastern Fleet.

September/October
British naval forces enter the Aegean, with seven escort carriers, seven cruisers, nineteen destroyers and frigates, to attack the German evacuation from Greece and destroy the remaining German naval units in the area.

17–19 October
Aircraft from *Victorious, Illustrious* and *Indomitable* attack the Nicobar Islands.

1945

4 January
Aircraft from *Indomitable, Victorious, Illustrious* and *Indefatigable* attack oil refineries in north-eastern Sumatra.

24 January
Aircraft from *Indomitable, Victorious, Illustrious* and *Indefatigable* attack oil refinery at Palembang on Sumatra.

29 January
The operation of 24 January is repeated.

1 April
British Pacific Fleet reinforces the US Fifth Fleet at the landings on Okinawa, providing the aircraft carriers *Indomitable, Victorious, Illustrious* and *Indefatigable* with 220 aircraft,

and the battleships *King George V* and *Howe,* with five cruisers.

7 April
Major Japanese kamikaze attacks with some 2,000 suicide pilots. Among the ships hit are *Formidable, Victorious* and *Indefatigable.*

11 April
British Eastern Fleet with the battleships *Queen Elizabeth* and the French *Richelieu* bombards Sabang on Sumatra, supported by two escort carriers, two cruisers and five destroyers.

26 March–25 May
The British Pacific Fleet operates as TF57 against the Sakishima Gunto group of islands, cutting Japanese reinforcements to Okinawa.

4 and 9 May
Kamikaze attack on *Formidable.* Latter date sees seven aircraft lost on deck and another twelve in the hangar.

15/16 May
British destroyers sink the heavy cruiser *Haguro* as she steams through the Straits of Malacca in a night torpedo attack, after the ship has been spotted by aircraft from HMS *Emperor.*

18 May
Armourer working on Corsair in *Formidable*'s hangar accidentally fires guns and starts fire in which thirty aircraft are destroyed.

9 August
Lt Robert Hampton Gray RCNVR, leading a strike of Corsairs from *Formidable*'s 1841 and 1842 squadrons, comes under heavy AA fire as he attacks a destroyer in the Onagawa Wan. He presses ahead with his attack despite severe damage to his aircraft and receives a posthumous VC.

BIBLIOGRAPHY

Published in London unless otherwise stated.

Akermann, P., *Encyclopaedia of British Submarines 1901–1955*, privately published, 1990.

Chesneau, R., *Aircraft Carriers of the World, 1914 to the Present*, Arms & Armour, 1992.

Cunningham, Admiral of the Fleet Sir A., *A Sailor's Odyssey*, Hutchinson, 1951.

Gelb, N., *Desperate Venture*, Hodder & Stoughton, 1992.

Hickey, D. and Smith, G., *Operation Avalanche: Salerno Landings 1943*, Heinemann, 1983.

Hobbs, D., *Aircraft Carriers of the Royal and Commonwealth Navies*, Greenhill Books, 1996.

Ireland, B., *Jane's Naval History of World War II*, HarperCollins, 1998.

Keegan, J., *The Price of Admiralty*, Hutchinson, 1988.

Kennedy, L., *Menace: The Life and Death of the* Tirpitz, Sidgwick & Jackson, 1979.

Kilbracken, Lord, *Bring Back My Stringbag: A Stringbag Pilot at War*, Pan Books, 1980.

Laffin, J., *British VCs of World War 2*, Stroud, Sutton, 1997.

Mallman Showell, J.P., *The German Navy Handbook 1939–1945*, Stroud, Sutton, 1999.

Moore, Capt. J. RN, *Escort Carrier*, Hutchinson, 1944.

Poolman, K., *Armed Merchant Cruisers*, Leo Cooper in association with Secker & Warburg, 1985.

——, *Escort Carrier: HMS* Vindex *at War*, Secker & Warburg, 1983.

——, *The Sea Hunters: Escort Carriers v U-boats 1941–1945*, Arms & Armour, 1982.

Preston, A., *Aircraft Carriers*, Bison, 1979.

——, *Destroyers*, Hamlyn, 1977.

——, *The History of the Royal Navy in the 20th Century*, Bison, 1987.

Roskill, Capt. S.W., *The Navy at War, 1939–45*, HMSO, 1960.

——, *The War at Sea, 1939–45*, Vols I–III, HMSO, 1976.

Sturtevant, R. and Balance, T., *The Squadrons of the Fleet Air Arm*, Tonbridge, Air Britain, 1994.

Thomas, D.A., *Battles and Honours of the Royal Navy*, Barnsley, Leo Cooper, 1998.

Thompson, J., *Imperial War Museum Book of the War at Sea, 1939–45: The Royal Navy in the Second World War*, IWM/Sidgwick & Jackson, 1996.

Van der Vat, D., *Standard of Power: The Royal Navy in the Twentieth Century*, Hutchinson, 2000.

Vian, Adm Sir P., *Action This Day*, Muller, 1960.

Winton, J., *Air Power at Sea, 1939–45*, Sidgwick & Jackson, 1976.

——, *The Forgotten Fleet*, Michael Joseph, 1960.

——, *The Victoria Cross at Sea*, Michael Joseph, 1978.

Woodman, R., *Arctic Convoys*, John Murray, 1974.

Woods, G.A., *Wings at Sea: A Fleet Air Arm Observer's War, 1940–45*, Conway Maritime, 1985.

Wragg, David, *Carrier Combat*, Stroud, Sutton, 1997.

——, *Combustible, Vulnerable, Expendable – The Escort Carrier at War*, Barnsley, Pen & Sword, 2005.

——, *Stringbag: The Fairey Swordfish at War*, Barnsley, Pen & Sword, 2004.

——, *Second World War Carrier Campaigns*, Barnsley, Pen & Sword, 2004.

——, *Malta: The Last Great Siege 1940–1943*, Barnsley, Pen & Sword, 2003.

——, *The Fleet Air Arm Handbook 1939–1945*, Stroud, Sutton, 2001 and 2003.

——, *Wings over the Sea: A History of Naval Aviation*, Newton Abbot and London, David & Charles, 1979.

INDEX

Warship names are only given when these appear in the narrative, rather than duplicating the extensive list of vessels given in Chapter 14. Similarly, Fleet Air Arm squadrons are dealt with in Chapter 16, with a brief summary of their aircraft and operations. To save space and avoid duplication, details of operations are given in the battle and campaign awards in Appendix II, with additional information in Appendix III on Victoria Cross awards.

Italic numbers denote illustrations.